MICROCOMPUTERS AND GOVERNMENT MANAGEMENT
Design and Use of Applications

■ BROOKS/COLE SERIES IN PUBLIC ADMINISTRATION

The Foundations of Policy Analysis
Garry D. Brewer and Peter deLeon

Public Administration: An Action Orientation
Robert B. Denhardt

Theories of Public Organization
Robert B. Denhardt

The Nonprofit Organization: Essential Readings
David L. Gies, J. Steven Ott, and Jay M. Shafritz

Organization Theory: A Public Perspective
Harold F. Gortner, Julianne Mahler, and Jeanne Bell Nicholson

Governmental Accounting and Control
Leo Herbert, Larry N. Killough, Alan Walter Steiss

Governing Public Organizations
Karen M. Hult and Charles Walcott

Democratic Politics and Policy Analysis
Hank C. Jenkins-Smith

Politics and the Bureaucracy: Policymaking in the Fourth Branch of Government, Second Edition
Kenneth J. Meier

Applied Statistics for Public Administration, Revised Edition
Kenneth J. Meier and Jeffrey L. Brudney

Fiscal Administration: Analysis and Applications for the Public Sector, Third Edition
John L. Mikesell

Managing Urban America, Third Edition
David R. Morgan

Classic Readings in Organizational Behavior
J. Steven Ott

The Organizational Culture Perspective
J. Steven Ott

The Job of the Public Manager
John Rehfuss

Microcomputers and Government Management: Design and Use of Applications
John F. Sacco and John W. Ostrowski

Classics of Organization Theory, Second Edition, Revised and Expanded
Jay M. Shafritz and J. Steven Ott

Classics of Public Administration, Second Edition, Revised and Expanded
Jay M. Shafritz and Albert C. Hyde

Managing the Public Sector
Grover Starling

Strategies for Policy Making
Grover Starling

Financial Management in Public Organizations
Alan Walter Steiss

Critical Issues in Public Personnel Policy
Ronald D. Sylvia

Program Planning and Evaluation for the Public Manager
Ronald D. Sylvia, Kenneth J. Meier, and Elizabeth M. Gunn

Classics of Public Personnel Policy, Second Edition, Revised and Expanded
Frank J. Thompson

A Casebook of Public Ethics and Issues
William M. Timmins

Introduction to Budgeting
John Wanat

Quantitative Methods for Public Administration, Second Edition
Susan Welch and John Comer

MICROCOMPUTERS AND GOVERNMENT MANAGEMENT
Design and Use of Applications

John F. Sacco
George Mason University

John W. Ostrowski
California State University, Long Beach

Brooks/Cole Publishing Company
Pacific Grove, California

Brooks/Cole Publishing Company
A Division of Wadsworth, Inc.

© 1991 by Wadsworth, Inc., Belmont, California 94002.
All rights reserved.
No part of this book may be reproduced, stored in a retrieval system, or transcribed, in any form or by any means—electronic, mechanical, photocopying, recording, or otherwise—without the prior written permission of the publisher, Brooks/Cole Publishing Company, Pacific Grove, California 93950, a division of Wadsworth, Inc.

Printed in the United States of America

10 9 8 7 6 5 4 3 2 1

Library of Congress Cataloging-in-Publication Data

Sacco, John F., [date]–
    Microcomputers and government management : design and use of applications / John F. Sacco, John W. Ostrowski.
      p.   cm. -- (Brooks/Cole series in public administration)
    Includes bibliographical references.
    ISBN 0-534-13200-6
    1. Public administration--Data processing. 2. Microcomputers.
I. Ostrowski, John W., [date]–   . II. Title. III. Series.
JF1525.A8S23   1990
350'.00028'5--dc20   90-36372
                                                                                     CIP

Trademarks and credits continue on pp. v and vii.

Sponsoring Editor: *Cynthia C. Stormer*
Editorial Assistant: *Cathleen Sue Collins*
Production Coordination: *Marlene Thom*
Manuscript Editor: *Margaret Tropp*
Permissions Editor: *Marie DuBois*
Interior and Cover Design: *Roy R. Neuhaus*
Cover Illustration: *Erin Mauterer, Bluewater A & D*
Art Coordinator: *Cloyce J. Wall*
Interior Illustration: *Cloyce J. Wall*
Typesetting: *Phyllis Larimore Publication Services*
Cover Printing: *Phoenix Color Corporation*
Printing and Binding: *Arcata Graphics/Martinsburg*

Trademarks

1DIR and **1DIR Plus** are registered trademarks of BourBaki, Inc.
Apple, Apple][, LaserWriter, and **Macintosh** are registered trademarks and **SuperDrive** is a trademark of Apple Computer, Inc.
ATI EGAWondergraphics is a trademark of ATI Technologies, Inc.
AutoCad is a registered trademark of AutoDesk, Inc.
Bernouli Box is a registered trademark of Iomega Corporation.
Compaq Deskpro 386 is a registered trademark of Compaq Computer Corporation.
Compuserve is a registered trademark of CompuServe, Inc.
Crosstalk is a registered trademark of Crosstalk Communications.
dBASE III, dBASE III Plus, dBASE IV, and **Framework** are registered trademarks of Ashton-Tate, Inc.
Dialog is a registered service mark of Dialog Information Systems, Inc., a Knight-Ridder Company.
Dr. Halo is a trademark of Media Cybernetics, Inc.
EGA Paint is a registered trademark of Rix Softworks, Inc.
Enable and **Enable/OA** are trademarks of Enable Software, Inc.
EnerGraphics is a trademark of Enertronics Research, Inc.
Epson FX85 and **LQ1000** are trademarks of Epson America, Inc.
ExSys is a registered trademark of ExSys, Inc.
Focus and **PC Focus** are trademarks of Information Builders, Inc.
Freelance, Hal, Jazz, Lotus 1-2-3, and **Symphony** are registered trademarks of Lotus Development Corporation.
Freestyle is a trademark of Summa Technologies, Inc.
GEM is a registered trademark of Digital Research, Inc.
GoldenGate is a registered trademark of Cullinet Software, Inc.
Grandview and **Time Line** are trademarks of Symantec Corporation.
Graphwriter is a trademark of Graphic Communications, Inc.
Harvard Total Project Manager, Harvard Total Project Manager II, and **PFS: Write** are registered trademarks and **Chartmaster, First Publisher,** and **Harvard Graphics** are trademarks of Software Publishing Corporation.
Hayes Smarmodem 2400 is a trademark of Hayes Microcomputer Products, Inc.
Hot Shot Graphics is a trademark of SymSoft, Inc.
IBM PC, IBM PC/XT, IBM PC/AT, IBM PC/2, PC-DOS, OS/2 Extended Edition, and

v

TRADEMARKS

Presentation Manager are registered trademarks and **DisplayWrite** is a trademark of International Business Machines Corporation.
Intel 8088, Intel 8086, Intel 80286, Intel 80386, and **Intel 80486** are registered trademarks of Intel Corporation.
InterPress is a trademark of Interleaf Corporation.
L-view is a registered trademark of Sigma Designs, Inc.
Mace and **Mace Gold** are trademarks of Fifth Generation Systems, Inc.
Motorola 6502, Motorola 68040, and **MC6800** are registered trademarks of Motorola Corporation.
MS-DOS, Microsoft Word, and **Xenix** are registered trademarks and **Excel, Microsoft Project,** and **Microsoft Windows** are trademarks of Microsoft Corporation.
Multisync and **GB-1** are registered trademarks of NEC Technologies, Inc.
Netware is a registered trademark of Novell, Inc.
NeXT is a trademark of NeXT, Inc.
Norton Utilities is a registered trademark of Peter Norton Computing, Inc.
Oracle is a registered trademark of Oracle Corporation.
PageMaker is a registered trademark of Aldus Corporation.
Paradox, Quattro, Sidekick, and **Superkey** are registered trademarks of Borland International, Inc.
Pathfinder is a trademark of MicroDecision Training Corporation.
PC Paint is a trademark of Mouse Systems Corporation.
PC Paintbrush is a trademark of ZSoft Corporation.
PC SAS is a registered trademark of SAS Institute, Inc.
PC Tools is a trademark of Central Point Software, Inc.
Pixie is a trademark of Zenographics.
Princeton Graphics HX-12E and **Max-12** are trademarks of Princeton Graphic Systems.
Procomm and **Procomm Plus** are trademarks of Datastorm Technologies, Inc.
Project Workbench is a registered trademark of Applied Business Technology Corporation.
Promis is a trademark of Strategic Software Planning Corporation.
Rbase is a trademark of Microrim, Inc.
Revelation is a trademark of COSMOS, Inc.
SPARC is a trademark of Sun Microsystems, Inc.
SPSS/PC is a registered trademark of SPSS, Inc.
Statgraph is a registered trademark of Statgraph, Inc.
Statpac is a registered trademark of Walonich Associates.
SuperProject is a registered trademark of Computer Associates.
TARGA is a registered trademark of AT&T Computer Systems.
Taxan 760 is a registered trademark of Taxan USA Corp.
The Genius monitor is a registered trademark of Micro Display Systems, Inc.
ThinkTank is a registered trademark of Living Video, Inc.
Unix and **X-Windows** are registered trademarks of AT&T Bell Laboratories.
Ventura Publisher is a registered trademark of Ventura Software, Inc.
Visicalc is a registered trademark of Software Arts, Inc.
VP Expert is a registered trademark of Paperback Software.
WordPerfect is a registered trademark of WordPerfect Corporation.
WordStar is a registered trademark of Wordstar International Inc.
XTree is a trademark of XTree Company.
XyWrite is a trademark of XyQuest, Inc.
All other product names are trademarks or registered trademarks of their respective companies.

Credits

This page constitutes an extension of the copyright page.

148, Figure 6.1 Copyright © 1984, 1985, 1986, Ashton-Tate Corporation. All rights reserved. Reprinted by permission.

334–338, Figures 10.1–10.7 Output shots produced using Harvard Total Project Manager II®, including text material, are used with the permission of Software Publishing Corporation, which owns the copyright to such products. Harvard Total Project Manager II® is a registered trademark of Software Publishing Company.

346, 349, Figures 10.13 and 10.16 Output shots produced using Harvard Graphics™, including text material, are used with the permission of Software Publishing Corporation, which owns the copyright to such products. Harvard Graphics™ is a trademark of Software Publishing Corporation.

343, Figure 10.11 PC Paintbrush screen print courtesy of ZSoft Corporation.

353, 354, Figures 10.18–10.20 © Aldus Corporation 1985–1989. Used with the express permission of Aldus Corporation. Aldus® and Pagemaker® are registered trademarks of Aldus Corporation. All rights reserved.

About the Authors

Dr. John F. Sacco is an Associate Professor at George Mason University. He obtained his Ph.D. from The Pennsylvania State University, where he majored in public management, research methods, and public policy. His major areas of research are government information systems and government accounting systems. Dr. Sacco has published articles and monographs on urban policy, program evaluation, and computer applications. Before joining the George Mason faculty, Professor Sacco was an evaluation officer with the U.S. Department of Housing and Urban Development.

Dr. John W. Ostrowski is an Associate Professor of Public Policy and Administration in the Graduate Center for Public Policy and Administration at California State University, Long Beach. He received his doctorate in public policy from Kent State University. Dr. Ostrowski specializes in systems theory, research methodology, and the use of computer-related technologies in management and decision making. Dr. Ostrowski has published widely on the management and use of microcomputers in public organizations.

Preface

The increased popularity of microcomputers has spawned numerous how-to books. The focus of most how-to books is on learning the commands of widely used software packages. These books are often helpful for the user who is beginning to apply microcomputers to analytical or managerial problems.

FOCUS AND FOUNDATION OF THE BOOK

This book, while incorporating several of the popular software packages, focuses primarily on the framework, logic, and design underlying the use of microcomputers as problem-solving tools. Its goal is to guide users in crafting popular software into effective applications for problem solving. The software—whether it be a spreadsheet, a database management system, or a word processor—represents raw, untapped power. To mold that software into productive applications, the user must possess an underlying problem-solving foundation and a set of design skills. In particular, it is necessary to understand the type of managerial problem at hand, recognize its degree of complexity, and identify general solutions that might be available. With this foundation, the power of the software is increased considerably. It is also critical to appreciate what constitutes an effective problem-solving application. Applications should not be so entangled that they add complexity and confusion to the problem-solving effort. Applications should reduce complexity and render the intractable manageable.

Several concepts lie at the heart of this effort to provide a logic and design for building microcomputer problem-solving applications. Combining ideas from past computer designers with the power of the latest microcomputer technology, this newly emergent framework emphasizes an understanding of the nature of the problem—particularly, where it falls on a continuum of routine versus novelty—a search for feasible solutions or models to weave into the microcomputer application, an effort to break problems into manageable parts, and a gradual refinement of the problem to the point where the software is shaped into an effective problem-solving application.

In short, simply knowing how to use the software, no matter how thoroughly, is not an adequate basis for use of microcomputers as problem-solving tools. Microcomputer application designers must appreciate the intricacies of the problem confronting them; they must have a set of conceptual tools to break down the problem; and they must know the software well enough to squeeze the most out of it.

In some respects, the route to productive use of microcomputers covers the same ground as learning how to use other computer technology effectively. Often, the initial emphasis is on the technology and its glitter. As experience is gained, successful users find that the logical and theoretical dimension is vital. In other words, good applications do not emerge from the technology alone. Good applications rest on the power of the technology, on a keen sense of problem-solving methodology, and on a set of tools that permits one to link this keen sense of the problem to the power of the technology.

This book not only covers fundamental problem-solving approaches and techniques, it also illustrates how to employ them in actual managerial situations. Case material used in building problem-solving applications has been drawn from numerous agencies and areas of responsibility, including finance, budgeting, control, planning, capital construction, evaluation, public safety, personnel, and telecommunications.

AUDIENCE FOR THE BOOK

This book is intended to be of value to several types of microcomputer users. For individuals just getting started with microcomputers, the book should provide a solid foundation for applying the popular software most offices now have. It traces the emergence of the microcomputer in the managerial environment, and it reviews the main types of software and hardware. The book also discusses general design and problem-solving techniques that can be used with almost any type of software.

For individuals with an extensive background in microcomputers, the book offers a review of the essentials and covers a number of sophisticated and advanced approaches to microcomputer use. Design of complicated databases, integration of powerful statistical and financial techniques, and development of decision aid applications are all part of the book.

For those using this book as a text, the book can be helpful to beginning and advanced students. The first four chapters lay a foundation for using microcomputers as problem-solving tools. Additionally, the initial cases in chapters 7 through 9 are easy to grasp and replicate. Beyond this introductory material, many of the chapters—especially chapters 5 through 10, including all of the later cases in chapters 7 through 9—offer more demanding and challenging topics.

ACKNOWLEDGMENTS

A number of people have helped us in our effort to develop a broad and fundamental understanding of the design of effective microcomputer applications. Over the past several years, we have called on numerous managers and analysts to see how they were using microcomputers and to share with them our ideas. Without the cooperation of these

PREFACE

busy people, we would have been cast adrift. The students and trainees in our classes have also given us the opportunity to test our ideas.

In terms of specific individuals, Mr. Bob Michael deserves our special thanks. He has listened to our ideas from the outset and has read and critiqued the manuscript. He has that valuable mix of conceptual and technical talents and a willingness to share them.

Special thanks also go to Mr. Charlie Collins and Ms. Gail Bohan, who not only gave us their time but also made arrangements for us to meet with other managers.

Ginny McCaslin, Kenny Moir, and Frank Wald offered stylistic and production ideas.

We thank our respective universities, George Mason University and California State University, Long Beach, for their support and encouragement. Additionally, we thank the following reviewers for their helpful suggestions and comments: David Billeaux, Oklahoma State University; Peter Haas, San Jose State University; Larry Jones, Naval Postgraduate School (Monterey); Alana Northrop, California State University, Fullerton; Sam Overman, University of Denver; and Herbert F. Weisberg, Ohio State University.

Perhaps most important, we need to thank our families for their support, their constant help, and their patience. If it is not a book or an article, it is a new class or a new piece of software. We only hope they have gained as much from us as we have gained from them.

Notwithstanding the important assistance, we are responsible for the content and material of the book.

John F. Sacco
John W. Ostrowski

Contents

PART I BACKGROUND, HISTORY, AND BASIC ELEMENTS 1

CHAPTER 1 Microcomputers in Public Organizations: Background, Impact, and Use 3

Introduction 3
Microcomputer Technology: Understanding Its Use
and Implications 4
Defining the Microcomputer as an End User Tool 5
Microcomputers in Public Organizations: A Brief History 7
Status of Microcomputer Usage in Public Organizations 9
    Growth 9
    Role 10
Purpose and Outline of the Book 14
Content of the Book 16
Conclusion 17
References 18

CHAPTER 2 Understanding Microcomputer Software 19

Introduction 19
    Categories of Software 20
Operating Systems 20
    Background, Purpose, and Definition 20
    OS/2 Presentation Manager 21
    Elements of DOS 22

CONTENTS

      Rudimentary Use of PC-DOS Commands   22
      A Cut Above Rudimentary   23
      Easy Ways to Use DOS   25
  Database Management Systems   26
      Background, Purpose, and Definition   26
      Elements of a DBMS   26
      Enhancement and Evolution of DBMS   31
  Spreadsheets   31
      Background, Purpose, and Definition   31
      Spreadsheet Elements   32
      Further Spreadsheet Enhancements   35
      Lotus 1-2-3 Version 3   36
  Statistical Packages   37
      Background, Purpose, and Definition   37
      Elemental Features   37
      Sophisticated Components   38
  Project Management   39
      Background, Purpose, and Definitions   39
      Project Management Concepts   39
      Supplemental Project Management Concepts   40
      Project Management Software   40
      A Note of Caution   41
  Word Processing   41
      Background, Purpose, and Definition   41
      Basic Word Processing Capabilities   42
      More Sophisticated Facilities   42
      Desktop Publishing Trends   43
  Graphics   44
      Background, Purpose, and Definition   44
      Business Graphics   44
      Processes and Structures   46
      Artistic Work   47
  Electronic Communications and Telecommunications   47
      Background, Purpose, and Definition   47
      Reasons and Circumstances for Data Mobility   47
  Utilities   48
      Background, Purpose, and Definition   48
      Disk Utilities   48
      Program Utilities   48
  Programming   49
      Background, Purpose, and Definition   49

CONTENTS   xv

    Building Blocks 50
  Conclusion 52
  References 53

CHAPTER 3 Hardware Configurations and Systems 54

Overview: From Hardware Components to Systems 54
System Components 55
 The Central Processor Unit 56
 Memory 58
 Input-Output Devices 59
 Storage Media 62
 Peripherals 65
Hardware Linkages 71
System Configurations 73
 Systems for Office Automation 74
 Systems for Management 76
 Specialized Systems 79
Conclusion 80
References 80

PART II FRAMEWORK FOR BUILDING MICROCOMPUTER APPLICATIONS 83

CHAPTER 4 A Framework for Developing Microcomputer Applications 85

Introduction 85
 Purpose 85
 Organization of the Chapter 86
Defining Microcomputer Applications 86
 Software Versus Applications 86
 A Sample Application 87
A Logic for Building Micro Applications 88
 How Not to Get There 88
 The Blueprint Analogy and Framework Approach 89
 Elements of the Framework 89
 Understanding the Nature of the Problem 91
 Types of Applications 94

Methods for Developing Micro Applications   95
Role of Microcomputer Software   98
Who Develops the Application and How?   98
An Illustration   100
Summary and Conclusion   103
References   104

CHAPTER 5 Database Development and Use in a Microcomputer Environment   106

Introduction   106
Background and Context   107
  Definitions   107
  Value of the Database and DBMS   107
  Databases in a Microcomputer Environment   109
Database Development and Use   110
  Building Databases for What   110
  Building Databases: The Process   110
  Preliminary Analysis   112
  Models and Diagrams   112
  Information Requirements Analysis   113
  Database Design   115
  Data Dictionary/Data Directory   125
  Implementation of the Database   127
  Consistency, Coordination, and Distribution   131
A Case Study   132
  Economic Development   132
  Preliminary Analysis   132
  Information Requirements Analysis (IFRA)   133
  Database Design   136
Conclusion   141
References   142

CHAPTER 6 Access Systems   143

Introduction   143
  Purpose   143
  The Costs of Poor Access Systems   143
Developing a Theory and Guidelines for Useful Access Systems   144
  Shared Knowledge and Familiarity   145

       Documentation 145
       Ease of Use 145
       Clear and Relevant Organization of the System 146
       Inclusion of Important Utilities 147
       Security and Preservation 151
       Summary 151
Access Mechanisms 151
       System-Internal Mechanisms 152
       System-External Mechanisms 163

PART III   USE OF THE FRAMEWORK IN DEVELOPING APPLICATIONS   171

CHAPTER 7   Structured Managerial Problems   173

Introduction 173
       Purpose and Scope 173
       Type of Problem: Structured 173
       Types of Micro Applications: Operational Applications 174
       General Design Tools for Microcomputer Applications 174
       Topics 174
       Software for Operational Applications: Spreadsheets 174
       Cases 175
Case 1: Revenue Inflow 176
       Background and Purpose 176
       Using the Spreadsheet 176
       Developing the Operational Application 177
       Displaying and Printing the Data 182
Case 2: Preparing and Aggregating Budget Requests 184
       Purpose and Background 184
       Using the Spreadsheet 186
       Developing a Bureau-Level Application 186
       Developing One Application for All Bureaus in the Department 187
       Developing the Application via Templates 188
       Using Lotus 190
Case 3: Tracking Capital Expenditures 195
       Purpose and Background 195
       Using the Spreadsheet 195
       General Goals and Mechanics of the Tracking System 195
       Divide and Conquer 196
       Design of the Spreadsheet-Based Capital Tracking Application 197
       Table of Contents 197

The Database 197
Beginning the Process: Finding Individual Items 198
Report: Overage or Savings 203
Automating Printing with Macros 205
Conclusion 206
Exercises 207

CHAPTER 8 Semistructured and Unstructured Managerial Problems 211

Introduction 211
   Purpose and Overview 211
   Topics 211
   Decision Support Applications 212
   DSAs and Spreadsheets 213
   Sophistication of Application Design 214
   Cases 214
Case 1: Budgeting Cash and Timing Bond Sales for Capital Projects 214
   Background and Purpose 214
   Using the Spreadsheet 215
   Developing the DSA 216
   First Attempt 216
   Second Attempt 218
   Third Iteration 224
   Fourth Iteration 226
Case 2: Financing Local Highway Improvements 229
   Purpose 229
   The Problem 230
   Background, Goals, and Constraints 230
   Model and Elements 231
   Exchange Among Computer Models 231
   Developing the Microcomputer DSA 232
   Beginning the Divide and Conquer: Major Funding Sources 232
   Building the First Worksheet 233
   The Power of Generalization 233
   State Contributions Module 235
   Business Extractions Module 241
   Local Government Contribution Module 246
   Integrative Module 246
Case 3: Menu-Driven Cost/Benefit Application 251
   Background and Purpose 251

       Using the Application 254
       Describing the Application 258
       The Heart of the Automation: The Macros 259
       Formulas in the Application 263
Conclusion 265
Exercises 266

CHAPTER 9 Data-Intensive Structured and Semistructured Problems 272

Introduction 272
    Purpose and Scope 272
    Type of Problem 272
    Topics 272
    General and Specific Design Elements 273
    Management Information Applications 273
    Analysis 274
    Data Organization and Relational Databases 275
    Development and Operation of the MINA 275
    Software 275
    Differences Among Applications 276
    Case Studies 276
Case 1: A Bare-Bones Telephone Service Application 277
    Background and Purpose 277
    Preliminary Analysis 277
    Data Organization 278
    Default Data-Entry Screen 280
    DBMS Query Commands 282
    Report Generators 283
    Limitations 283
Case 2: Enhancing the Telephone Service System 285
    Multifile Databases 286
    Relating Files 288
    Customizing Screens 290
    Menus 295
    Specialized Programs 296
    Summary 298
Case 3: An Application for Fire and Rescue Training Records 299
    Purpose and Background 299
    Identifying Objectives and Problems 299
    Identifying and Assembling Data 300

Normalization 301
Building the Application 305
Queries: Training Records 307
A Simple Expert System: Certification Status 311
Case 4: Using Database Information for Decision Making 318
Background and Purpose 318
A First Step: Calculating Time Taken 318
Building a Test Program 319
Generating a Report 321
Interpreting and Using the Report Results 323
Conclusion 324
Exercises 326

CHAPTER 10 Specialized Software and Applications 331
Overview 331
Project Management 333
Expert Systems 339
Presentation Graphics 342
Desktop Publishing 350
Conclusion 355
References and Additional Reading 356

Glossary 359
Index 371

PART I

BACKGROUND, HISTORY, AND BASIC ELEMENTS

☐ Microcomputers in Public Organizations: Background, Impact, and Use
☐ Understanding Microcomputer Software
☐ Hardware Configurations and Systems

CHAPTER 1

Microcomputers in Public Organizations: Background, Impact, and Use

INTRODUCTION

From time to time, technologies are introduced that substantially alter the way organizations operate. Examples include the typewriter, the telephone, the mainframe computer, and the copier (Chandler, 1977). It is our contention that another machine must be added to the list: the microcomputer. Although the microcomputer, or personal computer (PC), is a relatively recent innovation, there are indications that microcomputers are fundamentally reshaping the manner of doing business in public organizations (Garson, 1983).

This view may strike some as iconoclastic. Microcomputers were once (all the way back in the late 1970s and early 1980s) considered "toys" or "just another fad." No longer. Microcomputer use is a maturing technology in organizations (Raho, Belohlav, & Fiedler, 1987). For many public organizations, the microcomputer is an essential tool of productivity, problem solving, and creativity. As such, it deserves serious attention.

Set against the backdrop of the growth of personal computers and the expectations raised by this technology, the purpose of this book is to lay out a theoretical or logical foundation and to provide practical examples for using microcomputers in organizational problem solving. For a user equipped with a strong logical foundation, the microcomputer is capable of assisting with many aspects of organizational management, including searching for new ideas and information, assembling resources, coordinating projects, ordering compliance, and persuading associates.

Our image of the modern organization is one in which microcomputer power is available to managers and analysts at all levels of the bureaucracy and for many types of problems. In essence, the microcomputer offers the capability to help break down the complexity of programmatic, organizational, and environmental problems. With a powerful tool for handling complexity, managers are better equipped to improve the effectiveness and efficiency of organizations.

We focus on public organizations and the people in these organizations. Throughout the book, reference is made to analysts and managers. Although the analyst working for a manager is most likely to use the microcomputer directly, managers are integrally involved. Managers are requesting microcomputers for their own use, and managerial expectations and thinking are affected by the presence of the technology. Knowing that a quick "what if" or "reorganization" of the data can be done, managers are more likely to think in these terms and to ask for more analyses.

Although our contextual reference is to public organizations, the logical foundations we advance can apply broadly to the public or private sector. Moreover, the examples and illustrations can be of benefit to organizations in both spheres.

To expand on these points and to establish the groundwork for the book, we first provide background information on microcomputer systems and how these systems have been and are currently being used in public organizations. With this background, we proceed to a more detailed description of the purpose, goals, and content of the book.

MICROCOMPUTER TECHNOLOGY: UNDERSTANDING ITS USE AND IMPLICATIONS

Microcomputer technology can be viewed as a problem-solving and productivity-enhancing tool. It is a physical tool encompassing hardware, an analytical tool encompassing the different types of software, and a tool that facilitates expression for the creative and artistic mind. To use this multifaceted tool effectively, it is necessary to fathom the practical applications and, perhaps more important, the creative potential of this implement for problem solving and productivity.

Unfortunately, the capabilities of microcomputers are commonly misunderstood. An example of the consequences of not fully comprehending microcomputer technology and its power is the "tunnel vision" to which many new computer users fall prey. Typically, novice users are introduced to one or two software packages acquired for a specific purpose (e.g., spreadsheets for preparing a departmental budget or word processors for producing form letters). Although the user may become competent in that specific application, and the related syntax, the rote learning of the software and associated tasks neither encourages nor prepares the person to expand the use of the software into other applications. In contrast, analysts who understand the problem-solving fundamentals of this computer technology and its potential are able to see beyond a limited application to a broader range of uses—simply because they are more aware of the potential, and constraints, of the microcomputer system.

The manager who supervises individuals using microcomputers must understand not only his or her own uses of the microcomputer, but also the applications being undertaken by those being supervised. This burden goes far beyond a simple knowledge about technology to include an understanding of the uses, design, and implementation of microcomputer applications for what may be a broad range of agency tasks. This kind of knowledge has not been routinely covered in academic courses, nor is it something that is analogous to the manager's noncomputing experience. Even microcomputer training may be narrowly construed so that the focus is on the specific commands and syntax of a package, rather than on the general problem-solving capacity of microcomputer software. In short, it is important to appreciate that expanded and productive microcomputer use will depend in part on managerial understanding and support.

☐ *Syntax* is the logical structure of commands, comparable to the way a sentence in English is constructed. Proper syntax is necessary for correct command execution.

The literature brings little relief. A sizable portion related to microcomputer use is of limited utility in addressing the power and logic of microcomputers, because many of these texts take a "cookbook" approach to learning the commands and syntax of software and the physical configuration of hardware. Missing are the important links between the administrative wisdom of managers, general problem-solving principles, and how the microcomputer can leverage this knowledge base.

Without the ability to link managerial concepts and problem-solving approaches with the new technology, the manager is limited to using the PC to carry out only routine and repetitive tasks. Although this limited approach may still produce improvements in workflow and productivity, much of the potential of the microcomputer remains untapped.

The understanding of microcomputer technology needed to provide this vital link between managerial tasks and microcomputer use encompasses five basic elements:

- *Fundamentals:* knowledge of terms, concepts, and processes related to microcomputer system use, sometimes referred to as computer literacy
- *Practices:* knowledge of the development, current use, and potential application of microcomputers in public organizations
- *Theory:* ability to interrelate public management know-how, computer problem-solving logic, and microcomputer software into a theory of end user computing
- *Diffusion:* ability to communicate information about the technology and its products effectively to those who do not have a technical background
- *Integration:* capacity to link microcomputers to other computer information technology, as well as to the decision-making process

The first four of these elements are covered throughout this book. The last, integration, is touched on but not probed in detail. The microcomputer is basically a PC, and technical integration with other computing machines in the organization is still in the developing stages.

In the following sections of this chapter, we focus on the first of these elements, knowledge of fundamental terms, and then move to the second and third, practical and theoretical information related to the development and use of PCs in public organizations. Diffusion is part of the overall discussion.

DEFINING THE MICROCOMPUTER AS AN END USER TOOL

A microcomputer is a digital computer that uses a microprocessor chip as its central control unit (termed the *processor*). Although this definition conveys a technical image, it does little to define the current generation of microcomputers for the nontechnician. Nontechnically, the microcomputer has been described as a "small" computer (it fits on a desktop) with only one or two processor chips, limited in speed and memory compared with mainframes, and is used mostly by one individual at a time.

The *microprocessor chip* is the small device that contains the electronic circuits used to process information. These chips contain the functional equivalent of hundreds, or even thousands, of transistors. *Memory* refers to the ability of the micro to store and retrieve information. There are

PART I   Background, History, and Basic Elements

two basic types of microcomputer memory: RAM and ROM. RAM (Random Access Memory) is the memory used by the micro to hold information provided by the user (data) or software (program). RAM memory is temporary and is cleared when the machine is turned off. RAM can be accessed in multiple ways, hence the term *random*. ROM (Read-Only Memory) refers to chips that have instruction sets permanently encoded in them. ROM does not clear out when the machine is turned off. ROM is not changeable by the user and is often used to provide the rudimentary instructions necessary to make the computer function.

Machines that fit these characteristics are also known as *desktop computers* (for obvious reasons) and *personal computers*, or PCs. The microcomputer is often referred to as a PC because of the single-user characteristic and because the applications performed on the microcomputer tend to be more interactive and less complex than those performed on larger computers.

Although the desktop and single-user metaphors were adequate for early versions of the microcomputer, the rapid pace of development has obviated such simple definitions. In practice, current and future generations of microcomputers are distinguished from larger computing systems such as minicomputers and mainframes more by price and the internal electronic architecture than by use or size.

Even though the desktop characterization of microcomputers is still applicable, the term *desktop* can also be applied to many minicomputer systems that are not much larger than microcomputers. A similar problem arises when attempting to maintain the single-user status of the microcomputer. A single microcomputer is increasingly able to handle several users concurrently, in addition to being linked to other micros in networks. Multiple, concurrent computing sessions have traditionally been the domain of mini-or-larger computing systems.

The definition of microcomputers is also not found by examining the software used. The variety and sophistication of software available for microcomputers continue to expand dramatically. The microcomputer is now able to perform many of the same functions as mainframe computing systems. Sophisticated statistical packages such as SPSSX (Statistical Package for Social Science) and SAS (Statistical Analysis System) are now available in microcomputer versions. Many of the programming languages, such as FORTRAN, COBOL, C, PASCAL, and ADA, are available on microcomputers. Even such exotica as artificial intelligence languages, such as LISP and PROLOG, and "expert systems" are available on microcomputers. Microcomputers have also spawned entire generations of very sophisticated software packages that function more effectively in the microcomputer environment than on larger systems. Perhaps the best example is the maturation of the spreadsheet program, one of the most popular of the current management computer applications.

☐   FORTRAN, COBOL, C, PASCAL, and ADA are all programming languages. Each provides a powerful set of commands to input, manipulate, and output data. FORTRAN was developed primarily for scientific and engineering use; COBOL, for business needs; C, as a multipurpose language; and PASCAL, for teaching good programming practices. ADA has some of its origins in military and defense needs.

☐   *Expert system* refers to a software package that employs rules and information to arrive at the best possible decision given incomplete data and uncertainty. Expert systems usually consist of question/solution sets of information that help the user solve a problem by logically identifying information provided by real experts in the subject area and suggesting ways to use the information to provide answers to questions or solutions to problems. A *spreadsheet* is a type of software that closely resembles an accountant's worksheet. Divided into rows and columns, the spreadsheet facilitates numerical analysis on the micro.

In the current environment of fast-paced development and growing sophistication of systems, trying to define a microcomputer comprehensively is a formidable task. As a result of this increasing diversity, perhaps the only remaining practical way to define a microcomputer is by predominant use. Frequently, microcomputer systems are referred to as *end user* systems, implying that the entire system is controlled by the user(s) and not by a data-processing staff or other computer professionals. If the end user is in charge of the microcomputer, then it can be configured or set up to reflect the needs and preferences of the user.

Viewing the microcomputer as a user-configured system reveals some of its strengths. One advantage of this user-configurable computer is its flexibility, implying that the user has the ability to choose the software, applications, and operational activities to be carried out *independently* from other computer users. In fact, user independence may be the defining characteristic of the microcomputer. Other types of computer systems (mainframes and minis) are designed to operate with technical and programming support. By relying on the concept of end user independence to define microcomputers, we also gain a certain degree of independence from the development of technology. As technology expands, all of the technical indexes that may be used to define a microcomputer will invariably change, requiring a technology-based definition to undergo constant revision. The end user definition, however, should remain fairly consistent.

Another view of computer technology is that differences among computers will become invisible to users. Users will have "workstations" from which they will initiate sessions. In some sessions the user will operate independently, just as with the "old-fashioned" micro. In other sessions the user will tap resources from distant computers but never be aware that some of these resources are on a mainframe. The user may only know that he or she needs that particular resource.

MICROCOMPUTERS IN PUBLIC ORGANIZATIONS: A BRIEF HISTORY

Despite its attractiveness and rapid technological development, microcomputer use in public organizations has proceeded slowly. Early efforts were stifled because of the dearth of management-oriented software. When useful software such as spreadsheets and graphics packages became available, there continued to be a reluctance to invest seriously in the new technology.

Microcomputers began appearing in public organizations shortly after they were developed in the early 1970s. At first, only do-it-yourself kits were available, and those microcomputers were kit-built units owned by the individuals and used more because of their novelty than anything of significant value to either the employee or the organization.

With the introduction of commercially available microcomputers such as the Apple][and the Radio Shack TRS-80 Model I in the late 1970s, a few more usable microcomputers began trickling into organizations. These first "serious" microcomputers were quite restricted in memory and frequently treated merely as sophisticated calculators or fancy typewriters. The appearance of commercial software packages for financial calculations, simple database or file analysis, and word processing improved the functionality of these microcomputers. By and large, however, they were still seen as marginally useful.

> A *database* is a collection of related information that is organized for some purpose. A database may consist of one set of information (a file) or multiple files linked together. Databases are basic building blocks in computer applications.

In the early 1980s, the power of microcomputers continued to increase while prices began to drop dramatically. The introduction of the spreadsheet program for financial calculations and budget preparation signaled the first truly significant software designed for microcomputers in an organizational environment. With the growing usefulness of microcomputers and the sharp drop in prices, increasing numbers of managers and employees began to see value in acquiring a microcomputer-based system.

The desire to acquire the new microcomputer system was not easily satisfied. In agencies with existing mainframe or minicomputer systems, the data-processing (DP) department was usually responsible for acquisition of new equipment. Accustomed to dealing with very expensive, fragile, and complicated computer systems, these departments often balked at allowing untrained, nontechnical personnel to acquire and use a computer that was not under the control and supervision of the DP staff.

The reluctance of many DP staffs to allow microcomputers into organizations resulted in a number of interesting ploys used by employees to acquire the desired systems surreptitiously. Microcomputers were budgeted as calculators, typewriters, part-time consultants, and even office furniture. Potential microcomputer users saw the new computers as a way of achieving independence from traditional data-processing department control and procedures. Perceiving themselves to be victims of arcane and capricious data-processing department practices, they viewed the microcomputer as a way to meet their data-processing needs without having to submit to the control or authority of another department.

One should not get the impression from this sequence of events that the DP staff was always the bad guy. Many data-processing department objections to the acquisition of microcomputers were quite reasonable, ranging from concerns about maintenance and support to questions about the intended use of the microcomputer systems. Since most potential microcomputer users had little computing background, they tended to overestimate wildly the power and practical utility of the microcomputer. Often, managers and analysts expected to replicate easily their mainframe-based computing tasks on the microcomputer. Computing professionals recognized the futility of such expectations, but users chose to see their protestations as merely another attempt to maintain absolute control over computing resources.

The hesitancy of the traditional DP staff to accept the new microcomputer systems as anything more than toys or novelties, coupled with the unrealistic expectations of users, served to suppress the acquisition of microcomputers for more legitimate tasks. Early success stories with microcomputers came not from attempting to replicate mainframe computing applications on the microcomputer, but from developing new tasks particularly suited to the personal nature of the microcomputer. Word processing, office and departmental budget preparation, and small file management were the most successful of the early applications. In each case, the microcomputer was used to accomplish what was either impossible, too costly in computer use-time, or inordinately difficult to program on the mainframe.

Noticeable achievements with these applications began to change perceptions concerning the legitimate role of microcomputers in the organization. In addition, because these applications were not normally carried out in the mainframe computing environment, DP staff were somewhat more willing to accept the new role of the microcomputer. The introduction of the IBM PC in 1981 and the Apple Macintosh two years later also served to legitimize the microcomputer in the eyes of data-processing professionals. The resulting gradual acceptance of the microcomputer as a sanctioned computing tool in organizations led to the development of a new kind of computing, often referred to as *end user computing* (Porter, 1986).

End user computing, as we have seen, meant that control of the microcomputing system was placed in the hands of the user of the system and not a DP support staff. Moreover, the availability of quality commercial software packages meant that the user was not required to program the system before using it, nor were professional programmers needed to implement simple applications. Not all end users were created equal, however. Varying levels of competence and technical knowledge created significant discrepancies in the ability of the end user to use the new technology effectively.

The broad variety of possible applications, coupled with the dispersal of computing power to the individual level, produced a number of problems. For the first time, the managers confronted with these computing problems were not computer systems managers but managers who themselves were likely to be addressing the new technology for the first time. These managers faced the daunting task of trying to learn the new technology, adapt the technology to work tasks effectively, and manage the use of the technology—all concurrently. Little wonder that the pace of "microcomputerization" was somewhat slower than anticipated by early converts.

Beyond the problems immediately related to the direct use and management of the new technology, ancillary issues also developed with respect to general management and organization. One of the most common of these problems is computerphobia, or fear of the computer (Gardner, Render, Ruth, & Ross, 1985). This fear is widespread in organizations and can have a significant impact on personnel morale, productivity, and task acceptance. Other microcomputer-related externalities include job definition and pay problems, personnel assignments, security of information, planning, and health and safety concerns. Clearly, the microcomputer, far from being just a fancy typewriter, contributes to substantial changes in organizational function.

STATUS OF MICROCOMPUTER USAGE IN PUBLIC ORGANIZATIONS

Growth

Microcomputer system implementation in public organizations still lags behind implementation of such systems in private organizations. Although this situation has been generally true for all types of computer systems, only with the advent of affordable

TABLE 1.1 Microcomputer Application Typology

General applications	Office automation	Information management and decision support
Task, Applications, and Software	Word processing File management Electronic information transfer (e.g., electronic mail, messages, and bulletin boards)	Database management Spreadsheets Project management Statistics Graphics Expert systems
Primary Users	Secretaries Clerks Office managers	Managers Analysts Professionals

microcomputers have public organizations begun to make wholesale commitments to the use of microcomputers. In a 1982 study conducted for the International City Management Association (ICMA), the researchers found that only 13 percent of respondent local governments were then using microcomputers. A similar survey conducted for the Government Finance Officers Association (GFOA) in 1985 returned a usage rate of nearly 90 percent (Ostrowski, Gardner, & Motawi, 1986). At the federal level, the number of PCs estimated to be in service by the end of 1986 was 400,000, and that figure was growing by nearly 1,000 per day. Several public organizations, including major federal agencies such as NASA, have established goals to provide every white-collar worker with a PC system by the early 1990s. Clearly, there are major commitments to adopt microcomputer technology at all levels of government.

Role

Key to acceptance of the microcomputer is its role as a tool to enhance problem solving and productivity in the public organization. In an era of scarce resources and growing demands for services, governments are finding it increasingly necessary to do more with less. Beyond a certain point, it is counterproductive to attempt cost reductions by limiting personnel. Thus, a common response to resource scarcity is to incorporate technology designed to enhance individual productivity (Calista, 1985). The microcomputer is part of this technology.

The status of microcomputer use in public organizations can be more fully comprehended by examining a typology of applications, as presented in table 1.1.

This typology is based primarily on the general category of microcomputer use. The division between office automation and information management/decision support is a simple way of recognizing the difference between information *format* processing and information *manipulation* and *analysis*.

Office automation (OA) encompasses those tasks that transform information from one form to another. Word processing is one of these. It consists of two elements: text editing and text formatting. The goal of text editing is to establish the meaning of the text according to the principles of good grammar, usage, and syntax. The purpose of text formatting is to transform the text into its final form, including stylistic touches such as justification and boldfacing. In both cases, the meaning of the information imparted in the text should not be substantively altered, only the clarity and form improved (Madron, 1983, pp. 39–43).

Office automation functions are commonly carried out by personnel such as secretaries and clerks, although professionals, managers, and executives are finding it faster and more efficient to use OA techniques to produce their own memos and reports. This blurring of roles in OA is a frequent cause of conflict over job descriptions versus actual task performance. The traditional role of secretaries and clerks is undergoing substantial modification, producing a new generation of "information processors" whose tasks and responsibilities in the organization are more complex and sophisticated than indicated by traditional job classifications. At the same time, many managers and professionals are assuming routine information production tasks once reserved for support staff.

In information management and decision support applications such as those facilitated by spreadsheets and database management systems, information may be modified, searched, located, created, projected, and analyzed. With information management capacity, large pools of data are organized so that it becomes possible to access the data quickly, find specific information, and examine the data from a number of vantage points. This information management frequently replaces bulky paper files in which organization is limited to one facet, often alphabetical order by last name or bureau. For instance, there may be a personnel file that can easily be accessed by alphabetical order but not by magnitude of salary or some other characteristic of the employee. Information management tools associated with microcomputers (and other computers) would, in this brief example, open access to numerous employee dimensions, including name, salary, position, and work history.

With decision support capabilities, data can be investigated to determine the impact and consequences of change, whether in tax rate, size of work force, type of equipment, or any other factor. A brief example shows information management and decision support at work.

As an illustration of information management, consider a personnel database that includes information on current salary, date hired, and service grade. Using these three data items, an analyst could calculate a multitude of new information, such as an anniversary date for performance review (based on date hired), potential for salary increments within service grade, or a new salary factored for cost-of-living adjustments, merit increases, and any other salary adjustment factors. In a top-notch database management system, all of these calculations could be programmed to generate information automatically on all individuals in the database. In each case, the manager uses existing information and, through various forms of manipulation, produces new information that was not included in the original database.

The decision support process continues with subsequent analysis of this new information. In the updated investigation, the manager might apply a criterion to determine whether the new salary or other changes meet or exceed agency standards. Illustration of these manipulations and transformations is presented in table 1.2.

The elements of information management and decision support are often of greater concern to the manager; therefore, this text focuses mostly on these elements. Whereas

PART I Background, History, and Basic Elements

TABLE 1.2 Example of Database Information Manipulations and Transformations

Database information	Manipulations or transformations	New information produced
Date hired	Month and day of date hired added to current year	Date for annual performance review
Current salary and service grade	Maximum salary in grade minus current salary	Potential for within-grade salary increase
Current salary	Current salary multiplied by cost-of-living factor	Cost-of-living adjustment
Current salary	Current salary multiplied by percent merit increase	Merit pay increase
Current salary	Current salary added to merit pay increase and cost-of-living adjustment	New salary

office automation is a relatively well-understood field, with substantial available literature on system design, operation, and management, available literature in the field of information management and decision support focuses almost exclusively on major organizational problems and large computer routines, and not on the tools and techniques designed to enhance the microcomputer-based decision-making capacity of managers and analysts.

Although there are wide variations in tasks and software applications across organizations, recent studies indicate a relatively consistent pattern in microcomputer use for information management and decision support tasks, although generally at a rudimentary level (Mittra, 1986). The most common applications are those relating to spreadsheets, with budgeting the principal task. Database management systems (DBMS) are used for manipulating and searching through large pools of information. The other categories mentioned including graphics, project management, and statistics, are still somewhat limited in use. This is due, in part, to a lack of knowledge about both the function of applications in these areas and the technical processes required to employ the software in successful applications.

Use of microcomputers in the information management and decision support area is not without its problems. To begin with, problems arise when the user moves into decision areas that are rife with complexity. These difficulties are magnified because users do not have a full understanding of the power of microcomputer software and how to apply powerful software to complex decisions. The problems range from confusion over the proper role of microcomputer-based analysis in an organization, to unrealistic expectations of application performance, to management control and communication difficulties. Table 1.3 summarizes several of the more common problems encountered when public organizations implement microcomputer-based systems.

Table 1.3 breaks the microcomputer implementation process into three segments: pre-implementation, which covers strategic planning for the microcomputer system;

TABLE 1.3 Common Microcomputer Problems

Impact level	Pre-implementation	Implementation	Operation
Individual	Fear of the technology Lack of knowledge Nonparticipation in decision making	Differential learning curves Availability of time for training	Time management Task value Job redefinition Conflicting priorities
System	Design goals Budgetary constraints Acquisition	System integration Timing	Support and maintenance Obsolescence
Office	Compatibility with existing technology and procedures Management and planning authority	Timing Ergonomics System integration Training	Security Competition for use Management and control
Organization	Integration with organization goals and systems Authorization and acceptance	Timing System integration Process maintenance Scheduling	Impact on organization structure Job and task restructuring Budgetary impact

implementation, which focuses on those problems related to the actual installation of the system; and operation, which relates to problems that occur once the system is operational. At each of these stages, problems at several impact levels—from those that affect individuals to those that impact on the entire organization—are illustrated.

An example can highlight several of these problems. Consider the situation of a code enforcement agency that wishes to keep track of the work of its inspectors, evaluate their decisions, and then revise the code based on experience in the field. In addressing such an agenda, agency personnel may feel they can set up such a program on their (newly acquired) microcomputer but fail to fully appreciate that any revision in the code must go through myriad approvals. Even if approvals are considered when the microcomputer-based system is designed, users may find they do not have the time to develop all the facets of the program, or find that they cannot design the more complex parts. It is also possible that no one on the staff has sufficient time to enter the data and maintain the programs. Finally, there may be security problems in protecting the data or difficulties in persuading managers to consider information from the system.

As table 1.3 suggests, the problems that arise when microcomputers are adopted in an organization are diverse and extensive. Fortunately, many of the problems included in the listing are the kinds of problems amenable to analysis using microcomputers, but only when there is an adequate understanding of the needed microcomputer tools, techniques, and resulting applications. The need for managerial knowledge of the use of microcomputers to solve organizational problems is brought into sharper focus by the pervasiveness of these problems.

Drawing together the elements discussed so far, we can see why managers do not normally possess the knowledge and skills to manage effectively with the aid of microcomputers. In essence, the development of microcomputer applications in the public sector has occurred in something of a theoretical vacuum (Bozeman & Bretschneider, 1986). The reluctance of data-processing professionals to accept microcomputers as legitimate computer systems tended to slow the adoption of microcomputer systems and force many microcomputer users to operate without benefit of support or useful advice. Users who turned to the professional (and even popular) literature found little or no guidance on the use of microcomputers to solve problems, only extensive reportage on "cookbook" methods for using particular software packages, endless hardware descriptions, and programming tricks (seemingly) designed to befuddle all but the most esoteric hacker.

> *Hacker* is a slang term used to refer to individuals who become deeply involved in the functioning of microcomputer systems. Hackers are known for their love of complicated programming or "tricks and traps" of microcomputing. This term is also sometimes used derisively to describe a person who intentionally violates computer security or places a program (a virus) in use that destroys other people's data.

Essentially cast adrift to find their own way, microcomputer users soon discovered that the use of PCs in organizations generated substantial management as well as operational problems. Unfortunately, there was little information available on how to apply the management concepts appropriate to more traditional problems to those linked to the new technology.

The confluence of all these factors in today's public organization creates an environment in which the promise of microcomputer technology still far outweighs its performance. There is a clear need to provide guidance to the manager or analyst who wishes to use the PC effectively to manage, solve problems, and assist with difficult decisions. It is these needs that are addressed in this book.

PURPOSE AND OUTLINE OF THE BOOK

In broad terms, the purpose of this text is to provide a logic or framework for managers and analysts that will enable them to enhance their decision-making capacity through the use of microcomputers. Although this may seem a very lofty goal, the fact is that much of the knowledge needed to manage effectively with microcomputers is an extension of good management and suitable problem-solving theory and practice. It is our intent to bring together the basic information set that the manager needs to make best use of the new technology, thus providing an effective tool for planning, analysis, and decision making.

More specifically, this text incorporates three major objectives:

1. to provide a logical or theoretical framework for the development of effective microcomputer applications
2. to examine the range of managerial tasks suitable to microcomputer use
3. to illustrate and analyze the application of microcomputer-based solutions to managerial problems

Our first objective—providing a framework for the development of effective microcomputer management systems—is the functional linchpin of this text. It is our contention that through the use of contemporary theories in decision making, policy analysis, computer-based problem solving, and systems theory, it is possible to develop a general process for the engagement of microcomputers in managerial problem solving. In laying out this framework, we draw on several more generic problem-solving approaches from the professional literature, extract the relevant elements, and apply the resultant process to problem-sets amenable to solution using microcomputers. In this approach, we stress concepts of modularity or "divide and conquer," iterative or stepwise development, flexible organization of data, and a modified "top-down" method in order to offer the manager or analyst a flexible system for the application of microcomputer technology.

One of our central conceptual methodologies—referred to as *divide and conquer*—is deductive in process, since most problems facing the public manager or analyst are complex. These complex problems range from highly structured problems that are easily adapted to computer analysis, through semistructured problems that require more managerial resourcefulness and computer knowledge to solve, to unstructured problems that test a manager's intuition, creativity, and flexibility and may be only partially amenable to microcomputer-based analysis. By using a process that reduces complex problems to more manageable components and then links together the individual solution-sets, we offer the manager or analyst a framework that applies the new computer technology appropriately in a context of problem solving and does not defer to the technology alone.

Our second objective—examining the range of applications suitable for solution with microcomputer technology—is intended to assist the manager in selecting those tasks that will be carried out with the use of the computer. We recognize that not all problems are equally amenable to the problem-solving approaches afforded by microcomputers. To use microcomputers effectively, the manager must be able to recognize how far microcomputer-generated solutions can be pursued for different tasks. Throughout the text, we provide examples of various types of appropriate tasks, as well as more detailed analyses of the major categories of microcomputer software packages that can be applied to these tasks.

Since an important component of appropriate task assessment is an understanding of the systems orientation of microcomputers, an in-depth look at the composition and development of microcomputer hardware into functional work systems is also included. When it comes to the effective use of microcomputers, the old adage of "the right tool for the right job" has never been more true.

Our third objective—providing illustrative examples of microcomputer-based solutions to managerial problems—recognizes that, however well conceived the theoretical perspective, it may be difficult to apply the theory unless it is viewed in the context of appropriate examples.

An added reason for the use of examples in this text is to provide the manager or analyst with usable applications that can be adapted to common managerial problems. Given the paucity of relevant literature on the use of microcomputers in management and the absence of communication among users, many analysts spend an inordinate amount of time "reinventing the wheel" by struggling through the development of an application that may have already been successfully implemented elsewhere. Providing a broad range of illustrative applications may reduce the need for the manager to develop each application from scratch.

In a field that is developing as rapidly as that of microcomputers, where generations of technology are measured in cycles of months, the issue of timeliness regarding actual example information will invariably be raised. The references and examples used throughout this book are drawn from the real-world experiences of the authors and other professional microcomputer users. The development of new software tools, expansion of processing power, or improvements in the nature of the technology may quickly render some of the specific illustrations used in this text obsolete. However, we include examples not as "cookbook recipes," but as indicators of the processes and logic that are useful in problem solving. We believe this approach transcends a particular package, such as dBASE III or Lotus 1-2-3, used in an example and provides more elemental data about how the general class of software may be used. Essentially, the key to effective use of microcomputer technology is not the rote memorization of a task or the development of application-specific expertise, but the gaining of knowledge about the *logic*, *limits*, and *potential* of the technology as a problem-solving tool.

CONTENT OF THE BOOK

The book is organized into three major sections. This organization reflects the need to develop a comprehensive understanding of all facets of microcomputer use in problem solving. We proceed from background and basic tools through the establishment of an overall theoretical framework to the utilization of that framework in the development of systems solutions.

The first section of the text—chapters 1 through 3—provides the elements required for a basic understanding of microcomputers. The present chapter, chapter 1, defines microcomputers, gives highlights of the brief history of microcomputers, and notes that the focus of the book is on the logic or framework for using microcomputers as problem-solving tools, not on any particular software. Chapters 2 and 3 present the relevant elements of microcomputer systems: software packages and hardware design, respectively. Although specific software and hardware packages are described in these chapters, the emphasis is more on the categories of systems components available and how they may be combined to form functioning systems.

The second section of the book—chapters 4, 5, and 6—is the theoretical core. It examines the fundamental logic for building problem-solving applications, as well as the organization and accessing of information in a microcomputer-based environment. In chapter 4, the guiding framework for our approach is developed. This chapter establishes the theoretical genesis of our framework and reviews the contribution of key theorists in the field. Central to this framework for building problem-solving microcomputer applications are the complexity of the problem at hand, the specific type of application that best fits the complexity of the problem, and the general design tools that go with application development. Chapters 5 and 6 also focus on topics that are essential to application development and use: data and access. Applications need data and ready access to those data. When the application is being built, it is necessary to have some information about the problem and possible solutions. Once constructed, the application requires a fund of data on the problem in order to view the problem from different perspectives and to explore alternative remedies. All this translates into a need for a varied assortment of databases. A microcomputer environment is a fertile one for creation of these databases, because different interests and perspectives are represented by the microcomputer users. In view of the importance of databases, chapter 5 is devoted to a discussion of the development of relevant, flexible, and efficient databases.

Whereas chapter 5 deals with the structuring and development of databases, chapter 6 focuses on accessing information once it has been collected and stored. The very best data structure in the world is useless if the information cannot be productively accessed and used. This chapter covers the development of the elements that go into a good access system and provides illustrations of such a system.

The third section of the book consists largely of case studies designed to put the theoretical framework to use. Chapters 7, 8, and 9 are organized around one of the major concepts in the framework: how structured or novel are the problems facing the manager or analyst? Chapter 7 looks at structured problems—those that occur with some frequency and have a set of solutions available. Examples are taken from budgeting and expenditure control, and applications are developed from spreadsheet software.

Chapter 8 catapults to those problems that are novel and without much precedent. Often called semistructured and unstructured problems, these can benefit from microcomputer applications but depend mainly on the expertise and judgment of the decision maker for their solution. The case studies are drawn from finance and planning.

In chapter 9, the problems fall between the two extremes of routine and novel. More complex because of the large volumes of data, but not overwhelmingly complex, these often benefit from microcomputer applications. Case material comes from telecommunications management and public safety training.

In an effort to capture smaller or emerging items, the last chapter presents a collection of problems, software, and applications, including project management, expert systems, and desktop publishing. The capacity of each of these is discussed and illustrated with short cases.

CONCLUSION

This book is designed to offer a fund of theoretical and practical insights for using microcomputers as problem-solving tools. The theory draws on general problem-solving logic, information science, management perspectives, and policy analysis. The practical side comes from work with many software packages and from case studies.

As with any new technical area, microcomputers offer many opportunities for investigation and study. Our interests lie in building individual problem-solving applications. Other works will look at the process of employing microcomputers from different perspectives. Some will give attention to the organizational and decision milieu in which the applications are developed and used. Others will look toward the integration of microcomputers into the larger information and computer systems of organizations. Still others will exhaust all the ins and outs of specific software packages. It will be these different interests that will set the limits for effective use of microcomputers in public organizations.

REFERENCES

Bozeman, B., and Bretschneider, S. "Public Management Information Systems: Theory and Prescription," *Public Administration Review,* Special Issue (November 1986): 475–487.

Calista, D. J. "Microcomputer Applications to Productivity Improvements," *Public Productivity Review* 9 (Summer/Fall 1985): 121–128.

Chandler, A. D., Jr. *The Visible Hand: The Managerial Revolution in American Business.* Cambridge: Belknap Press, 1977.

Gardner, E., Render, B., Ruth, S., and Ross, J. "Human-Oriented Implementation Cures 'Cyberphobia'," *Data Management* 23 (November 1985): 29.

Garson, G. David. "Microcomputer Applications in Public Administration," *Public Administration Review* (September/October 1983): 453–458.

Kraemer, K. L., and Northrop, A. "Computers in Public Management Education: A Curriculum Proposal for the Next Ten Years," *Public Administration Quarterly* (Fall 1984): 343–368.

Madron, T. W. *Microcomputers in Large Organizations.* Englewood Cliffs, NJ: Prentice-Hall, 1983.

Mittra, S. S. *Decision Support Systems: Tools and Techniques.* New York: John Wiley & Sons, 1986.

Ostrowski, J. W., Gardner, E. P., and Motawi, M. "Microcomputers in Public Finance Organizations: A Survey of Uses and Trends," *Government Finance Review* 2 (February 1986): 23–29.

Porter, L. R. "Managing the Diffusion of End-User Computing Technologies: A Fifties Mindset with Eighties Tools." In *Managers, Micros and Mainframes: Integrating Systems for End-Users,* edited by Matthias Jarke, pp. 55–72. New York: John Wiley & Sons, 1986.

Raho, L. E., Belohlav, J. A., and Fiedler, K. D. "Assimilating New Technology into the Organization: An Assessment of McFarlan and McKenney's Model," *MIS Quarterly* 11 (March 1987): 47–58.

CHAPTER

2

Understanding Microcomputer Software

■ INTRODUCTION

The purpose of this chapter is to explore one of the tools critical to effective use of microcomputers—the software. It is this microcomputer software that is the central tool in crafting problem-solving applications.

Unfortunately, writing about microcomputer software is a frustrating venture because it is difficult, if not impossible, to be up to date. Not only new versions but entirely new packages are constantly being introduced.

Our strategy is not to attempt to cover the details or the evolution of specific software, but rather to lay out the general categories and general functions of major types of software. Our aim is to touch on the main tools of micro software and how these tools can contribute to building microcomputer applications. For each category, we look initially at the basic usage, and then move to more sophisticated functions. We also select specific packages from the more popular software to use as illustrations.

☐ A consideration for any office is the ever-changing nature of software. Each year virtually every major software manufacturer introduces a "major" change or upgrade. These advancements present the manager with two problems: should it be purchased, and where will the money for the upgrade be found? One thought is that an upgrade should only be made if the new features are specifically needed in the office.

The counterpoint to this argument is that failing to stay on the improvement path results in higher expenditures when a version of the software with needed features does appear. For example, many software companies charge approximately $150 for an upgrade to a new version. If, however, an upgrade is desired that skips a version, the cost may be double, or the user may be forced to pay full price. This means that there is a clear financial incentive to acquire upgrades.

Another argument in favor of update purchases is that the user is gradually introduced to evolutionary changes rather than abruptly encountering a totally unfamiliar command structure or user interface. Continuing to advance helps users to adapt more sophisticated features and reduces anxiety.

The overall point is that *software management* is an important element in ensuring the effective use of micros in the organizational environment.

Categories of Software

There are numerous ways to categorize micro software. The categories surveyed in this chapter are as follows:

- operating systems
- database management systems
- spreadsheets
- statistical packages
- project management
- word processors
- graphics
- telecommunications
- utilities
- programming tools

Admittedly, this listing is somewhat arbitrary. Integrated software programs can include all or some of these categories. Additionally, packages in some of these categories—a database management system, for instance—may offer capabilities that overlap other packages. The reason for proposing these categories is that they rely on common terminology used in today's organizations and instructional training (Curtin & Porter, 1987).

OPERATING SYSTEMS

Background, Purpose, and Definition

According to the premise of this chapter, a general appreciation of the functionality inherent in microcomputer software is necessary in order to use it wisely or to assemble it into microcomputer applications. Unfortunately, what the operating system (OS) does is not immediately apparent. A disk or set of programs referred to as a disk operating system (DOS) is needed to start or "boot" (Wolverton, 1984, p. 12) the micro, but why DOS is required is unclear.

When DOS is first loaded into a micro with floppy disk drives, the initial message on the screen is merely A>, which stands for A prompt or A drive. When it is loaded from a hard disk, the initial message is C>, for C prompt or C drive. These messages neither help nor encourage the novice. However, their days are numbered, since new versions of DOS (4.0 and 5.0), plus OS/2, and Windows will provide an easy-to-use graphics interface.

To clear up some of the mystery, an operating system can be thought of as standing center stage and directing the resources of the personal computer (PC)—that is, locating resources and then telling them where to proceed and what to perform. Resources include the data or information entered into the PC, the central processing unit (CPU), the memory, the keyboard, and the printer. An illustration of the use of DOS is storing a memo (i.e., a file with the memo in it) on a disk, then retrieving it at a later time. (Chapter 3 provides more detail on the hardware resources, such as the CPU.)

Another way to view DOS is by looking at the variety of "housekeeping" tasks it carries out. These include disk preparation, file management, information security, and file organization. In short, DOS helps keep track of and helps secure all the information on the PC. Because of the importance of these functions, familiarity with the operating system is the first step in gaining control over the computing system.

To accomplish many of these tasks, the disk operating system functions as an interpreter between the user and the machine. DOS allows users to work in an English-like environment (although at a cryptic English-like level) while the computer functions within its own language. The user may request a "directory" of files, but DOS communicates this request in a language (of 0s and 1s) the computer can understand.

Currently there are several basic operating systems in the PC arena. The best-established of these for IBM and compatible computers is PC-DOS or MS-DOS. These are nearly identical systems produced by Microsoft Corporation. PC-DOS is the trade name for the system licensed to IBM. As of the late 1980s, the vast majority of IBM-compatible micros depended on some version of the PC/MS-DOS operating system. The Apple Macintosh uses an operating system that is much more transparent to the user. The Finder, as it is known, uses aids, such as pictures, graphics, and menus native to the Mac. This approach insulates the user from the raw operating system command structure and presents a much simpler interface to the user.

An operating system that is gaining acceptance for use on microcomputers is the UNIX system, developed by Bell Laboratories. Also licensed as XENIX, this operating system was originally developed for minicomputers and is very sophisticated. As micros grow in memory and processing capacity, UNIX becomes a viable operating system.

A relatively new operating system is one designed as a replacement for PC/MS-DOS. This new system is called OS/2. The purpose of OS/2 is to handle efficiently the capabilities of the more advanced microcomputer systems, such as those based on the powerful 80386 processor (capable of handling more information faster than former processors). This operating system can manage larger amounts of memory and can accommodate more sophisticated demands.

OS/2 Presentation Manager

An integral part of IBM's strategy with OS/2 is the Presentation Manager included in the OS/2 Extended Edition. Presentation Manager is a graphics-based system similar in function to the Macintosh interface. With a graphics-based interface, the user selects objects on the screen, such as a garbage can, to communicate what the user wants the system to execute. By moving to a graphics interface, IBM hopes to reduce the complexity of the operating system command structure and enable the novice user to gain proficiency quickly. Presentation Manager is designed to be used with a mouse or other pointing device and allows the user to select commands from menus with a point-and-click action. By embracing a graphics interface, IBM also hopes to provide a standardized system across applications that will facilitate movement from one software package to another. In other words, whether the user is working with a word processor or a spreadsheet, the tools for access and manipulation will be guided by this standard graphics operating system. Such a system will also enhance data exchange among programs.

Some preliminaries are needed before we delve more deeply into the microcomputer operating system. First, because IBM-compatible software is widely used in the micro world, discussion of operating systems will be limited to MS/PC-DOS. We recognize that the specific syntax used may not be appropriate for other operating systems, such as UNIX or the Apple Finder; however, the logic and reasoning used in our discussion remain consistent. Second, to simplify the discussion, we will assume that one can use either a floppy disk system or a hard disk system, since both are widely used. (See chapters 3 and 6 for definitions and further details.)

Elements of DOS

DOS has myriad capabilities, but our focus is on how DOS manages and preserves files because these two functions are critical to the end user who wants to make the best and safest use of his or her files. These files are at the core of the user's work. They contain the data or information the user has compiled. A file could be a large spreadsheet that shows monthly expenditures; it could be graphs derived from that spreadsheet; or it could be a memo based on the information in the spreadsheet.

Rudimentary Use of PC-DOS Commands

In this section, four fundamental functions of DOS are covered:

- preparing disks to receive files
- listing the files on a disk
- backing up files
- deleting unneeded files

Setting up disks Before the user creates and manages important micro files and applications, some preparation is required—specifically, formatting or initializing the disks, whether floppy or hard. Formatting is actually related to file management, because the formatting blocks off any unusable parts of the disk and prepares the remaining good areas (often called *sectors*) to receive the files. Without proper formatting, a disk cannot be used.

Great care must be taken when using the FORMAT command because it is potentially a destructive command. Do not FORMAT a floppy or hard disk on which you have valuable information. The FORMAT will erase all the information.

Once the disks have been formatted, files are created with the micro software covered in this chapter—word processing, databases, spreadsheets, and others. For purposes of illustration, we assume the files have already been created with these software packages and the user relies on DOS to make the best and safest use of the files.

Listing files One common use of DOS is to call up or list the names of the files stored on a disk. This is an important facility because even with a few files it is difficult to remember the names. Knowing the exact name is critical because the PC will not ordinarily respond to any instructions for manipulating files unless the exact name is entered.

Chapter 2 Understanding Microcomputer Software

DOS has several ways of letting you peruse file names. Only a few are presented here, to give you a feel for the syntax of DOS.

```
DIR
DIR | SORT > PRN
DIR bud*
```

☐ The convention followed for any software commands is to capitalize the part of the command from the software language and to use lowercase letters for any part contributed by the user. For example, in DIR bud*, DIR is the DOS command to show the directory, and bud is the file name created by the user. The * is part of the command, but there is no way to differentiate it by capitalization.

The first command lists all the files on the current disk. The second sorts all the files in alphabetical order and then, to really help you remember the names of the files, the > PRN redirects the list of files to the printer. Finally, DIR bud* is the "needle in the haystack" solution. Assume that the disk has 50 files on it. You know that the one you want starts with "bud," but you cannot remember the rest of the name. In this case, the asterisk (*) comes to the rescue. The * is called a wild card (as in poker) and means, "Display all the files starting with 'bud' and ending with any set of characters."

Backing up or copying files With all these critical files stored on one vulnerable disk, backing up is essential. By now it should be obvious that there is "gold in them files." To preserve this precious commodity, DOS offers a variety of ways to back up or copy files from one floppy disk to another or between hard disk and floppy (or tape). Both the COPY and BACKUP commands can be used.

Deleting files Just as file management with DOS requires copying or backing up to ensure that files are preserved, file management with DOS provides a command to purge unwanted files. It does not take very long to accumulate an inordinate number of files that not only are unneeded but also take up precious space and make it difficult to find the really indispensable files. Any DOS manual (e.g., Devoney, 1986; Cain & Cain, 1986) will provide all the variations on the DEL, or delete, command.

A Cut Above Rudimentary

So far we have used DOS only at a rudimentary level. It is possible to use DOS in more powerful ways. Two of these are discussed below:

- packaging commands into programs
- organizing files into natural groups and subgroups

Programming Typing and retyping DOS commands can become tedious. For example, copying a file to a backup disk can be monotonous if done over and over. The planners behind DOS (as with most other operating systems) provided a way to package any set of legitimate commands, give those commands a short name, and execute them just by typing the short name. Figure 2.1 demonstrates an approach for transforming a set of commands into a program. Let's call the program save2b.bat.

How does this program, save2b.bat, work? The user types the name of the program, save2b, and some file name—say, budget—to execute the program. What happens next is that the file name to be archived—in this case, budget—is actually placed wherever %1 appears in the program. The percentage sign (%) is the means for generalizing the program and is referred to as a *replaceable parameter*. Consequently, if the user types save2b budmemo, the file budmemo is copied from the C drive to an archive disk in drive B, then deleted from the C drive if desired. With these tools, DOS not only lets the user write small programs to "automate" tasks but also allows the automation to be generalized, as is done in the save2b program.

```
COPY C:%1 B:
ECHO %1 has been copied to the disk in drive B:
ECHO If you want to delete this file, hit return when asked
ECHO Otherwise hit CRTL BREAK to abort the program
PAUSE
del C:%1
ECHO %1 has been deleted
```

FIGURE 2.1

The reason for the extension "bat" in the name save2b.bat can be found in most books on MS-DOS, but for now just think of "bat" as short for "batch" and as the computer's way of designating save2b as a program.

Organizing Another powerful tool is the ability to group files. Yes, DOS can list all the files, even alphabetically, but once the number of files becomes large, especially with the massive capacity of hard disks, it is essential to have additional means of organizing the files. DOS uses a system of "directories and subdirectories" that is essentially familiar to anyone who has seen a hierarchical chart of an organization. In this system, the top or main directory is referred to as the *root directory* and is symbolized by a backward slash (\). Directories tied to the root directory are called subdirectories. If a user had word-processing software, spreadsheets, databases, and special applications, the system in figure 2.2 might provide a way of clustering all this work. In figure 2.2, Main is the root directory, and Wordp, Spreadsh, Datab, and Appl are the subdirectories. Within each of these are all the files (such as wordprcs in the Wordp subdirectory). DOS has a command for creating or "making" these directories (MD) and one for "changing" directories (CD), used to switch from one directory to another.

The system of directories and subdirectories can be viewed as a way of organizing all the software, all the problem-solving applications, and all the data the user will eventually amass. Again, figure 2.2 is an example of how DOS enables users to structure the voluminous microcomputer work they are doing.

MAIN

Wordp	Spreadsh	Datab	Appl
wordprcs	spsheet	database	budgappl
budgrpt1	firstqbd	emplbkrd	finanapl
budgrpt2		perf 1988	persappl
		position.des	

FIGURE 2.2 Subdirectories

Easy Ways to Use DOS

DOS is a valuable tool, but, as we have seen, not always easy to use. Easy ways to use DOS turn control over to menu-driven systems. For example, if a staffer wants to copy an important file (as we did in figure 2.1), he or she must remember the exact syntax and type it correctly. Instead, there might be a sequence of prompts or menu selections that goes something like this:

```
Do you want to copy a file? Y/N

COPY OPTION

What is the name of the file?         _____
Do you want a new file name?          _____
Where do you want the file copied?    _____
```

Subprompts could be added to enhance these questions. For example, when the question about where to copy the file appears, a structure of directories could be placed on the screen so one does not need to remember the names of all the directories nor how to maneuver there.

There are essentially two ways to enlist these easy-to-use menus for DOS. If a user has the time and is so inclined, he or she can develop a personalized menu system to make DOS more cooperative. At the heart of constructing an attractive menu system are the two tools just discussed: the batch (i.e., bat) programming, and the hierarchical organization of directories and subdirectories. Any of the DOS manuals can provide a good starting point for creating one's own menus.

For those not inclined to create a menu system on their own, commercial systems are available. In fact, there are so many commercial systems in the marketplace that the frustration lies in deciding which is the best one. A few telephones calls to software stores will tell the story of the volumes of attractive menu systems. Some of the more popular ones are 1DIR, XTREE, PATHMINDER, DOS2OOLS (Puglia, 1986), and PCTOOLS.

As should be apparent, operating systems will continue to evolve, becoming at each step more powerful and easier to use.

DATABASE MANAGEMENT SYSTEMS

Background, Purpose, and Definition

DOS allows the user to organize and maintain all files, regardless of type (spreadsheets, database, word processing, etc.) or of the relationship among the files. In fact, DOS does not care whether there is gold or garbage in the files. It is the rest of the software and how it is used that determines the quality of information in the files.

Database management systems (DBMS) provide a powerful technology to create and manipulate large systems of files that can operate as an integrated whole. In essence, database management systems enable one to take a "data picture" of the important aspects of an agency (and its environment) and to explore and manipulate these data (Kroenke, 1983). For example, if an agency or division had 10 to 15 major dimensions to be tracked and analyzed, the database management system could create a data picture of these dimensions. This data picture might cover broad areas such as budgeting, social service, or recreation, or the focus might be on one area in great detail.

Database terminology varies considerably. In this book, databases are assumed to consist of several related files or a collection of files. In some treatments, the individual files are called databases, tables, or relations.

To achieve this data-modeling task, the DBMS has two components. One is the database (the actual information), which is the collection of files designed to represent the main features of the organization. The other is the DBMS itself, which is a collection of programs that create and manage the database.

Elements of a DBMS

To create and manipulate the data picture, database management systems have a variety of capabilities and functions that include:

- setting up a file or files to store the data picture
- entering and checking the data for accuracy
- modifying, changing, or updating to reflect new views or new data
- querying and reporting to tap and explore the database information
- indexing or sorting to order the information in the files
- joining files to create new ways of looking at the data
- programming to automate or customize applications

Each of these will be covered briefly, using dBASE III PLUS to illustrate the functions.

dBASE is evolving each year. dBASE III PLUS relies more heavily on a menu-driven approach than does dBASE III; the III PLUS version is used for most of the book when DBMS are discussed. dBASE IV will make the system even more powerful, more accessible, and easier to use. For example, it redefines the Assistant menu system from previous versions into a Control Center. This new interface provides greatly expanded access to dBASE functions through a menu system. Although the interface or menus have changed as the versions of dBASE have progressed, the

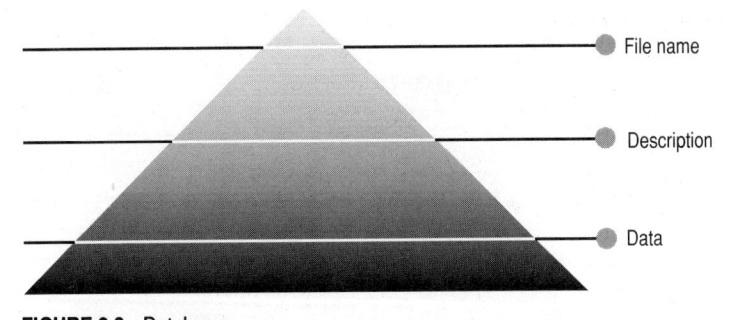

FIGURE 2.3 Database

actual commands that the menus represent are quite similar. In this book, we rely mainly on the commands rather than the menu interface.

The starting point for any DBMS is the design of the database: what data should be included, and how should the data be related to represent an accurate image of the organization? Because of the importance and complexity of database design, it will be dealt with separately in chapter 5. Here we will assume that a database has been designed and that dBASE III PLUS is available to do the actual implementation and manipulation.

Setting up files The initial task in implementing a database is creation of the files, which usually includes (1) *naming* the files, (2) *identifying* and *describing* the data that will go into the files, and (3) *entering* the data. It is important to distinguish among these three steps. The file name provides a "tag," or identifier, so that both the computer and the user can keep track of the file. The description of the data establishes the characteristics of the data; that is, it defines the "shape of the boxes" into which the data are placed. The entry step actually puts the data into the file. To visualize a file, think of a pyramid with the name at the top, then the description of the data, and finally all the data filling the bottom. Figure 2.3 provides a pictorial representation.

By way of example, consider building a file to hold information on the businesses in a community. The file will have a name, a list and descriptions of the data items, and the data themselves. Let's say the name of the file is typeofbs, with "create typeofbs" being the proper dBASE III PLUS command. The data items for each business will include the company's name, its address, and the number of employees as of January 1st. Ordinarily, each data item (company's name, for example) is called a *field*, and these are referred to collectively as a *record*. These fields must usually be thoroughly described.

Figure 2.4 diagrams this file. On the first line is the file name. Next is the record, which consists of or lists all the fields. Then, each field is described in detail.

For many DBMS, including dBASE III PLUS, a major task is providing a fairly detailed description of each field before any data can be entered. dBASE III PLUS requires a name, a data type, and a length for each field. This is illustrated in the lower half of figure 2.4.

Consider, for example, the last field in figure 2.4, labeled "number of employees." The name is num_of_emp; the data type would be numeric, because at some point the staff would want to do mathematical calculations; and the length is limited to five places

```
File Name:        typeofbs

                  Field           Field           Field
Record:           company         address         number of employees
                  name
Detailed
Description:

Field Name        co_name         address         num_of_emp
Data Type         character       character       numeric
Field Length      25              50              5
```

FIGURE 2.4

assuming no firm is likely to have more than 99999 employees in the foreseeable future. Again, this description is not the actual data. Later, when the description is finished, the data will be entered.

Of the three aspects of data description, data type requires further explanation. In technical terms, data type establishes what the user can and cannot do with the data. Below we discuss four data types: numeric, character, date, and logical.

If the data type is *numeric*, then mathematical calculations can be performed on these data. The previous example, "num_of_emp," illustrates numeric type. A second data type (in dBASE III PLUS and most other software) is *character* (or alphanumeric). Character data, such as the name of the firm, can be categorized, displayed, or printed.

The third type of data (again for dBASE III PLUS) is *date*. Date is self-explanatory. The first day of December in the year 1990 can be represented by 12/01/90. With date as a data type, calculation can be done via a special set of operations called *date arithmetic*. For example, how many days are there between 1/23/88 and 2/1/90? With date-type data, it is possible to find out.

A fourth data type (with dBASE III PLUS as a reference) is known as *logical*. The meaning of this data type is less obvious. Logical implies that the data can represent something that is either true or false. For the businesses in our file, each might be eligible or not eligible for state tax exemptions.

After going through the laborious process of giving the file a name and describing each data field, the analyst may think it is time to enter the data. But because people make errors or change their minds, dBASE III PLUS also allows a MODIFY STRUCTURE command. That capacity is important because organizations are plural entities and someone always wants a change. Thus, dBASE III PLUS allows modification of the descriptions before data are put in, and even after.

Data entry The actual data-entry task for most micro DBMS is simple. With dBASE III PLUS, a fill-in-the-blank menu appears, asking for the data for each record. For our business file, the first entry might be: Lambert's Clothing; 243 East Street; 34 (number of employees). Entering the data for each company is mere repetition.

Changing data After data have been inputted, it is very likely that some changes or updates will be needed. In other words, as our organization changes, so too must our data. dBASE, like many other DBMS, permits the user to change and update data. dBASE has a number of commands for this: EDIT, BROWSE, CHANGE, and REPLACE. The first three allow the user to make one or several changes at a time and are relatively simple; REPLACE takes a bit more care and thought. Using REPLACE, it is possible to alter one or more fields in the entire file, all at once. Under these circumstances, it is prudent to make a copy of the files and fiddle with the copy, just in case the REPLACE gets out of hand and makes changes not desired. In fact, if several people have access to the files, a potentially destructive command such as REPLACE might be disabled or configured so only selected people can use it.

Queries With the data described and entered, it is possible to query the database. This, of course, is what the analyst wants to do—obtain relevant information about the organization and its environment. dBASE III PLUS allows both simple and complicated queries. For example, it could provide a display of all the company names and number of employees from the file just created. The command

```
LIST co_names,num_of_emp
```

would do the trick. For a printed or "hard" copy, add a TO PRINT to the end of the above command.

Much more complicated queries can be developed by using what, in computer jargon, are called *operators*. These include:

```
=, <, >, <>
.and. .or. .not.
```

The only nonobvious operator is <>, which means "not equal to."

Using these operators, one can formulate more elaborate probes. One such probe would be to look at companies that have at least 500 employees but no more that 1,500.

```
LIST co_name FOR num_of_emp >= 500 .AND. num_of_emp
```

Sequencing An increment in sophistication is to add order or sequence to the queries. Would it not be more attractive and appealing to arrange the list of companies by alphabetical order? dBASE III PLUS can do that easily, with either its SORT or INDEX command. Additionally, DBMS can sort on more than one field. If the business file had a field for industrial code (e.g., banking, manufacturing, etc.), then a sort on both company code and number of employees would be possible. The result would be a file sorted by industrial code, from those in each code with the smallest number of employees to those with the largest.

```
USE business
INDEX ON indus_code TO busnindx
SET INDEX TO busnindx
LIST co_name,indus_code
```

FIGURE 2.5 dBASE III PLUS Program

Report generators Most DBMS also have what are called *report generators*. These can produce more detailed and more attractive output than the queries just discussed. For example, suppose an analyst has a file on contracts and wants to produce a report that lists all the contracts by type, the total dollars for each type of contract, and the total dollars for all the contracts. Such a report in dBASE III PLUS would require that the file for the report be first indexed or sorted by contract type. Once accomplished, using the dBASE III PLUS report generator is straightforward because of its fill-in-the-blank, menu approach.

Joining or relating files The DBMS examples thus far have dealt with single files. Quite frequently, however, the analyst must deal with more than one file at a time because of the need to consider interrelationships in the organization. Recall that we said the DBMS can provide a data picture of an organization or some part of it. A data picture of even minor complexity requires multiple files. Once there are multiple files, it is necessary to interrelate these to capture the interrelationships within the organization. DBMS, including dBASE III PLUS, are geared to handling demands for interrelating files. The logic behind designing and setting up multiple files is covered at greater length in chapter 5.

Programming The last facet of DBMS is their programming capacity. Using a programming language, it is possible to automate many of the routines a staff member might be doing through a slow, one-command-at-a-time method. Programming also allows customizing the DBMS so that the analyst can put together menu-driven applications (to be discussed in chapter 4).

Programming in dBASE III PLUS and other DBMS is not an overly difficult task so long as the problems tackled are not complex. Much of programming includes the very same commands as are used when the analyst is working interactively with one command at a time. However, programming demands that more thought be given to what commands are needed and to the sequencing of these commands.

A simple example can illustrate the value of programming. One set of commands a manager might employ quite often includes making a file available, indexing that file on a particular field, activating the index, and displaying certain information. With the programming capability of a DBMS, this complement of commands can be stored in a program, given a name, and "run" or executed when desired. In dBASE III PLUS, the program is shown in figure 2.5.

Once these commands are stored as a program, all four statements can be executed simply by running the program. In dBASE III PLUS, the command DO will execute the program. Moreover, as with DOS, dBASE III PLUS allows programs to be generalized so that the actual elements acted on are defined when the program is executed. In dBASE III PLUS the reserve word PARAMETERS serves a function similar to the percentage sign (%) used in DOS.

dBASE III PLUS and other DBMS have a wide assortment of programming capabilities and can be used for many types of programming tasks. In the applications chapters, particularly chapter 9, we will look at programming as a way of tying together various functions (such as data entry, updates, and reports) into more comprehensive micro applications.

Enhancement and Evolution of DBMS

As with any of the software we are covering, there are continual enhancements to DBMS. For example, the latest version of the venerable dBASE program is version IV. dBASE IV represents a substantial upgrade from the previous version. Most notable of the changes is a Control Center that replaces, and greatly enhances, the dBASE III PLUS Assistant. The new Control Center provides the user with a menu-driven interface that facilitates basic database commands and allows easy manipulation of more sophisticated programming and report generation capabilities. The new version of dBASE also includes a QBE (query-by-example) feature that enables the novice user to quickly develop sophisticated queries. Perhaps the most important feature of the new program, however, is its link to SQL (structured query language). SQL is a standard database language on IBM mainframes, and linking it to microcomputer DBMS software greatly expands the analytical power available to the user.

■ SPREADSHEETS

Background, Purpose, and Definition

Spreadsheets, in contrast to DBMS, are not oriented to storing large sets of data that render a general picture of the relevant features of the organization. Rather, the current generation of spreadsheets serve a more specific purpose. Ordinarily, these spreadsheets are most useful when they focus on one function or task, such as a departmental budget, travel vouchers, projection of client demand, or automation of inventory systems.

In this more specialized role, spreadsheets offer two important tools:

1. They are able to describe the state of affairs of some function, particularly the quantitative aspect. For example, how much was spent in the first quarter of the year, and is this amount greater than expenditures in the previous quarter?
2. They are capable of exploring alternatives and options. For example, what would happen to the budget if overhead were increased by 5 percent instead of 9 percent? This is called the "what if" capability.

As with microcomputer DBMS, there are several popular spreadsheet packages. From these we will select one to describe some of the features of setting up and using spreadsheets.

Among the more popular spreadsheet programs are Excel, Lotus 1-2-3, and Quattro.

Lotus, partly because of its ability to run on IBM and IBM-compatibles, holds the largest market share of spreadsheets. In many ways, it defines the nature of this software category. Lotus gives the spreadsheet what might be termed a highly "visual" orientation. It is an electronic sheet or matrix with rows and columns. The rows are numbered, and the columns are designated by letters. The user inserts a number or some other information into a particular cell (C14, for example), and the data remain there for the user to work on. Much of the following description of spreadsheets relies on Lotus 1-2-3.

Spreadsheet Elements

Our initial focus is on the elemental building blocks of Lotus that are integral to constructing simple spreadsheets. After these have been covered, then the more complex (and often more powerful) facets will be presented. Among the building blocks of Lotus are its:

- simplified information and data entry
- adjusting and formatting for appearance capabilities
- formulas
- labor-saving commands
- memory aids

Many of the spreadsheet building blocks that we will discuss are accessed through Lotus' *hierarchical-style* menus. The hierarchical menus are hidden from view except when called. As soon as the user strikes the slash key (/), which is usually toward the bottom right of the keyboard, the hierarchy of menus appears at the top of the grid without interfering with any of the cells in the worksheet (see figure 2.6). The menu is hierarchical in that the major commands appear on the very top row. On the second command row is a description of options associated with one of the main, or first-row, commands. To find out what one of the main commands does, just move to that command and look at the lower row. Figure 2.6 shows all the options associated with the WORKSHEET command. For example, the Insert option allows the user to insert a new row or column in the worksheet.

Design considerations In the following pages we will discuss various tools associated with Lotus; however, before beginning to use and take advantage of all these spreadsheet tools, it is vital to develop a plan or design of what the spreadsheet should look like and what it will do. Otherwise, the individual tools will be poorly used. Fuller discussion of designing spreadsheets will be given in chapters 7 and 8.

Data entry Once the user has laid out a design and knows what the spreadsheet is supposed to achieve, one of the first tasks in putting together a worksheet is data entry. This is straightforward in Lotus. Ordinarily, there is no need to specify data type or name the data, as in dBASE III PLUS. Simply go to the cell desired and type in almost anything. If a number is entered, Lotus assumes that at some point the user will want to perform mathematical operations on that number and thus automatically makes it a numeric data type. Following this logic, if a user puts words or phrases in the cells—Monthly Office Budget, for example—Lotus assumes this is a label (Lotus calls alpha or character data *labels*). If a label is entered, math operations will generally not be performed on it. Figure 2.7 shows the beginning of an unpolished Lotus spreadsheet with labels and numbers.

Chapter 2 Understanding Microcomputer Software

```
A1:
Worksheet  Range  Copy    Move    File    Print   Graph    Data    System  Quit
Global,    Insert, Delete, Column, Erase,  Titles, Window,  Status, Page
           A       B       C       D       E       F        G       H
1
2
3
4
5
6
7
8
9
10
11
12
13
14
15
16
17
18
19
20
```

FIGURE 2.6

Appearance Once data have been inputted, Lotus has extensive capabilities for adjusting information and formatting data. The main reason for adjusting or formatting is to make the worksheet more aesthetic. Figure 2.7 is singularly unappealing. Labels, such as JAN, FEB, and MAR, are not aligned over the numbers they represent; some labels, namely Categories, run into labels next to them; and none of the numbers is designated as representing dollars or percentages.

With Lotus it is possible to change the width of a column so that its contents do not overflow into the next column. Labels, such as JAN, can be placed on the left-hand or right-hand side of the cell, or centered. The numbers in the cells can have dollar signs or percentage signs. Figure 2.8 shows an enhanced spreadsheet.

Formulas Formulas for calculating are an integral part of spreadsheets. Lotus has a vast store of computational power for calculations. Much of this computational power falls under the aegis of Lotus formulas (often referred to as *functions*). For example, in figure 2.7 the subtotal for Jan (36000) is calculated by the command @SUM(C11..C13). For reference to cells, see figure 2.9.

The calculating power of Lotus includes formulas such as @AVG(RANGE), @MAX(RANGE), @COUNT(RANGE), @NPV(INT,RANGE), and @SLN(COST,SALVAGE VALUE). AVG stands for the mean; MAX finds the largest number in a list or range of numbers; COUNT tallies the number of observations in a list; NPV determines the net present value; and SLN does a straight-line depreciation.

```
                              Overhead      0.08
              Monthly Office Budget, First Quarter
  CategorieJAN         FEB          MAR         1QRT
  ------------------------------------------------
  Personnel    35000        27000
  Travel
  Supplies      1000         2000
  Subtotal     36000        29000
  Overhead      2880
  Total        38880
```

FIGURE 2.7

```
                              Overhead      8.00%
              Monthly Office Budget, First Quarter
  Categories    JAN          FEB          MAR         1QRT
  --------------------------------------------------------
  Personnel   $35,000      $27,000
  Travel
  Supplies     $1,000       $2,000
  Subtotal    $36,000      $29,000
  Overhead     $2,880       $2,320
  Total       $38,880      $31,320                  $0          $0
```

FIGURE 2.8

Lotus also lets the user create his or her own formulas. A good example of custom formulas is the calculation of overhead in figure 2.7. Usually, to signal a user-created formula, just type a plus sign (+). For overhead, the formula could be +.08*C14—that is, .08 (8%) times the content of C14, which is the subtotal. Specifically, .08 * the January subtotal of 36,000 is 2,880, or as figure 2.9 shows it, +$OVERHEAD*C14.

Labor saving Another particularly powerful facility for building spreadsheets falls under what might be called labor-saving commands. Because so much of a worksheet involves repetition, a major labor-saving command is the copy command. Note in figure 2.7 that only the January total has been calculated. Without a copy command, it would be necessary to retype or rekey the @SUM formula three more times. Lotus has a command called *relative* (address) *copy* that allows one to copy the formula from January total to February, March, and First Quarter totals. Lotus knows that when a formula is copied from column C to column D, for example, the formula must be adjusted to reflect the move. If you could look into the cell for February total, you would see that Lotus knew to change @SUM(C14..C15) for the January total to @SUM(D14..D15) for February (figure 2.9).

A relative copy, in which the formula is adjusted as it moves, is not desirable all the time. Take the overhead calculation, previously described. The percentage for overhead

```
         A         B              C              D              E         F
   1
   2
   3
   4
   5                                                         Overhead    0.08
   6
   7                       Monthly Office Budget, First Quarter
   8
   9         Categories            JAN            FEB            MAR      1QRT
  10         ---------------------------------------------------------------
  11         Personnel           35000          27000
  12         Travel
  13         Supplies             1000           2000
  14         Subtotal     @SUM(C11..C13) @SUM(D11..D13)
  15         Overhead     +$OVERHEAD*C14 +$OVERHEAD*D14
  16         Total        @SUM(C14..C15) @SUM(D14..D15) @SUM(E14 @SUM(F14
  17
  18
  19
  20
```

FIGURE 2.9

(8%) is contained in cell F2. If the formula for calculating January overhead were +F2*C14, and were copied from January to February, the F2 in the formula would be changed to G2. Unfortunately, there is nothing in G2. As a result, overhead for February would be zero. To solve this problem, Lotus has an *absolute* (address) *copy*. For our purposes, a dollar sign ($) is placed in front of the cell reference F2 (+$F2*C14). The $ means: use the cell location and content of that cell (F2) do not change when the formula is moved. When +$F2*C14 is copied to the D column, F2 remains F2, but C14 changes to D14.

Memory aids   Spreadsheets, like other software tools, become filled with "computerese," as in the formula +$F2*C14. Lotus allows the use of names in formulas to help the user understand what the formula is about. For example, instead of +$F2*C14, it is possible to assign a name to the contents of cell F2. The name OVERHEAD in +$OVERHEAD*C14 is an example. It conveys that we are multiplying the overhead percentage by whatever is in C14 (the monthly subtotal) to determine the monthly overhead. That is exactly what is done in figure 2.9.

Further Spreadsheet Enhancements

Lotus, like dBASE III PLUS, has the capacity to automate and customize the analysis by means of a programming language. In Lotus that language is generally referred to as a *macro* language; that is, individual instructions or commands are packaged into one large (macro) program.

By way of introduction to these programming tools, let us examine how they help automate a Lotus command, saving a file. In the course of a long worksheet session, the prudent analyst might save a worksheet file twenty times by using the following sequence of commands: /FS (for FILE SAVE), then the name of the file, and finally an R to replace the old file with the new file. Would it not be more convenient to bundle these keystrokes into a small program—a macro—and execute it by referring to the macro's name? The Lotus programming language makes it possible to store the sequence of commands as a label, name it with a one-letter name, and then run it with a simple keystroke combination. Below is the actual program, or macro, for saving a file:

```
'/FS{?}~R~
```

Admittedly, the macro looks more imposing than simply typing the entire set of commands. Why the single quote (') before the /, what is {?}, and why the ~ before and after the R? These symbols are all part of the programming, or macro, language. The ' before the / is necessary to store the entire macro. If the ' were not entered first, then as soon as one hit the slash key (/), the hierarchical menu would appear. The purpose here is to store the sequence, not bring up the menu. The rest of the macro is exactly what the user would do if typing it, except that Lotus provides a few special characters to replace some of the commands. The {?} is a prompt that allows the user to put in the name of the file to be saved. The ~, called a *tilde*, is the Lotus character for the enter key. If read from left to right, the macro contains all the commands to save a file, assuming that the file was saved the first time by directly keying in the commands.

One can be more ingenious with these programming macros. It would be possible, for example, to set up the Monthly Office Budget in figure 2.8 so that one could automatically access it and be able to enter all the data without knowing anything about Lotus. More complex, program-driven spreadsheets are illustrated in the problem-solving chapters, particularly chapter 8.

Lotus 1-2-3 Version 3

Most of the spreadsheet work done in this book draws from version 2.01 of Lotus. Version 3 of Lotus 1-2-3 continues the evolution of the integrated spreadsheet by adding features that allow larger spreadsheets, faster calculations, and the implicit linking of multiple spreadsheets. Although many of the features of the latest version of 1-2-3 are logical enhancements, the ability to link worksheets dynamically is a major improvement that dramatically expands the power of the spreadsheet. With the dynamic link, users can create three-dimensional worksheets that pass information from one worksheet to another.

For organizations with both IBM-compatible and Apple Mac systems, or those desiring a spreadsheet with extensive structure and format control, the Excel spreadsheet from Microsoft offers an alternative to the Lotus program. One attractive feature of Excel is the existence of both IBM and Apple versions. The common file structure of the programs makes data transfer between the systems a simple matter.

STATISTICAL PACKAGES

Background, Purpose, and Definition

Statistical packages typically consist of a wide variety of statistical analyses (averages, crosstabulations, correlations) collected into one large package and readily available to the end user. The user need only supply a description of the data, the actual data, and a few instructions about which statistic to use to obtain results from the statistical programs.

Statistical packages offer the user three powerful analytical capabilities:

1. They can summarize large bodies of data.
2. They can help untangle a complex causal pattern.
3. They can assist with projections into the future.

Statistical packages are similar to spreadsheets in that both offer significant number-crunching power. They differ in that statistical packages provide more tools for causal studies, whereas spreadsheets are more exhaustive when it comes to analysis of alternatives (what-ifs), particularly those alternatives that involve financial decisions. Because of these differences, it behooves one, when building applications, to examine closely what type of analysis is needed and what type of software can bring the largest arsenal to bear for that particular problem.

Elemental Features

To tap the power of statistical packages, it is necessary to understand the fundamental elements usually associated with these tools:

- Name the files.
- Describe the data.
- Input the data.
- Select the appropriate statistic.
- Manipulate the data, if necessary.
- Format the output, if desired.

One of the micro statistical packages that follows this format is STATPAC, and we will use it for purposes of illustration.

Of the several components listed, only the first four are essential for most statistical packages; the other two are optional. As a result, it is not difficult to begin using statistical packages. More problematic is choosing the appropriate statistic. Indeed, easy-to-use packages can make for dangerous situations when the user is not familiar with fundamental concepts of statistics and takes the results at face value.

File name, data description, and data entry These tasks are similar to the routines discussed in the database section and will not be detailed here. The syntax differs—for example, field names in STATPAC can have blanks in them (e.g., employ ID)—but the logic is the same. The file or files for the data description are named and the structure defined; then the data are entered. As with the DBMS, statistical packages have menus to assist in data description and data entry.

Selection of statistics Once the data have been described and inputted, the next task is to choose the appropriate statistics. This choice depends on what the analyst wants to know and on his or her knowledge of statistics, not on the syntax and rules of statistical packages.

A common scenario in statistical analysis is to start by examining the distribution of values or the averages (means, medians, modes). For instance, in a study of sick leave, what is the minimum number of days of sick leave taken? What is the maximum? What are the mean and the variability? To answer these questions, statistical packages offer descriptive statistics (means, medians, etc.) and frequencies (the number of cases that fall within each category, such as males and females).

After gaining an impression of the distribution of the data, the analyst may want to uncover the factors "causing" the differences—in this case, the differences in days of sick leave taken. For these questions, statistical packages provide crosstabular analysis, correlation, and regression. With these statistical tools, one can explore whether age or type of work is related to amount of sick leave taken.

Data manipulation Related to statistical analysis is data manipulation. One type of data manipulation deals with adjusting or modifying the distribution of the data. Many statistical tests assume that the data are distributed normally, which means if plotted from low to high values the plot would resemble a bell-shaped curve. If data fail to meet the normality criterion, it is often necessary to transform the data through data manipulation. An appropriate transformation might be a logarithmic transformation, using a command such as:

```
COMPUTE=LG(age)
```

After all the work of describing the data, keying it in, choosing the appropriate statistics, and making the necessary changes or transformations, it is important to have attractive output. More statistical packages are adding report writers and graphics. Report writers allow for clearly titled, well-placed, and nicely spaced output. Graphics take those mind-numbing numbers and translate them into mind-refreshing pictures. Common types of graphics are discussed in the section on graphics.

Sophisticated Components

Because of the complex nature of statistical analysis, statistical packages are beginning to offer what are called "smart statistics" (Minor, 1986). Here, expert statisticians are adding their knowledge to statistical packages. For example, instead of the user having to be fully aware of the normal distribution requirement for certain statistics, the package can look at the distribution and provide a message to the user such as: "Distribution of variable 1 not normal. Do you wish another run with a logarithmic transformation?" Although the user still may feel uncomfortable, at least he or she knows the type of question to carry to the expert.

Statistical packages for micros are advancing on all fronts, including not only the smart features just noted but also packages that run faster, have better graphics, and offer a wider range of statistics. As with spreadsheets and databases, statistical packages are receiving significant investments from the micro software developers. Currently available packages include SPSS/PC+, PC SAS, SYSTAT, and STATGRAPH.

PROJECT MANAGEMENT

Background, Purpose, and Definition

Project management software for microcomputers is a direct descendent of the same type of software used on mainframe computing systems. The term *project management* usually refers to a collection of analytical techniques that are used to:

- plan the details of carrying out large, complex projects
- determine the time and resource dependency among components of the project
- determine the time constraints on completing a project and how time can best be managed
- allocate resources in an appropriate and timely fashion
- track the progress of the project to determine potential time delays or resource misallocations and their consequences

Project management techniques first became popular in the 1950s. Perhaps the best-known early use of these techniques was in the Polaris submarine construction program. At that time, the Polaris program was considered to be the most complex undertaking ever attempted by the government and associated contractors. Many of the project management techniques were developed and refined to deal with the complexity of this project. For many years, project management required the use of costly mainframe computing resources, and its use was largely confined to technical experts in the field who dealt with the cumbersome syntax and inherent complexity of the project management techniques.

By the early 1980s, the power of microcomputers had progressed sufficiently to accommodate streamlined and simplified versions of project management techniques. With the publication of programs such as Harvard Project Manager, TIMELINE, Project Workbench, and SuperProject, the concepts and use of project management techniques became available to a much broader population of managers and analysts.

Basic Project Management Concepts

The set of techniques that comprise project management are all based on two related concepts. First is the technique known as Program Evaluation and Review Technique, or PERT. PERT is used to analyze the component parts of a project and how they relate to one another. Essentially, a project is divided into *tasks* and *milestones*. A task is an operative element of the project; it does something. For example, "pour the concrete for the foundation" is a task. The key feature of tasks is that they have duration, occurring over time. The length of time it takes to complete a task will affect both the overall time it takes to complete the project and the time it takes to complete subsequent tasks that are dependent on the prior task.

A milestone is a point in time that indicates the beginning or completion of a task, or both. Milestones are arbitrary indicators used to measure the progress of the project. They are frequently considered operational translations of objectives that indicate a specific start and end date and time for a task.

PERT is used to create a network diagram, called a *dependency network*, that graphically illustrates the time (serial) relationships and resource (dependency) relationships among project tasks. This dependency network is used both to plan the project by optimizing the dependency relationships and to facilitate time and resource allocations and track the progress of the project by matching planned milestone achievement with actual milestone achievement.

In addition to the dependency network, PERT is also used to create a time-relationship chart called a GANTT chart (named after its developer Henry L. Gantt). The GANTT chart is used to show the beginning–end time relationships of the project tasks in bar chart format. This makes it somewhat easier to track task completion and view whether a particular task is ahead of, on, or behind schedule.

The second major component of project management is the Critical Path Method, or CPM. CPM is a set of mathematical formulas that are used to indicate expected completion dates, likely completion dates, and actual completion dates for project tasks and how those times affect the overall completion date for the project. CPM gets its name from the fact that one chain of dependencies throughout the project will always consume the greatest amount of time. Any delay on this dependency "path" means that the entire project will be delayed. This is then known as the *critical* path. Since tasks on other dependency paths should be completed in less time than those on the critical path, they are said to possess slack or float. This means that there is some amount of delay that is acceptable in these tasks without disrupting the overall schedule of the project. By judicious analysis of these tasks, it may be possible to reallocate resources from a "slack path" task to one on the critical path. The result is that the project can now be completed in a shorter time with a more efficient allocation of project resources. CPM provides the mathematical formulas that permit such calculations.

Supplemental Project Management Concepts

In addition to PERT and CPM, many current project management software packages also include other techniques that facilitate resource management. Resource Allocation, or RA, is becoming a popular addition to the basic techniques. RA assumes that an organization has a finite pool of resources that must be allocated among competing projects. RA offers techniques to illustrate the various resource commitments among projects and warn when a resource has been overcommitted.

Another supplemental technique is Resource Leveling, or RL. RL is used to ensure that resources are being used efficiently. It can point out tasks or projects that are consuming an inordinate amount of a particular resource and allow that resource to be more efficiently reallocated. RL is a companion technique to RA, and when one is present in a software package, the other is as well.

Project Management Software

There are various levels of project management software available for microcomputers. Some programs, such as GANTT CHART and TIMELINE, focus almost exclusively on the GANTT feature, which is the easiest for the untrained manager to use. Other programs, such as Project Workbench, Promis, and Harvard Total Project Manager, offer the complete range of project management techniques, including PERT, CPM, GANTT, RA, and RL. These high-end programs look similar to their mainframe counterparts and require a considerably greater level of knowledge about project management in order to be used effectively.

It is difficult to illustrate the syntax of project management software packages because they vary so much. Some programs employ a matrix format that is equivalent to a spreadsheet format. Others have adopted a more graphic orientation in which the user actually constructs the GANTT chart or dependency network. Whatever the syntax, the program is usually capable of building the appropriate charts and graphs from a single data-entry format. This saves time and reduces the input needed from the user.

Current microcomputer-based project management software does not have the capacity to handle projects as complex as the Polaris submarine or space shuttle program. Limited to several hundred (as opposed to many thousand) tasks and milestones (generically called *nodes*), the micro programs are best suited to smaller, less complex projects.

A Note of Caution

While project management software can be a very useful tool, it is not for every manager or analyst. The appropriate use of this software requires a fairly extensive knowledge of project management concepts and procedures. Many novice users have found that the project management software requires far more prior knowledge than any other major category of software. For this reason, project management software must be considered as "niche" software designed to serve a specific set of functions. In later chapters, we will detail the appropriate use of this class of software.

■ WORD PROCESSING

Background, Purpose, and Definition

So far the focus has been on software packages that emphasize data management and data analysis. However, from a managerial perspective, data must be presented clearly and attractively to influence ideas and decisions. This brings us to the topic of word processing in this section, followed by graphics in the next.

Word processors are software packages that electronically store and manipulate characters or text. In this respect, word processing is not much different from many other types of software that also store and manipulate characters electronically. Word processors differentiate themselves by emphasizing editing and formatting functions to enhance the appearance, and perhaps the quality, of writing. In addition, word processors are being united with other powerful tools (outliners, indexers, style checkers) to bring more capacity to bear on the organization and presentation of data and ideas.

As with other types of software, there is no paucity of word-processing packages in the market. There are word-processing packages for the generalist who works on a wide range of documents; packages for people who produce long and complex documents; and packages for people who work with very technical documents in engineering and the sciences. What cuts across these packages is their ability to edit and format. Some widely used word-processing packages are Wordstar, Manuscript, XYwrite, Microsoft Word, and WordPerfect.

Basic Word-processing Capabilities

The basic features of word processing are as follows:

- wraparound
- maneuverability
- editing
- formatting

Each of these will be described in turn.

Wraparound Word processors facilitate typing with their "wraparound" ability. As the typist reaches the end of the line, the word processor automatically shifts the cursor to the beginning of the next line. With simple electronic typing, each end of line required pressing the return key to advance to the next line. For speed typists, and even the rest of us, the wraparound capability is a timesaver.

Maneuverability Maneuverability, or moving from one part of a document to another, is enhanced considerably by word-processing power. Word-processing packages allow one to jump directly to the beginning or end of the document, to a particular page, to the beginning or end of a paragraph, to the beginning or end of a line, to a particular word, or to the top or bottom of the screen.

Editing With the ability to maneuver around the screen and the document, it is possible to notice errors or poorly constructed phrases and to edit them. The editing capacity allows users to delete, insert, transpose, or transport anything from single letters to whole paragraphs. Just as editing can make all these changes, it can also undo them. If a line is accidentally deleted, it can be brought back with the "undo" command. Some word processors leave an "edit trail" so the reader can see what was taken out and what was added.

Formatting Effective written communication depends on stating your ideas clearly. Communication also depends on how appealing the document looks. Centering, indentation, underlining, boldfacing, and multiple columns (in newspaper format) can all enhance written communications.

More Sophisticated Facilities

Word processors have two other, more sophisticated facilities that involve modularizing and automating the writing process. *Modularizing* allows the writer or typist to enter previously prepared information into a document. Consider letters or memos that always include your name and address or name and title. Instead of retyping this information every time, type it once, place it in a separate file, and call it in when a document needs this information.

Automation A technique that falls into the class of automation is the search, find, and replace command. Think of a document where the name of your division or agency appears several times. Rather than typing the division name each time, many word processors permit the user to type a character or symbol, such as *. Later, when you are ready to complete the document, just use the search, find, and replace command to replace the * symbol with the agency or division name.

There is almost no end to the amount of automation in word processing. Some word processors guess at the word being typed and fill out the rest of the word as soon as it is apparent what the word is. Although this is new and still not used much, many other modes of automation are more common. A simple one is to take advantage of the "function" keys (usually F1 to F10) on the keyboard. During the installation of the word-processing program, these function keys can often be set to automate commands. Leaving the F1 for help menus, F2 might be set to go to the beginning of the document, F3 to do underlining, F9 to go to the end, and F10 to save the file.

In addition to these forms of automation, commands can be packaged into macros. If, after editing a paragraph, you typically go to the beginning of the paragraph, format it, and move to the end of the paragraph, all these commands can be stored in a macro and executed with one or two keystrokes.

Smart features Word processors have "smart," or intelligent, functions that go beyond simple automation. Spelling checkers were among the earliest smart add-ons. Now there are thesauruses, grammar checkers, and style checkers. A sentence such as "After the product was finalized it impacted myriad facets of the human support system" might just blow up a style checker.

One other convenient feature of word processors is an indexing capacity. For example, of the 200 agency memos the user has written, which ones discuss halfway houses? With an indexing capacity, the user can locate those memos that deal with a particular subject.

Another feature that is closely related to word processing is an outliner. Complex topics usually require preplanning and careful thought before one starts to write. Outliners can help in this preplanning and organizing task. Numerous outliners are on the market (including GrandView, Thinktank, and Freestyle), and many are able to transport the outline directly to the word processor to avoid rekeying the same material.

In one sense, the term *word processor* is a misnomer because so many features are now packaged with word processors. For example, the serious user might store small pieces of information, using the word processor, and then index these for further reference. When it is time to organize a particular set of ideas into a report, an outliner can be called. For each major point in the outline, the indexer can be used to find the pertinent material. Once the material takes shape, the user brings in relevant items, drafts the document, and then polishes with editing, formatting, and a host of checkers.

Desktop Publishing Trends

Further enhancing written presentations is the emerging world of desktop publishing, which allows users to integrate pictures with all sorts of text and enlarge or shrink images.

A trend among full-feature word-processing packages such as WordPerfect,

Microsoft Word, XYwrite, and Wordstar, is the inclusion of many features taken from desktop publishing packages. Nicknamed "word publishers," the new versions of these packages provide the user with extensive control over text placement, including columnar formatting, font selection and sizing, graphics insertion, and overall page layout. The programs also include sophisticated new page-preview functions that take advantage of the high-resolution graphics monitors (see chapter 4) to enable the user to view the layout of multiple pages at one time, thus reducing the need for continual trial printings.

All is not roses and light with these new packages, however. Their newfound power brings with it increased complexity and size as well as frequently slower operations. To take full advantage of the features of the new packages, users must have a fast computer system, high-resolution graphics, a hard disk, and a laser printer.

GRAPHICS

Background, Purpose, and Definition

As analysts and managers recognize, numbers and words are not enough to create attractive and convincing presentations. Graphics enable readers to digest otherwise complicated material. Graphics software can transform columns of dull numbers into vibrant charts and figures. Similarly, a mundane flow of paperwork can be made more dynamic, with simple flowcharts showing where the work originates and what happens as it makes its way through the various hands in the agency. For those with an artistic sense, a typical dull poster can take on new life with enhancements from graphic art. It is around these three topics—business graphics, flowchart graphics, and artistic graphics—that the discussion of graphics software revolves.

Business Graphics

Much of business graphics consists of the translation of numbers into pictorial representations. Our discussion will move from the elemental capabilities to the more sophisticated. For purposes of illustration, the graphics aspect of Lotus 1-2-3 is used. We will trace the evolution of a line chart that shows the monthly ratings of a given department. The data are given in table 2.1.

Obtaining attractive business graphics with Lotus involves:

- deciding on the type of graphics
- representing the data
- enhancing the graphics with titles, labels, legends, and scale adjustments
- saving the graphics

Ordinarily, the first decision in Lotus graphics is the type of graph desired. Three fundamental types—bar, line, and pie—are available. Next, the data are selected—in this case, the monthly ratings. The resulting graph can then be displayed on the screen. Figure 2.10 shows a simple graph for Departmental Performance Ratings.

Enhancing the graph includes adding descriptions for the x and y axes, providing titles, and inserting other critical information for the reader. The Lotus graph menu allows

Chapter 2   Understanding Microcomputer Software   45

TABLE 2.1   Monthly Department Performance Rating 19xx

Jan	90%
Feb	85%
...	..
...	..
Aug	60%
Sep	70%
Oct	80%
...	..

Dept Performance Rating
>90 good;70-89 ave;<70 poor

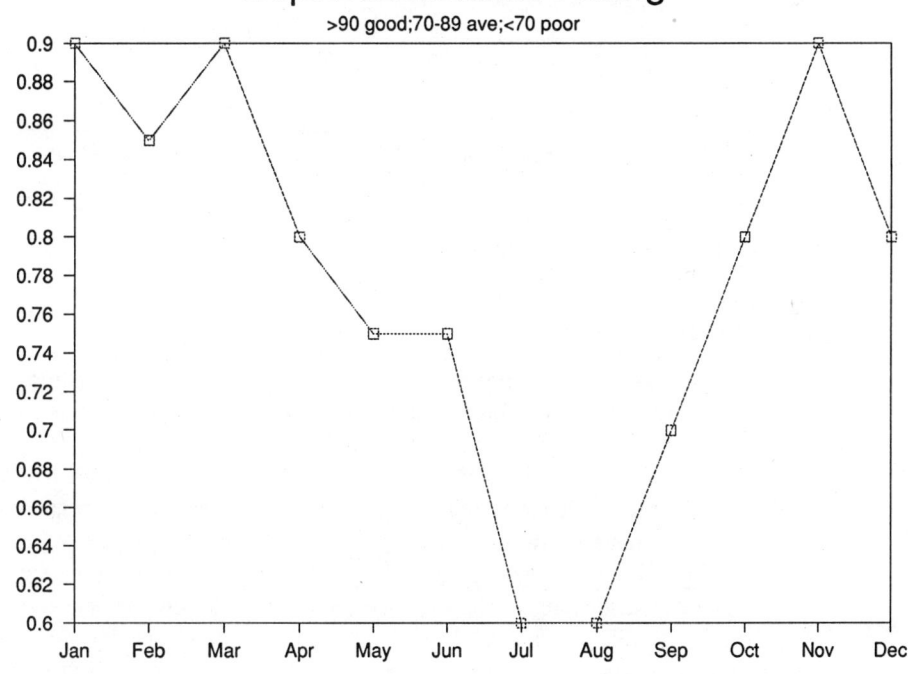

FIGURE 2.10

a first and second title, as well as titles for the *x* and *y* axes. Data labels and legends can also be interjected. In addition, the scale can be changed for either the *x* or the *y* axis, or both. Figure 2.11 shows an enhanced graph that outshines the initial effort.

As with other types of software, there are many packages that can do business graphics. These include Harvard Graphics and Pixie.

Dept Performance Rating
>=90 good; 70-89 ave; <70 poor

[Line chart showing monthly ratings: Jan 90%, Feb 85%, Mar 90%, Apr 80%, May 75%, Jun 75%, Jul 60%, Aug 60%, Sep 70%, Oct 80%, Nov 90%, Dec 80%. Y-axis: Rating (0.5 to 1). X-axis: Month.]

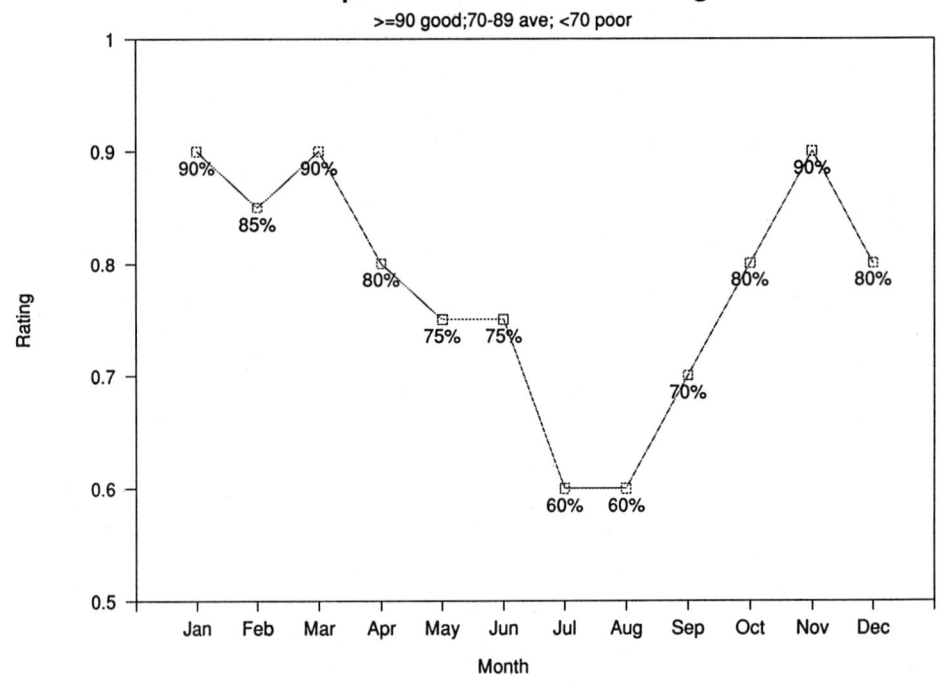

FIGURE 2.11

Processes and Structures

The next major category of graphics is the pictorial representation of processes and structures. *Process* refers to the flow of information in an organization; *structure* is restricted to the decision and authority lines of the organization.

To develop flow diagrams and organizational charts there are a number of graphics packages identified as "paint" programs—among them, PC Paint and Paintbrush. These programs have a variety of tools that make it relatively easy to create flows and structures.

The first category of tools in these paint programs allows the user to do lettering, to call on an assortment of shapes, to do some freehand drawing, and to move an item from one part of the screen to another. Typically, the work is guided by means of a set of *icons*, or pictures, on one side of the screen that represent the various tools. For example, the letter *A* might represent lettering capability; a square, the potential of creating a square of almost any size; and a chalkboard eraser the ability to remove mistakes.

For at least some of these tools, it is possible to add variations and enhancements. Lettering is a prime example. The size and type (fonts) of lettering can be altered. The title of a chart can be done in different sizes—for example, a scale of ½ inch or ¼ inch. The title can also be in bold lettering or in script, Greek or Roman, to mention a few options. Similarly, the boxes and other shapes can be of different thicknesses. Usually there is a set of lines of varying thicknesses, which, when selected, will translate into the desired thickness. Drafts of figure 2.2 were created with a paint program.

TABLE 2.2 Purposes and Types of Exchanges in Communications

Purposes	Types of Exchanges
Use programs	Micro to mainframe
Transfer data and information	Micro to micro
Develop programs	Networks, all types

Artistic Work

To add an artistic use of graphics requires not only a set of tools but also talent and an artistic eye. Not being able to draw a straight line should not prevent one from diagramming a flowchart. However, for that waterfall or artistic characterization of a recreation area, talent helps considerably.

If you are intent on doing more artistic work with graphics packages but "can't draw a straight line," you can use a set of tools known as *clip art*. For example, if most of your work revolves around outdoor scenes, there are software distributors who can supply you with birds, waterfalls, bike paths, sailboats, etc. Even those with artistic talent often find it helpful to have this added set of tools.

ELECTRONIC COMMUNICATIONS AND TELECOMMUNICATIONS

Background, Purpose, and Definition

Given all the data and analytical capability of micros, and given the intense exchange of information that characterizes organizations, it is important to be able to move data from location to location. In the computer realm, electronic communications and telecommunications provide this capacity. It consists of electronic access to data, programs, or information, and electronic movement of these resources among computing machines, memory storage, or display devices (monitors or screens). In general, telecommunications refers to communications over long distances, whereas electronic communications can be between two machines, one next to the other.

In the nascent days of micros, and even today, one of the major constraints on the "stand-alone" micro was its inability to work fully with other computing devices. The micro was a PC, a personal computer, designed mainly for the single user. Its architecture was contoured to make computing easy for the personal user, not for connecting to myriad other machines (Derfler, 1986).

Reasons and Circumstances for Data Mobility

Although the technology may pose some obstacles for data and program mobility, there are a variety of reasons and circumstances for communicating among machines. Table 2.2 lays out major reasons that underlie the need for communication among machines, plus the types of exchanges that can take place.

Purposes The first purpose for linking machines is to obtain a program that resides on another machine. Often, a person using a micro or workstation finds that a particular program resides only on the mainframe or minicomputer. The program may be a language such as COBOL, or it may be a financial package for projecting tax trends.

The second need revolves around transferring data or information from one machine to another. Two examples are: a micro user wants data from the mainframe database, or a micro user wants to send a report to several interested parties.

The third type of demand for communications occurs when a program is developed on one computer and then needs to be sent to another machine. A common scenario is to develop a program on a micro and then send it to the mainframe for wider access by people in the organization. Such micro-based development is often done to relieve the mainframe of computing burden.

Exchanges For each of these purposes there are different types of exchanges. The first two call for communication from one micro to one mainframe and from one micro to another micro. These capabilities are widely available. The third type of exchange, networks, refers to connection among machines regardless of whether the machines are micros, mainframes, or minis. A person on a mini could access data from the mainframe database, work on that data on the minicomputer, then send it to someone working on a micro. These exchanges are less common and more complicated to develop.

UTILITIES

Background, Purpose, and Definitions

The utility category of software is often overlooked until it is too late. Utilities are programs that enhance the user's ability to perform many tedious or routine tasks in a program or operating system. Although it is not possible to review comprehensively all the various forms of utility programs available, a brief overview of two important categories is included.

Disk Utilities

Disk utilities, such as the Norton Utilities and the Mace Utilities, offer the user an array of useful programs that recover erased files, prevent accidental reformatting of hard disks, test for bad sectors of disks, allow direct-code editing of object-code files, and allow extensive file manipulation. Easily overlooked in the annual budget cycle, this form of utility can be worth its weight in gold when it is needed. Every office should have some form of utility program for data recovery from both floppy and hard disk systems.

Program Utilities

Another class of utility programs involves those used within another program. Used with programs such as Lotus or dBASE, these utilities add functions not found in the original programs. For example, one of the most popular classes of utilities for Lotus is an add-in word-processing program that provides easy access to formatting functions not available in Lotus. For dBASE, add-in report writers and compilers offer functionality not provided by the manufacturer, Ashton-Tate.

■ PROGRAMMING

Background, Purpose, and Definition

Programming has been discussed in prior sections but not formally defined. *Programming* consists of a set of instructions that usually operate on data to produce a desired result. It is similar to giving someone detailed directions to get from point A to point B, but with the ability to handle very complicated and intriguing paths between points A and B.

Programming serves a number of useful purposes for analytical and management tasks. At a relatively simple level, programming allows the user to automate repetitive functions. Recall from the discussion of DOS and Lotus that there were many instances in which short programs could be written, stored, and called on later to execute a set of commands. Archiving, or copying files, was one such example.

Beyond the simple task of automating, programming can be used to create specialized modules, which are then tied together into sophisticated applications. The ability to combine modules is one of the more powerful facilities of programming. For example, in a financial management application designed to assure that money does not remain idle, one module can track cash available, another can keep abreast of the amounts invested in short-term securities, and a third can follow tax receivables. With these modules, information from tax receivables can be passed to the investment module and checked against the cash module to determine how much of current cash should be invested and for what period of time.

Most of the major software packages discussed in this chapter have programming languages. With DOS, it is the Batch language; dBASE III offers its own command language; and Lotus has macros that constitute its programming language. The advantage of these micro languages is that all the user-friendly commands that can be used outside of the programming language are perfectly acceptable as part of the programming language. For example, if dBASE has an edit command for changing or updating data, that command can be used in the dBASE programming language.

Although each of these languages has its own unique syntax, which is a drawback, all can be understood by examining several fundamental concepts. However, it is necessary first to clear up some misconceptions about programming.

People often equate programming with coding. The following three lines of code, for example, may be legitimate in a particular programming language:

```
READ(a,b)
y:=a+b
WRITE(y)
```

However, knowing the syntax, or how to code in a language, is only part of programming.

Programming is foremost a problem-solving process. If the problem is to subtract 10 percent from a client's annual recreation fee if the fee is paid before the first of the year, knowledge about programming code or syntax cannot help the user who is unable to enumerate the steps needed to solve the problem. In fact, a nicely printed answer generated by a computer program may give one a false sense of security.

Programming is also misjudged in terms of how difficult it is. Just looking at the cryptic code of a program suggests that any effort to program must be difficult. The conclusion is partly right, but for the wrong reasons. Programming is difficult if the problem is difficult. For small, easy problems, programming can be a breeze.

Building Blocks

In later chapters, programming will be examined in more detail. Here the intent is to present the basic building blocks of programming, which include:

- stepwise refinement and modularity
- algorithms and pseudocode
- data names, data types, and data structures
- read/write, or input and output
- control of flow
- expressions

Some of the language from these building blocks will become more familiar later because it parallels the language used in chapter 4 on building applications. It is similar because the focus here is on problem solving, just as it will be in chapter 4.

For large programs that are directed toward complicated problems, the place to start is not with the coding. Instead, start with analyzing the problem. How can the problem be broken down (*stepwise refinement* and *modularity*), and what appear to be the solution steps (the *algorithm*)? Even when the solution is well in hand, refrain from trying to plunge into the final coding; begin to write the program in *pseudocode*. Pseudocode is close to the actual code but lets one think about the solution and what the program should look like without having to know all the details of the programming language.

The advantage of this approach lies in breaking your task into manageable components. Complex problems are difficult enough to solve without having to figure out a solution plus all the correct coding.

The remaining building blocks are more directly related to writing the actual code. One of these building blocks is the data name. In many programming languages, it is essential to give names to all the items or variables that will be used in the program. In dBASE, they are called *fields* or *memory variables*. The purpose of the names is to define the entities and to reserve space in the computer so that actual data can be stored.

The next building block, data type, has already been mentioned in the discussion of dBASE III and Lotus 1-2-3. The data type specifies what can and cannot be done with the data. The data types are similar across programming languages. At a minimum, there are *numeric* and *character* types, with some breaking numeric into *integer* (whole numbers) and *floating point* (numbers with decimals). There can also be logical, or *Boolean*, types (true/false), date types, or even types defined by the user. For instance,

Chapter 2   Understanding Microcomputer Software

the user can denote that neighborhood is a type that includes Briarwood, Greenspring, Shallowgrove, and Mistyhollow.

Besides data names (or fields) and data types, programming languages may offer data structures that allow the manipulation of several pieces or types of data. The record discussed earlier (see figure 2.4) is a data structure. It may contain various fields, all of different data types.

The gamut of data structures is rather extensive. For example, *arrays* are data structures that usually hold many pieces of data of the same data type. The efficiency rating of a work crew for twelve months is a good candidate for an array. It could be called effic_rate(I), where I goes from 1 to 12 and holds the ratings for each month. Even processes can be put into data structures. A process that operates on a first-in/last-out basis is a candidate for a data structure.

Reading and writing, or inputting and outputting, are also common to programming. However, most of the microcomputer languages—dBASE III PLUS, for example—let the user get away without specifying an actual read or write. In dBASE III PLUS, you can simply say DISPLAY ALL and all the records will be displayed, without having to first say read all the records.

Another major aspect of programming is the control of flow in the program. Because programs are sets of instructions, there needs to be control over the order in which the instructions are followed or executed. The simplest control is to start at the beginning and proceed to the end. This is called *sequential.* Another type of control is *conditional.* If a condition is met, do one alternative; if not, do another alternative. For example, if a hearing is required, hold off on printing the regulations; if not, proceed with the printing. The general form of a conditional statement might be expressed as follows:

```
IF condition is true
THEN DO X
ELSE
DO Y
ENDIF
```

Conditional statements can cover more than two options. It may be necessary to check five or six options, but conditional statements can still handle the situation. A general form might look like this:

```
CASE OF
1: DO A
2: DO B

N: DO Z
ENDCASE
```

Menus often follow this case structure. Perhaps 1 stands for enter data, 2 for run reports, and so on. If the user chooses 1, then the program is routed into the module A.

Control can also correspond to looping. For example, keep printing until 100 has been reached or until there is no more paper. Many languages have this feature, often implemented with a DO WHILE command. In dBASE III PLUS, the DO WHILE . . . ENDDO command structure allows for repeated operation. Whatever falls within the DO WHILE . . . ENDDO command can be repeated or seen over and over again as long as the DO WHILE condition is true. The general form in dBASE III PLUS is:

```
DO WHILE some condition is true
  some operation such as the display of a menu of choices
ENDDO
```

The last facet of programming covered in this section is *expressions*. Expressions are very much like sentences in that they describe what is to be done. One type, called *Boolean* expressions, includes the operators AND, OR, and NOT. These Boolean operators might be used in the following expression: if a bill is thirty days late AND if there was any delinquency in the past six months, send this person a nasty gram. The NOT logic can give similar power to programming: give me everyone with NOT delinquencies and send them a pleasant gram.

Besides Boolean expressions, there are expressions that look very much like algebraic statements. However, the equal sign (=) in these expressions means: replace whatever value is in the item on the left with the value from the right-hand side of the expression. The expression roa=income/assets is one such statement. Any mathematical operator, whether addition, subtraction, multiplication, division, or exponentiation, is a legitimate part of such expressions.

Of course, the rules of order in algebra apply in programming. That is, move from left to right, do all calculations inside the innermost parentheses first, do exponentiation next, then multiplication or division, and finally addition or subtraction. The expression $a=k*(4.3/b)/c$ would mean: divide 4.3 by b, then multiply the result by k, then divide that result by c, and finally, store the results in a.

CONCLUSION

As a final point, it is important to return to one of the central themes of the book: microcomputer software is powerful, but it does not stand on its own as a problem solver. A spreadsheet, regardless of the facilities it possesses, does not solve budget problems. It provides the tools—indeed, a powerful set of tools. In later chapters, we will see how to use and craft these powerful tools into useful problem-solving applications.

This chapter has examined these software tools and provided the reader with a fundamental appreciation of the capabilities of micro software. The overarching goal of the book is to provide a framework and direction for using micro software as a problem-solving tool and for assembling micro software into problem-solving applications for public managers.

REFERENCES

Cain, T., and Cain, N. W. *Hard Disk Management.* New York: Prentice-Hall, 1986.
Curtin, D. P., and Porter, L. R. *Microcomputers: Software and Applications.* Englewood Cliffs, NJ: Prentice-Hall, 1987.
Derfler, F. J. "Micro to Mainframe," *PC Magazine* 5 (May 1986): 116–124.
Devoney, C. *Using PC DOS.* Indianapolis: Que Corporation, 1986.
Kroenke, D. *Database Processing.* Chap. 5. Chicago: Science Research Associates, 1983.
Minor, M. "Software Offers Financial-Forecasting Tools," *PC Week* (November 18, 1986): 190, 192, 195.
Puglia, V. "Extending DOS's Utility," *PC Magazine* 5 (May 13, 1986): 209–225.
Wolverton, V. *Running MS DOS.* Bellevue, WA: Microsoft Press, 1984.

CHAPTER

3

Hardware Configurations and Systems

■ OVERVIEW: FROM HARDWARE COMPONENTS TO SYSTEMS

Although software is integral to the use of micros in organizations, without the appropriate hardware there is no system. In this chapter, we examine the hardware side of the system equation, beginning with a brief look at the evolution of microcomputer hardware and its use in organizations. To examine more closely the expansion of hardware components into functional systems, we cover the various parts of a microcomputer system and then analyze how those parts may be assembled into useful work systems.

As suggested in chapter 1, the early days of microcomputer development were largely the province of the hobbyist or electronics expert. Early systems were built around a variety of microprocessor chips, circuit designs, and interface methods (including video terminals, paper tape readers, and cassette tapes). Trying to connect equipment such as printers, or even display terminals, was a job for a true electronics wizard. The reason for this state of affairs was a *lack of standards*.

Initial attempts to deal with these problems by organizations such as ANSI (American National Standards Institute) resulted in the proposal of several "connectivity" standards. These standards were intended to facilitate machine design (the S100 bus), printer connection (Centronics parallel standard), and communication (the RS 232C interface). Problems arose, however, when companies began to "improve" on the standards for their own purposes. This, of course, started a whole new round of even more exotic compatibility problems.

The proliferation of individualized "standards" continued to plague the microcomputer user until the introduction of the IBM PC in 1981. From a hardware perspective, this machine provided a set of easily recognized standard configurations for various connections.

The practical result of the entry of IBM into the microcomputer market has been a substantial reduction in the complexity of configuring a microcomputer system. As long as one is willing to acknowledge the IBM standards, the selection of input-output devices, expansion devices, and peripherals is greatly simplified. Almost all major manufacturers now routinely build their products to conform to the set of standards evolved in the IBM PC.

The principal exception to the "IBM standard" is Apple Computer, Inc., whose Macintosh line of computers continues to provide a viable alternative to IBM compatibility. Even Apple, however, is making an effort to reduce the complexity of data transfer between Mac and IBM systems through the use of a "super-drive" floppy disk drive capable of reading and writing IBM-format disks. In addition, an increasing number of software packages, such as Excel and PageMaker, use a common data format that facilitates data exchange.

Far from disappearing, though, the controversy over standards for hardware design has simply moved to a more sophisticated level. Now, the issues revolve around exotica such as graphics device standards, memory management techniques, and even central processor chip selection. In today's market, the rapid pace of development makes techhnology obsolete even before it is widely available. This rapid pace of technological development presents a real problem for the microcomputer manager. Although IBM compatibility is still the watchword for much of the basic hardware, even the influence of IBM has not been enough to stem the proliferation of cutting-edge technology. Thus, the microcomputer user who wishes to go beyond the basics and seek improved processing speed, better graphics, or improved information storage must often choose from among a number of competing "standards" that ultimately circumscribe future software and hardware selection.

The moral of all of this is that there will always be a certain amount of risk involved in selecting microcomputer system hardware. Axiomatically, a standard only becomes so after widespread acceptance. As long as the user desires to remain state-of-the-art, there is always the risk that the wrong avenue is being followed and the standard in the area will evolve around incompatible technology.

The trends examined above illustrate the common path of microcomputer evolution:

1. A new technology is introduced to the marketplace and struggles for recognition.
2. Competitive technologies arise to challenge for the market.
3. One technological approach gradually gains widespread acceptance (frequently after being adopted by IBM).
4. The new "standard" is rapidly superseded by new technology.

As the technology of microcomputers and their associated technology matures, this scenario is likely to be the dominant mode of hardware evolution. Fortunately, the development of *systems-based* solutions offers the micro user a greater measure of direction and guidance than was available in the infancy of the technology.

SYSTEM COMPONENTS

As a system, the microcomputer comprises several elements linked together to form an operational whole. Each of these component elements is discussed here. The purpose is not to develop technical expertise in the manager, but rather to create an awareness of the complexity of the microcomputer system and how it should be managed to produce effective results.

PART I   Background, History, and Basic Elements

The Central Processor Unit

The *central processor unit*, or CPU, is virtually the "brain" of the micro system. Although the CPU usually refers to all of the components that enable the computer to process information, the key to the CPU is a single microchip called a *microprocessor*. It is this single chip that endows the computer with its ability to perform the calculations that form the basis for all computer-based information processing. Since there are a number of possible microprocessor chips that may be used to build the CPU of a microcomputer, the selection of a particular chip provides the micro system with a particular range of powers and largely determines the overall speed of the system.

In the short history of the microcomputer, we have already seen the development of four distinct "generations" of microchips. Each of these generations has added considerable speed and power to the microcomputer.

The first generation of microchips designed for practical use in business-oriented microcomputers (as opposed to hobbyist toys) were developed by Intel Corporation and Motorola during the early 1970s. These chips—the Intel (Zilog) Z-80 and Motorola 6502—were known as 8-bit chips because they could process 8 bits of information at a time. In total capacity, these chips could address approximately 64,000 bytes of information. This translates roughly into the ability to deal with 32 pages of information.

When IBM decided to introduce a microcomputer, they broke with the current practice of using the Z-80 or 6502 and selected a microprocessor from a new family of chips developed by Intel (Moseley, 1987). The basic chip in this series was the 8086. This second-generation microchip was both faster and more powerful than the Z-80 or 6502 in that it was capable of dealing with 16 bits of data rather than 8. For its new PC, IBM selected a variation of the 8086 labeled the 8088. This chip was something of a hybrid: it offered the internal 16-bit processing power of the 8086, but still used the 8-bit method of passing information to and from the chip. This set of characteristics allowed the chip to be more readily adapted to existing technology, but at a penalty of processing speed. In many operations, the 8088 was no faster than the previous generation of 8-bit chips. It was, however, capable of handling about ten times the information of the previous generation, or 640,000 bytes. This tremendous jump in processing power enabled the microcomputer to handle operations and processes that began to encroach on the processing power of early mainframe computing systems.

In the mid-1980s, IBM introduced its next generation of microcomputers, termed the AT (Advanced Technology). It moved up from the 8088 to a new Intel chip, the 80286. This chip was a true 16-bit processor that enabled data to be sent to and from the chip, as well as internally processed, at that rate. The 80286 once again dramatically expanded the amount of data that could be processed, upping the limit to 4 megabytes (approximately 4 million bytes). Even as it was introduced, though, the 80286 was seen as a stopgap measure before the introduction of a 32-bit chip. The 80286, while offering substantial speed improvements over the 8088, was still limited in many ways to the same memory and processing restrictions as the earlier generation.

In 1986, Intel Corporation began to make available to manufacturers the next generation of microprocessor: the 80386 (*PC World*, 1987). Sometimes referred to as a "mainframe on a chip," this microchip moves the personal computer truly into the realm of mainframe computing power. The 80386 is capable of addressing tremendous amounts

Chapter 3   Hardware Configurations and Systems

of memory (4 gigabytes, or 4 billion bytes, of data), operates extremely quickly, and is capable of accommodating multiple processing sessions.

As the 80386 begins to make its presence felt in the microcomputer industry, industry experts predict that it will revolutionize the use of microcomputers in organizations. With chips such as the 80386 and its descendants—such as the Intel i486, introduced in 1989—the CPU of the microcomputer begins to resemble more and more the CPU of a mainframe computing system. Indeed, the distinctions between hardware configurations for micros and mainframes are becoming more and more difficult to recognize as the power of the personal computer CPU increases.

☐   It is interesting to trace the parallel development of the generations of microprocessors used in the IBM-compatibles and the Apple Macintosh series. The Intel (IBM) series began in 1978 with the 8086, a 16-bit chip that incorporated 29,000 transistors. The 8/16-bit 8088 used in the IBM PC appeared in 1979. That year also marked the introduction of the Motorola 68000, a 32-bit chip that became the foundation for the Macintosh. In 1982 Intel introduced the 130,000-transistor 80286 for the IBM AT, and Motorola produced the 195,000-transistor 68020 for the Mac II. Intel's next step was the 80386, with 275,000 transistors, and Intel's first true 32-bit processor, introduced in 1985. Motorola countered with the 68030, containing 300,000 transistors, in 1987. The next escalation of the chip wars came in 1989 with the Intel i486 (80486) and Motorola 68040, each with a capacity of 1.2 million transistors. Thus, in only eleven years, the industry produced a chip with 41 times the capacity of the state of the art in 1978. Although Motorola was the first to bring the full power of a 32-bit chip to market for use in the Macintosh, the Intel 80X86 series still dominates the market. In their latest incarnations, both the Motorola and Intel chips truly deserve the reference "mainframe on a chip" (Slater, 1989, p. 36).

For the manager or user of microcomputers, the selection of a particular CPU is usually determined by the uses to which the micro will be put. Each microchip is limited to certain operating systems and software packages. Therefore, the practice of selecting software and an operating system first serves to constrain the selection of a CPU. For several years, when the 8088 was the dominant processor, this choice was relatively simple. Now, however, with three distinct CPU types (8088 or 8086, 80286, and 80386 or i486) available, the choice is becoming more difficult again. Even IBM has served notice that new versions of the operating system (OS/2) for its business-oriented micros will not run on older 8088 machines or even on its new low-end PS/2 Model 30, which uses an 8086-based CPU (Pertzold, 1987).

The consequences of this CPU diversification are significant. Making the wrong choice of CPU now may dramatically reduce the service life and utility of the system. The manager must make a choice based not only on current uses but also on anticipated future needs. New, more powerful software for advanced CPU micros is inevitable. As that trend advances, the older 8088-based machines will not be able to keep up. For organizations where advanced applications are needed, investing in old technology is a waste of resources. For other organizations, however, where the micro is a more basic tool of productivity (word processing, simple recordkeeping, and small-scaled budgeting), continued use of the older technology offers no significant disadvantages and may prove to be significantly more cost-effective. With an installed base of several million units, the 8088-based CPU technology is likely to be around and supported at least well into the 1990s.

Memory

The second major component of the microcomputer system is memory, or more specifically, memory capacity. This is the capacity of the micro to store and process information. As indicated in the discussion of CPUs, the memory capacity is determined by the microprocessor that is used in the system. With the new microprocessors, the amount of memory that can be accessed has increased enormously.

There are two basic kinds of microcomputer memory: Random Access Memory (RAM) and Read Only Memory (ROM). Although there are exotic variations on both of these memory types, it is sufficient to understand the basic differences between the two types (Gupta & Toong, 1985).

RAM memory is called *volatile* memory because it depends on electric current for its operation. When the power to the computer is turned off, whatever is in RAM disappears into electronic never-never land and is permanently lost. This kind of memory is, however, the workhorse of the computer. Since information is readily passed into and out of RAM, it is where program information is stored for execution; it is also where information for processing is stored. The "random" part of RAM means that information can be accessed in any order. This facilitates information processing because information may be stored in widely separated areas of memory.

With the continuing drop in microchip prices and dramatic advances in RAM chip technology, the effective cost of memory in the microcomputer is drastically falling. For example, in 1984 the most common RAM memory chip was the 64-kilobyte (kb) chip; a set of nine of these chips provided 64,000 bytes of memory, at a cost of approximately $50. By 1986, the 64kb chip had been replaced by the 256kb chip. Nine of these chips provided 256,000 bytes of memory, at a per-set cost of about $30. By 1987, the 1 mb (one megabyte) chip was beginning to appear on micros. A set of these chips provided one million bytes of memory, at a cost of $75. Thus, in three years, the cost per 1,000 bytes of RAM had dropped from 78 cents to 12 cents to just 7.5 cents. Fifteen years ago, mainframe computer RAM cost in excess of $1,000 per 1,000 bytes. Although volatile market conditions create substantial swings in memory chip prices, the overall trend is clearly toward cheaper and cheaper memory. Combined with the increased capacity of newer processors, the result is bigger, more memory-intensive applications.

The availability of cheap RAM has encouraged microcomputer and software designers to develop systems that require more and more RAM. We seem to be caught in the same spiral as mainframe computers. As memory becomes available, programs are written to take advantage of it. The result is ever-increasing program size and sophistication, as well as a form of built-in obsolescence, since older micro systems cannot take full advantage of increased memory.

To illustrate this problem, consider the memory-related problems facing the user of a typical IBM PC–type computer. Running the PC-DOS or MS-DOS operating system, these machines have an effective RAM limit of 640 kilobytes. Although this may seem like a significant amount of memory, it can be allocated very quickly because of the ever-increasing size of software programs and the continuing development of utility programs that are termed "RAM-resident," since they remain in the computer's memory and are available at the stroke of a key or two. A typical system might offer the following RAM allocation:

Chapter 3   Hardware Configurations and Systems

DOS overhead	75k
RAM-resident utility	30k
Operating system shell	100k
Database software	384k
Total	589k
RAM available for data	51k

Clearly, one problem of increasing sophistication in programs and memory usage is the limit of older micro systems and operating systems. To overcome these limitations, new systems must be designed with the capacity to *address* more and more RAM. The latest generation of 80386 machines can do just that, with the ability to address *gigabytes* (billions of bytes) of memory. The problem is that the currently available operating systems (designed for the 8088 generation of computers) are still effectively limited to 640k. The lesson for the manager is simple: even though memory prices are almost negligible, simply adding memory to a system may not be possible. The system (processor hardware, RAM, and operating system) must be considered as a whole to achieve maximum performance. The ad hoc approach of adding capacity later to compensate for initial deficiencies may not always be a viable option.

The second kind of computer memory, ROM memory, is used somewhat differently than RAM. As the name *read-only* memory implies, ROM cannot be written to by the user. Essentially, the instructions (program code) contained in ROM memory are permanently encoded in the chip by the computer manufacturer. This code serves the function of helping the computer to start up, perform self-tests of memory and other computer components, and give instructions to the system on how to load additional information such as the operating system. Taken together, these functions of ROM are given the appellation "bootstrap loader" since they bring the system up to operation by its own "bootstraps," so to speak.

The amount of ROM in a micro is typically much less than RAM, usually less than 64k. Portable computers are an exception, since they may store entire software programs in ROM to free up the limited amount of RAM available in the portable configuration. As computers grow more sophisticated, ROM is being used to handle more sophisticated aspects of the system, such as communications or the video configuration. In the total micro memory system, however, ROM is likely to remain a small if vital part of overall computer memory.

Input-Output Devices

Third among the system components are input-output (I-O) devices, which allow communication to occur between the user and the CPU. I-O devices provide methods of inputting information (both data and instructions) to the CPU and outputting information in an understandable form from the CPU to the user.

The most common form of I-O device used with microcomputers is technically referred to as the *console*—a term borrowed from the days when mainframe computers were directed through the use of massive teletype machines. Today, the console refers to the use of a *video display* and a *keyboard*. The keyboard is the primary input device, since most instructions are issued in a language that at least resembles everyday English.

One problem with using the keyboard as an input device is that it was designed for another technology: the typewriter. The standard QWERTY key layout of most keyboards was actually designed to slow typing input on the old mechanical typewriters. On a micro, the keyboard effectively limits the speed at which the user can communicate with the machine. There have been attempts to overcome this limitation, including the redesign of the standard keyboard in numerous ways. Perhaps the most popular of these is the DVORAK layout, which enhances typing speed. Other problems have arisen out of the propensity of manufacturers to place ancillary keys in a variety of locations on the keyboard. Moving from one micro to another can be a confusing experience, especially for a touch-typist.

A good example of keyboard confusion is seen in the attempts by IBM to arrive at a "standard" keyboard layout. The keyboard provided with the original PC was criticized for not following the IBM Selectric typewriter format, particularly in the labeling and placement of the TAB and RETURN keys. When IBM introduced the PC Jr., it had an odd-looking keyboard frequently referred to as the "Chiclet" keyboard for its small and difficult-to-use keys. This keyboard was rapidly withdrawn from the market and replaced with another that differed from the original PC keyboard. Yet a third keyboard was introduced with the PC AT. This keyboard addressed some of the old complaints (RETURN key) but caused new ones by moving several important ancillary keys. An upgraded AT introduced another keyboard, with yet another layout. This last iteration seems to have gained favor with the company, since the latest generation of IBM micros, the PS/2 line, also uses it. It is doubtful, however, that we have seen the last of the keyboard changes.

The other element of the console, the video display terminal, or VDT—often, though incorrectly, called a CRT (cathode-ray tube)—is the primary means used for output. With the growing sophistication of micros, video displays have dramatically improved in resolution, color, and flexibility. The downside to this is that the manager must select a video display that is appropriate both to the environment in which it will be used and to the tasks that will be performed on the micro.

Video displays are classified most simply as either *monochrome* or *color*. Monochrome displays provide an image in one color, usually on a black or white background. The most common forms of monochrome monitor have either green or amber displays on a black background. Monochrome displays are most appropriate for those applications that are confined primarily to text entry, because monochrome displays are usually considered to have a higher resolution. That is, the characters on the screen are more fully formed, and the dots (or *pixels*) used to form the characters are not as apparent as they are on a color monitor. This makes the characters easier to read.

Applications that rely on graphics are more suitable for color monitors. To illustrate the confusing complexities of monitor selection, however, very high resolution graphics, such as engineering CAD (computer-aided design), are often done in monochrome to provide finer detail than is available with a color monitor. On the other hand, the latest generation of color monitors is capable of resolution equal to, or even greater than, the resolution of the basic monochrome monitor. Text-based software programs, such as word-processing programs, are taking advantage of this to offer color highlights that are not available when using a monochrome monitor.

Chapter 3 Hardware Configurations and Systems

Numerous studies have been done on the effect of screen color on users. Under some lighting conditions, the green screen was found to be superior; under others, the amber screen was best. Other reports suggest that the best combination is black characters on a white background, mimicking the printed page. Additional reports indicate that some individuals suffer from headaches when forced to work with certain screen colors (usually the green screen) and that individual users should be allowed to select their own color combinations because individual preferences vary so much (Bartlett, 1986).

Thus, what may seem a relatively simple equipment selection is really a very complicated process that involves an almost bewildering set of factors and choices. Later in this chapter, we will examine a number of hardware configurations and the appropriate monitors for those configurations. For the manager trying to put together a useful microcomputer system, selection of the appropriate video device is an important and complicated undertaking. Making an incorrect choice in this area can have serious health and productivity consequences.

Beyond the keyboard and video display, there are other I-O devices that perform specific functions, most often as a replacement or supplement to keyboard input. One of the most common of these supplemental I-O devices is the *mouse*.

A mouse is a small device about two inches by four inches in size. It has one or more buttons on its top and is connected to the CPU, either through the keyboard, a serial port, or a special connector card. The basic purpose of the mouse is to replace the use of cursor keys to move the cursor on the monitor screen. To accomplish this, the mouse is moved around on the desk. This movement is translated into cursor movement on the screen. The buttons on the mouse may be used to replace specific keys such as the ENTER key or the ESCAPE key.

The mouse first gained popularity with the Apple Macintosh, where the mouse served as a primary input device for the graphics-based user interface on the computer. The mouse has became familiar to PC users primarily as a mechanism for graphics input. Many software packages that rely on graphics, such as Microsoft Windows, Dr. Halo, PC Paint, and AutoCad, use the mouse for both command selection and direct drawing on the screen.

The mouse appears likely to become an integral part of many future hardware and software systems. As stated earlier, it is a primary input device on the Apple Macintosh and is also seen by IBM as an integral part of its new PS/2 line of microcomputers. As software moves more and more toward user interfaces based on high-resolution graphics, the mouse appears to be the supplemental input device of choice for both hardware and software manufacturers.

Other I-O devices, less widely used, are the light pen, the graphic tablet, and touch screens (*PC Magazine*, August 1987). The light pen is used by directing it at the screen, either to select a command or to draw a line or shape. Graphic tablets combine features of the mouse and the light pen. A stylus is used to draw directly on a pressure-sensitive tablet, and the stylus motions are translated to screen coordinates. The touch screen means just what it says. The user touches the screen to select a command or move the cursor to a different location.

All of these alternate input devices are designed to facilitate the entry of information into the microcomputer system. The problem is that data entry through the keyboard is often slow, error-prone, and awkward. This is especially true for graphics applications.

By employing an alternative means of data entry, the user is able to speed up the productive process and produce desired outcome in less time and with less effort. In designing a microcomputer system, the use of alternative input devices should be carefully considered if the application warrants their use. Significant productivity gains are possible with the right choice.

A final category of I-O device covers devices that are designed to facilitate a more wholesale entry of information. This class of I-O device is known generically as *scanners* (Stanton, Burns, & Vernit, 1986). Scanners are devices that can "read" information from the printed page (text or graphics) and translate that information into a usable format on the micro. Scanners are divided into two general classes: text scanners and image, or graphic, scanners.

Text scanners, also called *optical character readers* (OCRs), are used to input previously typed or printed text. The OCR is capable of recognizing the individual letters as they appear on the page and translating them through the use of special software into a text file that can be used by a word processor. Files produced using an OCR are treated like any other text file and may be edited or modified like a file entered from the keyboard.

The *image scanner* operates somewhat differently from the OCR and is used for a different purpose. The image scanner does not recognize individual characters on the printed page. Rather, the scanner interprets the image, whether text or graphics, and translates it into a pixel "map" that is stored in the micro as a graphic image. Text that is scanned using an image scanner is treated like graphics and cannot be edited using an editor program. This limitation makes the image scanner suitable only for graphics applications. Once the image has been translated into a computer file format, a software package such as a paint program can be used to enhance or otherwise modify the image.

As might be surmised, the process of image scanning is much more complicated than that of the OCR. The image scanner must be capable of reproducing both the *resolution* and the *shading* of the original image. Low-end image scanners have limited resolution, usually less than 200 dots per inch (dpi), which produces somewhat grainy images with jagged lines and rough circles. This class of scanner is also capable of recognizing only a limited range of shades, which means that the fine detail and subtle shade gradations of a photograph will not scan clearly. Low-end scanners are more suited to line art and simple illustrations than to sophisticated artwork.

More expensive image scanners expand the limits of both resolution and shading. Scanning at least 300 dpi, these devices match the practical limit of office-quality output devices such as laser printers. Many high-end image scanners also offer the ability to discriminate among an almost infinite number of shading gradations. These scanners are capable of reading photographic material and producing images of halftone or better quality. Many of these high-end scanners can also be equipped to perform OCR applications, thus enabling one device to produce both text and graphics. As scanner technology evolves, this dual capability is likely to become more prevalent, as well as less expensive.

Storage Media

A fourth major component of the microcomputer system is the class of devices known as *storage media*. Since information stored in RAM is not retained by the system when the power is shut off, and since programs and data must be loaded into the system to

Chapter 3   Hardware Configurations and Systems 63

function, there must be some way of permanently saving information. The most common form of this permanent storage is the use of a disk system.

Generically, a disk is a storage medium that borrows technologically from both the phonograph record and the tape recorder. Information is stored to, and read from, the disk with an electromagnetic head very similar to that found in a tape recorder. Instead of the streaming tape, however, the disk uses the tape-type recording medium in a circular format that is quicker to read. As the head moves over the spinning disk, it can quickly read or write information. The disk systems that rely on this basic technology are divided into two general categories: floppy disks and hard disks.

A floppy disk resembles a very thin phonograph record contained in a rectangular protective sleeve. This type of disk is the most prevalent now in use with micros. Virtually every microcomputer uses at least one type of floppy disk, with the notable exception of the new NeXT machine, which uses an optical disk. Aside from the relative inexpensiveness of the floppy disk, it is the medium used for commercial software. To load such software into the computer, therefore, requires the floppy disk.

☐ Like just about everything else related to microcomputers, floppy disks come in various sizes and capacities, and not all floppy disks are interchangeable with one another.

The most common size for a floppy disk is 5.25 inches. This disk, when used on an IBM-compatible system, holds approximately 360k of data. A high-density (HD) version of this disk is used with PC AT–type systems. It has a nominal capacity of 1.2 megabytes of data, or about 3.5 times the capacity of the regular floppy disk. These two disks, though the same physical size, are incompatible. Each requires a specific *disk drive* to function. A 1.2mb disk drive is capable of reading and writing 360k disks, but *only* if those disks are used with the high-capacity drive. A 360k drive simply will not recognize a high-capacity disk.

With the introduction of portable computer systems, where space and weight are at a premium, another type of floppy disk, termed a *micro-floppy*, began to gain in popularity. These disks are 3.5 inches in size. They are also encased in a hard plastic shell, making them much less susceptible to damage. The capacity of these micro-floppies is about 720k, since the hard shell permits a denser surface media. When IBM introduced the PS/2 line of computers in April 1987, the machines were equipped exclusively with micro-floppy disk drives. To make matters even more complicated, the capacity of the PS/2 micro-floppies was raised to 1.44mb.

A proliferation of floppy disk systems has substantial significance for the manager or users of microcomputer systems. Since there is no ready data interchangability among the different disk sizes and densities, offices with more than one kind of micro may find data exchange very difficult. In addition, if an agency decides to upgrade equipment to a newer generation of micros, it may be stuck with a substantial investment in incompatible disks and no easy way of transferring information from the old system to the new. Although there are solutions to the problem, including IBM's exotically named "data migration facility" (a plug-in 5.25-inch disk drive) and the Macintosh SuperDrive, mixing systems with different floppy disk formats in one office or agency does create compatibility problems that can adversely affect the productivity of the organization and the utility of the computer as a problem-solving tool.

Given the limited capacity of the floppy disk and the increasing sophistication and power of microcomputers, the floppy disk is no longer the disk of choice for serious mass storage. Although the floppy is useful for getting information into and out of the micro system, it is woefully inadequate to deal with contemporary information-processing requirements. The solution to this problem is the use of a hard disk system, in conjunction with a floppy disk for data transfer.

The hard disk is more sophisticated than the floppy system. It is usually permanently mounted within the computer system and is not easily removable (although removable hard disk packs are coming onto the market). The hard disk offers two substantial advantages over the floppy: size and speed. The typical hard disk in use today has a storage capacity of 20mb, or about 50 standard floppy disks. The hard disk system is also substantially faster than the floppy system, allowing quicker location, processing, and storage of data (Rosch, 1987a).

Rapid advances in technology have dramatically increased the capacity and speed of the microcomputer hard disk, while substantially lowering the price of the systems. It is now possible to purchase hard disk systems capable of storing more than 100mb, and capacities of 40mb to 60mb are becoming common. At the same time, the per-megabyte cost of these systems has dropped dramatically. During the early 1980s, the per-mb cost of a hard disk system was about $300–$400, or about $3,000 for a 10mb system. By 1987, the cost had dropped to about $25 per mb, and even less for larger disk systems.

It must be noted, however, that the capacity and value of the hard disk system come at a price. The sheer size of the storage capacity of these systems means that they must be carefully managed; otherwise, it is possible to "lose" information in the vast storage space available. Hard disk systems must be organized and carefully monitored to provide proper performance. Since many novice users are receiving their first microcomputer experience on hard disk systems, proper training is essential to prevent potentially costly mistakes. The most widely cited nightmare concerning hard disk usage is the user who inadvertently reformats the hard disk. This process is easy enough to do and does result in the potential loss of all information on the hard disk. In an organization relying heavily on such a system, this problem can be a true and very costly disaster involving the loss of expensive software and irreplaceable data files. With proper training and management, this problem is much less likely to occur.

The most effective solution to hard disk problems is the regular creation of a copy of all of the information contained on the hard disk on some other medium. Then, if there is a problem, the data can be restored from the archival copy. The problem is that making backups is a lengthy and tedious process if floppy disks are used. For example, to back up a 20mb hard disk on 360k floppies requires 56 disks and takes about three hours.

A more feasible solution is to employ an archival backup device, such as a *tape drive*. These devices are designed specifically for making backups of hard disk systems. When used properly, they are quick and efficient. A good tape system can back up a 20mb system in less than ten minutes. With the proper software, the backup process can be automated to create a backup only of files changed since the last backup. This reduces the volume of the backup and ensures that the most current version of any data file is always preserved. Any office that operates with hard disk systems on its microcomputers should consider the tape backup system a must.

Recent technological developments have introduced another category of mass storage device: the *laser disk*, or *optical disk* (Rosch, 1987b). Basically, the principle behind this technology is the same as that used in the compact disc (CD) for audio systems. A laser is used to mark the disk surface, instead of the electromagnetic approach used in traditional disk systems. There are two clear advantages to the laser-based disk system. First, the information stored on the disk is more or less permanent, being far more resistant to degradation than are magnetic disk media. Second, laser-based disks are capable of storing significantly greater amounts of data than their traditional counterparts. A 5.25-inch laser disk easily holds upward of 300–500 megabytes of data. Some systems are capable of storing more than one gigabyte on a single disk. Since the cost of the medium is relatively low, this works out to a cost of less than 50 cents per megabyte.

So, why haven't laser disks completely supplanted the traditional magnetic media? There are still several problems to overcome before this technology becomes commonplace. One major problem is the concept of reusability. Traditional magnetic disks can be erased and used again and again. The laser technology, which makes tiny holes or grooves in the disk surface, is not readily amenable to erasure and reuse. For this reason, most currently available laser-based disk systems are called WORM drives. This stands for Write-Once, Read Many. The WORM drive is most useful in those situations where a permanent record (e.g., for an audit trail) is needed. Once information is written to the WORM disk, it resides there permanently. Typically, the current WORM system offers replaceable media capable of storing 200–500 megabytes.

One very effective use of the WORM drive is as an archival backup device, since it creates an unalterable record of both program and user data. Another use for this system is as an on-line reference service. This variation of the laser technology is often referred to as a CD-ROM, reflecting the fact that the disk medium is virtually identical with the audio CD technology. The ROM refers to the fact that these disks cannot be written to by the user; they are read-only. Many companies are offering reference material on CD-ROM systems that can be accessed on the micro and extracted for use with other software. With this technology, it is possible to put an entire encyclopedia on just one disk. In the not too distant future, we may see the "reference-of-the- month" club offering CD-ROM disks with a multitude of reference libraries.

A clue to the future of laser technology is seen in the NeXT super-micro from Apple co-founder Steve Jobs. The NeXT computer is equipped with an erasable laser/optical disk system as its primary storage device. The inclusion of this type of drive in the NeXT computer portends the more widespread commercial introduction of read/write laser optical disk systems during the early 1990s.

Although there are other mass storage technologies currently available or under development, the magnetic disk, tape system, and laser disk are the major technologies in current use. Given the meteoric rate of development in this area, however, new technologies are undoubtedly on the horizon.

Peripherals

Peripherals are components that are connected to the microcomputer system and perform a specific function. The most common classes of peripherals are printers and communications devices.

Printers Printers come in a wide variety of types and technologies for differing purposes. Essentially, printers can be divided into two general categories, based upon the print technology employed: *impact* and *nonimpact*.

Impact printers use a technology that is similar to that employed in a typewriter. A "hammer" or other striking device strikes an inked ribbon, which presses on the paper to produce an image. Impact printers currently make up the bulk of printers in use with microcomputer systems. Within the category of impact printer, the most common technologies are the *dot-matrix* printer and the *formed-character* printer.

The dot-matrix printer uses a series of thin wire pins (usually either nine or twenty-four) that are fired in a specific sequence to place a series of dots on the paper. The sequence of firing determines the character that the printer will form. Dot-matrix printers have been around since the early micros and are still the most popular type of microcomputer printer. The advantages of the dot-matrix printer are speed and relatively low cost for reasonable output. The speed of these printers ranges from about 60 characters per second (cps) to more than 400 cps, at a cost of from $150 to more than $3,000 for heavy-duty, high-speed units. Dot-matrix printers also have the ability to print graphics, since the pin-firing sequence can be used to replicate individual dot-shapes and not just letter-forms.

The main disadvantages of the dot-matrix printer are the quality of its output and the noise it generates. Since the characters or graphics from a dot-matrix printer are formed by a series of dots, the quality of the print is not the best. It is usually very easy to discern dot-matrix output by the ragged, dot-formed edges of the letters. For graphics, circles and angled lines tend to be jagged, and the printer is not capable of truly high resolution. For example, phototypeset printed graphics may have a dot-resolution of 800 to 1,000 dots per inch (dpi). A dot-matrix printer has a usable maximum resolution of 100–200 dpi. Therefore, graphs produced on the dot-matrix printer are somewhat cruder in appearance.

The recent generation of 24-pin printers has significantly improved the quality of these printers. In many cases, the output from a 24-pin dot-matrix printer is indistinguishable from that produced by a formed-character printer. Graphics, unfortunately, do not benefit as much from the additional print wires. Although 24-pin printers are more expensive than their 9-pin counterparts, the price differential is rapidly diminishing. Some industry observers suggest that the 24-pin printer is likely to replace the 9-pin technology for all but the most inexpensive applications within one or two years. On the other hand, dot-matrix printer technology seems to have reached, if not an end, at least a broad plateau. Most of the research into printer technology has switched to other printer types, and little is being done to improve dot-matrix technology significantly. On balance, it remains the lowest-cost, best-supported of the printer technologies available for microcomputer systems.

The other kind of impact printer technology is the formed-character printer. These printers operate like a typewriter in that fully formed characters are struck against the paper to produce print. The most common type of this technology is the *daisy-wheel* printer. This type of printer gains its name from the print element, whose characters are positioned on long arms radiating out from a central hub. The effect is not unlike that of the daisy flower.

Daisy-wheel printers produce very high quality output, often termed "letter quality" because it is good enough to be used in official correspondence and formal reports. (Most dot-matrix printers are only capable of near-letter quality, or correspondence quality.) The disadvantages of daisy-wheel printers are their speed, which ranges from 10 to 50 cps, and their noise level, which is quite high. Some users compare the unmuffled sound of a daisy-wheel printer to a demented woodpecker. Although the number of daisy-wheel printers in use is second only to dot-matrix printers, this type of printer is considered "old" technology, and most new systems that require high-quality output are being equipped with more advanced printer technology (i.e., laser printers).

One final category of impact printer deserves mention: the *plotter*. The plotter is not, in the strict sense, a printer since it effectively draws its output. However, plotters are used as output devices, particularly for graphics. This technology uses a pen clasped to a mechanical arm that moves across the paper to literally draw the image. (Some plotters move the paper rather than the pen, but the effect is the same.) Plotters, as might be imagined, are specialized devices primarily designed for graphic output. In this area, they are capable of producing superior output that is the functional equivalent of a graphic artist. An organization that is required to produce substantial graphic output would find a plotter a worthwhile investment.

Most of the exciting research in printer technology is occurring in the area of nonimpact printers. Perhaps the most significant nonimpact technology is that of the *laser printer* (*PC Magazine*, 1987). Using a technology similar to that of the photocopy machine, the laser printer is capable of high-quality output at very high speeds, with very little noise. Laser printers for microcomputers first began to appear about 1983. Early models were very limited in their capabilities, often being unable to produce graphics and prone to breakdowns. The current generation of laser printers are faster, more reliable, and capable of producing quite attractive graphics.

The quality of output from a laser printer is so superior to that of older impact technologies that many users consider it good enough for formal documents, newsletters, and even magazines. When combined with the appropriate software, laser printers are frequently used for "desktop publishing," which is the in-house production of materials that were once professionally typeset.

Although laser printers offer very high quality output, they still are not capable of producing typeset quality (at least at reasonable prices). For example, the typical laser printer produces both character and graphic output at 300 dpi. While this is about twice the resolution of a good dot-matrix printer, it is still far below the 800–1,000 dpi used in typesetting equipment. Laser printers currently in use are usually limited to single-color output, although color laser printers are becoming commercially available at reasonable prices.

As the technology advances (a familiar refrain), the cost of laser printers is dropping dramatically. Early models sold for about $3,000 in the most basic configuration. Current generation printers offer far greater capabilities at about two-thirds the price. Further increases in capacity and reductions in price are seen as inevitable.

In addition to the laser-based technologies, there are other nonimpact printer technologies in current use. One popular alternative to the dot-matrix printer is the *ink-jet printer*. This technology uses a reservoir of ink that is "sprayed" on the paper to form the image. The output from ink-jet printers tends to resemble that of dot-matrix printers. Ink-jet printers, however are generally faster and quieter than the dot-matrix. They are also capable of producing color output that is second only to plotter output in clarity and resolution.

The disadvantage of ink-jet printers is that they frequently jam, particularly if a long interval elapses between uses. Most of these printers also require special paper that does not absorb the ink and smear. In many applications, particularly where color output is needed, the ink-jet is an attractive alternative to the dot-matrix printer. It is not considered to offer sufficient quality to compete with the laser printer, though.

A final type of nonimpact printer worth mentioning is the *thermal printer,* which uses heat to fuse ink to the paper to form the image. Similar in function to the dot-matrix printer, thermal printers offer the advantage of a very small, simple print mechanism. This makes the technology particularly attractive in portable applications, where size is a primary consideration. Since the thermal printer requires special paper and is generally slower (though quieter) than the dot-matrix printer, it is considered to be a specialty technology not appropriate for widespread, heavy-duty use.

From this discussion of printer technologies, it is apparent that the microcomputer system manager is confronted with a bewildering range of printer choices. Most experts agree that the office of the future is likely to employ at least two of the technologies discussed: dot-matrix printers for draft output, and laser (or equivalent) printers for final output. Other types of printer technologies are likely to be relegated to support roles in specific applications. Later in this chapter, we examine how the various printer technologies can be used in specific microcomputer system configurations.

Communications Peripherals that permit a microcomputer to communicate with another computer (micro or mainframe) are popular elements of the microcomputer system. As the communication networks available to users become more sophisticated, with the use of fiber-optic cables and high-speed data-links, the use of the micro in communication assumes greater importance in the organization.

At the simplest level, there are two types of microcomputer communication: micro-to-micro and micro-to-mainframe (or minicomputer). Within these basic categories, though, there are numerous variations designed to meet specific applications.

Micro-to-micro communication involves the linking of two microcomputer systems for the exchange of information. This linkage can occur between two micros located fairly close together, through a network, or over telephone lines.

The most elementary form of micro-to-micro communication involves physically linking, or "hard-wiring," two systems together. This form of linking is most often done to facilitate exchange of information between two different kinds of micro systems. For example, a user may desire to transfer a file created on a NeXT computer to an IBM PC. Since these machines use different operating systems and disk formats, it is not possible to simply exchange the file on disk. Instead, a communication link between the machines must be established and the appropriate software used to complete the transfer. Although this may seem a daunting task for the novice user, there are commercial packages available that facilitate such exchanges.

Linking several micros together occurs in a *network*. Since this kind of network is designed to accommodate machines that are located fairly close to one another (i.e., in the same building), the term Local Area Network (LAN) is often used to describe the configuration (Madron, 1983, pp. 21–34). Although there is a wide variety of possible LAN configurations, such as the bus, star, or wheel, the basic premise of the system is the same. The LAN is built around a high-capacity microcomputer (or sometimes, minicomputer) equipped with a high-capacity hard disk system of at least 50–100 megabytes. This central micro acts as the controller for the network, storing the software programs used and providing linkages to peripherals such as printers or modems. Since it is the machine that manages the network and is the location for most of the information used by the network machines, this micro is termed the *file server*. The file server is connected to other microcomputers or terminals through a cabling system. Each of the machines linked in the network is termed a *node* and is granted resources such as disk space, program access, and printer use priority through the file server.

With a network, several users are able to share computing resources. Since the nodes attached to the network do not have to possess individually all of the resources needed for sophisticated processing (such as a hard disk), their cost is substantially less than that of an equal number of independent, single-user machines. Each node gains the ability to use the maximum capacity of the network and file server, while still possessing some capacity for independent processing.

Local area networks have come into fashion of late, with many organizations enthusiastically pursuing the linking of micros in their offices. The LAN is not without complications, however, as many of these organizations have discovered. The LAN is a complicated system that requires knowledgeable support. For example, each LAN, whether supporting only two or three nodes or twenty, must have a network administrator assigned to oversee the functioning of the network. For a large network system, this is likely a full-time job that requires the addition of new personnel. In addition to the network administrator, the LAN requires a special operating system, such as Novell's NetWare, to handle multiple users in the network configuration. Many software packages do not normally support LAN installation and require new versions designed especially to work with the network. Many of these network software packages charge by the node, and not the single fee that is usual for the single-user version. Thus, beyond the physical connections, the LAN requires a new operating system, new software, and new personnel in the form of the network administrator. Clearly, this is not an inexpensive proposition. Unfortunately, many managers anticipate only the costs associated with installing the network and give little consideration to its operation.

A third type of micro-to-micro communication involves the linking of systems that are not located in close proximity. One solution for communicating over long distances is to use telephone wires and connect the micros via *modems*. A modem is a device that is used to translate the digital signals that the computer operates on into sound waves that can be broadcast through the telephone system. This process is known as *modulation*. At the receiving end, another modem is used to translate the sound back into digital pulses. This is known as *demodulation*. Combining these terms is the derivation of the word modem: MOdulation–DEModulation.

Of course, the process is not quite so simple. In order for the microcomputers to communicate, the modems must use the same *protocol*. Protocol is a set of parameters, such as speed (referred to as BAUD rate), word length (number of bytes that define a word), and signal compatibility (called *parity*). These parameters must be matched on both ends of the communications link in order for communication to take place. The easiest way to accomplish this task is through the use of special communication software, such as Crosstalk or Procomm, that allows the setting of parameters from the program.

This form of micro-to-micro link is generically referred to as *telecommunications* because the communication occurs over telephone lines. Telecommunications linking can be particularly useful to an organization that has geographically diverse locations or requires field agents to report data to a central location. Any organization that employs telephone access to its computer system must be careful, however, to protect sensitive information. It is quite easy for a "hacker" to gain access to a microcomputer system linked to telephone lines. Without proper safeguards, substantial damage may be done to the information on the system.

All of these micro-to-micro communication approaches rely on a common format of communication called *asynchronous* communication. This means that communication can take place only in one direction at a time. As with a two-way radio, there can be only one sender and one receiver at a time. This tends to limit the speed of transmission. The advantage to asynchronous communication is that it does not require special cabling or overly complicated protocols. When we move into the realm of micro-to-mainframe communications, however, asynchronous communication is not the only way to proceed.

Micro-to-mainframe communications are used primarily in those organizations that employ both kinds of computers. The link between these two kinds of computers occurs in three variations: dumb terminal emulation, intelligent terminal, and telecommunications.

The most elementary form of micro-to-mainframe communication is one in which the microcomputer is used to emulate a simple terminal. The micro is connected to the mainframe in either modem phone-link or networked configuration. Connected to the mainframe, the micro is used to emulate a terminal, usually through software. This means that the micro is not used to store mainframe information locally. Instead, the micro acts solely as a communications channel, and all of the processing is done on the mainframe system. This configuration is often referred to as a "dumb terminal." One of the more popular terminals used to connect with Digital Equipment Corporation's VAX mainframes is a VT100. By using the appropriate software (often the same programs used in micro-to-micro communications), the micro is configured to represent the VT100. It is then used just as if it were a VT100 terminal: all of the keys and communication protocols are the same as on a VT100. During this emulation, most of the capacity of the micro is not utilized, since only elementary communication is taking place.

One might logically ask why someone would want to hobble a perfectly good microcomputer to enable it to engage in simple communication with a mainframe. The answer lies in the way in which the two types of machines process information. Micros generally store and process information in the ASCII format. Mainframes however, use formats such as EBCIDIC or BCD for their processing. When used as an emulator, with no actual information being loaded onto the micro, this difference is moot. However, if the microcomputer user desires to transfer information from the mainframe to the micro (downloading) or vice versa (uploading), then both machines must be capable of matching the other's data protocol. Because these are different, the process is much more complex.

The second form of micro-to-mainframe communication, using the micro as an intelligent terminal, requires a great deal more sophistication than simple terminal emulation. As an intelligent terminal, the micro is used to download data from and upload data to the mainframe. In this incarnation, the micro makes use of all its resources, including processing power and storage devices. In order for this type of communication to work, there must be a *translator* at one end or the other that can provide the matching protocols so that the data formats are not scrambled in the communications exchange.

☐ A good example of how the download/upload process works is the relationship between mainframe and microcomputer products manufactured for IBM systems by Cullinet software. On the mainframe side, Cullinet supports a database package called IDMS-R. For the micros, a package entitled GoldenGate is used. If an organization using both of these packages wishes to engage in micro-to-mainframe communications, they need to add another Cullinet product called IDB. IDB is a subset of IDMS-R that is a translator facility with the GoldenGate package. With this translator package in place, the user of GoldenGate connects to the mainframe through normal sign-on procedures. Once connected, any data stored in the IDB database become available for downloading to (assuming that the user has the proper security clearance) or uploading from the micro. This is possible because the format of data stored in IDB is compatible with the microcomputer format. In a sense, the mainframe environment becomes transparent to the user, and mainframe data are treated just as if they were on the microcomputer.

Clearly, this process is a more complex and expensive undertaking than using a simple emulator program. For an organization with a substantial investment in both types of computer systems, however, it makes eminent sense because the cost of information-processing time on the micro is dramatically lower than it is on the mainframe. Using the micro as an intelligent terminal makes a vast array of mainframe data available for analysis and processing in the microcomputer environment. This considerably enlarges the analytical capability of the organization, since functions may be available or more cost-efficient on the micro. Of course, the micro is limited in the volume of information it can process. Thus, if the organization deals with databases numbering in the hundreds of thousands or millions of records, use of the micro is not possible.

A final form of micro-to-mainframe communication is the use of the micro to access designated mainframe databases outside, or not a part of, one's organization. A number of commercial ventures, such as Dialog, The Source, and Compuserve, provide information services for a fee. With these services, the micro is used to access the commercial database and download information ("Sophisticated Search Strategies," 1987). These services, as well as companies such as GE and MCI, also provide electronic mail functions. Since these commercial enterprises are designed to emulate a microcomputer at their end, the problem of data compatibility is avoided. Essentially, this process is closely akin to micro-to-micro communications.

HARDWARE LINKAGES

Having examined the various component parts of the microcomputer system, it is now appropriate to consider how these components are linked together to form a system. In order for a microcomputer system to function effectively, both the hardware and operating system software must work together. The reason for this is that a microcomputer functions with both physical and logical devices. Physical devices are the actual component parts of the system, whereas logical devices are the means by which the processor manages the physical devices. This cooperation becomes even more complicated when the logical devices are used to refer to more than one physical device. These complex system linkages require many elements to operate in precise harmony.

Central to the linkages in any microcomputer system is the *bus*. The system bus is essentially the electronic equivalent of its namesake, providing an electronic method for carrying information and tying various devices together. The bus is the link between the CPU and the console and peripherals. For the most part, the user does not deal with the bus. However, with the recent introduction of new microcomputer systems, such as the IBM PS/2 with its micro-channel bus (and the Apple Macintosh II with its nubus system), it becomes important for the system user to understand how the bus is related to the system. There are now at least three major buses in use, each of which requires its own specific hardware to operate; hardware, such as memory cards or disk systems, designed to work with one bus will not work on any other. Now, when designing a micro system, the manager or designer must be careful to coordinate the system bus with any desired optional expansion.

Even more important for the system designer are the devices related to the use of printers and communication devices. Previous discussion in this chapter touched on such devices as the Centronics parallel port and the RS 232C communications port. These are physical devices used by the system to link the various peripherals together.

Consider first the printer. Most printers now work on a parallel connections system. This means that the Centronics parallel port has become pretty much of an industry standard. So far, no problem. The difficulty arises when more than one printer is attached to the system. For the machine, each parallel port (to a maximum of four) is assigned a unique physical device description: LPT1: through LPT4:. Unfortunately, the operating system of the computer (DOS) can only deal with one logical printer: PRN:. This means that the user must instruct the computer which of the four physical printer ports is to be assigned the logical devices and, therefore, be available to actually print. Often, the assumption on the part of the user is that an additional printer is simply attached and automatically used. Unless the appropriate software is used or a series of specific machine-level commands issued, this is not the case.

The same situation arises with communication devices. While there may be two or more physical communication ports (RS 232C) on the system, the operating system must know what kind of device is attached to each physical port for it to function. Even though the operating system can address more than one communication device (serial port), the devices attached to each port must use different protocols; otherwise the command stream becomes confused, and the devices will not work properly. Consider a microcomputer equipped with two physical communication ports, designated COM1: and COM2:. Attached to COM1: is a modem used for telecommunications. Attached to COM2: is a mouse used for graphics. If the set of protocols (called *interrupts*) used by the modem and the mouse are the same, even though they are on different physical ports, the computer will be unable to separate the logical devices, resulting in malfunction of one or both devices. Since the configuration described above is a very common one, the problem surfaces more frequently than might be imagined. In cases of extreme conflict (which does happen between some mouse and modem devices), the only solution may be to remove one of the offending devices from the system. Careful planning and knowledge of the logical device requirements of a peripheral can forestall such problems.

Another kind of device connection that causes confusion relates to the use of floppy disk drives in the microcomputer system. Like printers and communication devices, floppy disk drives, which are connected to the system bus in a micro, have both physical and logical device designations. With disk drives, however, the situation is reversed from the other two. Even though a system may be equipped with only one physical floppy disk drive, normally referred to as the A: drive, the operating system will recognize it as two logical floppy disk drives: A: and B:. The reason for this confusion is to facilitate disk copying and the common practice of software to specify the B: drive as the disk that holds the program's data files. Thus, a system equipped with only one floppy drive, as are many hard disk equipped systems, is able to function in the same logical manner as a system outfitted with two floppy drives.

Considering all of this connective complexity together, the microcomputer system designer must exercise care not only in the selection of system components but also in how they are to be linked together. Fortunately, most connectors have been standardized so that the more difficult problem of early microcomputer users, finding the right cable or connector, is no longer a major obstacle. Instead, today's system designer must be concerned with matching expansion devices with the system bus and ensuring that devices that use the same logical ports do not conflict with one another. In many cases, the solutions to connectivity and compatibility problems will be beyond the technical knowledge of the typical manager or user. However, knowing that such problems can occur, and the likely cause of the problem, makes acquisition of technical support much easier.

SYSTEM CONFIGURATIONS

So far in this chapter, we have considered the various hardware components of a microcomputer system and the various ways in which the components are linked together. In this section, we consider various system configurations—that is, how the microcomputer can be configured to optimize select aspects of the system for specific applications. Several of the more common microcomputer configurations will be discussed—namely, systems for office automation, management productivity systems, and specialized systems.

Custom configurations of the microcomputer are the best way to ensure that a particular task or application is carried out most efficiently. Since the system designed for the application is what facilitates doing the application, the term frequently applied to micros configured for particular applications is a *workstation*. The workstation appellation is appropriate because it indicates that the micro and its ancillary equipment must function together as a system.

Before designing a workstation, however, it is necessary to understand to what use it will be put. This requires completion of a needs analysis that catalogs the desired uses of the system. Unfortunately, many organizations skip the needs assessment phase and proceed directly to making the wrong equipment selection. More appropriately, the organization should, at a minimum, carry out the following steps:

1. *Task assessment*. This involves the cataloging of what is currently being done in the organization—each specific task and who is doing it. Anticipated or desired task expansion should also be included in this assessment.

2. *Task appropriateness*. Not all tasks are equally suited to computerization. The manager should determine which of those tasks cataloged is most appropriate for computerization. This step should also explicitly include *who* is doing what, since there

may be employees particularly unsuited or unwilling to undertake computerization of their tasks.

3. *Resource availability.* Once a series of tasks has been identified for computerization, the manager must determine the computer resources needed to carry out the conversion, as well as the availability of organizational resources to sufficiently *support* the desired system.

4. *Organizational commitment.* If the resources exist for construction *and* support of the computer system, the final step is to ensure that there is organizational commitment to it. This must include both top-down commitment on the part of management, both to *use* the system and to continue to provide the necessary resources, and bottom-up commitment based on the desire of potential users to use the system. In many applications involving first-time computerization, this last may be the most difficult (but necessary) commitment to secure.

Once the determination has been made that there is both sufficient need and sufficient support to warrant implementation of a microcomputer workstation system, the designers must then choose the specific configuration for the system—based, of course, on the task assessment just completed.

Systems for Office Automation

Office automation (OA) is a field that is growing rapidly in both complexity and sophistication. Once considered to be simply word processing, the field of OA has expanded to include data entry and file management, communications, graphics, and even desktop publishing. To provide an overview of the use of specialized workstations in OA, three configurations will be discussed: a word processing system, a data-entry/file management system, and a desktop publishing system. Keep in mind that most real-world applications are likely to draw elements from at least two of these configurations, since seldom is an OA workstation dedicated to a single task.

In the examples that follow, an effort has been made to include the most up-to-date IBM, Macintosh, and other systems available. The reader should keep in mind, however, that new systems are constantly being introduced, and systems described in this chapter are meant as general examples only.

Word-processing system In designing a workstation for word processing, consideration must be given to the basic tasks that comprise word-processing applications: document creation and editing, document production (printing), and document filing. To accommodate these tasks, priority in system design must be given to:

- a clearly readable video screen that does not cause eyestrain or other problems with extended use
- high-quality printing capacity
- extensive storage capacity, with rapid retrieval for boilerplate and other often-used files

Word-processing systems, unless heavily graphics-oriented, are not dependent on the latest in high-speed processors for their effectiveness. Therefore, a system based on the standard 8088 or 8086 microprocessor is quite acceptable. To accommodate the need

Chapter 3 Hardware Configurations and Systems

for a high-quality video screen, a high-resolution monochrome screen is preferred. The color of the screen should be chosen by the user and not dictated as an agency policy. A hard disk system, to facilitate both storage of extensive numbers of documents and speedy file retrieval, is also warranted. Since the printed output needs to be of the highest quality, a laser printer should be included in the system, although a dot-matrix printer might also be incorporated to produce drafts for revision.

A sample word-processing workstation might consist of:

- an IBM PC clone or Model 30 with at least 640k RAM, one floppy disk, a 30-megabyte hard disk, and a streaming tape backup system
- a Princeton Graphics Max-12 or similar monochrome monitor
- an HP LaserJet Series II laser printer or equivalent
- as an alternative, a Macintosh SE with a SuperDrive, 30-megabyte hard disk, and LaserWriter II NTX printer

Data-entry/file management system This workstation is primarily designed to enter data into a database and produce simple data extractions, with perhaps basic report generation. In addition to the requisite software, the major considerations for such a system are a video screen with the capability to emulate a data-entry form, simplified methods of data entry, high-capacity disk storage, data transfer capability, and basic printing capacity.

Any microcomputer system designed with database manipulation in mind should be engineered with a fast CPU to handle extensive data searches and sorts rapidly. The video screen should be graphics-capable and usually color, to clearly identify data-entry locations. Depending on the nature of the data-entry task, a mouse or light pen can facilitate the data-entry process. A hard disk system is needed, with the capacity to accommodate the entire database. Since information entered into this system will likely be used by other analysts or transferred to a larger database, a network or telecommunications link would prove useful for data transfer. High-quality printed output is probably of less importance than rapid production of output, so a high-speed dot-matrix printer would be more cost-effective than a laser printer for this application. An illustration of the equipment that might comprise such a system is listed below:

- an IBM PC AT or equivalent micro with an 80286 processor, 640k of system RAM and another 2mb of expanded RAM, one high-capacity floppy disk, and a 40mb hard disk
- an NEC Multisync or similar high-resolution color monitor used with an EGA or VGA graphics card for maximum resolution
- a Microsoft mouse for supplemental input
- network linkage through an IBM Token-Ring adapter or other network link such as Ethernet
- an Epson FX 1000 high-speed dot-matrix printer

Desktop publishing The primary requirements of a desktop publishing system are very similar to those for a word-processing system. The major differences involve the ability to do on-screen layout and paste-up. This requirement is often referred to as a WYSIWYG (What You See Is What You Get) system requirement (Mullins, 1987). To accommodate WYSIWYG requirements, the system must be able to process far more information, much faster than the basic word-processing system. This requires a high-speed CPU with extensive memory capacity. Graphics are a requisite part of the desktop publishing system, so the monitor must be capable of producing detailed graphic images. These images, in order to meet the WYSIWYG criterion, must be of an *aspect ratio* that conforms to what they will look like on the printed page. There are several specialty monitors available that offer high-resolution, full-page viewing with 66- to 80-line resolution instead of the normal 25- to 40-line resolution of typical monitors.

Graphic images and full-page layouts consume a tremendous amount of disk space. For example, a full-page graphic with a resolution of 300 dpi takes more than 1.5mb of space to store on a disk. Thus, a high-capacity hard disk is a requisite. Graphics and the visual nature of most desktop publishing software programs also require use of a supplemental input device such as a mouse. The requirement for publication-quality output calls for a laser printer, perhaps supplemented with a plotter or color ink-jet system for color output. The final desirable component in this system would be a scanner system capable of both character and image input. To summarize, a sample desktop publishing workstation could include:

- an IBM PC AT or Model 70 class microcomputer with 1mb of system RAM and at least 2mb of additional extended RAM, floppy disk, 40–80mb hard disk, and archival backup system (perhaps a WORM disk drive)
- a specialized, full-page, black-on-white WYSIWYG monitor such as a Sigma Designs L-view with companion graphics card
- a Microsoft mouse and a scanner, such as the HP ScanJet, for supplemental input
- an Apple LaserWriter or similar high-end laser printer that supports the desktop publishing composition languages

With its high screen resolution and graphics orientation, the Macintosh II also provides an excellent platform for this kind of work. A Mac workstation might include:

- a Macintosh II with 4mb of RAM, an 80mb hard disk, and a page-white full-page monitor
- an Apple LaserWriter II NTX with additional memory and the built-in Postscript page description language

Note that there are several points of overlap among these three types of systems. In an organization where one workstation will be used to serve all three purposes, designing for the most sophisticated system (in this case, the desktop publishing system) also provides the capabilities needed by the other systems.

Systems for Management

Designing a microcomputer system for use by professionals, analysts, or managers in their work requires a system that, at base, is flexible. This means that management-oriented workstations tend to be less specialized than those described in the section on OA. Nevertheless, there are still a variety of fundamental systems that may be designed. In this section, three such configurations are described: an information review workstation, a communication/information retrieval system, and a generalized management productivity system.

Information review workstation A common microcomputer use by managers is to review work prepared by other staff members. Following on the adage that managers should manage people and not machines, many managers delegate the task of data analysis to subordinates. This still does not free the manager from managing the analysis of such information, a process facilitated when information can be reviewed by the manager on his or her own micro. An information review workstation needs to have four basic elements:

1. the ability to retrieve information from other microcomputer systems
2. the ability to display a wide variety of information (both text and graphics)
3. sufficient memory and storage capacity to handle the data under review
4. the ability to produce hard copy for more extensive review

A system that fulfills these four criteria will need a fairly powerful CPU because it will be required to handle large and sophisticated data-sets. It will also need a monitor with graphics capability, although super-high resolution is not a requirement since the system will be used for relatively short periods of time. Perhaps the most critical components of this system are those that allow connections with other systems. This connectivity may take the form of a network node, for direct data transfer, or multiple-format disk drives that can accommodate each kind of floppy disk in use in the agency. The key is that the manager must be able to read information from any of the other machines in use. This system should also include a hard disk with sufficient capacity to store, at least temporarily, any data under review. A basic dot-matrix printer would complete this installation.

One other key aspect of this or any other management-oriented system concerns the user interface and ease of use. Since the manager is unlikely to be a constant user of the system, remembering command sequences for many different software packages is likely to be a problem. The solution is to use a software package (or collection of packages) that stresses ease of use, along with a simple interface that facilitates use by the unschooled manager. More than any other aspect of the system, the selection of the correct software is the key to success or failure. In chapter 6, we will examine ways to enhance managerial productivity through these means.

Equipment that could be used to construct this type of information review workstation might include:

- an AT-class microcomputer with 1mb of RAM, high- and low-capacity floppy disk drives, a 30mb hard disk, and a network connector adapter
- an EGA-compatible monitor, such as the Princeton Graphics HX-12E, with an ATI EGAWonder graphics board
- a Microsoft mouse for graphics work and supplemental input
- an Epson FX 85-class dot-matrix printer
- a "DOS-shell" type software program, such as Microsoft Windows, to simplify system use

Communication/information retrieval system The second type of managerial workstation is primarily designed to allow the manager or analyst to capture data from a larger computer system, import it to the microcomputer, and proceed with analysis. The key to this system is its communications link with the larger "host" mainframe or minicomputer system. In addition, this type of workstation must have the capacity to perform sophisticated analyses on fairly large data-sets, requiring large amounts of RAM and high-capacity disk storage. Beyond these key elements, this system does not fully require a color monitor, but it must be capable of producing graphics. In addition, it must include a printer capable of providing rapid printouts of the data analyzed. Because this machine is used to perform primary data analysis, the user should also be capable of producing reports and other documents of sufficient quality for use internally and informal documents for external release.

This kind of workstation might include:

- a state-of-the-art, 80386-based microcomputer, such as the Compaq Deskpro 386, IBM PS/2 Model 80, or 68020-based Macintosh II CX, equipped with 2–4mb of RAM, high-capacity floppy disk, a high-speed 40–60mb hard disk, and an archival device such as a WORM drive
- EGA- or VGA-quality monochrome graphics with a monitor such as the TAXAN 760 and appropriate graphics card
- a bisynchronous communications adapter, such as an IRMA board, for high-speed communications with the mainframe
- an HP LaserJet Series II or similar laser printer capable of both high-quality and high-speed output

Management productivity system A management productivity system is the "typical" microcomputer system designed to support a wide variety of software and applications. This workstation must be able to handle word processing, spreadsheets, database management, project management, graphics, and a score of other tasks. Therefore, it must be designed with the capacity to accommodate each of these various tasks and applications.

A management productivity workstation should be designed around a powerful microprocessor, such as the 80386. The system must support expanded RAM and high-resolution color graphics. There must be a high-capacity hard disk to handle all of the possible software programs and data files, plus floppy disks to facilitate information transfer. If the office is networked, the system should be a node on that network with access to the larger file server, its disk capacity, and any other peripherals such as a laser printer. Since graphics development is a component of this system, a mouse (or some other supplementary input device) should be included, as should a graphics-capable printer. To access remote data sources, the system should be equipped with a communications port and modem. Taken all together, this system represents a "jack-of-all-trades" approach that provides the flexibility needed by the manager or analyst.

A sample configuration of such a system might include:

- an 80386-class microcomputer with 2mb of RAM, high- and low-capacity floppy disks, a 40mb hard disk, a network adapter, and a communications port
- a high-resolution color graphics monitor, such as the NEC Multisync, attached to the NEC GB-1 graphics card
- a Microsoft or compatible mouse
- a modem, such as the Hayes Smartmodem 2400
- a high-quality dot-matrix printer, such as the Epson LQ1000

Specialized Systems

The final category of systems to be considered are those designed for a specific purpose or application. These systems may employ specialized equipment that make them unsuitable for other uses. However, in an organization where a specific application is of significant importance, dedicating a microcomputer system to its accomplishment may be a very cost-effective measure. The two systems considered in this section cover presentation graphics and engineering.

Presentation graphics   A graphics workstation is designed to facilitate the production of sophisticated graphic images. Toward this end, the system must be capable of both developing sophisticated graphics and producing a variety of graphics output. The heart of the graphics workstation is a high-speed processor, since graphics are processor-intensive tasks. A super-high-resolution graphics monitor must also be included to produce the best images. Several input devices, from a mouse to a scanner to a digitizing tablet, should also be part of the system. Output should encompass a printer, a plotter, and perhaps an image-slide producer camera system.

Much of the equipment mentioned in the previous paragraph is dedicated graphics production equipment. For example, a super-high-resolution graphics system may be capable of "capturing" images from videotape or movies and incorporating them into the graphic. An image-slide producer system is capable of translating the screen image into professional-quality 35mm slides. Clearly, this kind of machine is designed with a specific purpose in mind. As an example, this workstation might be configured with the follwing equipment:

- An 80386-class micro, such as the Compaq DeskPro 386, with 4mb or more of memory (graphic images are very RAM-intensive), floppy disk, 60–80mb hard disk with archive backup device (WORM drive), and a CD-ROM drive for loading complex graphic images. This type of application is also ideal for a Macintosh IIX system with its ultra-high-resolution graphics.
- Specialized graphics device, such as the AT&T TARGA Board graphics system, to capture video images.
- Super-high-resolution graphics monitor, such as The Genius monitor, and a graphics card capable of at least 1024 x 1024 pixels.
- A Calcomp-type digitizing tablet, Microsoft mouse, and HP ScanJet scanner.
- An HP-type plotter, laser printer, and image processor such as the Polaroid Palette Plus for slide creation.
- This type of application is also ideally suited to the use of a "super-micro" system, such as the Sun SPARC station or NeXT, that operates on a variation of the UNIX operating system. These super-micros include the super-fast processors and extensive memory needed for calculation-intensive engineering applications.

Engineering workstation   A workstation designed for engineering purposes, primarily Computer-Aided Design (CAD), must be capable of handling the creation and manipulation of sophisticated images. Though similar in nature to the graphics workstation, this system manipulates a different kind of image for a different purpose. The objective of such a system is the production of engineering drawings that can aid in the manufacture of components, design of systems, or layout of a building, among others. This, of course, requires specialized software, and the workstation must be optimized to use it.

The engineering workstation should be built around the most powerful microprocessor available, make use of any available co-processor to speed up calculations, be capable of very detailed high-resolution graphics, have extensive storage and memory capacity, and have the ability to output high-quality hard copy of the results. Many of these components are similar to those needed in a graphics workstation: a digitizer, plotter, high-resolution graphics, mouse, and extended RAM. However, this application calls for subtle variations. For example, the graphics must be capable of producing very fine detailing, something that is often lost in a color system. Thus, the engineering workstation is likely to have a monochrome monitor. Given the design parameters described, an engineering workstation might include the following equipment:

- an 80386-class microcomputer, such as the IBM PS/2 Model 80, including 4–8mb of RAM, math co-processor such as the 80387, high-capacity floppy disk, 40–80mb hard disk, and tape backup system
- high-resolution monochrome monitor such as the Thorson engineering monitor, and companion graphics card
- a Calcomp-type digitizer and Microsoft mouse
- an HP or similar plotter
- an IBM PagePrinter-type laser printer

CONCLUSION

The various system configurations included in this chapter give an indication of the wide range of choices facing the designer of a microcomputer system. Throughout this chapter, reference has been continually made to the complex factors involved in designing an effective microcomputer system. Rather than dismiss it as a problem for a technician to handle, the manager or analyst responsible for the use of the system should play an active role in its design. Without a baseline of knowledge about microcomputer hardware and software, a manager is very unlikely to produce a system configuration that meets the needs of the users.

Reading chapters 2 and 3 will not make the computer novice into an expert in system design and implementation. With exposure to the different classes of software and hardware components and configurations, however, the system designer can make better-informed judgments about what is needed and how it should be developed. By creating systems that are efficiently and carefully designed, the microcomputer user provides a good base for developing the problem-solving applications that comprise the remainder of this book.

REFERENCES

"Alternative Input Devices," *PC Magazine* 6 (August 30, 1987): 95–202.

Bartlett, K. G. "Office Illness: VDT and Office Air May Be Hazardous to Your Health," *Trial* (May 1986): 62–68.

Gupta, Amar, and Toong, Hoo-Min D. "Bringing Everyman into the Computer Age." In *Insights into Personal Computers*, edited by Amar Gupta and Hoo-Min D. Toong, pp. 1–16. New York: IEEE, 1985.

Madron, Thomas W. *Microcomputers in Large Organizations.* Englewood Cliffs, NJ: Prentice-Hall, 1983.

Moseley, M. L. "The Intel Family," *Profiles* (August 1987): 26.

Mullins, Carolyn J. "The Layout of Desktop Publishing," *Information Center* 3 (June 1987): 19–25.

Petzold, Charles. "Smooth Operator," *PC Magazine* 6 (July 21, 1987): 157–170.

Rosch, Winn L. "Technical Knockout: Why Everyone Needs A Hard Disk," *PC Magazine* 6 (June 9, 1987): 109–119.

Rosch, Winn L. "WORMs for Mass Storage," *PC Magazine* 6 (June 23, 1987): 135–166.

Slater, Michael. "Hot New Chips," *Infoworld* 11 (May 8, 1989): 35–39.

"Sophisticated Search Strategies," *Online Today* (July 1987): 12–19.

"Special Issue on Laser Printers," *PC Magazine* 6 (April 28, 1987): 123–208.

"Special Report: The Future of Computing," *PC World* 5 (May 1987): 260–273.

Stanton, Tom, Burns, Diane, and Vernit, S. "Page-to-Disk Technology: Nine State-of-the-Art Scanners," *PC Magazine* 5 (Sept. 30, 1986): 128–140.

PART

II

FRAMEWORK FOR BUILDING MICROCOMPUTER APPLICATIONS

- ☐ A Framework for Developing Microcomputer Applications
- ☐ Database Development and Use in a Microcomputer Environment
- ☐ Access Systems

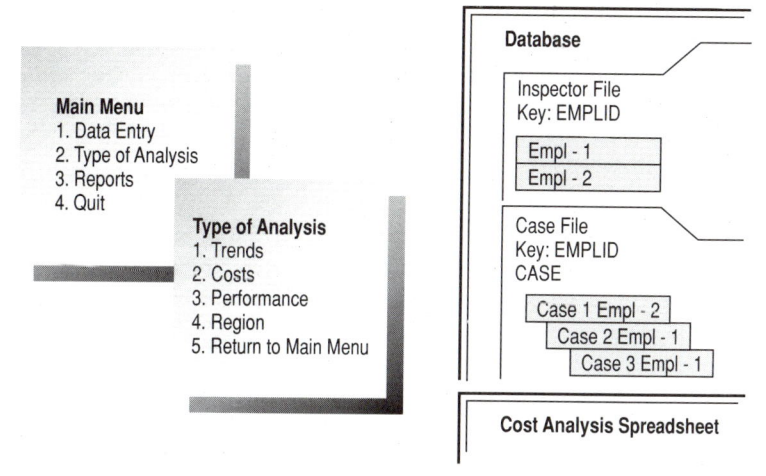

FIGURE 4.1 Customized micro application

A Sample Application

Figure 4.1 shows a typical end user application. It represents an undertaking for reporting on and analyzing government inspections. This sample application, like many applications, has four main components:

1. an access utility, often consisting of a set of menus
2. databases, which furnish the information
3. analytical tools, which operate on the information
4. modular structure, which contains the parts of the system

Each of these components has a distinct and critical role to play in a problem-solving application. The access system is designed to facilitate information interchange among the user, the database, and analytical tools. In this case, the access is provided by a set of menus. The menus show what analysis can be conducted, as well as providing easy passage to the analysis. In figure 4.1, the Main Menu accords initial entry to the microcomputer application. It can be designed to appear when the user begins execution of the application. Its function is to lay out the choices and options available to the analyst. Tied to the Main Menu are other sets of menus that enumerate the detailed options open to the manager.

Specifically, in figure 4.1, the Main Menu offers four choices, one of which is Type of Analysis. If this option is selected, a detailed menu for Type of Analysis is displayed.

While the menu provides the access, the database and analytical tools comprise the substance of the application. The database, or information base, holds the pertinent information about the problem or organizational function. The analytical tools provide ways to manipulate the data so that managers can summarize, track, or probe for alternative means to solve the problem.

In figure 4.1, the database and analytical tools are represented by the two open rectangles. The database contains two files: one for inspectors, and one for the cases they investigate. This is the information that will be analyzed. The analytical tool is represented by a cost analysis spreadsheet, which calculates, say, the cost per inspection. Other analytical tools, such as statistical packages, might also be available.

For these elements to work as a system, all menu choices are eventually linked to the database and analytical tools. In this illustration, the "2" choice from the Main Menu leads to Type of Analysis, where specific analyses can be executed. A request to explore trends, for example, would use the case file in the database, organize it by year or some part of a year, and then perhaps create a graph that plots the trend by type of case for a period of several years. Data and tools permitting, other analyses could be done to examine the causes of the trend as well as alternatives for improving performance.

The underpinning of all this activity is the microcomputer software. A forms-driven software package may provide the menus, a database management system, the information structure, and a spreadsheet for the cost studies.

☐ Forms software enables one to design attractive menus. Often driven by a hand-held mouse, these products enable one to easily draw boxes, triangles, or other shapes.

The application in figure 4.1 is quite involved. Efforts by managers and analysts to use microcomputer software need not always be directed from the start to produce fully developed, multifaceted applications. Indeed, with a modular approach, a simple start can be made and elaborated as time permits. Separate elements can be built, stored in software libraries, and implemented as needed, without the pressure to complete a comprehensive design at the outset.

Regardless of the scope of microcomputer applications—comprehensive and multifaceted, or simple and direct—it is essential to reiterate the characteristics that define the parameters for effective, problem-solving microcomputer applications:

- an access facility, or menu system, that makes it easy for the manager or analyst to understand and use the application
- a flexible organization of stored information, so that users can manipulate data according to their needs
- appropriate analytical tools
- a modular structure, so that development is manageable and so that individual parts can be used before customized, fully developed applications are ready

■ A LOGIC FOR BUILDING MICRO APPLICATIONS

How Not to Get There

There is little doubt that well-thought-out and well-designed microcomputer applications can be effective and productive. Attainment of those goals, however, is often a formidable feat. Of particular importance is not being misled into thinking that some magical software will forge good applications. Unfortunately, even with all the lessons demonstrating that technology alone cannot solve problems, the method for developing microcomputer applications is too often perceived as one of selecting the most powerful or sophisticated microcomputer software available and redefining the application to fit the capabilities and constraints of that software package.

Thus, if the software has a host of power tools, as with an integrated software package, and if the application developer learns these plus any hidden tricks, the novice designer might feel that the answers to managerial problems are only a short distance away. Certainly this powerful-software, crafty-programming approach has its place. It can, however, lead to wasted energy and futile applications if careful thought is not given to the problem and what the application ought to do to solve it. For example, even with an attractive-looking application, an effort to project outflow of cash in a capital budget might go astray if all the accounts are formulated to use cash at the same rate, regardless of type of project or past experience. Another possible flaw in this example is to have a system in which one set of accounts runs on a monthly basis and another on a quarterly basis. In short, sound thinking about what is at the heart of the problem and its solution leads to sound applications for solving the problem.

☐ *Integrated software packages* contain a variety of tools, such as database management systems, word processor, and spreadsheets. Results from one can be used in another. Analysis from a spreadsheet, for example, can be accepted directly into a word processor that is being used to write a final report on whatever analysis was undertaken.

The Blueprint Analogy and Framework Approach

Solving managerial problems with any set of tools is a difficult and complicated task. What is required, regardless of the technology exploited, is clear thinking about the problem and careful design of the solution. Unless both are present, reaching an effective, workable solution is unlikely. In brief, clear thinking and careful design are a must in order for microcomputer applications to have ease of use, flexibility, appropriate analytical tools, modularity, and accurate and realistic results.

One analogy for the planning and work required to develop viable applications is the *blueprint* used for putting together large construction projects. Blueprint design begins with a rough sketch of the finished project. As the blueprint is developed, additional information is used to refine the crude approximations of the first designs, until the formal construction blueprint is produced. Only then is the implementation and building process begun, with the blueprint serving as a road map. Just as complicated construction projects need plans and designs, the same holds true for developing microcomputer application programs. Central to building an application for even a modestly complex managerial problem and for avoiding the trap of a trial-and-error approach is a blueprint, or plan of attack, that rests on clear thinking and careful planning.

In the language of computer applications, the term *framework* or *logic* is more commonly used than blueprint. The framework or the logic encompasses the general guidelines and tools for moving from the rough-edged, poorly defined managerial problem to a productive microcomputer application. It suggests where to start with the development, what concepts are important in the problem-solving effort, and what tools can be beneficial for dealing with complexity and assuring accuracy.

Elements of the Framework

The framework for moving from a managerial problem to an effective microcomputer application consists of five major elements:

1. a typology for understanding the nature of managerial problems that distinguishes between easy-to-graph, routine problems and more complex problems

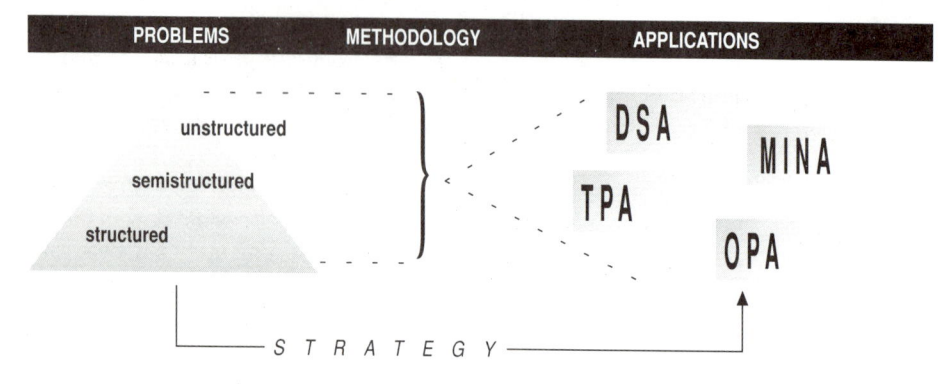

PART II   Framework for Building Microcomputer Applications

Legend:
DSA-decision support application
MINA-management information application
TPA-transaction processing application
OPA-operation processing application

FIGURE 4.2 Framework elements

2. a typology of computer-based problem-solving applications that is linked to the complexity and demands of the managerial problem
3. a methodology specifically designed for building computer applications
4. a dual role played by the software and other applications (a) as an interactive tool for searching for key information to build the application and (b) as part of the resources or modules that constitute the new application
5. organizational strategies for assigning responsibility and authority for building the applications

   Figure 4.2 is a schematic representation of these elements and how they operate together. The starting point is a typology for better understanding the nature of the problem confronting the manager. By distinguishing three types of problems—unstructured, semistructured, and structured—the typology differentiates between the more difficult, complicated problems and the more routine.

   With a broad perspective on the nature and difficulty of the problem, it is possible to form a general notion of the type of microcomputer application needed. As suggested in figure 4.2, certain generic types of applications—namely, decision support applications (DSAs) and management information applications (MINAs)—are linked to the more demanding unstructured and semistructured problems, whereas transaction (TPAs) and operating applications (OPAs) are connected to the more routine managerial problems.

   Although the typology of problems and the link between problems and applications provide a basic guide for developing the microcomputer application, the guide is too general to build the details required for a problem-solving application. Necessary to developing the details is a methodology specifically designed to break down the complexity of managerial problems and build a computer-based program. Central to this methodology is a technique known as *divide and conquer*. It emphasizes partitioning problems into manageable modules and refining solutions until they can be translated into computer applications.

To each of these elements, the availability of micros appends a special dimension. In general, the micro brings the user added and more immediate power in sifting through information to understand the problem better and in reorganizing information to offer more creative and quicker solutions.

Finally, an organizational strategy for assigning the responsibility and authority for putting the application together is indispensable. Such a strategy may incorporate a number of approaches, including information centers, life cycle development, and prototyping.

Understanding the Nature of the Problem

In any type of managerial problem-solving exercise, it is vital to have a broad understanding of or perspective on the nature of the problem. Such an understanding constitutes a solid basis from which to configure the application. One approach used successfully for comprehending the nature of the managerial problem is to view problems in terms of how structured they are. This results in a typology with three categories:

1. unstructured
2. semistructured
3. structured

The fundamental difference among these categories lies in the amount of complexity, uncertainty, political influence, novelty, and conflict inherent in the problem. Unstructured problems are inherently complex, uncertain, conflictual, and subject to extensive political influence. Structured problems, on the other hand, are more likely to be routine, organized, and subject to rational solutions. Semistructured problems fall between these two extremes.

To fully appreciate this problem typology and its contribution to designing microcomputer applications, it is essential to define each of the categories more thoroughly. These definitions emanate from the work of several scholars who have characterized organizational tasks in terms of the degree of structure associated with the task.

Herbert Simon contributes to the discussion with his characterization of problems as *programmed* (structured) or *nonprogrammed* (less structured or unstructured):

> Decisions are programmed to the extent that they are repetitive and routine, to the extent that a definite procedure has been worked out for handling them so that they don't have to be treated de novo each time they occur. Decisions are nonprogrammed to the extent that they are novel, unstructured, and consequential. There is no cut-and-dried method of handling the problem because it hasn't arisen before, or because its precise nature and structure are elusive or complex, or because it is so important that it deserves a custom-tailored treatment (Simon, 1960, pp. 4–5).

Robert Anthony also contributes to the investigation of the nature of managerial problems. Anthony (1965) uses the terms *strategic, tactical,* and *operational* to define problem/decision categories. Strategic decisions cover the more unstructured and often long-range problems. Tactical decisions are semistructured and cover many middle-level managerial problems. Operational decisions apply to structured problems, in which a standard operating procedure may suffice to handle the decision. Starting with strategic and moving to operational, Anthony (1965) offers these definitions:

> [Strategic:] The process of deciding on objectives of the organization, on changes in these objectives, on the resources used to attain these objectives, and on the politics that are to govern acquisition, use and disposition of resources (p. 24).
>
> [Tactical:] The process by which managers assure that resources are obtained and used effectively and efficiently in the accomplishment of the organization's objectives (p. 27).
>
> [Operational:] The process of assuring that specific tasks are effectively and efficiently carried out. Operational control is concerned with performing predefined activities (such as manufacturing a specific unit) whereas management control more often relates to the organization's policies (p. 69).

A third important contribution to the nature of managerial problems is provided by Ken Kraemer and James Perry (1983). In an article directed toward public management, these authors characterize *developmental* (unstructured) problems as those "that involve determining objectives for future systems." *Programming* (semistructured) problems include those "involving the integration of various systems and operations to attain some objective." *Operational* (structured) problems "include those found in day-to-day operations of government."

Using the typology in application development This typology and its emphasis on the differing nature of managerial problems, from unstructured to structured, can help in a number of ways with developing microcomputer applications:

1. It suggests how amenable each category of problem is to microcomputer-based solutions.
2. It points to possible solution models for different problem types.
3. It indicates the data needed for one or another problem type.
4. The typology presages the type of computer application that can be developed for the type of problem being examined.

How amenable are problems to microcomputer software solution? It is apparent from the definitions given in the typology that unstructured problems are the most difficult to comprehend and solve. Not only are they complex and frequently without precedent, but there is often little in the way of quantitative data that can be used to develop a solution. For this reason, the role of judgment and political insight will be important, and micro applications will play more of a support role. Nonetheless, the fact that the microcomputer sits on the manager's desk and offers "power-easy" software opens the possibility of combining managerial creativity, judgment, and savvy with the micro and advancing a microcomputer-inspired solution that might not have emerged if application development were left to a long and involved bureaucratic process. In fact, some writers feel that the fourth generation language (4GL) characteristics of micros open considerable possibilities for development of applications in top-level, managerial decisions. Inmon (1986, p. 6) argues:

> The primary need faced by the enduser is for decision support–type systems. These systems are generally small . . ., quick to construct, and easy to change. . . .
>
> Enduser systems [including micros] are designed to manage . . . while yesterday's DP [data processing] systems were designed to run the company.

Moving down the ladder from unstructured to semistructured situations opens additional possibilities for development and use of microcomputer applications. Semistructured problems are problems that have at least some precedent. In addition, rules governing problem analysis and solution development are easier to derive and apply, and there is more reliable data for problem solving.

In the case of a structured problem, microcomputer-based solutions are often practical. It is possible in structured problem situations to input the data to a microcomputer application, complete the pertinent analysis, and produce acceptable results. Often the application is an automation of existing processes and decisions.

Solution models Another payoff from a better understanding of the problem is aid in identifying the *solution models*. In general, solutions models articulate the theory that applies to the identified problem. These models point out critical factors, criteria, and the relationship among the factors that influence the solution.

With respect to unstructured problems, fraught with political considerations and uncertainty, a particularly appropriate solution model is termed *disjointed incrementalism* (Lindblom, 1959). Disjointed incrementalism means that those involved with the solution will most likely take "pieces" (small subsets) of the problem and search for compromises and limited changes. With compromise playing a central role, the solution criteria are not based on a rigid conceptual model, such as economic rationalism, but include a variety of influences such as community values, past organizational practices, and the political capital, or influence, built up over time. Works by Banfield (1961) and Williams et al. (1965) discuss decision making by incrementalism, and the multiple values (economic and others) that go into it.

At the semistructured level, solution models begin to rely more on rational economic resolutions. However, even at this level, it is necessary to keep in mind what the people in the organization historically have been willing and able to do. For example, a microcomputer-based economic analysis might indicate to a local government that one-person police patrol vehicles are far more cost-effective than two-person patrols. However, other, more value-laden factors, such as safety concerns, union requirements, or public perceptions, might indicate a greater overall value in two-person patrols. Simon (1957) and Argyris (1964) have both contributed to the development of this "satisficing" model through studies of complex organizations and the motivational elements involved in getting workers to put forth an effort when their goals clash with the goals of the organization.

Structured problems offer greater opportunity for the generation of optimized, formal, or standard operating procedure solutions. In these cases, quantifiable indicators, such as a productivity index, margin of variance, trend line, or rate of return on investment, facilitate computer-based solutions premised upon rational/economic criteria designed to produce optimized results. Even here, however, the bureaucratic reality is that old, more familiar patterns that worked well, but not optimally, may persist. For this reason, implementation is not as straightforward as the optimization solution suggests. Those carrying out the program can see opportunities for discretion—either to enhance productivity, for example, or to relax the rational/economic criteria somewhat to accommodate organizational or community values. Studies and models by Lipsky (1980) are particularly relevant to the issue of compromising the optimal productivity decisions with on-the-spot discretion on the part of those implementing the program.

Types of data   In viewing the differences among the problem types, it is also possible to conjecture about the type of data needed for each problem category. Keen and Morton (1978, p. 82) develop such a matrix. Using Anthony's terms for describing the nature of managerial problems (strategic, tactical, operational), they see data needs varying in terms of sources, quantification, detail, and use. For long-range, strategic decisions, made at the top of the organization, data come largely from outside the organization, are in aggregate form, are qualitative, and are not frequently used. A major decision on altering an important section of a tax law or local charter would fit into this category. At the other end of the spectrum—lower-level, operating decisions—the data come from internal sources and are more detailed, quantitative, and frequently used. Revamping recreational areas according to set procedures falls into this category. In between, where middle managers struggle to coordinate goals with resources, the data take on some characteristics from both worlds, although the middle manager is often hampered in obtaining outside data because of lack of authority or perspective.

Types of Applications

The typology of managerial problems provides one more significant contribution. From the insight and knowledge generated by the trilogy of problem types—unstructured, semistructured, and structured—it is possible to outline the type of computer application that can be developed. A tacit link (Kroeber & Watson, 1987, p. 250) suggests these combinations (see also figure 4.2):

- Unstructured and semistructured problems are associated with decision support applications (DSAs).
- Semistructured and structured problems are connected to management information applications (MINAs).
- Structured problems are identified with transaction processing (TPAs) and operation-processing applications (OPAs).

Decision support applications are considered appropriate for addressing unstructured and semistructured problems. According to Sprague and Carlson (1982), decision support applications exhibit several characteristics that make them appropriate for these less structured tasks. They consist of carefully crafted or carefully selected analytical tools that fit the novel dimensions of ill-structured decisions. Decision support applications also have access to databases, with information from both inside and outside the organization. For these reasons, they are geared to the complexity and novelty of less structured problems.

Management information applications are better suited to semistructured and structured problems. These applications work more directly with databases to summarize and check the status of programs, projects, and personnel (Kroeber & Watson, 1987, chap. 9). Much less emphasis is placed on major, goal-setting decisions or critical agency choices than is the case with decision support applications. Typically, middle managers tap these management information application systems. Managers either receive regular reports or make spur-of-the-moment queries to determine how some program is progressing.

Transaction-processing applications are essentially data-recording systems and fall in the structured category. They keep track of important events and transactions between the organization and its environment, or within the organization. A ticket issued for a violation, amount of overtime recorded, payment to a client, and disbursements to a vendor are all transactions that the organization must follow and record. Transaction-processing systems are designed to capture and store these transactions accurately. Transaction-processing applications are largely directed at the more structured problems in an organization and are often managed by mainframe computers because of the large volume of data involved. However, original entry can be done on a micro, as can later reanalysis.

Operation-processing applications are also directed toward structured managerial decisions. They often incorporate well-defined statistical, mathematical, or rule-based models for taking input data and calculating or determining optimal solutions (Ottensmann, 1985, chap. 6–7). Although they may harbor very complex calculation, they can also be based on very simple calculations. Routine scheduling, supply problems, or allocation issues fall within the purview of operation-processing applications.

Often it is the simple operation-processing or transaction-processing application that agencies develop first. Once analysts and managers feel comfortable with these, they move on to more demanding applications, such as management information and decision support applications.

A potentially significant impact of micros on the link between problems and applications is the opportunity for managers to be more involved in defining and generating a tie between problems and applications. With the immediacy and fourth generation (4GL) qualities of micros, managers can be more aggressive in initiating a link and, given the propensity of managers to deal with unstructured and semistructured problems, can move more quickly to initiating decision support and management information applications.

Methods for Developing Micro Applications

The typology of problems is an important starting point. It provides general direction by suggesting the practicablity of computer solutions, the general solution models, the type of information needed, and the type of computer application appropriate. However, it does not provide the step-by-step process for moving from the unhewn problem to the final microcomputer application. For example, an analyst may decide that a problem is a semistructured one and that a management information application is the application of preference, but there is still the question of developing the application. This more detailed work requires a set of methodologies designed specifically for translating complex problems into computer applications.

To fully appreciate the role of this methodology in a microcomputer-based environment, we want to look at it from two perspectives: first, what constitutes the methodology, and second, how does the microcomputer abet the implementation of this methodology.

Divide and conquer Central to design methodology is a divide-and-conquer strategy that enables the application developer to break down the intricacies inherent in managerial problems. By reducing the complexity of a problem, the complexity of the solution, as well as the resources needed, is also reduced. In addition, the divide-and-conquer strategy is a logical extension of one of the goals of the framework, which is to produce a clearer, more understandable representation of the problem to be solved. More generally, the divide-and-conquer approach refines the major dimensions into solutions, moving closer with each iteration to a working microcomputer application.

Unfortunately, the tendency is to approach such managerial complexity in one of two ways: either to attempt a "big picture" solution that solves the whole problem, or to retreat from proposing any solution because of the seemingly overwhelming complexity of the task. By following the strategy inherent in the framework, the analyst has a third, and far more productive option: to reduce the complexity of the problem solution by focusing on smaller components defined in the problem definition phase.

The process of applying the divide-and-conquer strategy is itself divisible into five serially related steps. Although these borrow heavily from traditional computer science logic (Graham, 1982, chap. 10), they capture the essence of repeated refinements that move not only to a solution stage but also to solutions that are implemented via microcomputer software. The five steps are:

1. a preliminary *statement of goals or objectives* associated with the problem
2. a first cut at breaking the problem into its logical parts, or *modules*
3. *stepwise refinement*, which consists of breaking the major parts into even smaller modules if necessary
4. the *algorithm* (set of problem-solving formulas or techniques) that leads to the solution proposed for each of the modules
5. the *pseudocode*, which is the English-like expression of the algorithm or solution that leads to implementation in the selected microcomputer software

The terms *stepwise refinement, algorithms,* and *pseudocode* derive, in part, from traditional computer science. One might wonder why these terms are introduced when the purpose of micros is to make computing easier and more congenial to the end user. The reasons are twofold. First, these terms are common in the computing community, and it is therefore wise to add them to one's vocabulary. Second, and more important, the logic they convey is a powerful one. This logic is based on the premise that problems, whether those faced by computer scientists or by managers, are complex and require a problem-solving logic that can handle complexity. The terms also provide a common language for problem solving.

In applying the divide-and-conquer technique, the first step is to define a preliminary set of goals and objectives. From these goals and objectives, guidelines are produced that define the actions to be taken to solve the problem. In other words, the goal is a general statement of what is desired or what is sought in solving the problem. Objectives and criteria provide greater specificity to goals, detailing such things as who, what (usually in some quantifiable term), and when.

Although the goals provide some direction and structure, it is important to recognize that in public organizations goals tend to be unclear or sometimes in conflict with each other, especially at the start of a project. For this reason, tentative goals are proposed at the beginning of the problem-solving effort, then more specific objectives and criteria are elaborated as work progresses.

After setting out a preliminary expression of goals and objectives, it is necessary to make a first cut at breaking the larger problem into smaller modules. These modules may reflect actual divisions in the organization, common ways that professionals view the problem, elements from the solution model, or subgoals of the overall problem that began to emerge in the problem definition stage. By replacing disorganized complexity with a series of less complex and more understandable modules, the manager substantially improves his or her ability both to understand the problem and to solve it. Moreover, in dealing with a very complex problem, modularizing allows the manager to delegate specific components to staff that may be familiar with that module but not possess sufficient knowledge or expertise to solve the overall problem.

The remaining three techniques—stepwise refinement, algorithm development, and pseudocode—are particularly helpful in doing the detailed work that leads to the final microcomputer application. The simple fact is that even breaking down a problem into major parts is still not sufficient to specify the solution or the details of the application. These techniques encourage an approach of gradual refinement to create specific application solutions.

Stepwise refinement Stepwise refinement is an effective means for avoiding the trap of overly hasty applications development. Stepwise refinement means accepting that each subpart of a problem may be at a level of complexity requiring more subdivision (refinement). If an element, separated out from the overall problem, seems too complex or unwieldy, it may require further simplification through more extensive subdivision. In effect, the actual construction of solution elements should not begin until the level of complexity of the problem has been reduced sufficiently to allow the analyst to deal with a single, logical aspect of the problem.

Algorithm development Algorithm development refers to the actual crafting and specification of the solution. The algorithm comprises the steps one follows to produce a workable answer. More technically stated, the algorithm consists of the logical processes and relationships used in establishing causal linkages, dependency relationships, and procedures that are employed in the actual construction of the solution. In many software packages, this translates into specific formulas, data structures, or control statements that determine the logic of the program used to solve the problem. For example, the steps taken to decide whether an expenditure is legitimate constitute an algorithm.

Pseudocode Pseudocode is an exotic term that means nothing more than writing out the solution (i.e., the algorithm) in an English-like language *before* attempting to construct the actual software code or format for the application. Pseudocode is a combination of English and the language, or syntax, used in the software (e.g., Lotus 1-2-3 or dBASE) that will be employed in developing the application. By using pseudocode initially to design the application, managers and analysts who are not comfortable working in a structured programming language or with the specific syntax of a software package are still capable of making vital contributions to the application design.

A distinct advantage with respect to these design tools is that it is not necessary to know every detail of the syntax of the selected software to derive a solution that produces reliable answers. The use of nontechnical language (pseudocode) to specify the application structure and processes enables review by staff or professionals with widely varying degrees of technical competence. This process has an added advantage of producing a feeling of substantial participation by those who work on the application, whether or not they are responsible for constructing the final code.

Role of Microcomputer Software

The point at which microcomputer software and technology enter the methodology depends, in part, on the sophistication of the user and the degree of automation in the work environment. A person versed in various types of software and operating in a highly automated organizational environment will use software to implement the logic outlined thus far. For instance, in an employee study that falls in the category of semistructured problems, a manager might use a database management system (DBMS) to take a quick look at employee records to see what performance data are automated and where people fall in terms of performance. A graphics software package can act as a design tool to lay out the modules and show how the application will appear to the end user. Queries of the library information base can be made to see what literature or studies exist on this problem.

More generally, microcomputer software enables an interactive implementation of the divide-and-conquer strategy. As ideas are formulated, the micro can be used immediately to test the idea. If the results show gaps or flaws in one's thinking, a second or third iteration can be conducted to close the disparity. Additionally, some "blind" or "guess" searches can be conducted if the application developer comes to an impasse. In this manner, the micro can be used as a tool to help build its own applications. There is a recursive or self-generating quality to problem solving with micros. The tools and applications of micros can be used to form more microcomputer tools and applications.

Who Develops the Application and How?

The last major dimension of this framework is the organizational strategy for developing the microcomputer application. In organizations it is necessary to assign people, resources, and authority for completing an application. Below we look at who develops the application and how.

Developing a microcomputer application can be a considerable undertaking. In fact, for the busy manager, or for the staff just getting started with using micros, it may not be feasible as an individual undertaking. As a result, development of microcomputer applications may involve several people in the organization. One person may have expertise with the software, another might provide the insights for clarifying and solving the problem, and a third person might envision the best layout for the application given the preferences of the users.

Chapter 4 A Framework for Developing Microcomputer Applications

However, this does not rule out application development as a unitary activity with one person playing the driving role. Some of the most exciting applications can come almost exclusively from one person, with that person originating the idea, deciding on the essential solution ingredients, designing the application, writing it, testing it, and being the sole user. What cuts across both modes is the use of management knowledge, the divide-and-conquer strategy, and the drive to make the application easy to use and dependable.

In terms of recent experience (Rockart & Flannery, 1986; Quillard & Rockart, 1986), several patterns have evolved for developing microcomputer applications. The one that captures the imagination and fits nicely with the personal nature of micros is the solitary individual grinding away at a problem and its solution. Sometimes this person is referred to as the "office guru"; sometimes he or she is called, more formally, a "functional support person." Whatever the name, the individual takes advantage of all the power and personal qualities of the microcomputer and crafts an application that is often the marvel of others, with at least some of these others becoming users or even "apprentice gurus."

As microcomputer application development becomes more integral to an office or to an organization, the development process becomes more formal. Typically, problems are placed on a priority list for allocation of organization resources, a premium is placed on the accuracy of the results, and individuals are assigned responsibility for the development of the application.

One formal organizational mechanism that has emerged for microcomputer application development is the information center (IC). The information center often has responsibility for developing, or at a minimum outlining, microcomputer applications. Individuals bring problems or partly finished products and work closely with the information center to develop the application. Where information centers exist, the process of microcomputer application development and implementation becomes more formalized and, in some cases, resembles the process of developing applications on mainframes or minicomputers.

Outside consultants provide another vehicle for microcomputer application development. During the nascent stage of microcomputer use, outside consultants can play an important role. Few individuals in the organization have either the time or the skills to develop useful microcomputer applications. However, if interest in and demand for microcomputer applications are high, then the outside consultant can bring added value to the micros. Consultants can also play a role when a highly specialized need, one not handled by the organization, appears.

Besides the issue of who develops the application, there is the issue of how to develop it. Two approaches are *prototyping* and *life cycle systems development*. Prototyping takes a quick, hands-on approach, in which a simple version of the final product is developed; life cycle systems development involves a more elaborate, step-by-step approach before an actual application is put together.

Of the two, prototyping is more closely associated with the emergence of end user computing (Inmon, 1986). With smaller but powerful microcomputers directly available to end users, individuals seek a development strategy in which they can be involved and in which a sample or prototype of the application will be quickly produced. Under such circumstances, the users work with the prototype application to get a "feel" for its responsiveness and power. Continued solution and development are carried out largely with the prototype. At some point, when the participants think the prototype has provided as much information as possible, either a full-scale application or some smaller-scale application is built.

The prototyping process is somewhat similar to, but not as detailed or involved as, the classical life cycle development. A strict life cycle systems analysis and design approach necessitates a much clearer definition of goals and information requirements than is followed in the prototyping strategy. Additionally, life cycle systems analysis and design engenders a very elaborate process, one that does not conform to the end user nature of microcomputers. Generally, there is an initial investigation and feasibility study, an extensive statement of the requirements for the new computer-based system, and then a detailed design followed by testing and implementation. All this is usually performed by professional systems analysts who work with the user. The user is important in describing needs, but passive in setting up the computer application. Life cycle systems development has been more closely associated with large mainframe projects geared to heavy amounts of data processing.

Prototyping trades off some of the rigor and sophistication of full-scale systems analysis for speed, experimentation, individuality, and innovation afforded by the microcomputer. The prototyping approach, as part of the framework for developing microcomputer-based systems, demands care and thoughtfulness, but lets the user be involved in the development of the solution and of the microcomputer application.

AN ILLUSTRATION

At this point, it will be helpful to examine a specific managerial problem in order to show how the framework operates and how it moves us toward a microcomputer application, such as the one in figure 4.1. Consider an agency that has hired a number of people to meet growing demands for a particular service. After a period of time, it becomes clear that a reduction in force is necessary, either because demand has leveled off or because technology has rendered delivery of the service less labor intensive.

This problem falls between the unstructured and semistructured categories. Although it is not novel, it is not likely to be a regularly occurring issue. Additionally, like unstructured and semistructured problems, it has a political dimension.

The general solution model is likely to emphasize a host of compromises, extending from how many employees will be displaced to the criteria used. More detailed solution models are possible, but this is sufficient to serve for this example. The application will fall in the category of decision support application but with a sizable management information application component because of the considerable demand for employee data.

Using the general solution model as a guide, the application builders can begin the process of stating preliminary objectives and then moving to a working microcomputer application. In this case, the preliminary objective might be to reduce the work force, but to do so in a fair, equitable, and nondisruptive manner. Of course, at some point the number of people who will lose their jobs must be established.

Chapter 4 A Framework for Developing Microcomputer Applications

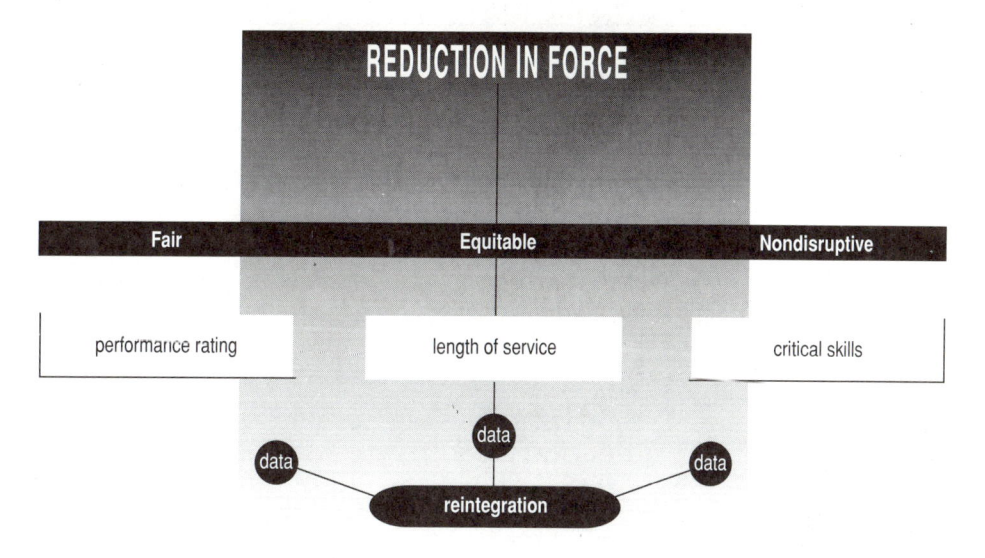

FIGURE 4.3 Hierarchy chart

Although these objectives provide a start, they are at too general a level to help render any concrete decisions. Some further refinement is necessary. One route, using the divide-and-conquer method, is to take each of the criteria—fair, equitable, and nondisruptive—and make each a separate application module. Detailed refinement can proceed within each module. Graphically, this process of divide and conquer and stepwise refinement can be characterized in terms of hierarchy charts, where each successive level points to further specification of the solution. Figure 4.3 shows a hierarchy chart for this problem.

Once the larger problem has been subdivided into modules, it is possible to begin with the more detailed work of analysis within each module. For example, it may turn out that past performance can be used for the fairness module as long as it is melded at some later point with length of service and how critical certain skills are to the agency.

With the modules defined, the specific solution (the algorithm) begins to take shape for each of the modules. For the performance module, it could be stated that performance is a function of annual awards, annual rating, and sick leave. Exactly what weight or importance is attached to each factor will eventually need to be specified.

As the algorithm takes form, it is possible to begin writing the pseudocode. In the case of performance, the pseudocode can start as simply as: "Provide me with the percentage of all persons who received an award, scored at least 4 on performance rating, and took less than five sick days." A simplified version of the pseudocode might look like this:

- Get the necessary employee files.
- Join or relate the data items needed from the various files.
- Get the joined file.

```
Below are factors for gauging performance:
A. sick leave taken
B. annual reward
C. annual rating
D. positive letters
E. negative letters

Select up to three:
____  ____      ____  ____        ____  ____

All equal weight              y       n

Rank factors:
    most important       ____
    least important      ____
```

FIGURE 4.4 Employee performance

- Find who received an award and scored greater than 4 on the performance scale and missed less than five days.
- Calculate the percentage who fall within the above criteria.
- Do a report showing employees who do and do not fall within the above criteria.

When the pseudocode has been satisfactorily developed for this module, a team member may be able take the pseudocode and write a generalized application program to share with other members of the application development team. At least for this module, the generalized application can be constructed so that the end user is presented with a menu option on performance. In this option, the list of factors (awards, performance, and sick leave) can be presented to gauge performance, allowing the end user to select and weigh each factor. A generalized module on performance would allow the end user to experiment with different cutoff points, different weights, and perhaps even different factors and then see the results in terms of rankings of individuals or other types of consequences, such as loss of vital positions.

Figure 4.4 shows the selections a manager or analyst might have in a working application directed toward the employee performance module of this problem. First, the factors are listed, with the list proceeding from sick leave to appraisal letters. From this list, up to three factors are selected. Next, the user assigns a ranking to the factors selected. The final output for this module could be a report on the employees as they rank on performance. It would be possible to implement most of this module through a package such as dBASE or another database management system (e.g., Rbase, Paradox, Revelation). It would also be possible to use a statistical package (such as PC SAS, SPSS/PC, or Statgraph) or even a spreadsheet, although the latter might not be the best choice.

From each of these separate modules, and the results produced, will come some idea of who is expendable. Of course, as with all real-world problems, the solution lies not in any one criterion but multiple criteria. As a result, findings from one module would have to be compared or integrated with the others. A final decision must be made based on the analysis, the criteria, and the objectives.

In looking at this example, it is particularly important to understand that a good deal of "interactive" work will take place in developing the application. Indeed, this is part of the special allure of micros. With the assistance of micros, the application builders will probe actual data as they proceed with the project. They will test different solutions and alternatives. And, perhaps, they will try different access or menu systems.

Besides the interactive quality, there is also the chance to tap modules built for similar projects. Using this strategy, not all of the system needs to be built from scratch. At least some of these questions have probably been asked in the past. A good computing practice is to keep a library of modules. These modules comprise the building blocks of new projects.

One other reality that must be mentioned in this example is the possibility that the application will never be fully developed. Time and resource pressures may force a cutoff at some point short of full development. Nonetheless, with the constant interactive processing, with the modular approach, and with the use of prototyping, a satisfactory application and set of answers may be available even with a partially developed application.

In summary, this example represents a difficult and complicated problem, the type that falls in the class of semistructured or unstructured problems. The framework provides guidelines and information to carry it out (although there is a good deal of skill and interpretation in defining and weighting the relevant factors). At the outset, the typology sets the tone for the nature of the problem, the type of information, and the application needed. The divide-and-conquer method, with its iterative refinement and modular approach, its algorithms and pseudocode, helps to break down problems into more manageable elements. This is followed by the task of synthesis, comparing and analyzing results from different modules. Added to the power of this problem-solving logic, the micro gives the manager more opportunity to use computer power for ill-defined problems, makes the application-building process more interactive, and perhaps pushes decisions closer to where the problems occur.

■ SUMMARY AND CONCLUSION

The microcomputer application is a critical element in using microcomputers for problem solving and productivity enhancement in public organizations. The application should consolidate the best thinking on the problem and transform that thinking into an easy-to-use automated system. One deterrent to developing sound problem-solving applications has been the emphasis on how-to approaches to microcomputer software. Micro software, though fascinating and powerful, is simply a tool for building applications. Needed is a conceptual basis or logical framework for capturing and making good use of this tool.

A logic that takes advantage of traditional problem-solving theory and integrates the user-friendly, 4GL power of microcomputer provides the basis for using micros as problem-solving technology. With this combination, it is possible to appreciate the underlying nature of the problem, pose plausible solutions, and be more aggressive in attacking tough, ill-defined problems. This combination of traditional problem-solving techniques and micro software also makes it possible to apply the powerful divide-and-conquer methodology, to test modules interactively as ideas are germinated, and to give the end user a direct role in developing the microcomputer application.

In sum, we have a sound conceptual basis from which to start. Micros have the potential to extend this basis more fully to difficult problems, to make the process more interactive, and to bring the manager and his or her insight and knowledge directly into the fray of developing and using microcomputer problem-solving applications.

The next two chapters probe more deeply into several of the elements of the problem-solving framework. Chapter 5 looks at the task of organizing large pools of data for use in microcomputer applications. Chapter 6 examines how easy-to-use access systems can be used or built into the microcomputer applications.

REFERENCES

Anthony, R. N. *Planning and Control Systems: A Framework for Analysis.* Boston: Graduate School of Business Administration, Harvard University, 1965.

Argyris, C. *Integrating the Individual and the Organization.* New York: Wiley, 1964.

Banfield, E. C. *Political Influence.* New York: Free Press, 1961.

Gorry, G. A., and Morton, M. S. Scott. "A Framework for Management Information Systems," *Sloan Management Review* 13, no. 1 (1971): 55–70.

Graham, N. *Introduction to Computer Science.* 2nd ed. New York: West, 1982.

Inmon, W. *Managing End User Computing in Information Organizations.* Homewood, IL: Dow Jones–Irwin, 1986.

Keen, P., and Morton, M. S. Scott. *Decision Support Systems: An Organizational Perspective.* Reading, MA: Addison-Wesley, 1978.

Kraemer, K. L., and Perry, J. L. "Implementation of Management Science in the Public Sector." In *Public Management: Private and Public Perspectives,* edited by J. L. Perry and K. L. Kraemer, pp. 256–279. Palo Alto, CA: Mayfield Publications, 1983.

Kroeber, D. W., and Watson, H. J. *Computer-Based Information Systems.* 2nd ed. New York: Macmillan, 1987.

Lindblom, C. E. "The Science of Muddling Through," *Public Administration Review* 14 (Spring 1959): 79–88.

Lipsky, M. *Street Level Bureaucracy.* New York: Russell Sage Foundation, 1980.

Milter, R. G., and Rohrbaugh, J. "Microcomputers and Strategic Decision Making," *Public Productivity Review* 9 (Summer/Fall 1985): 175–189.

Nagel, S. "Using Microcomputers to Aid in Governmental Decision Making." Unpublished paper. Urbana: University of Illinois, July 1986.

Ottensmann, J. R. *Using Personal Computers in Public Agencies.* New York: John Wiley & Sons, 1985.

Quillard, J. A., and Rockart, J. F. "Looking at Micro Users." In *The Rise of Managerial Computing,* edited by J. F. Rockart and C. V. Bullen, pp. 311–322. Homewood, IL: Dow Jones–Irwin, 1986.

Rockart, J. F., and Flannery, L. S. "The Management of End User Computing." In *The Rise of Managerial Computing,* edited by J. F. Rockart and C. V. Bullen, pp. 285–311. Homewood, IL: Dow Jones–Irwin, 1986.

Scoggins, J., Tidrick, T. H., and Auerback, J. *Computer Use in Local Government.* Washington, DC: International Managers Association, 1985.

Simon, H. A. *Administrative Behavior.* 2nd ed. New York: Free Press, 1957.

Simon, H. A. *The New Science of Management Decisions.* New York: Harper & Row, 1960.

Sprague, R. H., and Carlson, E. D. *Building Effective Decision Support Systems.* Englewood Cliffs, NJ: Prentice-Hall, 1982.

Williams, O. P., Herman, H., Liebman, C. S., and Dye, T. R. *Suburban Differences and Metropolitan Policies.* Philadelphia: University of Pennsylvania Press, 1965.

CHAPTER

5

Database Development and Use in a Microcomputer Environment

■ INTRODUCTION

Chapter 5 is directed toward understanding, developing, and implementing databases. As such, it focuses on how to organize and structure the considerable amount of information managers and analysts wish to access. This information can comprise data specific to one's division, data from other parts of the agency, and data from outside the agency.

Figure 5.1 suggests how databases fit into the overall computing and information structure of organizations. The databases, depicted as barrels in the figure, provide what can be called a *data picture,* or model, of the important facets of the agency and its environment (Kroneke, 1983, ch. 5). The lines between the organization (represented as

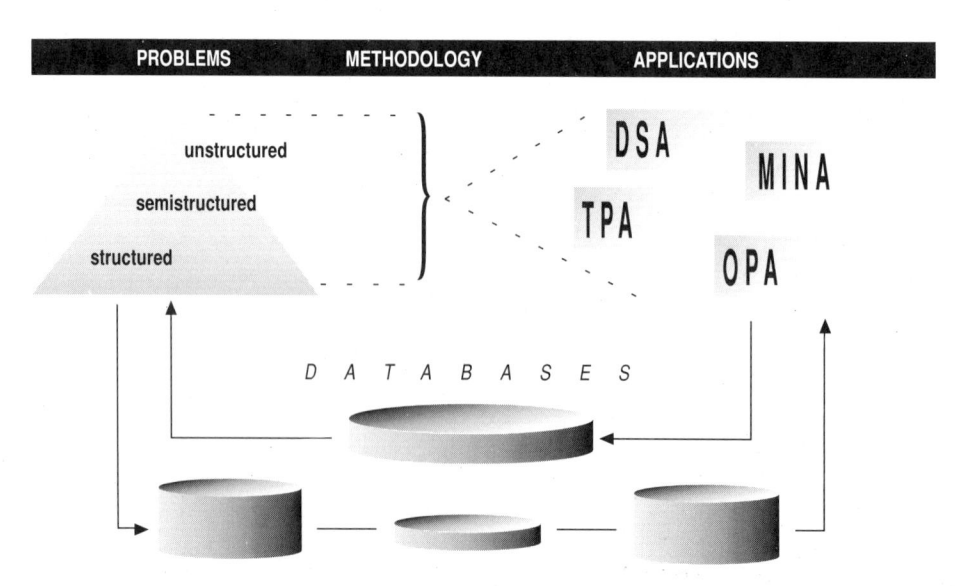

FIGURE 5.1 Databases in a micro environment

a triangle) and the databases indicate that the databases reflect the major events and activities of the organization.

In a micro, or end user environment, there is likely to be a large number of dispersed databases. Databases can reside on the personal computers (PCs), on a central micro accessible to several end users, or on larger computers. In figure 5.1, the large database (barrel) denotes the mainframe databases; the smaller ones, micro databases.

As a model or picture of the agency or some portion of the agency, databases are an integral part of microcomputer application development and use. Existing databases are counted on as a source of ideas and information for building problem-solving applications. Once constructed, applications again rely on databases for raw information to analyze. Finally, databases are expanded as a result of the findings and analyses produced by the new applications. The lines going back and forth between the applications and databases represent this interchange.

Databases are useful beyond helping to construct customized applications. They provide an important repository for ad hoc or spur-of-the-moment inquiries managers routinely make. More generally, using the information in databases, managers can summarize the status of programs and events, locate unique data patterns, trace occurrences over time, or integrate data from different parts of the agency and environment. For these reasons, it is essential to understand how to devise databases, and how to build *quality* databases that are capable of serving managers and analysts.

To handle this complex subject, chapter 5 is divided into three parts:

- definitions and context
- database development and use in complex computer environments
- case study on PC and shared databases

The first section sets the stage by providing a definition of databases and of the tool for manipulating databases: database management systems (DBMS). Also covered is the value of databases to the organization and its managers, as well as the nature of databases in micro environments.

The next section, database development and use, is the core of the chapter. Addressed in this section are the qualities databases should have and the steps or elements necessary to achieve these qualities.

The case study, which is designed to illustrate the process of building microcomputer databases, makes up the last section. To reflect a situation representative of microcomputer environments, the case is one that draws data from multiple sources, including the agency's environment, the central data-processing unit, and other PCs and divisions within the agency.

BACKGROUND AND CONTEXT

Definitions

Database Two of the central terms in this chapter are *databases* and *DBMS*. The database is a specially designed repository of information that contains a data model, or data picture, of the organization or some part of it. The database encompasses one or

108 PART II   Framework for Building Microcomputer Applications

more files and the relationships among the files. In this structure, each file may represent one distinct domain, such as the demographic characteristics of the employees or the principal attributes of all businesses in the community.

The file itself is made up of *fields* and *data values*. Conceptually, fields symbolize or represent characteristics of events, people, programs, organizational divisions, and the organizational milieu. Technically, the fields are the names of the items in the file. A file containing demographics information about employees might have fields for employee name, identification number, date of birth, and work department. The values are nothing more than the actual data: the worker's name, ID number, date of birth, and the name of the department where he or she is assigned.

One set of values for all the fields in the file is sometimes referred to as a *record*. Thus if there were thirty people in this file on demographic characteristics, there would be thirty records, each holding four fields.

Frequently, there are several files in a database, capturing different dimensions of a function or operating bureau. For example, in addition to a file on the employees, there might be a file describing the departments where the employees work. When multiple files are present, a way of relating these files must exist. The relationships symbolize the more complicated or aggregate features of the task, organization, or agency. It is this ability to show relationships that sets databases apart from other, simpler modes of organizing large bodies of data. By displaying relationships, the database is able to capture a more realistic picture of the dynamic interchanges and cross-references in bureaucratic agencies.

As noted in previous chapters, the nomenclature for databases varies widely. In this book, the terms chosen are database, file, data field, and data value. Databases consist of files; files of fields; and fields of data.

Figure 5.2 gives a concrete illustration of a database that captures information about employees and the departments where they are assigned to work. In the employee file are four fields: name, identification number, date of birth, and department name (e.g., AGR). The department file holds three fields: name of the department, budget code, and number of employees at the last update. The files can be related through department name because both files have that field in common. Thus, for any employee, we can find information on that employee, such as date of birth, and we can find related information, such as the budget code of his or her department, in the event we need to charge expenses incurred by that employee.

DBMS   Closely associated with databases are the DBMS. The DBMS is the software used to create, store, and manipulate the database. Modern DBMS are powerful tools. They handle technical tasks, such as distinguishing among types of data (character, numeric, logical, and date, as described in chapter 2) and keeping track of where the data are stored in the computer. They can also add data to the database, alter or summarize it, and produce complex queries, reports, and applications.

Value of the Database and DBMS

In an environment populated by many databases, the databases can be viewed as the place where a manager can request and obtain information on the many dimensions of the

Chapter 5 Database Development and Use in a Microcomputer Environment

```
Employee File
Key: Employee ID
  Name    ID       Date_birth    Dept
  ----------------------------------------
I ZK    147-34    09/13/54      AGR
I BN    187-33    12/01/65      PWK
I AB    222-12    03/22/59      ADM
I SD    321-22    06/03/66      ADM


          Department File
          Key: Budget_Code
          Name    Budget_Code   Num_Employ
          ----------------------------------------
       I ADM    01-ADM-44         20
       I AGR    02-ARG-55        100
       I PWK    03-PWK-66         80
```

FIGURE 5.2 Employee file

organization or activities associated with the organization. Once managers and analysts are familiar with the set of databases most relevant to their own functions, the databases provide considerable convenience because essential information is close at hand.

Added to the convenience afforded by databases, the tools for manipulating the database—the DBMS—are relatively easy to learn and use. Sometimes referred to as fourth generation languages (4GL), these DBMS are designed for nontechnical end users. Typically, the DBMS follows a consistent set of rules, and the terminology for working with DBMS is English-like. Terms such as CREATE, APPEND, LIST, DISPLAY, and SORT are commonplace.

Databases in a Microcomputer Environment

The microcomputer environment opens new vistas for databases. Historically, databases resided on mainframes, and development and use were centralized. Managers and analysts wishing to develop a new database or obtain access to ongoing databases worked with a central information department. In a microcomputer environment, there are multiple databases with no clearcut centralized control. Some of the databases will be a product of agency policy, but others will be created by individual analysts or managers on their own PCs with little or no agency guidance. Databases created by the agency are often called *public*, while those built without agency supervision are sometimes referred to as *private* databases.

This more diffused climate offers advantages and challenges. The advantages lie in the richness of data that can be assembled. Data that previously might not have been automated because of restricted interests or resources now find their way into PC databases. This gives managers what might be termed a strategic edge. Data relevant, and perhaps critical, to decisions are under the direct control and purview of managers, rather than at substantial organizational and physical distances. The challenge of this new environment is to coordinate and share the knowledge of these private databases (Inmon,

1986, p. 7). People in different parts of the organization should not be "reinventing the wheel" each time they proceed with developing a database. Additionally, consistency needs to be maintained across departments and divisions, so that dissimilar results are not reached simply because one section has more up-to-date data than another.

DATABASE DEVELOPMENT AND USE

Building Databases for What?

Before we delve into the question of how to develop databases, we need to consider the question: for what purpose are we building these databases? In the mainframe environment, a database is built with the intent that many applications will access the database. Furthermore, over a period of time, new applications will be added that will also access the database. Such a database might serve countless departments, including finance, budgeting, and a whole host of operating agencies. In a microcomputer environment, the intent may not be as global. A database can be developed that serves one person and one application or a narrow set of applications.

Although these agendas appear dramatically different, the issue of scope should not drive a wedge between mainframe and microcomputer databases. Similar guidelines and principles can benefit both efforts. The person constructing a microcomputer database can benefit from a broader horizon—seeing the database as growing to encompass more applications. The individuals building mainframe databases can profit from the more action-oriented, implementation-driven inclination of the micro environment. Especially with the user-friendly 4GL, mainframe database systems can be started and placed into use more quickly.

Ultimately, these databases should be capable of working together. Microcomputer databases, which are often the brainchild of an astute and energetic analyst, should not remain the exclusive province of that analyst. They ought to be known and accessible to others. Mainframe databases, which are frequently the grand edifice of a central information department, should not be considered the private domain of those who created them. They, too, should be accessible.

In all this discourse, it is important to emphasize that databases are built not as ends in themselves, but to be used by analysts and managers. Although much of this chapter focuses on building databases, the objective is to build databases that will be used and useful.

Building Databases: The Process

As we have seen, databases are an important repository of data in organizations and have a formidable role to perform. The intent of this section is to discuss in detail what goes into building databases. This process consists of several steps, or elements, each of which is meant to ensure particular qualities. It is these qualities that make for useful databases. Table 5.1 shows the steps and the associated qualities.

In brief, the process begins with a preliminary analysis to assess whether the opportunity or problem merits the attention and investment associated with database

TABLE 5.1 Steps and Qualities in Database Development

Steps	Qualities
Preliminary Analysis	Worthwhileness
Models and Diagrams	Visual Representations
Information Requirements	Goals/Relevant Data
Design	Flexibility/Efficiency
Dictionary	Codification of Knowledge
Implementation	Use of Knowledge
Distribution	Consistency/Coordination

development. Somewhere at the end of the preliminary analysis or at the beginning of the information requirements, models or diagrams can be used to provide an overall picture of the main data dimensions and interrelations that will make up the database. Once the merit and general scope have been established, an information requirements analysis is undertaken. It is directed toward identifying the goals, objectives, and problems, as well as the data relevant to these dimensions. Next, the database structure is designed so that the database will have the flexibility and efficiency necessary to address the many demands and needs of managers. Creation of a data dictionary follows, allowing all potential users to know what is contained in the database. Then comes the actual implementation of the database—that is, using the DBMS to create, store, and manipulate the database for more effective management. Building the applications that will access the databases is integral to this implementation step. Final concerns have to do with distribution—that is, sharing and coordinating any single database with other users or other databases.

In viewing this sequence, it is important to appreciate that the steps are more of a pedagogical device than a blueprint of what will actually occur in the field. In practice, one file may be developed, used, and then amended without ever preparing a fully customized data dictionary or a formal model of what the total database might represent. Particularly with micros and their fourth generation languages, separate aspects may be developed quickly and used without waiting for a more elaborate system to be devised.

Notwithstanding the pedagogical flavor, these steps provide an extensive and important list of the elements that go into database development. Even if a user is putting together a database under time pressure, the user should still understand the formal process and not compromise it to the extent of diminishing the usefulness of the database.

The other overarching point is the balance or trade-off between the traditional life cycle development (LCD) method of launching databases and the prototyping method. Although the elements of building the database—from preliminary analysis to distribution—are nearly always important, the methodology or sequencing can differ. The more classically devised database approach, life cycle development, puts off instituting any actual operating database system until the information requirements analysis and design are finished. The prototyping approach introduces a different compass to guide database development and needs to be clearly understood. With prototyping, the development process jumps from one state to another. A small sample system is built as quickly as possible, then tried and evaluated. Based on the evaluation, a new or altered system is presented for the next iteration.

Of the two methods, we assume that development of databases in the microcomputer environment will lean toward prototyping. However, the reflective aspect of life cycle development can be extremely valuable. A pause of a day or two for reflection and discussion can minimize mistakes and wasted effort (Achituv, Hudass, & Newmann, 1984).

Preliminary Analysis

The preliminary analysis is a quick but pointed examination of the problem or opportunity facing the manager. Its purpose is to avoid wasting time or money on unimportant or futile efforts. It is also a time to see if others have faced similar issues and perhaps have laid some groundwork.

During the preliminary analysis, the opinions of those most intimately involved in the subject matter are tapped to gauge the extent and criticalness of the issue, because for every issue pursued, there is an opportunity cost, or cost of not doing something else. Even if only one person in the division is considering building a personal database, that person should conduct a preliminary analysis. Often a chat with co-workers reveals whether a particular project is worth the effort.

The preliminary analysis should conclude with a sketch showing the priority of the issue relative to the goals of the division, the major types of data to be collected, possible software needed, and the payoffs of the database. If all or most of these point in a positive direction, then the detailed work necessary for developing a database should proceed, acknowledging that the project can still be aborted if negative feedback is encountered on the worth of the effort.

Models and Diagrams

Models and diagrams represent the problem or task to be addressed by the database through visual images, rather than turgid prose and dull data. A general model highlights the major dimensions of the issue at hand and some of the important relationships among these dimensions. Somewhere during the preliminary analysis and the information requirements analysis, the model can be sketched and shared with other people who are involved or interested.

In actuality, model construction can occur at any time in the database development process. It can be used at the start to speculate on what is important, and it can be used later as the database unfolds.

These overall models are not to be confused with more elaborate diagramming, sometimes referred to as *data flow diagrams* (DFDs). Data flow diagrams are the result of an elaborate process designed to capture both general and detailed facets of the origin, flow, storage, and processing of information. A full set of data flow diagrams for even a small project may require from twenty to fifty pages to cover all the details of the process. With 4GLs available, these data flow diagrams sometimes take a backseat to prototyping, or iterative development. Instead of laying out all the details on paper before undertaking the database system, the system is produced in smaller increments on the microcomputer.

A set of computer-aided technology is emerging that focuses on constructing and presenting these models and data flow diagrams. One of the goals of this effort is to create the models and diagram, then permit the structure of the database and the outlines of the applications to unfold from the more pictorial representation. However, such technology is still in the experimental stage, with only rudimentary tools commercially available.

Information Requirements Analysis

The function of the *information requirements analysis* (IFRA) is to generate a list of data fields that provides information relevant and pertinent to the goals, problems, and tasks of the division or bureau creating the database (Davis, 1982). The importance of this function cannot be overestimated. All the technology and all the dollars are wasted if the system contains data that fail to address the concerns of the agency or the end user. Without relevant information, it is difficult to advance or evaluate agency goals, it is difficult to define the scope and nature of the problem, and it is cumbersome to track projects and programs. What follows is an examination of *who* does the information requirements analysis, *what* sources or questions might prove worthwhile, and *how* to collect the data.

Who The end users, including managers and their staff, play a central part in the information requirements analysis. They are the ones with knowledge of the problem, and it is they who will ultimately decide what data to include. Kozar and Mahlum (1987), in a study of user development of data systems, found, "The approach of using the system's users to document the system . . . is using the strength of user groups. They are the systems people in the sense that they understand their system" (p. 172).

People who are professionally trained to build computer-based information systems also have a role to play. Often called *systems analysts*, they can provide initial guidance, critique decisions of users, set technical standards, and offer their own independent observations. Generally, the smaller and more delineated a project is, the more users dominate in the process. As projects grow in size and breadth, professional systems people play a greater role.

What The question of what to probe focuses on identifying sources and perspectives that might be important. Included are the master plan (if one exists), the type of problem (unstructured versus structured), the solution models associated with particular problems, critical success factors that separate data fields on the basis of degree of importance, underlying assumptions behind the plans and models, and the actual inputs and outputs needed.

The first source is the organization's master plan, assuming that one exists (Davis, 1982). Master plans for information resources can arise at either agency or departmental level. The value of seeking out the master plan is the discipline it imposes on data collection. In a PC environment, each department and individual within the department is likely to identify his or her own set of information needs, perhaps independent of overall organizational goals. A master plan for data collection can foster a balance among agency goals, departmental objectives, and individual aspirations. Without this balance, the results may be suboptimal in that a department or individual may push some task beyond its reasonable contribution to agency objectives.

4. In that framework, problems faced by managers were divided broadly into unstructured, semistructured, and structured (or strategic, tactical, and operational). For each type of problem, certain kinds of information are more appropriate. With unstructured problems, information is often siphoned from the outside social or political environment. Semistructured, or tactical, problems rely more on internal program information, especially aggregations that demonstrate performance. Structured, or operational, problems require detailed internal information on transactions and work progress.

The solution model is another general source, but not as broad in scope as the master plan or type of problem. Solution models are peculiar to a problem or set of problems. As noted in chapter 4, solution models are selected when the microcomputer application is being developed. As such, these models impart information needed for the problem at hand. For example, the solution model may suggest that data on political influence are most vital, followed by data on financial assets.

Similar to the role played by the solution model is that of *critical success factors* (CSF). Both solution models and critical success factors look to what is most important in getting the job done or the problem solved. However, critical success factors concentrate almost exclusively on what is most essential in solving a problem or taking advantage of an opportunity. Unlike solution models, they do not delineate how the several variables affecting the problem might interrelate. For this reason, critical success factors do not deliver the richness of information that comes from solution models.

Underlying assumptions do not necessarily add more detail; rather, they impel one to think more carefully about what is behind the solution model or critical success factors (Mitfoff & Emshoff, 1979). When underlying assumptions are examined, factors that initally seemed important may turn out to be spurious.

Though worthwhile, probing underlying assumptions is taxing. People's deeply held feelings are questioned. Moreover, if the users are the prime movers in the information requirements analysis, they may be too involved to challenge their own basic assumptions. At this point, professional systems analysts from outside the department can play a valuable role in a collegial type of questioning of assumptions.

A final source is the input and output requirements: that is, exactly what data will go into the database, and what types of reports or queries will be requested? In a sense, this is a culmination of probing all the other sources. It also has the effect of forcing one to be specific. Such an exercise can uncover variables not apparent before or prove some factors to be superfluous.

In pursuing this list of sources and perspectives, it is important to recognize stepwise refinement (discussed in chapter 4) at work. Some of the sources are at a general level, and others are at detailed levels. The more general elements, such as solution models, may be broached first, followed by a probe of assumptions and rounded out with the detailed input and output requirements.

Although the stepwise refinement perspective can be a helpful guide, it is not imperative to start with master plans and solution models—the general level—and then work down to the details of inputs and outputs. What is important is an appreciation of the distinct levels and how they reinforce each other. Starting with the details of inputs and outputs is acceptable so long as those conducting the information requirements analysis understand that these details must be compared to the general problem or goals at stake. Otherwise, data collection may not be germane to major concerns.

Chapter 5 Database Development and Use in a Microcomputer Environment

How So far we have discussed who should do the inquiring and what sources ought to be considered, but not how to collect the data. To fill this gap, three approaches are suggested: (1) questioning managers and colleagues about goals, solutions, and critical success factors; (2) rummaging through documents and past decisions; and (3) experimenting with prototype systems.

Questioning others offers a relatively quick and easy way to assemble information. With this approach, it is possible to follow up, probe, and return to ask more questions. What detracts from this technique is the tendency of managers to request too much information and not to differentiate between the most important and less important considerations (Louata, 1987). The other problem is getting some managers to stop long enough to give serious thought to future systems.

A way of circumventing the weakness of questioning is to examine past documents and decisions. These can fill gaps in people's memories, disclose patterns that may not be apparent to managers, and provide background for in-depth questioning. Together, the questioning and document search present a more complete picture, one not available when either technique is used alone.

To these traditional techniques it is important to add the method of experimenting, or prototyping (Kraushaer & Shirland, 1985). With prototyping, a small-scale system is built and presented to the users. The advantage of this style lies in giving users an opportunity to explore, in a hands-on way, the value of different pieces and arrangements of information. Specific information needs are likely to emerge when users are concentrating on a problem and gaining immediate feedback from a working system.

Given the 4GLs associated with microcomputers, prototyping is a feasible technique for information requirements analysis. Small or sample databases can be created quickly. Similarly, sample input screens and output queries and reports can be designed so that users can actually work with the products rather than only discuss them or see them on paper.

The end result of the information requirements analysis is a list of data fields the managers and analysts feel will satisfy their information needs for a particular problem. Ordinarily, users and others involved in the information requirements analysis review the list for omissions or unnecessary fields.

Table 5.2 lists the data fields that might arise from an information requirements analysis of a local taxing and billing system. These items will be carried through the remaining theoretical presentation of designing databases. The concrete data provide a way of interjecting case material along with the theoretical discussion.

Database Design

The next step in building the database is the design, or more precisely, the design of the data files. In this step, the data fields identified in the information requirements analysis (which, even on micros, can number in the hundreds) are grouped or organized into separate data files that will eventually make up the database.

In the literature, the terms *tables* and *files* are often used interchangeably. Both simply refer to a grouping of data fields and the values for each field. The term *table* comes from the fact that the data fields and associated data values look like a table of values. Among those who write about

TABLE 5.2 Items for Finance Charges Database

Resident ID
Resident name
Resident address
Resident phone
Development name
Acreage
Parcel ID
Water bill
Adult education fee
Library fees
Rate(s) for services
Total charge
Real estate tax
Real estate tax rate
Total tax
Resident's occupation

the theory of databases, *table* is part of the common parlance. Among practitioners, *file* is more commonly used.

The goal of grouping fields into files is to ensure flexibility and efficiency in the way the data are organized and accessed. *Flexibility* refers to the ability to rearrange and access the data and data files according to the needs of the managers. *Efficiency* represents a guard against waste and unintended data loss.

The design step is a critical one in building databases. If the data are organized poorly or improperly, then it may take a great deal of time and money to rectify the situation. Database design can be akin to quick-drying concrete: once set, the original work is not easily altered. The more grievous the error, the more likely it is that the design will have to be abandoned and replaced with a new design.

Relational logic The primary vehicle for the design of databases is referred to as a *relational logic*. Almost all microcomputer databases, and many mainframe and minicomputer databases, follow this logic. The relational approach to building databases is useful because of its inherent flexibility in organizing large amounts of information. In essence, relational databases consist of numerous data files and the facility to extract, combine, or relate data from any of these files. It helps to evade the "quick-drying concrete" effect and provides a more malleable context in which to work.

Built largely on relational algebra, the relational logic provides a powerful conceptual tool for dealing with tables of data. Seminal work was done by E. F. Codd (1970). Some of the relational algebra and set theory that support the relational logic can be found in Vetter and Maddison (1981).

A few brief examples will show the flexibility of databases using the relational logic. In essence, as long as any two or more files share a data field, information from these files can be linked or related. Once these two fields are linked, the user has access to all

```
File R                                    File S
Resident   Resident    Household          Service          Service
ID         Address     Size               Type             Rate
---------------------------------         ----------------------
I 1467                                    I ad ed IV       $25
I 1433                                    I water rate     $75
I                                         I inspection     $50


                       File RS
                       Resident       Service
                       ID             Type
                       ----------------------
                       I 1467         ad ed IV
                       I 1467         inspection
                       I 1445         ad ed I
```

FIGURE 5.3 Linking files

the data in both files. For example, if a manager wished to examine payment records across a variety of files, such as water bills, adult education classes, and real estate taxes, the manager could extract such information for all residents as long as each file containing the pertinent data had a field identifying the resident.

In figure 5.3, file *R* and file *RS* contain a mutual field: resident ID. Thus, we can link files *R* and *RS* and find all the services that each resident has received. Going one degree further, it is also possible to relate two files that do not have a data field in common as long as each file shares a common field with a third file. If one file contained resident ID (file *R* in figure 5.3) and another file (*S*) had the cost or rate of certain services, it would be feasible to link these original files if a third file (*RS*) existed with both resident ID and service type as data fields. The linking occurs when service type in file *S* finds service type in *RS* and resident ID in *RS* finds resident ID in file *R*. Called *chaining*, this indirect link is shown in figure 5.3. It would permit analysis of, or cross-references among, the fields in all three files.

Many other manipulations can be accomplished under the relational logic. Selected records can be identified, whole fields from a file can be extracted out and made files unto themselves, and files can be joined in a variety of ways.

This relational approach fits the changing, multidimensional world of the manager. Managers wish to extract and combine different data fields depending upon the nature of the problem facing them at a particular time. Relational databases allow this flexible manipulation.

Prior approaches to database design, often called *hierarchical*, were more rigid. Relations among the fields had to be specified in advance, and subsequent analyses were limited to these relations only.

Relational databases, at least in theory, offer a smooth way to integrate data from broad and diverse agency functions or from different departments. Simply because relational databases have the potential for flexible and efficient organization, however, is not sufficient to bring this capacity to the public manager. To achieve the potential, it is necessary to design the database so that it captures rather than loses the power of relational databases. If data fields are not properly organized into the appropriate files, the advantages of the relational logic are dissipated.

Part of the perplexity of designing flexible and efficient databases emanates from the sheer volume of information managers and analysts want to assemble. If fifty or a hundred data fields are identified in the information requirements analysis, the design task constitutes placing all these fields into the appropriate files so that access, interrelationships, and analysis proceed smoothly.

Two sets of rules for designing databases and maximizing the potential of the relational logic are *normalization* and *Bachman Charts*. Each will be discussed in turn.

Normalization Normalization consists of three stages or steps. The initial stage is the information requirements analysis, previously discussed; it consists of identifying and listing all the data fields important to the objectives of the project. The second stage involves grouping all the fields into files. The third and final stage is a refinement of the initial groupings so that any serious flaws—namely, those that would detract from achieving a flexible and efficient organization of the data—are removed.

Assuming that a satisfactory list of data fields exists, the mission is to group the fields into the files that will eventually form a well-designed database. The guide for the initial grouping is to designate the dominant fields (or categories) in the list, and then to find like or related sets of fields that are dependent on each of the dominant fields, and only on the dominant fields. Each dominant field and its related set of fields then form groups of fields, or what will eventually be the files.

These main or dominant fields ought to be the fields of primary concern to the projects or goals of the bureau or division. These fields should drive or shape the other fields. These dominant fields are usually termed *keys*.

Key has a more technical connotation in addition to the general notion that it is the dominant or main item in a file. Technically, the key is the unique identifier of each record in a file. The key can be one, two, or more fields, depending on how many fields it takes to uniquely identify a record. Consider, for example, the files in figure 5.3. In file *R*, the key consists of one field, since each resident ID is unique (assuming the person is not a resident at two places). In file *RS*, the key consists of two fields, ID and service type, because ID is not likely to be unique. A resident can use or purchase many services. Thus, ID in combination with service type is more likely to produce a unique key. In some cases, a unique identifier must be created because no combination of fields will be unique. That is possible in file *RS* if a resident takes the same course twice.

In our first cut at the groupings, we will show how groupings are often poorly conceived. Then we will use a set of tools to correct the design flaws.

This first cut (figure 5.4) has three files. The first file is what might be called a resident file. It has resident ID as the key and includes all the characteristics of the resident. The next file is a service or service charge file. With resident ID again serving as a key, we show all the services for which the resident has been billed. The last file is built to accommodate fields allied with real estate taxes paid by the residents.

The pattern of choice shown in figure 5.4 is quite typical. Designers perceive

Chapter 5 Database Development and Use in a Microcomputer Environment   119

```
File I
Residents
Key: Resident ID

  ID  Name   Parcel Address   Assessment    Development    Acreage
----------------------------------------------------------------------
I  KY                227 Ven    123,000       Concord        323
I  LM                278 Ren    167,000       Concord        323
I  BF                 14 Kar     75,000       Beach          100
I   .
I   .
I  JG
----------------------------------------------------------------------


File II
Residents and Charges
----------------------------------------------------------------------
                     Adult      Adult     Library    Water
   ID   Name         Ed. I      Ed. II    Fees       Bill
----------------------------------------------------------------------
I  AK                                                 X
I  BR                  X          X
I  FR                  X          X          X        X
I  SS                             X                   X
----------------------------------------------------------------------




  File III
  Real Estate Taxes
  Key: Resident ID
  ID    Type of Tax    Total     Paid      Rate
----------------------------------------------------------------------
I  JG    real estate    1231      1231      1.20
I  LU    real estate    4321      4000      1.20

----------------------------------------------------------------------
```

FIGURE 5.4 Finance department database (first-cut groupings)

individuals (residents, employees, trainees) as "owners" of characteristics and proceed to build the files around the individuals.

This intuitive grouping is a first-cut effort. It originates from the knowledge and design sophistication of those involved in the program or department. Essentially, users and managers select fields that are considered central to the functions and establish groupings around these keys. This grouping usually represents a commendable start. From here it is necessary to do the more precise refining.

Detailed refinement consists of a series of tests meant to reduce or eliminate inflexibility and inefficiency. These tests, often expressed in the highly specialized and technical language of normalization theory, can be communicated in a more practical nomenclature. In effect, normalization tests for three problems:

- repeating fields
- modification anomalies
- redundancies

In the technical approach to normalization, the design revolves around transforming the files into first normal form, second normal form, and so on. For each normal form, certain types of dependencies must be removed. Expository pieces on normalization can be found in Kroneke (1983).

In actuality, all the files must past each test, starting with the repeating fields test and moving to the redundancy test. When the initial files are cleared of these flaws, the resulting files should exhibit the two important qualities of databases: flexibility and efficiency. That is, the files should be amenable to a wide range of rearranging and should not exhibit waste or unintended loss of data.

The tests start with repeating fields, which can be the most damaging of the flaws if not detected and removed. When repeating fields inhabit a set of files, huge amounts of storage space and data-entry time are wasted, and interrelationships among the files are often difficult.

The danger of repeating fields occurs when an event takes place over and over again, usually for an unknown number of times. A resident can draw on a number of services, but no one can predict how many or how often. Designers fall prey to this trap when they endeavor to allow enough fields (or space) in a file to accommodate the estimated maximum number of events.

Among the files in figure 5.4, one exhibits repeating fields. It is file II, which includes data fields on service charges. Not knowing how many services (bills or fees) a resident will accumulate in a given period, space is apportioned for a maximum of four bills or charges.

Two serious problems arise from repeating fields: empty cells and not enough space. As can be seen in figure 5.4, waste is a nemesis of repeating fields. Some records in the data file will have few or no events (data values), while others will have the maximum. Under some circumstances, only a small portion of records will have all the fields filled while most records have just a couple of values. An enormous amount of storage space is wasted because most of the file has no data. In figure 5.4, only resident FR has all four bills.

The other problem is how to enter the data when a new service is added. For instance, what if the community now offers a mooring service at a nearby inlet? No space is allocated for this fee. The only hope is that the DBMS allows for adding new fields after the database has been established. Finally, imagine what the file would look like if the community eventually had fifty services and the designers sought to place them all in one file.

```
Bills
Key: Resident ID, Type of Bill

    ID    type of bill    total     paid     rate   units used
    ---------------------------------------------------------------
I   KR     water bill     32.20    32.20     .04
I   JG     water bill     42.33    20.33     .04
I   KI     adult ed I     22.00    22.00      22
I   DN     mooring fee    44.00    22.00      44
    ---------------------------------------------------------------
```

FIGURE 5.5

The solution (or normalization) of repeating fields is to make a generic category or categories from the fields that repeat. Instead of having a field for each time an event occurs, simply have one category, such as charges for services. The file would then repeat vertically (the data values) not horizontally (the data fields). The file will now look like the file in figure 5.5 rather than the repeating setup in figure 5.4.

This idea of having one generic category shows what should have emerged initially in the design. In attempting to identify the dominant fields or categories from the list of original fields, it should have been apparent that the many charges represented one category. This category is then taken as the dominant field. The fields related to the charge for service are the like fields to be included in the file. The rate, the units used, and the charge itself are related to the type of charge. In essence, what we are doing is raising the level of abstraction. Instead of seeing individual charges assigned to residents, we see a category of charges.

Assuming that repeating fields have been adequately addressed, the next test is for modification anomalies, of which there are two: deletion and insertion. Deletion in a data file means that the sole occurrence of a data value is unintentionally lost. The record may be deleted because most of the data values are no longer needed. For example, deleting the record of a resident who moves is acceptable, but if the parcel number or address is also stored in that record, and that is the only place the parcel number is stored, then an important fact is lost. In this case, there is no longer any record that the land parcel exists, even though the parcel is still there.

Insertion anomalies arise when no one engages in an activity or event, even though it is available. With insertion anomalies, the data value never gets into the file. A jurisdiction may have a particular activity with a given rate structure, but if no one partakes, then the activity is not captured in the database.

Deletion and insertion anomalies creep into files when the files include a mix of fields, wherein some fields are dependent on or linked to nonkey fields. One illustration comes from figure 5.5. The user's ID, the activity or type of charge, and general information about the activity (such as the rate for the activity) are all in one file. In this case, rate is dependent on activity, which is not the key; the key is ID and activity. With this structure, if one record were deleted, the file is susceptible to deletion anomalies if that record were the only one with a particular activity. The activity and general

```
File I
Bills
Key: Resident ID, Type of Bill

    ID    Activity         total     paid
    ------------------------------------------
    I KR    water bill      32.20    32.20
    I JG    water bill      42.33    20.33
    I KI    adult ed I      22.00    22.00
    I DN    mooring fee     44.00    22.00
    ------------------------------------------

        File II     Activity
        Key: Activity

            Activity        Rate     Description
            ------------------------------------------
        I   adult ed I       20       aaaaaa
        I   mooring fee      44
        I   water bill      .04
```

FIGURE 5.6

information about it are now totally lost. Similarly, if no one participates, then there is no record of the activity or the information that is normally included with the activity. Note that in figure 5.5, a deletion of resident DN causes loss of information about mooring. For instance, if DN pays his or her bill and the record is deleted, there is no longer any information on mooring and the fee for it. Moreover, if the jurisdiction offered adult education III but no one participated, then the file would not contain any information on it.

Deletion and insertion anomalies are corrected by splitting the data file to remove the mix of dependencies. For example, in figure 5.6, the activity remains in one file to show who is involved and what they are doing, but there is a separate, comprehensive file for all the activities and their attendant information. This structure not only removes the anomaly, but the two files can still be related because each has the activity field.

The final test relates to certain types of redundancies. In this circumstance, a data value must be added to a file simply to maintain the symmetry of the file. When a new record is placed in the data file, the redundant data value must be added even though it has nothing to do with the new information. For example, if a file comprises a manager's ID, project assignment, and department, the department must be added every time the manager is given a new assignment. Figure 5.7 shows the problem, and figure 5.8 shows the correction. In figure 5.8, a three-file setup, with manager ID and department in one file, manager ID and project assignment in another, and project information in a third file, would satisfy the redundancy problem. It also avoids modification anomalies and opens up multiple possibilities for interrelationships among the files.

```
Manager ID      Assignment      Department
-------------------------------------------
I  DF           recruiting      ARG
I  BC           evaluation      ARG
I  AS           budgeting       PWK
I  DF           budgeting       ARG
```

FIGURE 5.7

```
Manager ID         Department
-----------------------------
I  DF              ARG
I  BC              ARG
I  AS              PWK
I  DF              ARG


    Manager ID         Assignment
    ----------------------------
    I  DF              recruiting
    I  BC              evaluation
    I  AS              budgeting
    I  DF              budgeting


        Assignment      Description
        ------------------------------
        I recruiting
        I evaluation
        I budgeting
        I budgeting
```

FIGURE 5.8

Even with these guides and tests, there is still considerable subjectivity in forging the general groupings, because what constitutes a key or dominant field to one person may not hold the same predominance for another. As a result, there is a back-and-forth movement between the subjective grouping and the more technical facets of probing the files for design flaws.

Bachman Charts Another recognized technique for designing flexible and efficient files is the use of Bachman Charts (BCs). Bachman Charts start in the same fashion as the normalization process—with a list of data fields. Bachman Charts differ in that they build files on the basis of specific types of relationships among the fields. That is, for any pair of data fields, the three possible interrelationships are:

- one to one
- one to many
- many to many

To determine which relationship exists, it is necessary to compare each data field with the others in the group. Once a relationship is determined for two fields, then it is possible to spell out the file structure.

In a one-to-one relationship, one data value relates only to only one other value. A particular person signified by an ID number has only one age; an address has only one zoning or ZIP code designation. According to the Bachman Chart approach, all data fields with one-to-one relationships, such as ID and age, should be placed in separate files. To determine which fields go where, all the one-to-one relations that fit into a particular conceptual category go into their own file, while other one-to-one relations must make up their own distinct categories. For example, all one-to-one relations that comprise basic information on residents would go into a resident file, and all one-to-one relations pertinent to categories such as municipal services would go into another file. A service, its ID number, and rate might constitute such a file, assuming each service had only one rate.

For a one-to-many relation, any data value that can be associated with many other data values becomes the target. For example, an inspector can make many inspections, and a resident can use many services. In the construction of these files, the one and the many are placed together in a separate file, and the many item is also given a file of its own, yielding a two-file configuration. Interrelations can be drawn between the two files because both contain the many item. For inspectors and cases, there would be a single file to record all the efforts by the inspectors and a separate file to list all the types of cases and any general information consigned to these types of cases.

The many-to-many situation searches for data values that can be associated with many others, which, in turn, can be associated with many of the original values. Drivers can use many cars in a car pool, and each car can be driven by various drivers. The files for this more complex relationship consist of one file to record who is driving which cars, one file just about the drivers, and one file solely about the cars. In other words, one includes both objects, while the other two files are only for one of the objects.

Typically these relationships are represented by the following symbols:

- <-------> for one to one
- <------>> for one to many
- <<----->> for many to many

Either technique, normalization or Bachman Charts, can be used to take the numerous data fields and produce flexible and efficient files. With normalization, the initial grouping around dominant fields and the three tests are central; with Bachman Charts, the three types of relations are critical.

Systems expertise Because of the potential complexity in the design component, a team approach or the availability of consultants is of particular value. Integral to the team or consultants should be a member who has experience with database design. Users can be their own experts in the information requirements analysis, but the design requires special expertise and experience that users may not have. The role of the user is to set the basic parameters for the design. The expert works within these boundaries to establish the specific design or to check designs developed by the users.

Data Dictionary/Data Directory

Like other elements of the database, this one can begin at the completion of the design or earlier and continue as the database is built. We place it here because once the design is set, so too are many of the fields (or variables) that make up the database.

A number of reasons lie behind the need for a data dictionary and directory. One is the large amount of data and information that can be involved in databases. It is possible to have fifty, a hundred, or even more data fields in any given database. No one is capable of keeping track of or remembering the names and definitions of all these fields. Additionally, with micros as an integral part of the information system, there can be numerous databases, each with its own set of data fields. To use all these data prudently, it is necessary to describe the data so that the user is aware of the content and makeup of the data fields.

Besides the need to describe the data fields, other exigencies are associated with good database development. One is control of the integrity and use of the data. Who is permitted or not permitted to use the database is an example of control. Databases also produce ancillary types of information, such as indexes, reports, and format layouts. Although these have not yet been discussed, they add to the information that is part of the database, and they add to the details that must be described so that users know what the database embraces.

The tool traditionally used to describe the content of the database is called a *data dictionary/data directory* (often referred to as DD). The data dictionary/data directory does not incorporate the actual data or any of the ancillary material (such as an index or report). Rather, it itemizes the names of what is contained in the database and information about or descriptions of the data. More abstractly, the DD is sometimes referred to as *metadata*—that is, data about data.

Typically, a data dictionary/data directory holds:

- the name of all the data fields
- technical descriptions, such as whether the field is numeric or character
- substantive descriptions, which are essentially definitions
- aliases, which are other names the data fields go by
- update frequency
- descriptive communications on ancillary attributes, such as indexes, reports, and form layouts

By way of example, if the database holds data on residents, such as address, assessed value of property, and taxes due, the data dictionary/data directory would name each of these fields and describe the content. Additionally, the narration could be divided into technical description for computer operations people and nontechnical descriptions for managers and analysts. If there were special forms for data entry, these forms might also be described. Any ancillary material, such as reports or indexes, may be described as well.

The traditional data dictionary/data directory serves well for the centralized database. One or several major databases exist, and the DD covers these. Moreover, one person, often called the database administrator (DBA), is charged with maintaining the database and the data dictionary/data directory.

In a microcomputer-based environment, the predicament is compounded. Besides the central databases, there are many databases on PCs, and these are spread throughout the bureau or agency. In addition, some micros have private databases, not known to the overall management of the agency. As a result, a centralized data dictionary/data directory cannot adequately serve this situation. Nonetheless, some form of codification is needed.

The data dictionary/data directory system envisioned for a micro environment consists of four parts: a data administrator (DADM) to set guidelines and parameters for amassing and describing data in the organization; traditional DD systems for central databases; modified or simplified DD systems for official microcomputer databases; and some form of personal data dictionary/data directory. Behind this structure is the notion that data and information should be managed just as other valued organizational resources are.

An academic specialty that arose well over a decade ago addressed itself to the notion that information ought to be managed just like any other resource. Called *information resources management*, it has made inroads into most government agencies, though not as successfully as early proponents had hoped.

The data administrator is the point person in this structure. This position is different from the DBA and perhaps above the DBA on the organizational chart. The position of data administrator exists partly because of the dispersed data environment created by micros. The more encompassing role of the data administrator is outlined by Henderson (1987, p. 42):

> Data Administration parallels the management of an organization's other resources. . . . Like [these] officers, the DA uses appropriate tools and procedures to determine the status of the organization's data: what are available, what have been used, and what are needed?

Under this umbrella, the more traditional mainframe-based data dictionary/data directory systems can continue to serve their purpose. They are well established and can assist many users. End users in particular should be familiar with the DD system for centralized databases to take advantage of the vast store of data in mainframe databases. These DD systems shed light on what databases exist, the data in these storehouses, who can access the data, how often the data are updated, and the ancillary information in the database.

In addition to showing what data are available from larger computers, the mainframe data dictionary/data directory can help shorten the learning curve for those building a PC data dictionary/data directory for official departmental databases. Although micro DD systems may not need all the options available on a mainframe data dictionary/data directory, the latter provides an example of what goes into a data dictionary/data directory. In general, DD systems for official PC databases can borrow some of the basic elements of mainframe DD systems.

The last question is what to do about personal data dictionary/data directory systems. In the microcomputer environment, users will collect and gather information from a variety of sources, as well as develop their own ancillary information from the database, such as their own reports and forms. Since the information in these databases can be important, end users need to be disciplined in developing DD systems, lest they forget what is in their databases.

Fortunately, micro DBMS are coming up with more and more tools to cover the need to track and organize what is in a database. dBASE III Plus, for example, has a CATALOG facility. With this service, one can place all the files, applications, and ancillary material that depend on one another in one catalog. Then a call to this CATALOG excludes material not related to it.

Finally, there is the problem of sharing information from departmental and personal data dictionary/data directory systems. Even if users are conscientious about keeping up with DD systems for these various databases, this information is not easily shared. One possible device for tying departmental and personal DD systems together is the electronic bulletin board. As a device that is familiar to the PC user, it can serve to identify what databases are available. Barring severe competitive strains in the organization, electronic bulletin boards may provide a mode of communication among database builders.

An activist role by the data administrator is also a way to share information about the various databases. Frequent visits and discussions between the data administrator and the departments can give the data administrator insight into what databases are being built. This intelligence can be shared with others in the organization.

All in all, the data dictionary/data directory is a necessary component of the database. Given the complexity of databases and the public organizations in which they reside, it is vital to have a mechanism for codifying what information is held.

Implementation of the Database

Up to this point, the discussion of databases has been on a conceptual or planning level. The data fields important to a division or agency have been identified, the fields have been grouped into data files (normalized), and a data dictionary/data directory has been created to describe the data.

The next major task is actually implementing the database, which includes creating and manipulating the database. In reality, the implementation need not be delayed until all of the previously mentioned planning is finished. With the fourth generation character of micro software, small or trial aspects of the database can be implemented as the planning takes place. For example, as soon as one data file is established, that file can be implemented and used for demonstrations or a trial analysis.

Again for pedagogical reasons, we describe the development of databases in a linear fashion, which means covering implementation after planning. This implementation section consists of six subparts:

- defining the data structure, which entails naming the file and describing the data
- designing the input screens

- establishing checks to make sure the data entry is accurate
- creating important relationships
- designing the outputs, including queries and reports
- integrating the database into the problem-solving applications

Defining the database structure In chapter 2, under the topic of database management software, we noted that a number of preliminary steps are indispensable in many of the DBMS before data can be inputted to the database. These steps include naming the file(s) and describing the data that will go into the file. Figure 2.3 shows a pyramid structure, with the file name at the top, followed by a description of the data, and finally, at the bottom, the actual data.

Rather than repeat the process of defining the database structure, we will simply list the steps and delve into only those that have not been discussed in prior chapters. The several steps are:

- Name the file.
- Name the data fields.
- Give the maximum length of the data for each data field.
- Identify the type of data (numeric, character, etc.) for all the fields.
- Set legitimate range of values to enter, and other edit parameters.
- Establish names other than the main one assigned.

Most of these descriptors are fairly obvious or have already been presented. The last descriptor—names other than the prime name—calls for additional explanation. Two common reasons for alternate names are shortening the original name and accommodating different user preferences. The original name for a data field may be rather long. ZONE_CLASS is an illustration. Typing those ten characters, including the underscore (_), can be tedious. For this reason, the option of an alternative name is offered. ZONE_CLASS can have an alternative called ZC. The other reason is to keep different users happy. As micros become more powerful and as they are linked to other computers, several users may have access to the same database. One user may adamantly want one name, while another user may be just as insistent on a different name. If this is the case, then alternative names can satisfy different users.

Designing the input screens Once the data fields have been adequately described, data entry can commence. Two different formats for data entry are generally available. One is called the *default* format; the other, a *customized* format.

dBASE, Rbase, and Paradox all have a default screen to guide entry of the data. These might be called utilitarian or no-frill options. A blank record is displayed, and the data-entry person moves along entering data for each field in the record.

Default data-entry screens are adequate if the person inputting the data is the same person who generated the data description. This individual will know what each item means and what should and should not go into the field. However, input in the micro realm is being separated from the planning and descriptive function. The individuals entering the data are not the same as those who design the system. As a result, it is advisable to provide a more elaborate layout for data entry.

For a more exhaustive and comprehensive data-entry effort, it is incumbent to design customized input screens. These are attractive in appearance, to cut down on the boredom of data entry, and they are automated in a variety of ways to increase productivity and decrease errors.

The appearance of customized screens can be enhanced by titles, spacing, different screen intensities, and colors, if a color monitor is available. These attributes simply make the screen more interesting and pleasant. The designer and input personnel can work together to agree on an attractive presentation. Illustrations are given in chapter 9.

Besides improving the appearance of input screens, it is also important to devise a means of catching inadvertent errors. Several types of acceptability criteria, or *edit checks*, can be built into the screen as a way of alerting the data-entry person that an entry error has occurred.

One type of edit check is directed toward assuring proper designation and spelling. For a given data field, such as zoning classification, it is possible that only three categories are legitimate. Wording on the screen lists the proper designations, which are backed up by supporting programs to catch any errors. If the entry is improper, a message flashes, noting the incorrect entry and listing the proper categories.

A second type of edit check deals with proper range. For a particular data field, there may be acceptable minimum and maximum values. Entries cannot fall outside this range. A third check is forced input, meaning that an entry absolutely must be made for a given data input. Blanks or skips are unacceptable. Nothing can proceed unless an entry is made. A fourth acceptability criterion is uniqueness. This dictates that each entry for a data field must be different from any other. If two values for one item are the same, something is amiss. The classic example is social security number.

Custom screens, with all their design enhancements and edit checks, sound involved but are not necessarily difficult to produce. Most modern DBMS provide various tools for easy generation of these screens. Some DBMS allow the designer to literally "paint" the screen in the fashion desired. With this paint capacity, designers can create boxes to highlight where the data input should go; wording can be inserted anywhere to describe what data are to be entered; and different screen intensities or colors can be used to give the screen an attractive appearance.

Updating and changing the database In a typical agency, new data and changes in old data are a fact of life. Easy-to-use routines must be established for this function, since updating and changing can be extensive and complex. Imagine the potential work in finding the record to be changed, then locating the field to be modified, and finally, checking to determine whether the transformation was made correctly.

Most DBMS provide automated routines for updating and changing databases. In some of these routines, an entire file can be updated in one run or pass of the data. Other routines are more iterative and interactive. These present one record or one field at a time, ask whether a change is to be made, then move on to the next record.

Regardless of the type of update, special caution is needed because large parts of the database are likely to be altered and thus possibly damaged or lost. Before proceeding with the update, it is prudent to make a backup copy of the original database file in case the update goes astray and damages the content of the database. The backup not only preserves the database in case of malfunctions or errors; it also provides a prior generation of the database so that comparisons can be drawn over time. With these precautions, the information is protected, and past records are available for running comparisons over time.

Using the relational power of DBMS After the data have been inputted and modifications made, it is often necessary to relate two or more files in order to have all the data needed for the desired analysis. The relation of one file to another permits the user to tap data fields in both files. In fact, more than two files can be related through the process called *chaining,* described earlier. A detailed discussion, with illustrations, is given in chapter 9.

Designing the outputs One of the finishing touches, though not the last task in database implementation, is design of the output. For output to be useful and effective, it is important to present the results in a simple but attractive format. Three types of output are discussed: queries, reports, and graphics.

Queries are quick or short-term responses, whereas reports are more detailed and absorbing. The two can work together, however. A query might be made initially to acquire a general sense of the problem, then followed by a detailed report to cover the issue more fully.

Because of their quick response nature, queries are apt to be displayed on the screen, with a hard copy printed if the results prove interesting. For reports, the screen also provides the medium for a quick glance to determine if the report is ready and worth printing.

The presentation format for queries can be less polished than for reports. As quick response tools, it is the results that matter for queries. Nonetheless, there are certain guidelines that can enhance the understandability of queries and reduce any confusion over meaning. Title, date, and scope are important ingredients. A query without a date or information showing the scope of coverage can be meaningless.

Scope refers to the part or parts of the database that were queried. Was the entire database covered, or just a segment of it? For example, was the query based on all residents or only those with dwellings valued at more than $150,000? One simple way to capture the scope is to *echo,* or print, the command used to generate the query.

With reports, greater attention must be given to presentation format. More people are likely to see the report, and the report is likely to be in circulation longer. Titles and subtitles need to be clear and descriptive. Supplemental information, such as legends and notes, are often indispensable.

In some cases, a report may have both a detailed and a general version, with the detailed edition serving managers who are deeply involved in day-to-day operations and the general version serving managers who take on more global responsibilities.

The third category of output—graphics—is customarily an extension of the results from queries and reports. A pie chart can vividly compare the percentages of revenue from real estate taxes versus service fees. A bar graph can show the areas of a jurisdiction where new real estate growth is taking place. A line graph can portray the trend in service fees. Ordinarily, the job of producing graphics from query or report results is a matter of finding suitable software that interfaces with the DBMS software. For example, data or results from dBASE can be transferred to Lotus 1-2-3 for graphics presentation.

Chapter 5   Database Development and Use in a Microcomputer Environment   131

Making the database a part of the micro application   The final topic in this section on implementation is the use of databases in constructing and using problem-solving applications, such as an application for evaluating and apportioning raises to employees. As a rule, these applications represent a considerable undertaking, with the database often playing a significant role in application development and use. Three modes of using a database with an application are reviewed:

1. The application is built with the same DBMS used to develop the database.
2. The application is built around software other than a DBMS (such as a statistical package, spreadsheet, or project manager) but relies on database files generated from a DBMS.
3. The application must rely on a database that is downloaded from a larger computer (or from another PC) and must accept or reformat the data so that it is appropriate to the host application.

The first of the three situations presents the simplest way to integrate the database with the problem-solving application. In this context, the database is always directly available to the application, since the same DBMS is used to create both the database and the application. Accessing the database is simply a matter of using the name of the database.

More complex, but still feasible, is conversion of database files developed with a DBMS software package to an entirely different type of software that houses the application. Examples include moving from a database created under a DBMS to an application created with a spreadsheet. The process usually includes several steps—first getting the database into a format the operating system can read, then translating that format to a format the host software can read. A common transfer is from dBASE III to Lotus 1-2-3.

The last mode adds one more element of complexity. The database is on a larger computer or another PC and must be moved to the environment holding the application. This means changing the format of the data so the host application can read and use the database. Fortunately, all these transfers are becoming more common and easier to execute.

Consistency, Coordination, and Distribution

The last formal topic in building databases in a microcomputer environment involves consistency, coordination, and distribution of these databases. The key lies in agencies using a similar logic in putting together databases, so that duplication is minimized and the fruits of work in one department can benefit and not hinder other departments.

With numerous micros available to users, not to mention the presence of larger computers, a government agency will have many databases, both private and public. Private databases, as already defined, are those built without agency knowledge or approval; public databases have approval at some level in the agency. If an agency is to employ its resources wisely in developing and using databases, the agency must find ways of coordinating these efforts without stifling the innovation and ingenuity of the many users who want to be involved with databases.

One common problem is duplication. In an agency that shares similar goals and functions, it is likely that two or more units will need similar data. With micros available, each may collect the same data.

Another problem occurs when several units download the same data but hold it for different periods of time and add different elements to it. For example, a finance department downloads data from a mainframe database to a micro, holds those data for a long period of time, and also adds privately collected information. Another department downloads the same data but goes back to the main database for updates and does not add the same private information. The two departments are now working with different sets of information, and their conclusions can be dramatically different.

Several approaches and tools are available for promoting consistency, coordination, and distribution. These have been alluded to previously. One is to have a data administrator who possesses an overview of data needs and existing data resources. The data administrator is responsible for data use and can impose control over what data are collected and used in analysis.

Another, more informal approach, takes advantage of electronic bulletin boards to help keep users informed of what projects are taking place and what data are being used.

A third system makes it a matter of policy to include in all databases a list of data used, where they came from, and when they were updated. This system is similar to footnoting. References are made in the text, and fuller "citations" are given in the "bibliographic" section.

A CASE STUDY

The bulk of this chapter has been devoted to the theory behind developing databases. In this section, the focus turns to a particular case study. The purpose of the case material is to further illuminate the database development process.

Economic Development

The case selected involves setting up a database for an economic development agency. The case was chosen because it involves identifying and gathering data from outside as well as inside the government.

In a pure pedagogical exposition, the initial step would consist largely of defining the problem (or opportunity) and establishing goals. In practice, database development steps can occur in parallel, or sporadic data collection can take place before any explicit database planning occurs. For instance, if an agency were under pressure to examine one particular economic development issue, hectic data-collecting efforts might go forward without a general database design.

In this presentation, the more pedagogical model will be followed. Later cases will reflect the sporadic, start-and-stop process that frequently characterizes data collection and data organization.

Preliminary Analysis

Definition Given the "rational" context for building this database, the starting point is the definition of the problem or opportunity facing the agency. In general, the definition

Chapter 5 Database Development and Use in a Microcomputer Environment

would comprise these items: What are the specific trouble spots or opportunities? What information and decision systems are currently in place to address the issues? Is there an existing database? If not, is one necessary?

Typical concerns or problems of an economic development agency are: declining central business district, competition from surrounding jurisdictions, need to diversify, dearth of jobs for minorities, ambition for new development, and loss of a major employer.

Goals For this case study, the local economic situation is not one of distress, but rather promotion and continued growth. With this orientation, agency goals might include:

- Strengthen the existing economic base.
- Encourage a cooperative spirit on the part of government units that have major dealings with business.
- Solicit new business prospects.
- Provide information to prospective businesses.
- Assess the impact of new economic development or loss.
- Receive early warning of any problem areas.

This array of aspirations is quite encompassing. Even a well-funded and well-established economic development agency might start slowly, selecting only a few goals from which to generate a database. In appreciation of this realistic constraint, four of these goals have been selected:

- solicitation of new businesses
- support for prospective businesses
- cooperative spirit
- early warning system

Information Requirements Analysis (IFRA)

With the concerns and goals understood, the task turns to the information requirements analysis: that is, what data fields can help track and achieve these goals? The methodology for the information requirements analysis revolves around the personnel assigned to the task (who does it), the sources or perspectives used (what to collect), and the means for collecting the data (how to gather the data). Personnel assignments can be divided between systems people and end users; sources range from agency goals to input-output requirements; and collection can be via interviews, experimentation, or a host of other techniques.

Personnel If the unit proposing the database possesses a good deal of expertise, much of the information requirements analysis can be conducted by the staff, with a small team taking the lead. In this case, with the agency being intimately involved in and knowledgeable about economic development, users can take the lead role in the information requirements analysis.

One caveat necessarily follows this assumption about leaving the information requirements analysis to in-house personnel. Although the economic development unit has considerable expertise, there are still tasks in the information requirements analysis that could benefit from outside assistance. One of these is gathering information about the decisions, activities, and cooperative spirit of other local departments and divisions involved with new businesses or ventures. Economic development personnel may be too committed to development and thus generate some hostility from other actors in the government. If these differences interfere, the information requirements analysis will suffer.

Typically, if outside assistance is needed, it comes from the central systems analysts. The systems analysis group consists of professionals trained in conducting information requirements analyses. These individuals understand what goes into gathering data from a diverse set of bureaus. Involving systems analysis personnel in a small part of the study has payoffs in a number of ways. Later, if highly technical issues arise, the systems staff has already gained familiarity with the project and can move more easily to aiding the end user.

Sources Information sources will depend, first of all, on goal statements, since it is a set of goals that is driving the construction of the database. It may be that the agency already has articulated goals and measures for the goals. If so, these would be especially valuable in identifying the data needed. For example, if one of the goals were to increase the proportion of the tax base coming from commercial development and if a specific objective were given, such as increasing the proportion from 7 percent to 15 percent, then the agency would have several very definite indicators to include in its information requirements analysis.

Another perspective on what information to identify comes from the type of problem. In this case, the problem—encouraging and supporting economic growth—falls in the semistructured or unstructured category. As such, much of the information will come from outside the agency, including information on site availability, extant rents, and sources of capital.

A third possible source is a solution model directed to gauging cause-and-effect relationships among the variables involved with economic growth. Most of the agency personnel probably have views on what affects growth and how these factors interrelate. However, an extensive solution model does not appear to be critical because the goal of deciphering the impact of economic growth on the environment, transportation, and housing was eschewed. The economic development agency feels that these impacts are the province of other departments. Their task is to attract business.

Other sources, such as critical success factors, may help in the information requirements analysis. The critical success factors identify what is important in achieving a particular goal. For example, what factors are most critical in getting other government units to display a cooperative and supportive attitude toward new business?

These sources are not mutually exclusive. Items deduced from the goals may be the same as items generated by a critical success factors analysis. Some redundancy and overlap is helpful in that multiple sources provide a mechanism to assure that important information is not missed.

Collection techniques Surveys constitute an important means of data collection because much of the data may be peculiar to the needs of the economic development division and

```
                        Contacts
                           │
                           ▼
Adversarial Groups ──▶  ┌─────────┐
                        │Prospects│  ◀── Relevant Agencies
Local Providers   ──▶   └─────────┘
                           │
                           ▼
                 Sites and Real Estate Facilities
                           │
                           ▼
                  Startup and Employment
                           │
                           ▼
                  Impacts on the Community
```

FIGURE 5.9 Relevant elements in finding business prospects

thus not readily available from general secondary sources or from the central data-processing department. For example, no bureau in the government may collect data on prevailing rents for commercial offices and buildings. Traditional interviews also play a role. The economic development staff and systems analysts would talk with people in other divisions to determine what these divisions do vis-a-vis economic development and what their attitudes are. Lastly, experimenting or prototyping with sample databases constitutes a way of determining which data stay in the information requirements analysis and which do not. Quick demonstrations of the database may reveal data fields that are needed but were not considered in any of the previous methods.

In this particular case, we will assume that the economic development division relies heavily on original data collection, on the assumption that finding business prospects and supplying these prospects with information is a function peculiar to the economic division. No one else has either the interest or the mandate to gather such data. Only very general data, such as population figures, school information, and housing data, are assumed to be assembled from secondary sources in the government.

Overall models and data diagrams A helpful by-product of the information requirements analysis is an overall model of the major data components and the flow of data among the components. For the economic development function, the components and flow are represented in figure 5.9. The process starts with the contacts, or individuals who help identify business prospects, then moves to the agency working with the prospects. Working with the prospects involves providing them with needed information and assistance, as well as identifying who else (other bureaus, banks, real estate firms) can offer help. Success is measured in terms of those prospects that decide to stay.

Also in this picture are other relations that emerge independent of economic development initiatives. These could be adversarial relations that the division needs to understand, perhaps emanating from an elected official who is not enamored of growth. Other roadblocks can arise from companies currently in the area who do not wish to reckon with more competition for the labor pool.

TABLE 5.3 Data Items for Business Prospects Database

contact name
contact address
specialty of contact
contact's affiliation or event
prospect's name
prospect's phone
real estate needs of the prospect
capital needs of the prospect
type of business
important business ratios
site needs of the prospect
capital providers
real estate available
involved agencies
agency contact

Data fields The primary result of this data requirements endeavor will be a long list of data fields and a semblance of how these fields ought to be organized into a database. With respect to the data fields, it is important to scan the list to determine whether there are any gaps, whether there are redundant fields, and whether there are any needless fields. Table 5.3 presents the list.

A quick glance at the list reveals that more work is needed. Items such as "site needs" are too general. What, specifically, is meant by site needs? Does it include acreage, ownership, assessed value? A data dictionary/data directory can be of help in firming up the specifics and ought to be started at this point.

Database Design

Initial groupings Once the staff has signed off on the data fields, the database building can proceed with a first cut at grouping the fields. The initial groupings do two things: (1) identify dominant fields and (2) list items that reside within each grouping. In some respects, the groupings are similar to the model or data diagram shown in Figure 5.9 and can be borrowed from the data diagram.

Based on the work and thought that have gone into the project so far, the initial groupings for the economic development database are:

- contacts or people (or events) that locate prospects
- the prospects
- sites where prospects may locate
- local real estate facilities that prospects may lease or purchase
- relevant agencies
- economic attractiveness based on important business ratios
- local providers (banks, suppliers, etc.)

These initial groupings revolve around the dominant fields. Contacts who locate prospects constitute a dominant entity in the environment of the economic development

```
Contacts
   ID    Contact    Affiliation  Phone      Tickler Expert  Special
   key   person     or event     #          date    area    notes
---------------------------------------------------------------------
   I
   I
   I
```

FIGURE 5.10

agency. In the business of finding prospects, very little can happen without the work the contacts do. Similar reasoning lies behind the selection of other dominant fields. Information on sites is critical because the competition to attract prospects often revolves around the type and cost of sites available.

As for the fields to include with each dominant factor, the criterion is to find like (i.e., conceptually similar) sets of items that depend on the dominant item. The placement is sometimes obvious. Items pertaining to the contact, such as affiliation of the contact, belong in the contact grouping.

After the initial groupings have been stipulated, the more rigorous normalization can ensue. This is directed to enhancing the flexibility and efficiency of the database. One practical way of achieving this quality is by inspecting groupings for three danger traps: repeating fields, anomalies, and redundancies. For each grouping, we will list the fields that make up the file and then go through the normalization checks.

Using the data field "contact person" as a main element, the contact file is shown in figure 5.10.

☐ In this file, a special ID key is used because it would be too complex to develop a key from the existing fields in the file. Because the key must uniquely identify each record, it is possible that combinations such as contact person and affiliation/event will not yield a unique record. If one person is from the same affiliation/event, but has two specialties, then contact plus affiliation/event is insufficient for a key.

Some normalization problems are apparent in this first grouping. A person can have more than one area of expertise, giving rise to repeating fields. Insertion and deletion anomalies are also present. If an affiliation or event has not been used by or associated with a contact person, then there will be no information on it (insertion anomaly) in the file. This absence, or insertion anomaly, may not be critical, however. The economic development division may decide that important affiliations and events are best discovered through contacts. Thus, affiliations and events are added to the file only as contacts become involved with the process.

For now, the file will remain unaltered. Perhaps experience has shown that contacts tend to have only one area of expertise and that focusing on contacts adequately covers important affiliations. Of course, if the situation changes, this does not prevent staff at some time in the future from developing a separate file to handle more than one type of expertise or to develop a more generic list of affiliations or events.

The second grouping in the database is the business prospects. Quite a few fields are listed under this grouping, ranging from telephone number and other typical identification

```
Prospects

Prospect   Contact   Phone   site   nearness   nearness   sq_ft   price
name       person    #       size   to rail    to ....    avail   rent
------------------------------------------------------------------------
I
I
```

FIGURE 5.11 Grouping for prospect file with repeating fields

information to a host of needs the prospect may enumerate. It is this spectrum of needs that creates snags. In particular, the problem involved is repeating fields. Figure 5.11 shows a file layout for prospects, with the repeating fields trap.

The problem with the above file organization is the indeterminant number of needs. Some prospects may articulate one need, whereas others may articulate many. As a result, there is no way of knowing how many needs to include. If a large number is incorporated as repeating fields, considerable waste is almost inevitable.

A preferable design is to break the single file in figure 5.11 into two files. One file carries the fundamental characteristics of the prospects, and the other holds the needs. Figure 5.12 shows the second file arrangement.

With this two-file layout, the second file is able to hold any number of needs for a given prospect. Each time a prospect enumerates a new requirement, the prospect's name and requirement are added as another record. Additionally, it is possible to link the needs file with other related files. The needs file can be linked back to the basic prospect file

```
Prospects

Prospect   Contact   Phone
name       person    #
-----------------------------
I
I




     Prospect            Articulated
     name                need
     -----------------------------------
     I  Blue Chip        near airport
     I  Green Diamond    near truck depot
     I  Pizza Grande     near intersection
     I  Blue Chip        1 million line of credit
```

FIGURE 5.12

```
Site

Parcel  Acreage  Zone    Purchase  Purchase  Assessed
#       amount   class   price     date      value
------------------------------------------------------
I
```

FIGURE 5.13

via the prospect ID; or the needs file can be related to resource files that contain data on what resources are available to meet needs.

In fact, the next set of files are the resource or support files. Two are discussed: one is a site file, and one is a real estate file. Others could be developed to cover capital, training, and employment.

The purpose of the site file, displayed in figure 5.13, is to identify what land is available, who owns it, and how it is zoned. A prospect may need certain acreage, zoned in a particular way, and available at a given cost. The site file can provide much of this information. This type of file is probably available from the central data-processing department.

Examining the site file reveals no serious normalization traps. As a result, it can stand as it is.

The real estate file is shown in figure 5.14. From this file, one can obtain information on space available, cost of lease or purchase, and perhaps important features of the space.

One possible difficulty with the real estate file is repeating fields. There are no limits to the number of important features. Some companies may want to know whether rail is nearby, others want information on airports, others want specific information on the building itself. The same resolution taken with the prospects file—namely, dividing the original file into two files—can be taken here. Whether the change is made depends on the stability of these important features. If there are two or three needs that are usually requested, a repeating of important features presents little problem; if not, then a separate file is needed to track real estate requirements.

Moving to the file(s) for relevant agencies shows the potential complexity and subjectivity of database design. With respect to this dimension, users in an economic development division would want to know which agency decisions or activities have a

```
Real Estate

Address   Present  Broker's  Sq_Ft   Price  Prox.  Prox.  Prox.
location  owner    name      avail   rent   rail   air    HW
----------------------------------------------------------------
I
I
I
```

FIGURE 5.14   Real estate file

```
Agencies
Agency        dec_activity    contact    notes
----------------------------------------------
I planning    zoning          JKG        .....
I water auth  rates           BBK        .....
I council     zoning          LLM        .....
I planning    site approval   KSD        .....
```

FIGURE 5.15

direct impact on business location. This, however, can lead to an overwhelming amount of information. Every agency in some way touches business operation.

Because of the complexity inherent in agency business relations, the economic development division might pursue a much simpler route. One modest approach is a database that acts like a specialized, automated phone directory. In this approach, a file is established to include four items: the relevant agency, selected decisions and activities, agency contact, and notes about the decision or activity. Figure 5.15 shows a sample file.

This file, though quite simple, can be helpful to the economic division. One attractive feature of this approach is that a query can be made to cross-reference any decision or activity. For example, all the agencies involved in zoning can be identified quickly.

More complex and sophisticated elements can be added to this topic of agencies involved with businesses. A significant increment would be to add a file on the business side—that is, identifying the agencies currently dealing with business prospects. This would not only provide a picture of which decisions are affecting business prospects, but it would also permit a link between businesses and agencies. With this link, we could determine whom to call in particular agencies dealing with particular business prospects.

The next complement of information in which we are interested are industrial ratios broken down by standard industrial code (SIC). These ratios show the "average" performance of a particular industry. Individual companies can be compared to the average to determine how "attractive" they are. One of the commonly used ratios is return on assets, measured by net income over total assets. If we have an insurance company looking to locate in our jurisdiction, we might get some indication of the economic strength of that particular company by comparing its return on assets to that of other insurance companies.

If we want to set up a database file on SIC and industrial ratios, a critical decision is the jurisdiction level at which the data will be summarized. Should the SIC industrial ratios be broken down by region, so that both regional and national ratios can be used for comparison? Or should the jurisdictional level be lower, such as the state or county? For now, our decision is not to incorporate these data into our database. The agency receives a national publication (Dun and Bradstreet's Key Business Ratios, for example). Keying these data would not be worthwhile, since they are so easy to retrieve from the printed volumes.

The last category—local business providers— is not detailed here. It might include specific banks, their address and phone number as well as similar information for other providers.

Finally, in looking closely at these various groupings, it should become apparent that the technical process of normalization does not address certain database limitations. The database we will be setting up will be a traditional database, with a rigid format for numeric and character data. It does not always capture the richness of information available. For example, in the first file on contacts, if one of the fields pertains to the specialty of the contact, such as the type of business or industry the contact usually handles, and this is the only item of data wanted, then it is easy to code that field and do various queries on it. However, as variables become more text-oriented, with complex passages necessary to describe the variable, then traditional databases are circumscribed. For example, several contacts may all have expertise in the financial area, but one may do well with start-up firms while another has strength in contacting major companies. All of this information does not fit easily into a character field.

Needed for a richer expression of information are text-oriented databases that allow searches within a variable to pick out special topics. Traditional databases do have some capacity in this respect (usually called "contained in" operators), but it is not very powerful.

In some databases, it is possible to take advantage of the varied content of the specialized notes by searching through the notes for certain key words and phrases. If the implementing database management system has this capability, then searches can be done to identify all contacts with certain characteristics. Unfortunately, traditional relational databases generally do not have this ability to conduct extensive text searches within a field.

■ CONCLUSION

Database development is an important part of building microcomputer applications. The database supplies the information that is eventually analyzed (sometimes by routine models, sometimes by complex models) to produce answers to or insights into management problems.

Development of databases entails a number of steps, with each step designed to capture or assure that the information is pertinent to the issues at hand and well organized. Too often large amounts of data are gathered and then stored in a single file without any consideration to whether the data are relevant to the problems or goals of the unit or whether the data can be easily accessed and manipulated. Efforts such as preliminary analysis of the problem, checks into the type of databases others have set up, and examination of potential inefficiencies, such as repeating fields, all help create useful databases.

This chapter has introduced and covered the various steps of database development, discussed these steps in light of the numerous microcomputers in an organization, and offered a number of examples and illustrations of how to construct viable databases. The overall lesson is that simply putting data into a user-friendly database management system is insufficient to good database development. Thought and care about the management problem for which the database is intended as well as careful specification of the individual files in the database are critical.

REFERENCES

Achituv, N., Hudass, M., and Newmann, S. "A Flexible Approach to Information Systems," *MIS Quarterly* 8 (June 1984): 69–78.

Codd, E. F. "A Relational Model of Data for Large Shared Databanks," *Communications of the ACM* 13 (June 1970).

Davis, G. "Strategies for Information Requirements," *IBM Systems Journal* 21 (1982): 4–30.

Henderson, M. "The Importance of Data Administration in Information Management," *Information Management Review* 2 (Spring 1987): 41–47.

Inmon, W. H. *Managing End User Computing in Information Organizations.* Homewood, IL: Dow Jones–Irwin, 1986.

Kozar, K. A., and Mahlum, J. M. "A User Generated Information System: An Innovative Development Approach," *MIS Quarterly* 11 (June 1987): 163–176.

Kraushaer, J. M., and Shirland, L. E. "A Prototyping Method for Application Development by End User and Information System Specialists," *MIS Quarterly* 9 (September 1985): 189–197.

Kroneke, D. *Database Processing.* 2nd ed. Chicago: Science Research Associates, 1983.

Louata, L. L. "Behavioral Theories Related to Design of Information Systems," *MIS Quarterly* 11 (June 1987): 147–149.

Mitfoff, I., and Emshoff, J. "On Strategic Assumption Making: A Dialectical Approach to Policy and Planning," *Academy of Management Review* 4 (January 1979): 1–12.

Vetter, M., and Maddison, R. N. *Database Design Methodology.* Englewood Cliffs, NJ: Prentice-Hall International, 1981.

CHAPTER

6

Access Systems

■ INTRODUCTION

Purpose

Prior chapters have focused on a number of topics important to microcomputers, including the logic of building microcomputer applications, the fundamentals of microcomputer software and hardware, and the tenets of building databases. In order to use all these microcomputer resources effectively, it is vital to understand how to construct and to choose capable access systems. Thus, in this chapter, we examine the problems created by poor access systems, guidelines for useful systems, and a number of current, easy-to-use access systems.

For the purpose of this chapter, when we refer to *access systems*, we are concerned with passage to computing resources located on a microcomputer's hard disk or passage to other computers from a microcomputer. The resources may include custom applications such as those described in chapter 4, various types of software such as a word-processing program, and information stored in databases.

The importance of easy access to computing resources derives from the growing quantity of material stored in computers, the necessity of encouraging non-data-processing end users to take advantage of this quantity of material, and the variety of different computer systems confronting the end user. If some application or piece of information is buried deep within the computer or if it is not obvious how to obtain and use a program, then the value of the computer and its resources is either diminished or rendered worthless.

The Costs of Poor Access Systems

As many managers discover, often too late, a well-designed database or application does not mean much if these resources are not easily accessible. Case in point: The director of a small state government office responsible for processing historical site preservation requests considered it particularly good fortune that he was able to hire a computer "whiz kid" fresh from college to carry out the conversion of the office from a paper-based

143

processing system to one completely automated through the use of the office's new microcomputer system.

Within a short period of time, the new employee had designed a computerized database to efficiently store information that had previously resided on a variety of paper forms, index cards, and miscellaneous slips of paper. Upon witnessing a demonstration of the new system, the director decreed that, henceforth, all incoming requests were to be filed using the database system.

For several months, the director delighted in being able to request the most detailed and complex reports from the new "database manager," as the whiz kid was now called. Response was always swift and efficient. Of course, all good things must come to an end, and the database manager soon left the office to take a position in private industry with a substantial salary increase.

The day after the departure of the erstwhile whiz kid, the director was horrified to discover that no one else in the office had the foggiest notion of how to gain entry to this system and produce the beautifully detailed reports that had become the pride of the office. Attempts by other employees to manipulate the highly sophisticated database resulted in frustration, anger, destruction of data, and virtually no progress in producing reports. The office was left with no choice but to ignore the microcomputer database system and resort to the old paper-bound methods.

DEVELOPING A THEORY AND GUIDELINES FOR USEFUL ACCESS SYSTEMS

The general goal of information access is simple: to provide the resources or information needed, when needed, and in a useful form. As might be expected, the achievement of this goal increases in difficulty in direct proportion to the complexity of the required information. There are, however, a number of general guidelines that can be applied to access systems.

In the case just described, no one else besides the "whiz kid" was knowledgeable about or even familiar with the database system. The database manager had not trained anyone else nor familiarized anyone with the details of operating the system. Documentation was also absent. No manuals existed to guide one through the process of penetrating and using the system. As a result, accessing the system was neither easy nor apparent, and no one was able to unlock the secret keys. Because users could not make even the simplest foray, they knew nothing about those valuable kernels the database managers used so astutely. Similarly, if the access system possessed important utilities, such as transforming the database information to a spreadsheet, no one knew that either. Finally, the system provided no security for the precious data stored in it. When a naive user tried to work with the system, he or she destroyed the valuable data.

From these errors comes a list of guidelines that can be helpful in building or choosing access systems:

- shared knowledge and familiarity
- formal documentation
- ease of use
- clear and relevant organization

- inclusion of important functions and utilities
- security and preservation of the data

Shared Knowledge and Familiarity

As witnessed in the short example, it is important for more than one person to know how to access vital applications and databases. If a second person had been somewhat familiar with the system, he or she could have called for assistance, perhaps from the agency's information center or the vendor who provided the microcomputer. The backup person could then have become more literate in a short period of time. Such was not the case, and all too frequently this is not an exaggeration of what actually happens.

Unfortunately, the stand-alone, personal nature of microcomputers works against shared knowledge and familiarity. The microcomputer is often located in someone's office, and one does not transgress another person's office. Moreover, developers of microcomputer systems are often office staff with many other jobs, and teaching someone else how to use a system is not a priority.

A number of approaches are available for circumventing proclivities toward highly personalized systems with unknown access methods. Among them are an office policy for documentation and sharing of operating knowledge, periodic review of microcomputer systems by "auditors" who can catch potential disasters, and formal ties or backups with the agency's information center. Any of these would have minimized the problems encountered in the case study.

Documentation

Tied to shared knowledge and familiarity is documentation of access systems. If it is not common procedure for one office staffer to share the ins and outs of his or her system personally, then a minimum of documentation can act as a damage control agent. The documentation can be as simple as a list of screen prints showing the steps in accessing and running a given application. Of course, more elaborate documentation can supplement this "quick and dirty" approach. Formal user manuals can be prepared, and common access techniques can be agreed upon and published for the office.

☐ On many PCs and with much of the software, it is possible to print exactly what is on the screen with the combination keystrokes: SHIFT PRINTSCREEN (often labeled, PRTSC). All one needs to do is depress the SHIFT key, then depress the PRTSC key.

Ease of Use

Another feature of an effective access system is ease of use. Sharing and documentation are futile if the access is confusing and convoluted. Ideally, access should be designed in such a way that the process of entry is transparent to the user. It should require only minimal knowledge of the syntax and procedures of the software that form the basis of the approach. Unlike mainframe systems, microcomputer-based access applications are likely to be used by individuals with little or no knowledge of programming concepts, application syntax, or program commands. This lack of knowledge should not, however, be an obstacle to use of the system. As far as possible, access applications should be constructed to present a *user interface* that consists of simple, English language commands that make intuitive sense to the user.

Easy-to-use access systems are not always simple to devise. Routine, structured information requirements are the most yielding to our ease-of-use expectation. Because standardized and repetitive queries or reports form the basis for this level of admission, the access system itself can be standardized. Menu systems, which give users limited and specific choices, are widely used for this type of access. This mechanism is examined in more detail later in this chapter.

Situations or problems that are semi-structured must be designed with greater flexibility than those dealing with routine requests. An access system designed for this level usually requires more substantial knowledge on the part of the user because information needs vary. It should still be possible, however, to insulate the user from many of the more complex and obscure elements of the access procedures. Although there are a number of mechanisms that can be employed to reduce the complexity of semistructured information access problems, the key factor is consistency in procedures. If the number of commands and the complexity of command syntax can be kept to a minimum, the user is much more likely to tailor requests without cumbersome and frustrating experiments. Later, in chapter 8, we will show how some simple tables of contents in spreadsheets allow users to maneuver around applications developed for semistructured problems.

Unstructured information access problems represent the greatest challenge in designing access applications that are easy to use. In fact, the two requirements may be mutually exclusive. At this level, there may be no alternative to extensive knowledge of the software (and hardware) being used in the application. Although there may be no way to facilitate access in unstructured situations, care should be taken that the access application does not hinder the user.

Clear and Relevant Organization of the System

A fourth element in effective access systems is clear and relevant organization. The organization of an access system can benefit by a design that is parallel to tasks and functions in the agency. If one of the major functions of the office is personnel administration and if everybody looks at personnel in terms of recruiting, performance, and training, then access systems should give serious consideration to these prevailing concepts.

Organization, like ease of use, may also occur on several levels. At the most general level, organizing for effective access begins with the application. As defined in chapter 4, an application usually consists of software for data storage, data access, and data analysis. Although these functions may be found in one software package, more commonly they are found in several specific programs. This means that the programs that comprise an application should be organized to facilitate movement from one component of the application to another. For example, consider the organization of a hard disk around an application involving the use of a database program and a spreadsheet. If a primary focus of the application is the ability to pass information from the database to the spreadsheet for analysis and then back to the database for storage, the use of a *common directory or location* to hold all the data reduces the complexity of this process. Gathering all of the information used by an application in a common location is one way to enhance our organizational principle. In this instance, a separate subdirectory is set aside to receive the data from both the database management system (DBMS) and the spreadsheet.

☐ In MS-DOS operating systems, the PATH command allows one to use a program from a subdirectory other than the one where the program resides. For example, if all the pertinent data are in a subdirectory, appldir, the DBMS might be reached via the command: PATH C:\main\dbplus. If in the directory setup, both appldir and dbplus branch from main, then the PATH command will take us back to main and down to the dbplus subdirectory where the DBMS is located.

More generally, files related to a common application should be organized to facilitate their usage. Again, this may mean location in a common disk directory, or a specified set of directories.

Another type of access organization relates directly to the data. This may involve organizing data in a variety of ways that correspond to the multiple ways in which the data may be used. This level of organization is usually handled in an application within a program. For example, a database application may require that data be organized alphabetically for a summary report, by department for data review, and by ZIP code for mass mailings. A useful access system will make such temporary data reorganizations as simple as possible.

As with any application, be it an access system or not, a good design or organization requires that the users be consulted as to their needs prior to the design. Talking with others in the office or showing them the development as it progresses can unearth what is common or relevant and what is understood and what is not.

Inclusion of Important Utilities

The next objective of an access system is to include functions and utilities that will help manage the computing resources being accessed. Two such utilities are data retrieval and data transformation.

Data retrieval *Retrieval* means making data available for review, modification, or output. Efficient data retrieval depends on both an effective design of data and appropriate organization. To facilitate data retrieval, an access application should provide the user with three categories of information:

- data location
- data structure and organization
- essential commands for effectuating retrieval

Information on data location may start with something as general as a *catalog* of available information. In mainframe applications, the catalog is often contained in a data dictionary, which defines the information available to the user and specifies its location/access. For microcomputer applications that are large or complex, this method is also appropriate. For smaller applications, the "catalog" may be a simple narrative statement, describing the location and availability of information in the application, that

PART II   Framework for Building Microcomputer Applications

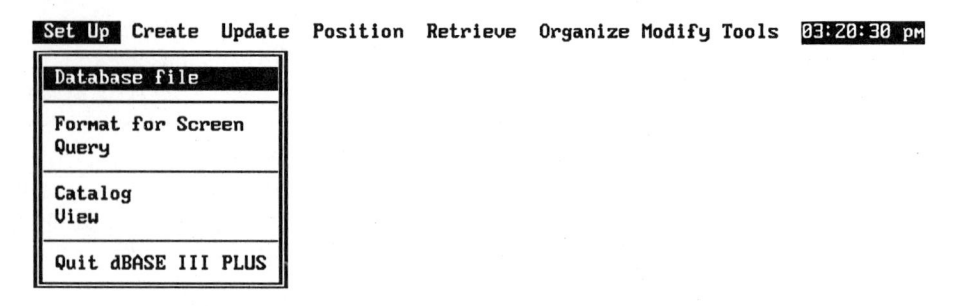

```
 Set Up  Create  Update  Position  Retrieve  Organize  Modify  Tools    03:20:30 pm
┌─────────────────────┐
│ Database file       │
├─────────────────────┤
│ Format for Screen   │
│ Query               │
│                     │
│ Catalog             │
│ View                │
│                     │
│ Quit dBASE III PLUS │
└─────────────────────┘




 ASSIST        <C:>                        Opt: 1/6              Num
Move selection bar - ↑↓. Select - ↵.  Leave menu - ←→. Help - F1. Exit - Esc.
                          Select a database file.
```

FIGURE 6.1

appears when the application is started. For example, the opening menu might state that the data available for the present application go back two years only.

A second method of cataloging information location is a tree diagram of the disk organization that specifies the name(s) of the directories that contain the relevant information. If this approach is used, it is incumbent on the developer to use descriptive names for the directories that leave no question about their content.

Within an application, such as a database that may contain a large amount of complex data, specifying the location of relevant data speeds up the use of the application. Although specific software packages vary in their ability to limit and direct the user to specific elements of the data, most offer some facility for limiting the data made available to the user (e.g., the dBASE III FILTER command). Of course, if the data are not appropriately organized prior to the retrieval request, specifying information location may be a tedious and cumbersome task. This points up the critical need for effectively organizing data *prior* to access attempts.

Finally, data retrieval can be expedited by the command set used to retrieve the data. For simple and structured applications, retrieval can be effectively handled through a menu system. Other modes of retrieval are the built-in retrieval tools associated with popular software, such as the Assistant function of dBASE III Plus and the HAL (Human Application Language) available in Lotus 1-2-3.

The dBASE Assistant provides the user with a menu system that makes use of drop-down "windows" of subcommands that walk the novice user through many of the dBASE functions, including both file and data retrieval (see figure 6.1). This feature allows a user to exploit some of the power of the program without having to be an expert in the program's command structure or syntax. In many retrieval situations, the Assistant

Chapter 6 Access Systems

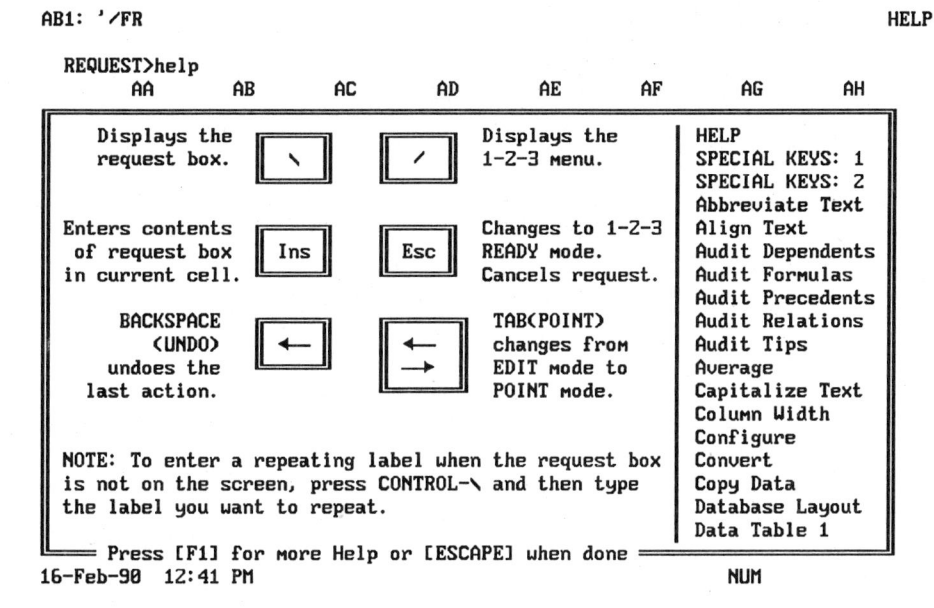

```
AB1: '/FR                                                           HELP

REQUEST>help
    AA         AB         AC         AD        AE         AF        AG              AH
┌─────────────────────────────────────────────────────────────┬──────────────────────┐
│  Displays the    ┌───┐        ┌───┐   Displays the          │ HELP                 │
│  request box.    │ \ │        │ / │   1-2-3 menu.           │ SPECIAL KEYS: 1      │
│                  └───┘        └───┘                         │ SPECIAL KEYS: 2      │
│                                                             │ Abbreviate Text      │
│  Enters contents ┌───┐        ┌───┐   Changes to 1-2-3      │ Align Text           │
│  of request box  │Ins│        │Esc│   READY mode.           │ Audit Dependents     │
│  in current cell.└───┘        └───┘   Cancels request.      │ Audit Formulas       │
│                                                             │ Audit Precedents     │
│     BACKSPACE    ┌───┐        ┌───┐   TAB(POINT)            │ Audit Relations      │
│      (UNDO)      │ ← │        │ ← │   changes from          │ Audit Tips           │
│    undoes the    └───┘        │ → │   EDIT mode to          │ Average              │
│    last action.               └───┘   POINT mode.           │ Capitalize Text      │
│                                                             │ Column Width         │
│                                                             │ Configure            │
│ NOTE: To enter a repeating label when the request box       │ Convert              │
│ is not on the screen, press CONTROL-\ and then type         │ Copy Data            │
│ the label you want to repeat.                               │ Database Layout      │
│                                                             │ Data Table 1         │
╞═════ Press [F1] for more Help or [ESCAPE] when done ════════╡
16-Feb-90   12:41 PM                                                  NUM
```

FIGURE 6.2

acts as a tutor, helping the user to select the appropriate commands and procedures for the desired retrieval.

The HAL add-in for Lotus 1-2-3 works on a slightly different principle from the dBASE approach (see figure 6.2). HAL allows the user to specify a vocabulary of ordinary language terms that supplant the program's native command syntax. This enables the user to create a data access system that is executed with a simple phrase instead of the more complex (and difficult to learn) program command syntax.

The approach taken in the HAL program is becoming commonplace in many microcomputer software programs under a variety of names such as "query by example" (QBE), as in Rbase's Clout. The key to all of these approaches is that they are designed to substitute a less complicated and cumbersome ordinary language structure for the often arcane command syntax found in programs. This approach allows the program and application to be tailored to the knowledge level of the user without sacrificing the flexibility needed to deal with more complex problems.

Data transformation The other utility that we include in our discussion of access applications is one that assists in any needed *transformations* of data from one form to another for analysis. Typically, this means restructuring data from a database for use in a spreadsheet, graphics, statistical, or other analytical program. It may also cover returning data from an analytical program to a database. As an additional complicating factor, it may also be necessary to transform data from a mainframe to a microcomputer format, or vice versa.

During the early years of microcomputing, data transfer was a serious problem. Not only were there structural differences in data from mainframe and microcomputer systems, but each microcomputer program seemed to have its own unique data format.

PART II   Framework for Building Microcomputer Applications

Transferring data from one program or application to another was at best difficult, and frequently impossible, without re-keying the data into the new program. Fortunately, this situation has improved significantly.

Most major microcomputer programs now provide the ability to read and write data in the formats of other major programs. dBASE, for example, will transform database data directly into the Lotus worksheet format. It is also capable of transforming Lotus worksheets into the dBASE data structure. Lotus also offers similar transformation capabilities.

To accommodate data from programs for which a direct translation procedure has not been provided, most programs now accept data in one or more "standard" data formats. One of the most common of these standard formats is DIF (Data Interchange Format). The DIF procedure arrays data in a row/column format, referred to as *tuples* and *vectors* in the arcane procedure syntax. Once data have been transformed into the DIF format, they can be freely transferred among a number of programs. Another common standard is ASCII (American Standard Code for Information Interchange), also referred to as SDF (System Data Format) or Delimited format. This format is a plain-English data structure that does not contain any special formatting or control characters. An ASCII file is readable, whereas other formats appear on the screen with special symbols and control codes embedded.

To build effective data transformation into an access application, the developer must know both the format for the program in which the data originate and the format of the destination program. With that information, transformation of data should be a fairly easy procedure. The only caveat is to ascertain any ancillary requirements for the transfer. For example, dBASE requires that data be imported into a predefined database structure.

Data transformation between micro and mainframe environments is a somewhat more complicated problem. The difficulty of transfer stems from the fact that micros and mainframes store data in very different formats. Whereas most micros store data in some variation of the ASCII standard, mainframes employ schemes such as EBSIDIC or BCD. Thus, even though data may *appear* readable on a terminal screen, when they are actually transferred from one system to another the data *formats* are incompatible. The answer to this problem is some form of *translator* utility at either end of the transformation process (usually placed at the mainframe end).

One limitation to these translator programs is that they are frequently keyed into only one microcomputer software package. For example, programs such as Focus, Oracle, and GoldenGate are all designed with both micro and mainframe components. However, each of these programs uses its own data format, which requires yet another translation if the data are to be used in another package such as Lotus. Another limitation of these translators is cost. The mainframe component can cost several thousand dollars. A few translator programs are designed to accommodate a variety of mainframe and micro programs—among them, T.A.C. (The Applications Connection), produced by Lotus. These programs are still limited in their applicability and also remain quite expensive. There is reason to believe, however, that this situation will improve in the next few years as companies such as IBM bring their SAA (System Applications Architecture) to micros, enabling an almost seamless transfer of data.

☐   The term SAA (System Application Architecture) is used by IBM to denote a common user interface designed to be implemented across all of IBM's applications, from the largest mainframes to PCs.

The philosophy of SAA is that a single user interface will facilitate use of whatever computing system is needed and reduce user fear of unfamiliar systems.

Security and Preservation

Finally, there are times when the most important form of access in an application is no entry. Protecting files from unauthorized entry is facilitated when the files are organized in a way that makes access to any one file subject to the same restrictions as access to all the files. Whether this means password protection, file locking on a network, or physical removal of the files from the hardware, security procedures are enhanced when the files are organized to take advantage of these procedures. A comprehensive application that includes sensitive data files should contain a method of protecting against unauthorized access to those files as part of the access procedure.

Along with the need for security is the need to ensure preservation of application data. Here, the primary concern is the ability to back up data files quickly and conveniently to an archive medium (disk or tape). When the files for an application are organized in a common directory or set of directories common to a program directory, backup and restoration of data are easier to accomplish, faster, and less likely to inadvertently include extraneous data or exclude critical data.

Ideally, an access application should contain a simple procedure for creating backups of vital data files. Since backing up data is a procedure more frequently honored in the breach than in the practice, anything that facilitates it is highly desirable.

Summary

The analysis presented in the previous pages details the theory behind the development of effective access systems. Using these concepts—shared knowledge, documentation, ease of use, organization, helpful utilities and functions, and security and preservation—steers the developer toward the generation of systems that provide effective access to needed information.

In the world of microcomputers, there is a wide range of access mechanisms and systems that can be employed to facilitate information acquisition. Not all of these mechanisms meet all of the tenets of the theory, just as all applications do not always need to meet all of the theory requirements. The next section of this chapter explores a number of access mechanisms and procedures. In reviewing these options, the applications developer should always keep in mind both the theoretical concepts *and* the real-world needs for successful access.

ACCESS MECHANISMS

This section describes a number of useful access mechanisms and procedures. It is not intended to be a comprehensive encyclopedia of such mechanisms, because the variety is extensive and ever-changing, but to suggest alternate solution-sets for the applications developer. To simplify the presentation, it is divided into two parts: system-internal mechanisms, and system-external mechanisms.

System-Internal Mechanisms

The term *system-internal* refers to those applications that are contained within one microcomputer system. This means that access requirements are limited to information physically stored on one machine, and no need exists for communication connections to external data sources. Within this category, access applications can be further divided into those mechanisms and procedures that function at the *operating system* level and those that function at the *application*, or *program*, level.

Operating-system access   Essentially, any operating system (OS) is designed as a de facto access mechanism. (See chapter 2 for a detailed discussion of operating systems.) Since it is the operating system that monitors and controls disk access, access to information is channeled in some fashion through the OS structure. The native commands of microcomputer operating systems vary in their level of effectiveness as access applications. The most popular microcomputer operating system, MS/PC-DOS, is rather crude in its ability to act as an access application. Basic commands in the system are limited to copying and displaying the contents of files. Location and organization commands are provided, but operate in only the most elementary fashion. The MS/PC-DOS environment does provide for a reasonably sophisticated *batch* file language that can be used as the basis of menu systems (examined in detail later in this chapter).

A new entry in the microcomputer OS field is the joint Microsoft-IBM product, OS/2. OS/2 was designed specifically to take advantage of the power of the latest generation of microprocessor chips, provide *multitasking* ability, and remedy many of the access deficiencies of the older MS/PC-DOS. Two key features enhance the ability of OS/2 to work as an effective access mechanism.

First, the operating system's advanced Presentation Manager is specifically designed to provide a consistent user interface across applications. Similar in theory to the Apple Macintosh Finder OS, the Presentation Manager includes a graphics-based user interface that expedites the organization, location, and transformation of data between OS/2 applications. Very similar in appearance to Microsoft's Windows operating shell (described later in this section), the consistent interface and designed-in features of the Presentation Manager dramatically reduce the complexity of data access through application-common commands. Thus, the user need only learn one set of commands and procedures, which can then be applied across all compatible applications. This is the approach that Apple has been following successfully since the introduction of the Mac—a machine that is generally considered to offer the novice user the most intuitively logical and useful interface.

The second feature of OS/2 that relates to information access is its ability to *multitask*. Multitasking means to run two or more tasks, or programs, at the same time. By opening more than one program under the Presentation Manager, the user is offered a seamless environment for locating data across applications, transferring data between applications, and organizing data among applications. In terms of access management, OS/2 is a significant advance over the single-task, arcane command structure of MS/PC-DOS.

The trade-offs with OS/2 are size, cost, and limited ability to run many existing microcomputer programs and applications. Since OS/2 runs only on 80286 and 80386 microprocessor-based micros, it excludes the multimillion-unit installed base of PC-class

8088 machines. The full implementation of OS/2 consumes more than one megabyte of disk storage and many megabytes of RAM to permit effective multitasking. The cost of full implementation of OS/2 is several times that of MS/PC-DOS and may well be out of financial range for single-user systems.

The third major OS available to microcomputer users is the UNIX system and its derivative for microcomputers, XENIX. The UNIX OS was originally designed for use on minicomputers. Ported to the microcomputer environment, UNIX retains many elements that facilitate access management. Similar to OS/2 without the Presentation Manager, UNIX includes a number of powerful commands for data organization, retrieval, and transformation. Since most applications used under UNIX are written in the "C" programming language, exchange of data among programs is facilitated, as is the development of new applications. The limitations of UNIX as a microcomputer OS stem from its size and complexity. The complete UNIX kernel occupies several megabytes of disk storage and requires extensive RAM for operation, as does OS/2. UNIX, through X-Windows, now offers the graphic interface that eases use of the powerful access commands.

Recognizing the limitations inherent in the OS as an access mechanism, many software developers have created add-on products designed to supplement (and supplant) native OS commands. Generically, these OS extensions are referred to as operating system *shells*. The term *shell* refers to the way in which the program overlays a new user interface or command structure on top of the basic OS commands. Although there are shell systems available for each of the OS designs previously described (including AT&T's shell for UNIX and the OS/2 Presentation Manager), the greatest effort has been directed toward developing shells for MS/PC-DOS. These shells can be classified as either *command* shells or *windowing* shells.

Command shells are designed to extend the commands available in the OS. Often using either basic menu systems or shorthand control-code sequences, these shells seek to simplify the issuing of OS commands. This kind of shell is well suited to semistructured applications where most access requirements are routine but occasional exceptions are required. Some shells facilitate routine functions even more by offering some form of macro command processor. A *macro* is a command issued with one or two keystrokes that may contain several longer or more complicated commands. For example, the sequence ESC-C may be used to represent the command COPY *.* B:;DIR/W B:. The use of such macros allows the user to predefine routine access commands, enhancing both parsimony and ease of use.

☐ The command COPY *.* B:;DIR/W B: means copy everything from the current directory to the disk in drive B: and then display everything on the disk or directory in B:.

Command shell systems may specialize in functions such as location and organization, data retrieval, program execution, or data transformation. For example, the shell X-Tree is designed to facilitate hard disk management through the graphic representation of the disk directory structure and shorthand methods for the management of both directories and files. It is most useful, therefore, in data organization and data retrieval. 1-DIR, on the other hand, is a replacement for much of the MS/PC-DOS command structure. Its strength is in the simplification of command sequences and the execution of programs.

When considering a command shell system for an access application, care should be exercised to choose the shell that will expedite the kinds of data access desired. On balance, shell systems are best suited to applications involving mostly routine access needs and in situations where novice users are more likely to be put off if required to deal with the native OS command structure and syntax. To more advanced users, the shell may seem cumbersome and slower than execution of the basic MS/PC-DOS commands. Since shell systems are, by nature, limited in their flexibility, they are also not usually appropriate for use in unstructured problem applications.

Windowing shells, while incorporating most of the features found in command shells, are designed as a new *environment* for the user. The key to the windowing shell is its complete substitution of the DOS user interface with one that enables a much greater degree of flexibility in information and program management. Perhaps the most widely known and used windowing shell system for MS/PC-DOS is Microsoft Windows. This shell system, which also forms the basis for the OS/2 Presentation Manager, replaces the command-line interface of DOS with a graphics-based interface that employs drop-down command menus and a mouse to select commands. Windows also permits the user to perform editing and file manipulation functions and multitasking. As illustrated in figure 6.3, Windows looks similar to the interface used by Apple on the Macintosh.

There are two advantages of a windowing shell system for application access. First, most windowing environments permit more than one program to be open at a time. This allows the user to switch rapidly between programs without the need to restart each one. Applications created to run in a windowing environment approach the concept of multitasking very closely. Some windowing environments, such as DesqView, do provide multitasking, which involves multiple programs running *concurrently*, each performing a specific function in data manipulation (see figure 6.4).

Second, windowing environments facilitate the transfer of data from one program to another. This feature is implemented using a clipboard, whereby data elements can be extracted from one program, held in RAM, and then "pasted" into another application. This procedure significantly reduces the need to go through the data translation utilities offered within individual software packages. With the expanded ability to switch between programs and an easy method of data transfer, windowing shells are more suited for use in semistructured or unstructured problem situations. The one disadvantage of the windowing approach is that it tends to slow down the experienced user by requiring menu selections and point-and-click actions to carry out procedures. There is little question, however, that windowing interfaces seem to be the wave of the near future in microcomputer systems.

> The term *point and click* refers to the use of a pointing device (usually a mouse) instead of cursor keys. To point and click, the user moves the pointing device until a menu item or icon is highlighted, then presses a button on the device to select the item.

A somewhat less complicated (and less powerful) approach to creating an operating-system-level access application is to use the OS command set to create *menu systems* for data organization, data retrieval, or program execution. A menu is a simple device that allows the user to select an option from a list of provided alternatives by choosing a number or letter. Selection of the number or letter begins execution of a *batch* program

Chapter 6   Access Systems

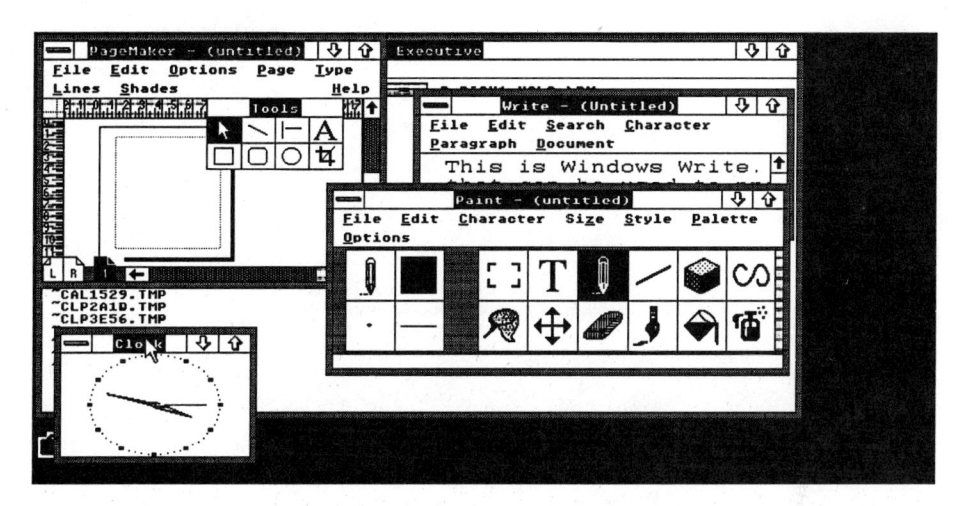

FIGURE 6.3

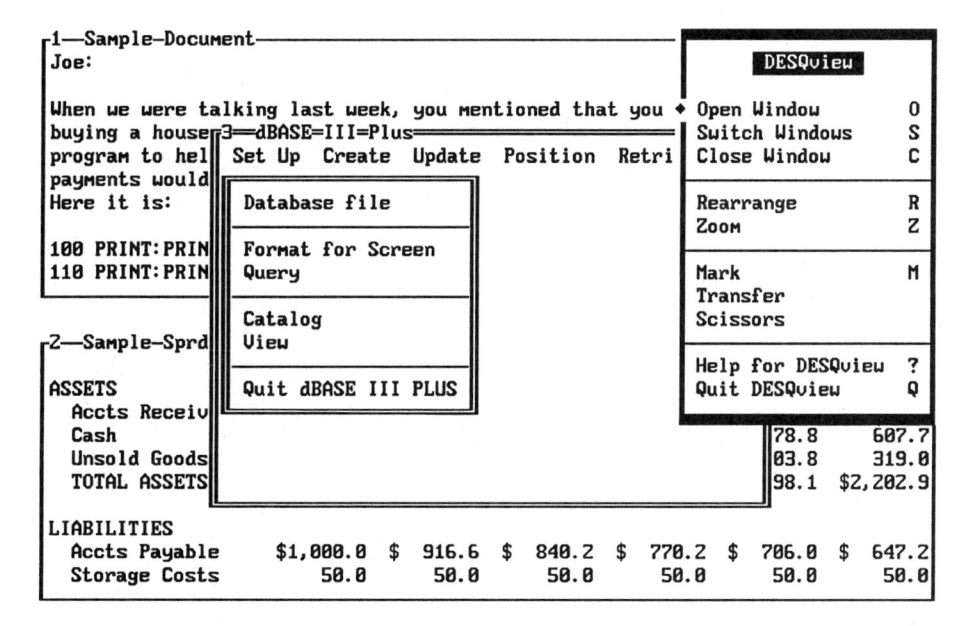

FIGURE 6.4

that activates the desired procedure. Although the level of sophistication in menu systems varies widely, there are always two basic components to the menu system itself:

- A text file that provides the list of available options. Each option is selected by choosing the appropriate letter or number.
- A series of small batch files, each with a name that corresponds to one of the menu choice letters or numbers. Each batch file is responsible for carrying out any needed

```
xxxxxxxxxxxxxxxxxxxxxxxxxxxxxxxxxxxxxxxxxxxxxxxxxxxxxxxxxxxxxxxx
                       PROGRAM SELECTION MENU

              Lotus 1-2-3 . . . . . . . . . . . . . . 1

              dBase III Plus . . . . . . . . . . . . 2

              Harvard Project Manager . . . . . . . . 3

              WordStar 4.0 . . . . . . . . . . . . . . 4

                    ENTER THE NUMBER OF YOUR CHOICE
xxxxxxxxxxxxxxxxxxxxxxxxxxxxxxxxxxxxxxxxxxxxxxxxxxxxxxxxxxxxxxxx
```

Example Batch Files:

```
    1.BAT                        2.BAT

    CD \123                      CD \DBPLUS
    LOTUS                        DBASE
    CD \                         CD \
    CLS                          CLS
    TYPE MENU.TXT                TYPE MENU.TXT
```

FIGURE 6.5

relocation, opening the appropriate application or program, and, upon termination of the application or program, returning to the menu.

An example of a simple menu system written for MS/PC-DOS is provided in figure 6.5. Note the basically repetitive nature of the batch files used to execute the menu choices. The common structure of these files makes it very easy to create the menu system or modify it once in operation.

Menus are designed to provide a specific set of options for the user, making them most suited for structured applications. Although the use of a menu system restricts the variety of operations that can be carried out, it also facilitates application access for the novice user. For very structured, routine applications, the menu provides the most intuitive and easy-to-use interface available. Figure 6.6 illustrates how a series of menus is used to create an access application for word processing. Use of this menu structure permits a secretary who has only rudimentary knowledge of MS/PC-DOS commands, and virtually no experience in organizing or managing a hard disk, to access and manage word-processing files for a variety of individuals. With a menu, the user sees only one of two interfaces: the menus or the word-processing system. At no time does the user have to deal with native DOS commands. As an access application, this system fulfills all of the theoretical criteria presented earlier. An added benefit of this system is the ability of a new user to employ the system with virtually no training (word-processing program commands excepted).

The key to each of the OS-level access application mechanisms is that they are designed to link programs and data. This means that they are *not* limited to working with only one program or application. For situations in which more than one program is involved in an application, or where data may be needed in a variety of locations and formats, OS-level access applications are the preferred instrument.

Chapter 6　Access Systems 157

```
******************************************************************
                    WORDPROCESSING MENU

              AGENCY MEMOS . . . . . . . . . . . . 1

              DIRECTOR'S CORRESPONDENCE  . . . . . . 2

              MONTHLY REPORTS  . . . . . . . . . . . 3

              STAFF CORRESPONDENCE . . . . . . . . . 4

              MISCELLANEOUS  . . . . . . . . . . . . 5

                    ENTER NUMBER OF YOUR CHOICE
******************************************************************

Example batch file:    1.BAT
                       SEARCH C:\WS4
                       CD \MEMOS
                       WS
                       CD \
                       CLS
                       TYPE WPMENU.TXT
```

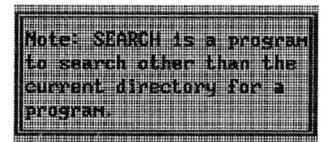

Note: SEARCH is a program to search other than the current directory for a program.

FIGURE 6.6

Application-level access mechanisms　These mechanisms operate from within a specific application or program. Although they may replicate some of the functions and interface modes available in the OS-level mechanisms, they are more limited in the nature of the data manipulated and primarily associated with the command structure of the host program.

One of the most common application-level access mechanisms is the now familiar *menu system*. Not surprisingly, menu systems at this level resemble those designed at the OS level. Application menus are usually more concerned with the execution of procedures from *within* a specific program rather than among programs.

Procedurally, applications menus are constructed in a manner similar to the OS-level menus. Because they are operating with specific programs, however, the menu systems can take advantage of program commands designed for menu applications. Figures 6.7 and 6.8 illustrate two menu systems.

Figure 6.7 depicts a dBASE III Plus menu. Although the two basic elements of a text section and separate choice programs are present in this system, note that the menu makes use of a built-in dBASE control structure command called CASE. The CASE command is used to call other command programs which actually carry out the desired procedures.

Figure 6.8 shows a menu created in Lotus 1-2-3. The approach taken in the Lotus program is quite different from that of MS/PC-DOS or dBASE. Lotus makes use of a command recording procedure that uses macros to create the menu choices. Included in the macro commands are several designed solely for use in menu creation and execution, such as the XM and MENUBRANCH commands. Instead of appearing as a separate text file, the Lotus menu appears exactly as other commands in the program. This degree of consistency is made possible by the command structure of Lotus, which is itself menu-driven.

These two examples demonstrate that although menus are a common form of access

158   PART II   Framework for Building Microcomputer Applications

```
Edit: B:master.prg                                      Num
USE MYFILEA
SET TALK OFF
SET ECHO OFF
STORE " " TO CHOICE
DO WHILE .T.
CLEAR
?"================================================================"
?
?"                    DATABASE MENU CHOICES"
?
?"      Append a Record to the Database           A"
?
?"      Edit a Record in the Database             E"
?
?"      Generate a Report                         R"
?
?"      Generate Labels                           L"
?
?"      Quit the Command Program                  Q"
?
?"================================================================"
?
wait "What is your choice? (Enter choice letter) " to choice
DO CASE
```

FIGURE 6.7

```
BE5: U [W15] '\M                                              READY

              BE           BF              BG              BH
 5   \M                    {GOTO}A1~
 6                         {MENUBRANCH PROC_MENU}
 7                         {BRANCH FINISH}
 8
 9   PROC_MENU   DATA ENTRY      RESULTS         CALCULATIONS
10               ENTER RAW DATA  VIEW RESULTS    INTERMEDIATE CA
11               {BRANCH DATA}   {BRANCH RES}    {BRANCH CALCS}
12
13   FINISH      {RETURN}
14
15   DATA        {GOTO}A10~
16               {QUIT}
17
18   RES         {GOTO}A36~
19               {RETURN}
20
21   CALCS       {GOTO}AA1~
22               {RETURN}
23
24   PRT         /PPA~
16-Feb-90  12:49 PM          UNDO              CALC       NUM
```

FIGURE 6.8

mechanism within a program, each software package approaches the creation and execution of menus in a unique fashion. For the user or developer, this means that each application-level menu system requires knowledge of the program command structure

Chapter 6   Access Systems   159

and the available procedural options. As with the OS-level menu system, menus designed within applications are best suited for structured or routine applications. Obviously, dealing with any exception to the menu options requires the user to deal with the native command language of the program, contravening the ease-of-use criterion for an effective access application.

Both the dBASE and Lotus examples make use of other access mechanisms in the creation of the menus. These additional mechanisms and procedures include *command programs* and *macros*. Although both of these mechanisms are used in creating menus, that is not all that they can do. There are a number of other access applications that can be created through their use.

Command programs make use of commands indigenous to the program. By structuring these commands in a batchlike format, one can create very complicated and sophisticated procedures. Since most programs that support a command language also support the use of variables, an application command program can be made interactive. This means that the program is a more effective mechanism for dealing with semi- or unstructured situations. Through the use of a variable (the value or content of which can be changed), the user can explore a range of options and compare results before deciding on a final selection. This is clearly an asset when confronting complex or difficult problems where solution-set parameters may vary considerably.

A sample command program from dBASE III Plus is presented in figure 6.9. This simple program is designed to facilitate a "what if" scenario regarding property tax rates. The purpose of the program for this semistructured situation is to allow the user to examine a range of alternate values and evaluate their impact on overall property valuation. The key to the utility of the program is the use of variables to indicate the two tax rates being compared, thus allowing frequent and easy modification of the tax rates.

The structure of this program reflects the way in which command programs can be structured as access applications. At the outset, the program retrieves the appropriate data through the USE command, reduces the complexity of the available information with the SET FILTER command, and organizes the information appropriately with the SET INDEX command. Once the application information has been properly structured, the program interactively defines two variables for the comparison tax rates and prints a report detailing the comparison. Thus, although the ultimate purpose of the program is to provide the tax comparison, the first part of the program also functions as an access application.

Lotus 1-2-3 uses a different mechanism to enhance information control: the macro. Within the Lotus program, macros are used both to automate command sequences and to produce sophisticated procedures (including the menu program presented earlier). Macros resemble command programs in that they sequence commands that are executed in batch fashion. Also like command programs, use of macros requires the software to contain built-in macro functions and a mechanism for both accessing and storing macro functions. Just as dBASE has a built-in command language for program creation, the Lotus program contains an equivalent macro language. Macro-based access applications in Lotus are primarily confined to the autoexecute macro that carries out a predefined procedure or the menu macros discussed earlier.

Figure 6.10 presents a simple access-related macro for the Lotus program. In this autoexecute macro, every time the worksheet is loaded in Lotus, the user is automatically

```
Edit: prop.prg                              Ins      Caps
SET TALK OFF                                                    <
SET ECHO OFF                                                    <
USE PROPTAX                                                     <
SET FILTER TO CLASS = 'RES'                                     <
SET INDEX TO PARCELNO                                           <
REINDEX                                                         <
CLEAR                                                           <
?' ======================================================'      <
?                                                               <
?'         PROPERTY TAX RATE COMPARISON FORM'                   <
?                                                               <
INPUT 'WHAT IS THE FIRST RATE TO BE USED?' TO A                 <
?                                                               <
INPUT 'WHAT IS THE SECOND RATE TO BE USED? TO B                 <
?                                                               <
?' ======================================================'      <
CLEAR                                                           <
?'             PROPERTY TAX COMPARISON'                         <
?                                            PROPTAX is the name of a
?'The first rate selected was: '+STR(A,4,2)  dBase report which is run
?'The second rate selected was: '+STR(B,4,2) by the program.
GO TOP                                                          <
REPORT FORM PROPTAX                                             <
```

FIGURE 6.9

presented with the selection of existing worksheets for retrieval. Consider a situation in which a user has a number of unrelated worksheets to be stored on a hard disk system. Normally, Lotus is configured to access only one directory. Storing all the available worksheets in that one directory is a poor access strategy because the logical and effective method is to store related worksheets in subdirectories under the default directory. Within the default directory, the only worksheet is the AUTO123 worksheet, which contains an autoexecute macro that makes each of the subdirectories available for retrieval. Selecting a subdirectory immediately presents the user with a list of worksheets available in that directory. Use of this macro, in combination with efficient hard disk management, creates an access environment that is more efficacious for the user than the native Lotus command sequence.

In addition to macro languages that may be built into specific programs, there are a number of freestanding macro programs, such as Superkey, that can be used with an extensive variety of programs. These commercial macro programs are often referred to as keyboard macro programs because they are principally designed to substitute one or two keystrokes for a complicated command procedure within a program. To use one of these programs, the user creates a macro library of commands that is loaded as part of the application prior to execution of the program in which the macros will function. Once activated, the macro key sequence is simply substituted for the native command in the program. The macro makes the appropriate syntax substitution and carries out the procedure. For programs that do not support either a native command language or a macro function, these stand-alone programs offer an attractive alternative for application development.

Another kind of application-level access mechanism is the *query system*. Query systems are database functions and can be found within database programs. A query

Chapter 6 Access Systems

```
AB1: '/FR                                                              FILES
Name of file to retrieve: D:\123DATA\*.wk?
AUTO123.WK1     22FILES\        30FILES\       CLASSES\      GRADES\
       AA          AB       AC       AD       AE       AF       AG       AH
   1   \0          /FR
   2
   3
   4
   5
   6
   7
   8
   9
  10
  11
  12
  13
  14
  15
  16
  17
  18
  19
  20
16-Feb-90   12:51 PM                                          NUM
```

FIGURE 6.10

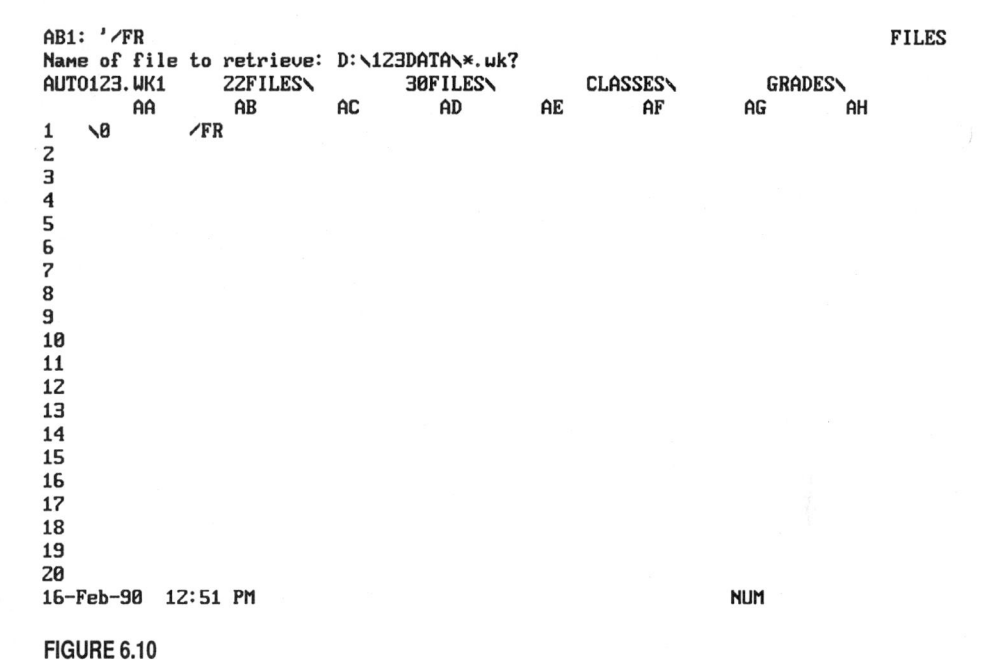

system enables the user to "ask" the program to provide information that meets a specific set of criteria. This process may be accomplished through direct specification of the information parameters needed or through a procedure referred to as *query by example* (QBE). Under the QBE procedure, the user provides the program with an example of the information needed; the program then extracts the critical parameters from this example and provides all of the data that match the example.

Although sophisticated query systems are a hallmark of mainframe database systems, they are still relatively new at the microcomputer level (with Paradox as an example). This seems to be changing, however, with the adoption of the mainframe-standard SQL (Structured Query Language) methodology. Ported to the microcomputer environment, SQL provides a standardized set of procedures for carrying out queries. The downside to this approach is that it is a relatively sophisticated methodology requiring a good command of programming language syntax to be used effectively. In the long run, SQL query applications may follow two roads: simplified menu-based derivations for use by novice users in structured and routine query situations, and more sophisticated command-line applications for experienced users. Given the power of the full implementation of SQL, it is an appropriate tool for use in semi- and unstructured query situations.

In a more generic vein, the use of the QBE methodology is also developing rapidly. QBE seems to be most appropriate when used in conjunction with other 4GL procedures to provide users with a more "natural" way of communicating with a program. A promising development of QBE is its use in an *artificial intelligence* environment, where the program can "learn" patterns of inquiry and continually refine and simplify the user's task based on previous actions. This form of interaction is ideally suited to semistructured applications, in which an accumulation of experience in the application would effectively reduce the need to constantly "reinvent the wheel" through redundant queries.

A final form of application-level access mechanism is the *integrated program*. Integrated programs combine several specific tasks in a common environment that facilitates information transfer from task to task. Most integrated programs, such as Enable, Framework, Symphony, and GoldenGate, combine five functions: database management, spreadsheet, word processing, graphics, and communications. Since each component, or tool, in an integrated program utilizes a common command structure and user interface, the theory is that the user will be able to make better use of the variety of tools provided in the program. As an added feature, many integrated programs also offer some form of command language or macro function to enhance information manipulation among tools.

Although it may seem, on first glance, that integrated programs solve most of the access problems a user is likely to encounter, they have a number of problems that reduce their utility. Most integrated software packages are designed around one of their tools as a core element. For Symphony, it is the spreadsheet; for GoldenGate, it is the database. Because these core elements are the main reason for the program's existence, they tend to be quite good. However, the attention lavished on the core element is often taken from the other components of the program. This means that the ancillary tools, such as word processing, graphics, and communications, are substantially less powerful than the equivalent stand-alone programs of the same type. The result is that the user of an integrated package is faced with trade-offs that reduce the ability to manipulate data as effectively as if separate programs were being used.

A second problem with integrated packages is their sheer size and complexity. Even though each tool in the package may have a similar (or identical) user interface, the range of commands needed to cover all contingencies creates a long learning curve for the user. Many users of the Lotus 1-2-3 package found this out when Lotus introduced the Symphony package. Spurred on by a low-cost upgrade offer, many 1-2-3 users traded their package in on the integrated Symphony package. Confronted with a substantially more complex command structure, and a spreadsheet that was not any more powerful, a substantial number of users soon wished that they had kept their former software. Based on this kind of response, software manufacturers began to orient the integrated package toward the user who needed to do a variety of things, but none with any great degree of sophistication.

Sophisticated users, termed *power users* in the literature, found the power of the integrated package to be inadequate and preferred to stay with familiar stand-alone software packages. In recent years, integrated programs have come to be viewed more as niche programs with a limited audience. Although they may be effective in building elementary access applications, the lack of power and sophistication across all of the incorporated tools precludes the integrated program from widespread adoption for more complex semi- and unstructured applications.

☐ The term *power user* refers to a professional or management-level user who needs to make use of extensive analytical applications. Power users require highly sophisticated programs and fast, powerful computers.

System-External Mechanisms

Access application mechanisms that go beyond a single microcomputer system are referred to as *system-external mechanisms*. These applications must enable the user to access, organize, retrieve, and analyze information that is not physically located on the user's micro system. System-external access applications can be arranged in two basic categories: *micro-to-micro* links and *micro-to-mainframe* (or minicomputer) links.

Micro-to-micro Micro-to-micro access mechanisms are designed to facilitate information exchange between microcomputer systems. As explained earlier in this chapter, this kind of information exchange is facilitated by the fact that the *basic* form of data stored on microcomputer systems is similar. This means that once a physical connection has been established, transfer of information requires only a common *protocol* employed by compatible software at each end.

On a conceptual level, micro-to-micro communication takes one of two forms: superior-to-subordinate or equal-level. In a superior-to-subordinate link, one machine serves as a repository of data, programs, or both. The subordinate system relies on the superior system to provide either data or programming that it lacks. In this form of access link, the subordinate system may not have the internal capacity to carry out the needed analysis; therefore, it must rely on the superior capacity of the linked machine to enable the analysis to be carried out. This kind of access relationship is the basis for Local Area Networks (LANs), as well as remote-access database systems.

Equal-level, or peer-to-peer, access applications are designed to facilitate *sharing* of data or resources among computer systems. In this situation, there is no clear superior-subordinate relationship; the systems involved are of approximately equal capacity and power. This form of linking is becoming common in work-group processing situations, where each member of the group is responsible for one component of analysis and must be able to exchange information easily with other group members.

☐ *Work-group processing* is a term that is used to describe the process of creating a final product through the input of several individuals, each with a specific contribution to make. Work-group processing is particularly useful in a networked environment.

In either case, certain basic requirements for connection must be met before any access application can be implemented. First, there must be a physical link between or among computer systems. As discussed in chapter 3, this link may take the form of a hard-wired connection or a telecommunications link. Second, each system participating in the exchange must run software capable of sending and receiving information via a common protocol. Third, each system must run the same applications programs or have the capacity to translate any data acquired from another system. With these elements in place, it is then possible to develop access applications.

The micro-to-micro link that is growing most rapidly in popularity is the LAN. Access mechanisms available to LAN users are similar in function to those described in the system-internal section. The reason is that most LANs employ the superior-subordinate structure: one system on the network is dedicated as a "server" to control resources, store data, and provide program access for other nodes on the system. As with a stand-alone system, access may occur at either the LAN OS or application level.

To work, any LAN must employ an OS, such as Novell's NetWare, to control the flow of information and allocation of resources. This means that the OS-level access mechanisms discussed earlier may also be used in this context. In particular, the operating shell and menu approaches are commonly employed. Since the LAN is predicated on multiple machines linked together, OS-level access applications tend to be somewhat more complex than their single-system counterparts. For example, on a single system, a locate access function need only provide information for a single system. On a LAN, to locate information requires determining on which system the information resides (server or another node), locating the information on that system, requesting access to the information (if limited by the controlling user), and then accessing, copying, or transferring the information to the user's node for processing. If not properly organized, extending such a procedure across several machines can be a lengthy and frustrating process.

An additional access concern with a network system is the file cloning and update problem. Consider that multiple users may request access to a single file. This access may take one of two forms: access through creation of a copy on the requesting system, or direct access to the original file. If access is not controlled very carefully, problems arise in either case.

If local copies are made of the file and then modified, there may be substantial confusion over which version is the "official" version of the information. Because each copy of a file is independent, there is no effective means of preventing multiple, incompatible modifications from being carried out.

In the case of access to the original file, if multiple users access the same file—a spreadsheet, for example—and each user makes different modifications, the user who finishes modifying the file last "wins." This means that that revision replaces all previous modifications, thereby undoing any other changes made by other users.

Clearly, in a system designed to facilitate information access, either of these situations can result in serious problems. The LAN OS should offer at least minimal protection against such occurrences through command procedures that prevent file duplication and provide *file locking* to prevent more than one user from accessing a file at once. For the development of LAN access applications, these two problems must be considered and the appropriate safeguards built into the application. This obviously raises the level of complexity of the application. In a well-designed shell or menu system, however, the functioning of the safety procedures can (and should) be made transparent to the user.

Another major OS-level access concern for a LAN system involves *levels of security*. Not all users on the LAN may be allowed access to all information on the network—hence the need for some method of security to prevent unauthorized access. Once again, most LAN operating systems provide a level of access security that can be controlled by the network administrator from the network server. Caution must be exercised, however, because some forms of security are activated at the *machine* rather than *user* level. Thus, an unauthorized user can gain access to restricted information simply by logging on at an unrestricted machine. Unquestionably, the better procedure is to employ a user-based security system with individual access codes.

At the application level, access mechanisms include all of those already discussed plus several others related specifically to application-level access. Typically, an application designed for use on a network makes use of either programs or information stored on the server or another network node (if everything were on one machine, why bother with networking?). This means that the application must have the capability of directly accessing information or of making use of the native LAN OS commands for information access. One problem is that many programs are not designed with multiple-machine access in mind. Programs such as Lotus, dBASE, and Framework are all designed as *single-user, single-machine* programs. Unless augmented through the LAN OS, applications designed around these and other single-machine programs are severely limited in their ability to make use of network data.

A corollary to this problem is the naive expectation of novice network users that one copy of a program, located on the server, is all that is necessary because it can be accessed by any network node. Unfortunately, unless the program is designed for network use, it will still be limited to one user at a time, negating any advantage of the network system. Applications designed to facilitate multiple use of a program through the network server are restricted to use of network versions of the software. Fortunately, as networks grow in popularity, the availability of such software, such as the dBASE LAN Pack, is increasing.

Depending on the application needs, the programs being used to access network information must also be capable of supporting either file locking, record locking, or both. For example, if the application involves access to database files located on the server, more than one user may have legitimate reasons for accessing the same file simultaneously (to work on different records). A program capable only of file locking would not support this access situation. In this case, the accessing program must support *record locking* of the individual records in the database file, leaving the remainder of the database available to other users without restriction. Although this form of access restriction is common on mainframe database systems, it is still fairly rare on micros, probably because of the continuing single-user orientation of most software.

☐ Record locking is similar to file locking, but it works at the record level in a database rather than at the file level. This allows more than one person to access a single database, but only one person at a time to access a specific record.

If the application involves use of a spreadsheet on the other hand, record locking is an impractical device because there are effectively no "records" in a spreadsheet. In this case, users must be restricted from multiple file access or even serial access-replace actions. One possible solution to this dilemma is use of a macro or command program within the spreadsheet that allows the user to *extract* necessary information for manipulation in another worksheet. In concept, this resembles the common mainframe practice of designing *transaction* files for routine access and modification. If this access approach is chosen, the network administrator (or some other delegated individual) must be responsible for aggregating the transaction files back into the main file. Once again, the possibility of multiple changes to the same data must be accommodated.

When a large database needs frequent updates, a procedure known as *transaction processing* is often used. This process involves creation of a small transaction database that is a subset of the main database. Updates are made initially to this transaction database and later transferred to the production database. This process reduces the chance of errors or corruption of the production database.

As the foregoing discussion indicates, developing access applications for networks involves additional complexities compared to single-system applications. Not only must the network access application meet the criteria proposed at the outset of this chapter, it must also deal with the access limitations imposed in a multi-user system. Clearly, developing such applications is not normally within the realm of the inexperienced user. It is often not well understood by managers that implementation of a network system requires an investment not only in hardware and software but also in commensurate human resources to professionally design and manage the network functions. Too often, users are left without guidance in network applications, resulting in numerous problems.

The equal-level, or informal network, configuration of a number of micros linked together to facilitate exchange of information (without a designated server or unequal distribution of resources) may either facilitate or inhibit access, depending on the application instituted. Frequently, equal-level networks are designed with limited kinds of information or resource sharing required. In some cases, it may be as simple as sharing a printer. It is becoming increasingly common to find this kind of micro-to-micro link in a *group process* situation. This configuration is designed to facilitate the linear development of some product, whether it be a report, an analysis, or a final document. The process of the application is linear in nature, with each member of the group contributing to the final product in sequence. As long as the process is one-way or single-task, the access problems are minimal and center on the efficient transmittal of needed information from one workstation to the next. Concerns about file and record locking are moot because only one user accesses the application data at a time. Access concerns in this kind of application are directed more toward efficient design of the application itself so that there is no duplication or need to "loop" the process back on itself. These concerns are more appropriately considered in the basic design of the production application than in a specific access function.

A form of micro-to-micro linking quite different from the various network configurations just discussed involves the use of telecommunications. Remote links, as they are sometimes termed, have three basic design purposes: communication, data exchange, and remote control.

Linking for communication is the most elementary form of remote link. It is designed to facilitate exchange of "electronic mail" or electronic conferences. In this case, the access requirements are quite simple. Beyond the hardware requirements of modems and available phone lines (see chapter 3 for a full discussion of remote link setups), each micro must have access to a terminal emulation program that the other machine can recognize. Creating the access involves establishing one system as a "host" to receive incoming calls (set by hardware and software) and the other system(s) as communication originators, setting any access restrictions such as passwords, and deciding on a common communication protocol. Since communication occurs in ASCII, there is no need to worry about data conversion.

Limiting the remote link to the simple exchange of messages is a rather primitive form of linking that can often be done more efficiently with a normal telephone call. The link has greater value when actual data can be exchanged. Consider the example of a state pollution control agency that must collect routine water quality reports from a dozen collection agencies around the state. Use of an access system that would allow each collection agency to connect its computer with agency headquarters and directly transmit the needed data would certainly facilitate the collection of information. To accomplish this, an access application must be created that allows the exchange of data as well as simple communication. As indicated in chapter 3, the procedures involved are termed *uploading* (from remote to host) and *downloading* (host to remote).

Hardware requirements in this case are no different from those for simple communication. The key difference is that instead of terminal emulation, each system must run telecommunications software that expedites data exchange. Because data may be in the form of a database file, graph, spreadsheet, or other non-ASCII format, the software must accommodate *binary* data transmission. This form of data exchange occurs without disrupting any special format or control codes that may be embedded in the data file. It is essentially occurring at the most basic level of computer communication—binary machine code.

A successful access application in this case is one that ensures that all participants are using compatible protocols and provides (at the host end) any data translation facilities that may be needed to restructure data from disparate sources. Thus, the remote ends of this process have fairly simple access requirements. The host, on the other hand, must be sophisticated enough to deal with the access concerns just outlined. To this end, a variety of programs designed for host operation are available, both commercially and through user groups as public domain software, or *shareware*. Preprogrammed to handle many of the access issues raised in this discussion, programs such as RBBS-PC (Remote Bulletin Board Systems), Colossus, and FIDO greatly simplify remote access development. It must be noted, however, that these packages are not designed for the novice user. Their creators expected the user to have a reasonable level of knowledge concerning microcomputer data communication and transfer protocols. Users without that level of knowledge should seek professional help in establishing such systems.

These remote link systems are proving very effective mechanisms for government agencies wishing to collect or disseminate information. Agencies such as the IRS, Veterans Administration, NASA, and Office of Personnel Management at the federal level and numerous state agencies, local governments, and school systems have implemented RBBSs.

A form of access application unique to telecommunications, particularly with RBBSs, is the use of *scripts*. A script is a series of automated commands issued by a telecommunications program that facilitates signing onto the host system and may automatically review specific files or functions or quickly take the user through a series of commands necessary to accomplish a specific task. Many telecommunications programs, such as Crosstalk and Procomm, provide scripting capability. In practice, a script functions like an autoexecutable macro, running a command sequence without the need for user intervention. Because each remote linkup requires a specific and unique script, most programs with scripting capability provide a means for linking a specific host system with a stored script. By employing a menu system from within the communications program, the user may only need to select a single number or letter in order to dial the appropriate number and access the host computer system.

The third purpose of a remote link system is *control*. In this situation, one computer system is used to control another. The directing unit uses the resources of the "slave" system as if they were its own. In a telecommunications situation in which a RBBS is not practical or desirable, use of a remote-control program can facilitate access to external information. A practical example of this form of access is a field agent making use of a portable computer to access the micro in the agent's office, enabling both transfer of data and, more important, *analysis* of the information on the more powerful office computer. Access of this type requires specialized software at both ends of the communication link. The ideal is to provide a link that is transparent to the user, enabling any existing access applications on the host computer to function through the remote link. Of course, since this form of access takes place over phone lines, it is necessary to guard against unauthorized access because the complete operations of the host system are open to the user. Remote-control access applications are most appropriate where the capabilities of a sophisticated microcomputer are needed—for access to large data sets or complex programs—but it is impractical to provide the computer at the location of the needed work.

Micro-to-mainframe The second form of system-external access, micro-to-mainframe, is becoming increasingly popular in public organizations. The logic behind such linking is simple: the mainframe offers nearly unlimited information storage capacity, while the micro offers the benefits of flexible analysis and reduced analytical costs. Given this logic, micro-to-mainframe access applications are usually designed (1) to extract data from a large mainframe database and download it to the micro for analysis or (2) to upload data from the micro for incorporation into a mainframe database.

The key to developing any successful micro-to-mainframe access application is translation of data between the two systems. As discussed earlier in this chapter, micros and mainframes use different data storage formats. Thus, the task of exchanging data between systems is complicated by the need to provide the appropriate format translation. This requirement effectively limits micro-to-mainframe access applications to those programs explicitly written to translate between two particular systems. Fortunately, systems such as GoldenGate and T.A.C. make use of macro or scripting functions that greatly simplify the access task.

The access application for this kind of communications link is designed around four components, although not all four are always used. First, at the mainframe level, a component must be developed that allows the user to extract the needed data from the mainframe database. This may be accomplished by the user directly but is more likely to occur indirectly through a user request to the mainframe database analyst (DBA). A file is then created, on the mainframe, containing the data needed by the user.

The second component of the access application is the transfer of the mainframe data to the user's micro. This requires the user to log onto (gain access to) the mainframe with the appropriate user code and password, access the storage area (termed the *library* or *catalog*) where the file resides, and copy the file to an appropriate directory on the microcomputer. A well-designed micro-to-mainframe application will make these steps as transparent to the user as possible. For example, the application might begin with a menu to select the data transfer process. The menu executes a macro (script) that logs the user onto the mainframe, opens the appropriate library, and displays the files available for downloading. This can be automated even further if only one file is made available at a time. By using a single file name, the macro can continue with instructions to download that file, copying it into a predesignated directory on the micro.

The third component of this access application involves any required micro-level data transformation needed to enable data analysis. If the data are to be analyzed within the program used for downloading (e.g., GoldenGate), this may be a moot point. However, if they are to be examined using another software package, the appropriate data structure must be created. Once again, this may be facilitated by creating a macro or command program that automatically translates the data and places the resulting file in the appropriate directory.

The final component of this application involves returning data to the mainframe environment. Although this is not usually any more technically difficult than downloading the data in the first place, it does offer an interesting problem that is the micro-to-mainframe equivalent to the "last in wins" dilemma discussed in relation to LANs. In this case, the question is whether to allow a user to upload directly back to the original mainframe database (referred to as the *production* database). This avenue is dangerous because any errors are immediately transferred into production. It also provides the potential for multiple, differing updates to be made to the same records. A more practical approach is to permit uploading only to a separate file. It then becomes the duty of the DBA to effect data integration into the production database. Procedurally, this process is the simple reversal of the downloading method. The user simply copies the file back to the appropriate library on the mainframe. Data translation back to the mainframe format is then handled at that level.

In a sense, micro-to-mainframe access is a cut-and-dried proposition. Either the appropriate programs are used, in which case it is quite simple, or it is virtually impossible because of the data format incompatibilities. Creating effective access applications for this kind of situation is almost always a highly structured process because the specific translation requirements do not permit unstructured queries.

PART III

USE OF THE FRAMEWORK IN DEVELOPING APPLICATIONS

- ☐ Structured Managerial Problems
- ☐ Semistructured and Unstructured Managerial Problems
- ☐ Data-Intensive Structured and Semistructured Problems
- ☐ Specialized Software and Applications

CHAPTER 7

Structured Managerial Problems

■ INTRODUCTION

Purpose and Scope

Chapter 7 marks an important juncture in the book. Up to this point, we have been preoccupied with laying the groundwork for deploying personal computers in managerial problem solving. In this and subsequent chapters, the emphasis turns to building and using actual microcomputer applications.

This task entails taking actual managerial problems and showing how to use the framework and tools of the first and second sections of the book to develop microcomputer applications. In this chapter, we start with simple managerial problems that are referred to as *structured problems*. In dealing with these structured problems, we rely heavily on what are called *operational applications* and on spreadsheets to develop these applications. Topics come from rudimentary but common revenue, budgeting, and expenditure control tasks.

Three simple operational applications will be developed, all designed to automate routine but tedious managerial chores. In the process of developing these applications, we will see the general steps involved in moving from managerial task to microcomputer application, including a good deal about using and molding spreadsheets.

Type of Problem: Structured

According to the framework set forth in chapter 4, it is important to appreciate the type of problem at hand before embarking on development of any application. In this chapter, the focus is on structured problems. Structured problems are routine and recurrent. They are simple and mechanistic, but burdensome in terms of the time required to deal with them. Sometimes they are viewed as "drudgework" problems. Tallying the proceeds from all revenue categories for one month and comparing the total to the same month from a previous year is an example of a structured problem. Microcomputer applications can reduce the tedium of such tasks.

Types of Micro Applications: Operational Applications

Referring back to the framework again, there are generic types of applications that offer specific guidelines for dealing with different types of managerial problems. One type of application relevant to the structured problems chosen for this chapter is termed an *operational application* (OPA). Operational applications are designed to capture and summarize the continuous flow of activities in an agency, or to take a static snapshot of activities. Tracking revenues, as we will do later, is one example.

The operational application provides a relatively rudimentary level of analysis. It does not possess sophisticated what-if capabilities to aid in decision making, nor does it have powerful manipulative capabilities to arrange and rearrange data or to permit extensive querying or probing. Rather, it provides a solid base from which analysts and managers can make basic calculations.

The specific makeup of the microcomputer operational application depends on the functions or tasks it is designed to capture. If, for example, daily revenue or fee totals are to be recorded and tallied, then the operational application is not much different from the pencil-and-paper system it replaces or supplements. The principal advantage is the reduction of labor. Making a minor change and recalculating the new total is facilitated with the aid of the microcomputer and the operational application.

General Design Tools for Microcomputer Applications

Regardless of the type of application, the general design tools still provide overall guidance. Prominent among these tools is divide and conquer—the technique of breaking larger problems into more manageable modules. Another is stepwise refinement, which means gradually refining the work until a satisfactory solution emerges. These tools, as well as the use of pseudocode, will be used repeatedly in building the applications in this chapter.

Topics

Limiting ourselves in this chapter to structured problems, we have drawn our three cases from simple revenue analysis, budgeting, and expenditure control. Revenue analysis often starts with projections, then continues with a close scrutiny of how inflow compares with past collections. Our case study focuses on the latter question. In budgeting, there is generally a set process of sending out policy guides for the forthcoming budget, collecting budget requests, summarizing all the requests, comparing these summaries with policy guides and revenue projections, and adopting the agreed-upon budget. Our second case study is concerned with the common task of summarizing budget requests from individual units to the department level. Expenditure controls, our third case topic, include who supplies the product, how much of the product is kept on hand, how purchases are financed, and how much should be spent on the product. We examine how to stay within the constraints set on the cost of individual items.

Software for Operational Applications: Spreadsheets

In actuality, there is no preferred category of software for an operational application. The software used depends on availability as well as the type of software with which the staff is most conversant. Spreadsheets, database management systems (DBMS), statistical packages, project managers, even languages such as BASIC and C can all serve for operational applications.

In this chapter, spreadsheets are used because they handle the monetary input and the numerous calculations required by revenue, budgetary, and expenditure control data. More generally, spreadsheets are valuable because they are easy to learn and use. The open, visual display of spreadsheets invites users to input data easily, incorporate mathematical assumptions, and run calculations as often as needed. Extensive preliminary definitions or elaborate programming are not imperative.

Spreadsheets offer a flexible and open format. Almost any type of quantitative analysis can be incorporated into a spreadsheet, ranging from simple percentages, through complex equations such as net present value, to linear regression and linear programming. To round out these capabilities, spreadsheets offer graphic tools to represent the results visually in the form of graphs, bar charts, and pie charts.

In using spreadsheets, a number of broad guidelines are beneficial in transforming the spreadsheet into an effective application:

- Divide the spreadsheet into sections or modules to reflect the main issues or items of interest.
- Take advantage of the many formatting options to enhance the appearance of the spreadsheet.
- Use tables of contents or menus to identify the different parts of the spreadsheet.
- Combine or link modules or spreadsheets together to form summative pictures.
- Automate where feasible and productive.

Throughout the cases, in both this and the next chapter, examples and illustrations of each guideline will be offered. Also, note how these techniques simply reflect and amplify the more general design tools associated with the divide-and-conquer technique.

Cases

To demonstrate how microcomputer operational applications are developed and used, the nucleus of this chapter is a set of three case studies: tracking revenues, aggregating budget requests, and controlling capital expenditures. These cases bring together all the points relevant to application development. In particular, they illustrate how to use spreadsheets, and how to do so with good design techniques, so that the applications are effective and easy to use.

Throughout the presentation of these cases it is critical to recognize that we separate the *logic* from the *implementation* of the application. The logic shows how, in general, the problem is solved with a spreadsheet. The implementation draws on the specific rules and syntax of Lotus 1-2-3, version 2.01. Taking this approach, a good deal of learning can take place just from understanding the logic, because the logic can be applied to almost any spreadsheet.

By way of summary, we characterize the problems of this chapter as structured problems—problems that are fairly routine, but may involve moderate amounts of data and calculations. For these problems, we rely on operational applications for guidance in building our microcomputer applications. Such applications tend to replicate the nonautomated pencil-and-paper solutions but capitalize on the speed, accuracy, and memory of microcomputer software to reduce the "drudgework." Spreadsheets are selected as the particular category of implementing software.

CASE 1: REVENUE INFLOW

Background and Purpose

This first case demonstrates application development for a tedious but important task: keeping abreast of revenue inflow and comparing the current status to the previous year's revenues. In any government, knowing whether revenues are ahead or behind prior collections is a critical piece of information. If revenues are lagging, then expenditures may have to be followed more closely. In contrast, if revenues are running ahead, then investment strategies may need to be altered to take advantage of excess cash.

Jumping ahead for a moment, figure 7.6 on page 184 shows the final revenue-tracking application for a three-month period, January to March. Overall, it contains three sections: the sources of revenue (real estate, gas utilities, etc.) on a monthly basis, a month-by-month analysis, and a cumulative analysis.

From the simple spreadsheet in figure 7.6, we can obtain basic data such as the revenue for any month. For example, real estate yields $1,399,000 in February. Perhaps more important, we can check whether we are running ahead or behind in comparison to last year. The "Mo Difference," or monthly difference, in the month-by-month analysis section shows whether revenues are above or below the previous year's total for that particular month (parentheses around a number, as in ($41), mean a negative number or value). The "Cum Difference," or cumulative difference, in the cumulative analysis section tells whether revenues are running above or below last year's pace for all the months up through the most recent month.

> For those with an interest in finance, there is the technical question of when revenue is considered revenue on the books of the government. Is it when the bills are sent? When the money is actually collected? Governmental accounting books cover such questions.

The remainder of this case study shows how the spreadsheet application in figure 7.6 was constructed. As with most applications, we will start at a simple level and improve and amend as we proceed.

Using the Spreadsheet

In pursuing this application we have the opportunity to see how several of the basic characteristics of spreadsheets are used in application building. In particular, we will see how effortlessly titles and headings can be handled (Lotus refers to all titles, headings, etc., as *labels*); how different types of calculations can be accomplished with spreadsheet formulas; how easily data can be entered; and how work-saving features, such as the copy command, can facilitate implementation of the spreadsheet.

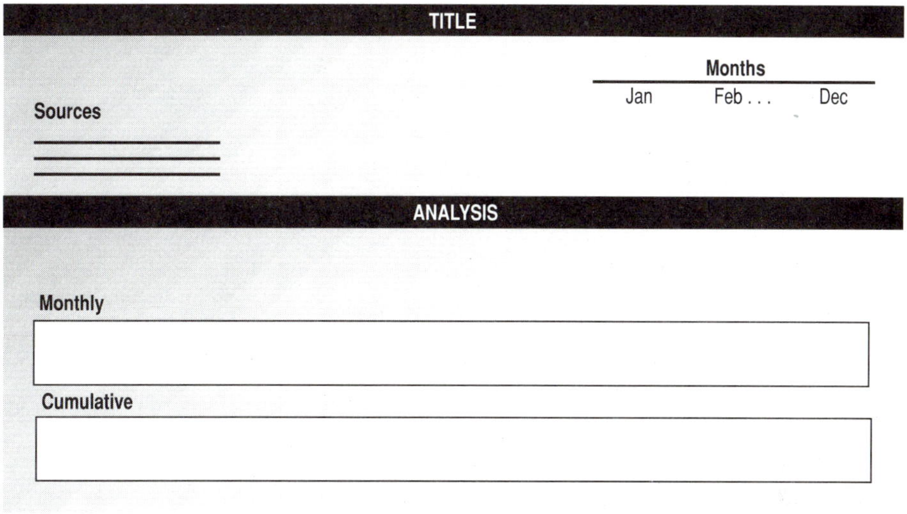

Chapter 7 Structured Managerial Problems 177

[Sketch showing a spreadsheet layout with TITLE bar at top, Sources section on left and Months (Jan, Feb..., Dec) on right, ANALYSIS bar in middle, and Monthly and Cumulative sections below]

FIGURE 7.1 Sketch of revenue spreadsheet

Developing the Operational Application

Although this is a relatively simple application, adherence to the tenets of the conceptual framework, including divide and conquer, stepwise refinement, modularity, and pseudocode is still beneficial. In the discussion that follows, we highlight the use of several of these techniques.

Stepwise refinement To begin the application, we first produce a rough sketch. Figure 7.1 shows two main parts (a hint of modularity): one that will track revenue inflow by month, and one that will do the comparative analysis. As it turns out, the tracking part is the tedious element. The revenues must be entered for each month. The comparative analysis involves more mathematical operations and gives us an idea of how we are doing in comparison to last year.

With this outline providing the overall picture of what the application will look like, we move to the next level of detail—actually entering the main features of the worksheet—but without logging in the data. Figure 7.2, which is not yet very attractive in appearance, describes the worksheet to this point. It has all the titles, headings, revenue sources, and analytical categories. One advantage of delaying data entry is that the thinking, or logical, aspect is separated from the effort needed to enter the data. Another advantage of this approach is that design errors are easier to spot and correct. With all the data in place, reconfiguring the appearance of the application is much harder. Additionally, destroying or altering data is a real danger if changes are made to the overall design after all the data have been inputted.

The work in figure 7.2 also exhibits some of the easy to use facilities of the spreadsheet. The titles and heading are typed directly into the spreadsheet without any special or preliminary work. For the main title—XXX FUND REVENUES—simply go to the cell and type in the title. If it does not look centered, it is possible to edit in Lotus

178   PART III   Use of the Framework in Developing Applications

```
                            XXX FUND REVENUES

                                  Month

Sources         Jan       Feb       Mar       Apr       May       Jun
Real Estate
Delinquencies
Personal Property
Delinquencies
Bank Franchise
Land Transfer
Recordation
Gas Utility
Amusement
Business License
Building Permit
Swimming Pool
Bingo
Dog License

Totals
Current Yr
Current Cum
Last Yr
Last Yr Cum
Mo Difference
Cum Difference
```

FIGURE 7.2

with the F2 function key. In this case, a few blanks were placed in front of the title to "push" it to the right. The rest of the labeling is just as easy. Follow the preliminary sketch in figure 7.1 and simply type character data (titles, headings, sources, and totals) into the cells in the spreadsheet.

Pseudocode Our next level of detail is to develop the formulas. Recall that we must do a good deal of adding and comparing. Under the Totals heading in figure 7.3 (bottom left) are five formulas for each month. Although the formulas are straightforward, we will use pseudocode before explaining the actual Lotus formulas. A statement for each formula follows:

- Current Yr (year) is the sum of all revenues, from real estate to dog licenses, for one particular month.
- Current Cum (cumulative) is a mite more complicated, with two different formulas. The cumulative for the first month is the first month; there is nothing to accumulate. For the second and subsequent months, it is last month's cum plus the current for this month. For instance, the cum for Feb is the cum for Jan plus the current for Feb.
- Last Yr is the month-by-month revenues from last year and requires no formula.

```
 1
 2
 3                        XXX FUND REVENUES
 4                             Month
 5
 6
 7  Sources       Jan          Feb          Mar          Apr
 8  Real Estate   1345         1399         1400
 9  Delinquencies 9            9            2
10  Personal Pro  325          326          333
11  Delinquencies 2            2            1
12  Bank Franchi  25           25           12
13  Land Transfe  14           26           27
14  Recordation   21           29           31
15  Gas Utility   176          167          130
16  Amusement     14           9            11
17  Business Lic  453          455          461
18  Building Per  123          132          142
19  Swimming Poo  2            0            4
20  Bingo         5            2            2
21  Dog License   1            2            3
22
23  Totals
24  Current Yr   @SUM(B8..B21) @SUM(C8..C21) @SUM(D8..D21) @SUM(E8..E21)
25  Current Cum  +B24          +B25+C24      +C25+D24      +D25+E24
26  Last Yr                2499         2566         2600         2700
27  Last Yr Cum    +B26          +B27+C26      +C27+D26      +D27+E26
28  Mo Differenc+B24-B26      +C24-C26      +D24-D26      +E24-E26
29  Cum Differen+B25-B27      +C25-C27      +D25-D27      +E25-E27
         A           B             C             D             E
```

FIGURE 7.3

- Last Yr Cum follows the same logic as Current Cum.
- Mo (month) Difference is Last Yr subtracted from Current Yr.
- Cum Difference is the same as Mo Difference, except it is Last Yr Cum subtracted from Current Cum.

Up to this point, the design suggestions for this application would apply almost regardless of the brand of spreadsheet used. A general sketch, pseudocode, and entering the labels and formulas before the data are all good design ideas. The remainder of the description is the specific implementation with Lotus. It is designed to highlight some of the tools available in Lotus for building microcomputer applications.

Formulas With the pseudocode completed, the actual Lotus formulas can be inserted into the worksheet. Two types of formulas are available: built-in Lotus formulas, which come with the software and are referred to as *functions*, and user-designed formulas.

Figure 7.3 shows all the formulas. Finding the current-year total for any given month is based on a built-in function: @SUM(RANGE). The @ signifies that the formula is a built-in function. The SUM, of course, means to sum everything in the RANGE. From the pseudocode, we know that the range includes all the revenues for the month.

To enter the sum formula for the Jan column, place the cursor in the Jan Current Yr cell (which is actually cell B24 in figure 7.3) and type @SUM(. Then, move the cursor to the first revenue item for Jan (cell B8). Once the cursor is in this cell, enter a period (.), which "anchors" the pointer at this cell. Next, move the cursor down to the last revenue row (cell B21) and notice that, as you do so, the RANGE is "painted." The painting is a highlighting that shows the range that will be used in calculating the sum. As soon as you reach the last revenue row for Jan, enter a close parentheses [)] and press the enter key. The formula will then read @SUM(B8..B21). The two dots, or periods, were created when you entered the period at the top of the range—that is, in the first Jan revenue cell. In actuality the sum, not the formula, would appear in the Jan Current Yr cell, although we have displayed the actual formula in figure 7.3 to make it easier to see how to create the formula.

The method just used to enter the sum formula is called the *pointing* method. In fact, once you start moving the cursor, the panel or mode indicator in the upper right-hand corner of the Lotus worksheet will read "point." The formula could also be entered directly—that is, by actually typing @SUM(B8..B21). However, this method invites errors. In order to type the sum formula directly, one must make sure that the first cell in the range is B8 and the last, B21. As the work moves farther and farther away from the upper left-hand corner of the worksheet (cell A1) it becomes increasingly difficult to discern the cell location accurately.

The next formula of note is Current Cum for Feb (Jan Current Cum is simply Jan Current Yr). From the pseudocode, recall that we must take the last month's cum and add this month's current revenue to get the cum. Following this guide, the formula for Feb Current Cum is +B25+C24 (see figure 7.3, which contains all the formulas). It does exactly what the pseudocode specifies. It takes the cum for Jan, which is in cell B25, and adds the current for Feb, +C24. The plus sign (+) between B25 and C25 is an addition sign. The + in front of B25 plays a different role. It means that a custom-built formula is being prepared, not a Lotus built-in formula. Without the +, Lotus would think that the B was a label, rather that a formula or cell reference. Thus, when you are designing your own formulas, you place a + in front to convey this fact. Remember that Lotus guesses whether an entry is a label or some sort of math by looking at the first character entered.

The other formulas are relatively straightforward and need no comment. Mo Difference and Cum Difference are merely subtractions of last year's totals from current totals.

Labor-saving copy command After the initial formulas have been entered for Jan or Feb, what remains is duplicating them for the remaining months. Almost all the formulas are a repeat of those in the Jan column, except for the exact range. To avoid typing all those formulas, Lotus provides a way of copying from one cell to another while adjusting for the differences in the range. This device is called the *relative copy*.

For example, it is possible to copy the @SUM(B8..B21) from the Jan Current Yr to all the other months, with Lotus making the necessary adjustments so that the range changes as the formula is copied from column to column. This operation begins by

```
                         XXX FUND REVENUES
                              (000)

                               Month

Sources     Jan       Feb       Mar       Apr       May       Jun
Real Esta   1345     1399      1400
Delinquen      9        9         2
Personal     325      326       333
Delinquen      2        2         1
Bank Fran     25       25        12
Land Tran     14       26        27
Recordati     21       29        31
Gas Utili    176      167       130
Amusement     14        9        11
Business     453      455       461
Building     123      132       142
Swimming       2        0         4
Bingo          5        2         2
Dog Licen      1        2         3
Totals

Current Y   2515     2583      2559         0         0         0
Current C   2515     5098      7657      7657      7657      7657
Last Yr     2499     2566      2600      2700      3100
Last Yr C   2499     5065      7665     10365     13465     13465
Mo Differ     16       17       -41     -2700     -3100         0
Cum Diffe     16       33        -8     -2708     -5808     -5808
```

FIGURE 7.4

activating the Lotus menu system with a slash (/) and then requesting the copy command. (The spreadsheet section in chapter 2 discusses, in general terms, how the Lotus menu system works.) The complete command is: /COPY FROM B24 TO C24..G24. In other words, copy the content of cell B24 (figure 7.3) to cells C24, D24, E24, F24, and G24. As the formula is copied across the row, Lotus knows to change the range. In C24, for example, Lotus changes the range from B8..B21 to C8..C21 (again, see figure 7.3). Using this copy facility, one can type the formula once, then copy it to the other relevant cells.

Entering the data For purposes of exposition, only three months' data are entered (see figure 7.4). Starting with 1345 for Jan real estate (actually $1,345,000, because we are reporting in the thousands) and ending with 3 for Mar dog licenses, we input all the necessary data. Because the formulas have already been entered, the results will appear as the data are entered.

Enhancing the appearance With the data entered, a rudimentary worksheet is available (figure 7.4). We can see the collections for this year and the comparisons with last year. However, the appearance of the worksheet must be improved. The names of the months are poorly placed with respect to the data; the names of the revenue sources run into the data in the Jan column; there are no clear demarcations among the modules; the data are in raw form, not in dollars and cents; and the analysis section looks crammed.

Lotus has an array of tools to deal with all these appearance, or formatting, problems. The names of the months (or any label, for that matter) can all be shifted to the far left of the cell, the center, or the far right. In this case, a shift to the far right will probably align the labels better with the data. The command for this is /RANGE LABEL RIGHT and then the range to shift. The column holding the names of the revenue sources can be widened by the command /WORKSHEET COLUMN-WIDTH SET and then either a number to designate the width or use of the right arrow key (->) to make the column just wide enough so it does not overlap the column next to it.

To separate clearly the components of the worksheet, borders should be inserted. First, a new row must be inserted between "Sources" and the individual revenue items. New rows can be inserted with the command /WORKSHEET INSERT ROW and then use of the arrow key to indicate the number of rows to insert. With this row insert completed and the space available, a border at the top and bottom of the inflow part of the worksheet can be inserted quickly by means of the repeat and copy commands. The special backslash character (\) means to repeat whatever is placed after it. Thus \- puts borderlike lines in the cell between "Sources" and the revenue items. The line can then be extended to the end of the revenue inflow table by using the copy command. Once completed, the entire line can be copied to the bottom of the revenue inflow table.

All the raw data can be converted to dollar form by means of the range format command. Using /RANGE FORMAT CURRENCY, then a decision on how many decimals (to include cents, 2 decimals; to exclude cents, no or 0 decimals), and finally what range to format will convert the data to the designated currency format. Figure 7.5 shows the results of these improvements, producing a far more legible spreadsheet than in figure 7.4.

Displaying and Printing the Data

Before the data are presented to others, either by "letting them look over your shoulder" or by printing, two more appearance problems need to be addressed. First, the analytical section is not clearly differentiated from the body of the revenue data. With a series of row inserts and moves, the designations in the analysis section can be moved around until the right visual mix is achieved. Figure 7.6 shows these improvements.

Figure 7.6 also shows a second improvement in the analysis section. Because all the formulas were entered before all the data, the analysis in figure 7.5 shows results for months for which no revenue has yet been collected. For example, there are Current Yr, Current Cum, Mo Difference, and Cum Difference entries for April even though the April revenues have not been received. To conceal the results for these months, without destroying all the work you put in when you copied the formulas, Lotus has a HIDE command that takes a display off the screen without erasing what is in the cell. The HIDE command is part of the range format command: /RANGE FORMAT HIDE and then the range to be hidden.

Figure 7.7 represents what is called a *screen print*, showing the exact rows and

Chapter 7 Structured Managerial Problems

```
                         XXX FUND REVENUES
                              (000)

                               Month

Sources                Jan       Feb       Mar       Apr       May       Jun
-----------------------------------------------------------------------------
Real Estate          $1,345    $1,399    $1,400
Delinquencies            $9        $9        $2
Personal Property      $325      $326      $333
Delinquencies            $2        $2        $1
Bank Franchise          $25       $25       $12
Land Transfer           $14       $26       $27
Recordation             $21       $29       $31
Gas Utility            $176      $167      $130
Amusement               $14        $9       $11
Business License       $453      $455      $461
Building Permit        $123      $132      $142
Swimming Pool            $2        $0        $4
Bingo                    $5        $2        $2
Dog License              $1        $2        $3
-----------------------------------------------------------------------------
Totals

Current Yr           $2,515    $2,583    $2,559        $0        $0        $0
Current Cum          $2,515    $5,098    $7,657    $7,657    $7,657    $7,657
Last Yr              $2,499    $2,566    $2,600    $2,700    $3,100
Last Yr Cum          $2,499    $5,065    $7,665   $10,365   $13,465   $13,465
Mo Difference           $16       $17     ($41)  ($2,700)  ($3,100)        $0
Cum Difference          $16       $33      ($8)  ($2,708)  ($5,808)  ($5,808)
```

FIGURE 7.5

columns where everything is placed on the spreadsheet. Additionally, all the formulas are presented, so that one could completely recreate this spreadsheet by putting everything in the exact cell where it is displayed in the screen print.

With all this done, the final application is ready. A short memo can be put together and submitted along with a printout of the results as displayed in figure 7.6. In that memo, we might say that we were doing fine until March, but with the slowing of revenues in March it may be necessary to contemplate some corrective action. More specifically, for this March $41,000 less was collected than for last March. This difference was so large that the cumulative excess of $33,000 realized up to February was wiped out, leaving ($8,000) less than was collected from January to March of last year.

Note that this type of operational application does not indicate what action to take. Operational applications help summarize events or activities; they do not necessarily emulate or promote decision making. In chapter 8, we will look at applications designed to provide direct assistance with decision making.

```
                         XXX FUND REVENUES
                              (000)

                              Month

Sources                 Jan      Feb      Mar      Apr      May      Jun
-------------------------------------------------------------------------
Real Estate           $1,345   $1,399   $1,400
Delinquencies             $9       $9       $2
Personal Property       $325     $326     $333
Delinquencies             $2       $2       $1
Bank Franchise           $25      $25      $12
Land Transfer            $14      $26      $27
Recordation              $21      $29      $31
Gas Utility             $176     $167     $130
Amusement                $14       $9      $11
Business License        $453     $455     $461
Building Permit         $123     $132     $142
Swimming Pool             $2       $0       $4
Bingo                     $5       $2       $2
Dog License               $1       $2       $3
-------------------------------------------------------------------------


                              Month-by-Month Analysis
                              -----------------------
Current Yr            $2,515   $2,583   $2,559
Last Yr               $2,499   $2,566   $2,600
Mo Difference            $16      $17    ($41)

                              Cumulative Analysis
                              -------------------
Current Cum           $2,515   $5,098   $7,657
Last Yr Cum           $2,499   $5,065   $7,665
Cum Difference           $16      $33     ($8)
```

FIGURE 7.6

CASE 2: PREPARING AND AGGREGATING BUDGET REQUESTS

Purpose and Background

Our second case deals with a fairly common budgeting task: preparing budget requests at a bureau level within a department and then combining the several bureau requests into a single, total department request. If all the bureaus in the department use the same format, aggregating into one department summary presents few, if any, problems. However, we will start by looking at a single bureau and how it develops a budget

Chapter 7 Structured Managerial Problems

```
    1       A                 B              C              D              E
    2
    3
    4                                  XXX FUND REVENUES
    5                                       (000)
    6                                       Month
    7
    8   Sources              Jan            Feb            Mar            Apr
    9   ------------------------------------------------------------------------
   10   Real Estate          1345           1399           1400
   11   Delinquencies           9              9              2
   12   Personal Proper       325            326            333
   13   Delinquencies           2              2              1
   14   Bank Franchise         25             25             12
   15   Land Transfer          14             26             27
   16   Recordation            21             29             31
   17   Gas Utility           176            167            130
   18   Amusement              14              9             11
   19   Business Licens       453            455            461
   20   Building Permit       123            132            142
   21   Swimming Pool           2              0              4
   22   Bingo                   5              2              2
   23   Dog License             1              2              3
   24   ------------------------------------------------------------------------
   25
   26
   27                              Month-by-Month Analysis
   28                          ------------------------------------
   29   Current Yr      @SUM(B10..B23) @SUM(C10..C23) @SUM(D10..D23) @SUM(E10
   30   Last Yr              2499           2566           2600           2700
   31   Mo Difference   +B29-B30       +C29-C30       +D29-D30       +E29-E30
   32
   33                                 Cumulative Analysis
   34                          ------------------------------------
   35   Current Cum     +B29           +B35+C29       +C35+D29       +D35+E29
   36   Last Yr Cum     +B30           +B36+C30       +C36+D30       +D36+E30
   37   Cum Difference  +B35-B36       +C35-C36       +D35-D36       +E35-E36
```

FIGURE 7.7

summary largely on its own. Then we will move to the model in which all the bureaus cooperate. Like the first case, this one presents an excellent opportunity for developing an operational application. It is a relatively routine problem where we want to take a snapshot of events or capture the flow of events.

Using the Spreadsheet

The spreadsheet is more than adequate as a software tool for this task. The dollars and cents and rows and columns characteristics of budgets fit squarely with the matrix layout of spreadsheets and the ability of spreadsheets to handle all types of quantitative data. Additionally, the capability of spreadsheets to change data entries or to adjust titles and headings, and to calculate quickly and accurately reduces the drudgework often associated with the routine collection and calculation of budget data.

Developing a Bureau-Level Application

We assume that individual bureaus are given general policy guidelines for how much spending to propose, but fewer common rules regarding format. We will trace how one bureau sets up its summary and what happens when it comes time to consolidate all the bureau summaries.

Our bureau shows three years of budget data: prior year, current year, and next year, which follows the request from the central office. The data are organized in three major categories: personnel, operations, and capital expenditures. The bureau also shows the percentage change between prior and current years and between current year and next year's request. All this seems prudent and rational. Figure 7.8 shows the final product for this bureau's budget request.

Stepwise refinement As noted in the first case, a general outline of the major features of the application is a good starting point. It suggests where the items ought to be placed on the worksheet. From here one can refine the outline until there is a fairly detailed picture of what goes into the worksheet. However, since we have already demonstrated how to proceed from general sketch to a first-cut application and then to more refined iterations in the prior case, and because this part of the present application is relatively straightforward, we will move directly to the final product.

Formulas and names in formulas Because this is a fairly simple spreadsheet with only three years, three categories, and a few calculations, all that is required is a discussion of how to develop the formulas for the calculations. Two sets of formulas are needed: one for totals and one for percentage change. The total for each period (prior, current, request) is merely the sum of the three categories. The percentage changes are a bit more complicated, requiring a basic appreciation of algebra. Using shorthand names, the first change can be captured by the formula (Cyr-Pyr)/Pyr, where Cyr is current year and Pyr is prior year. The parentheses are needed because computers have rules for the order in which mathematical operations are performed. According to these rules, division occurs before subtraction, so without the parentheses, the Pyr/Pyr in (Cyr-Pyr)/Pyr would be executed first, then the result subtracted from Cyr. Parentheses evoke an overriding rule: do the work in the parentheses first. As a result, the quantity Cyr-Pyr is calculated first. Following this same logic, the second percentage change can be depicted by (Ryr-Cyr)/Cyr, where Ryr stands for request year.

Lotus permits using names in formulas instead of cell locations. Names are helpful in making formulas somewhat more readable. A name for the content of a cell is created

```
                    Budget Request: Bureau X
-----------------------------------------------------------------
                              YEAR
-----------------------------------------------------------------
        CATEGORY          PRIOR       CURRENT      REQUEST

Personnel Services       $95,894     $194,275     $259,795
Operational Expenses     $76,644      $95,194      $50,050
Capital Equipment             $0      $24,600       $8,189

    Total               $172,538     $314,069     $318,034

% Change                              82.03%        1.26%

-----------------------------------------------------------------
```

FIGURE 7.8

with the command /RANGE NAME CREATE and then the name to be used. In figure 7.8, a name for prior year total (Pyr) can be created by placing the cursor in the cell where the total ($172,538) is located and then invoking the command /RNC Pyr. When Pyr is used in a formula, Lotus knows that Pyr refers to $172,538, or whatever total happens to be in the cell for prior year total in figure 7.8. If we name the total amount in the cell for prior year Pyr, the total for current year Cyr, and the total for request year Ryr, we can then use these names in the formulas to calculate the percentage change from year to year.

☐   After spelling out a command sequence in full, such as /RANGE NAME CREATE, we will often move to the short, single-letter version. In Lotus, depressing the single keys is sufficient to execute the command. Thus, depressing the keys /R N C and then giving a name to the range is a quick way to perform this particular command.

To close out the explanation of figure 7.8, the percent signs in this figure are obtained in a manner similar to the way we added dollar signs to various amounts in prior examples, except that in the command /RANGE FORMAT we ask for % instead of currency when prompted for the desired format.

Developing One Application for All Bureaus in the Department

At this point, the problem of aggregating all the bureau requests into one department total could present a veritable Tower of Babel. In a department such as this one, with multiple bureaus, if a common, consistent format is not adopted, attempting to combine the information provided from each of the bureaus into a single budget may prove problematic. For example, if expenditure categories differ, nothing more than a grand total can be given for the department. So far, we have seen that one bureau uses personnel, operating, and capital expenditures. If another bureau uses personnel, supplies, and travel as its summary categories, then aggregations will not be possible.

Ultimately, the director of the department needs to produce a budget summary that is common to all bureaus. Once again, the elements of a general problem-solving logic can assist—in particular, the top-down approach and modular development.

Top-down strategy The product of this application is a departmentwide budget summary. Therefore, it is the responsibility of top management to see that a usable report is produced and that it is achieved without confusion and wasted energy. By starting with the requirements for the end product and working down to the individual bureaus, the application design proceeds logically from the general to the specific. This approach produces appropriate components of the application that are parsimonious, providing only the information needed—no more, no less.

Modularity The modular approach is used in the institution and replication of the bureau budget requests. In effect, each bureau uses the same categories, thereby providing a means for aggregating all bureau requests into a total department request.

From a managerial standpoint, the top-down, modular nature of application development enables the manager to exert a substantial degree of control over the production of information. Because each bureau is required to conform to a common reporting format, there is greater assurance that the needed information will be provided. This method is more desirable than allowing each bureau to develop and use its own (nonconforming) reporting format.

In this case, the final model chosen by management resembles the format from the first bureau reviewed. Figures 7.9 and 7.10 show it in two forms: the formulas in 7.9, and ready for data entry in 7.10. The idea of presenting the prior year, the current year, and the request remains unchanged. Also the same are the three categories: personnel, operating, and capital. Two alterations have been made, however. The percentage changes from prior to current and current to request have been dropped, and a new set of entries has been added. The new entries seek to capture whether a unit is operating at a "surplus" or a "deficit." Any income generated by the unit is recorded, then the total cost of running the bureau is subtracted from this income. Apparently someone in management wants to give a "business look" to the budget process.

Developing the Application via Templates

The actual mechanics of developing this application could require the preparation of four worksheets: the departmental master and three bureau summaries for our three fictitious bureaus. Rather than approach the development of each of these worksheets as a separate entity, it is useful to view each of the bureau spreadsheets as identical in format to the departmental master. This makes the developmental task somewhat easier because only one worksheet—the departmental—must be developed from scratch. The other three will be copies of the master.

With all the formats the same, the development of the master worksheet is best accomplished through the creation of a budget reporting *template* that will be used by the department and each of the bureaus. A template is a partially completed spreadsheet,

Chapter 7   Structured Managerial Problems

```
                    Budget Request: Bureau Template
------------------------------------------------------------------
                                    YEAR
------------------------------------------------------------------
      CATEGORY            PRIOR         CURRENT        REQUEST

Personnel Services
Operational Expenses
Capital Equipment

     Total            @SUM(C9..C11)  @SUM(D9..D11)  @SUM(E9..E11)

Income

Surplus/Deficit         +C15-C13       +D15-D13       +E15-E13


------------------------------------------------------------------
```

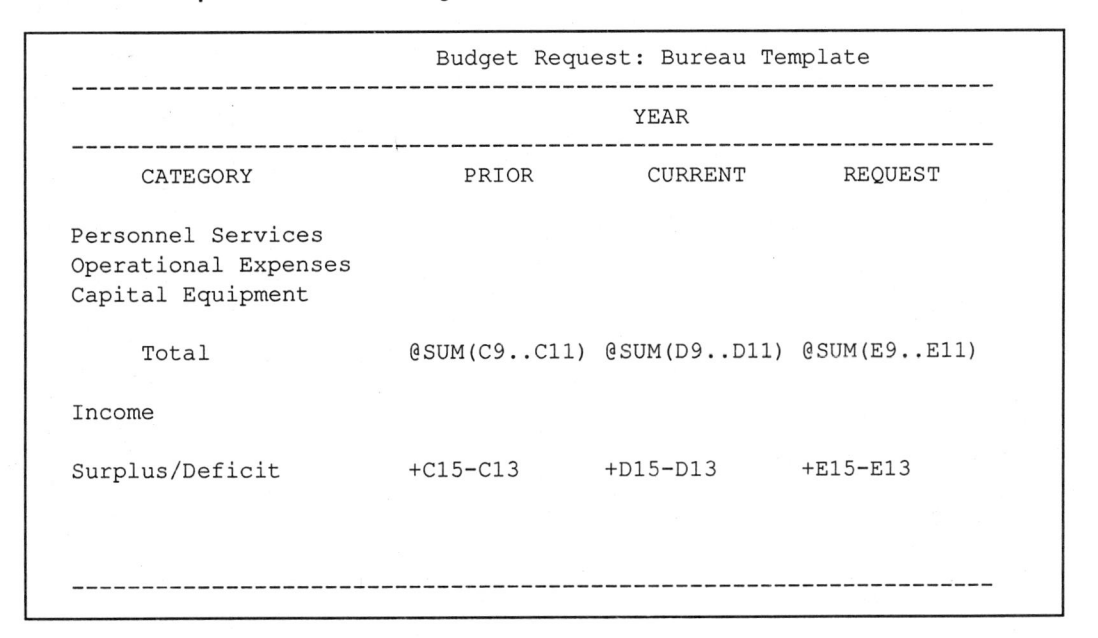

FIGURE 7.9 Template with formulas

```
                    Budget Request: Bureau Template
------------------------------------------------------------------
                                    YEAR
------------------------------------------------------------------
      CATEGORY            PRIOR         CURRENT        REQUEST

Personnel Services
Operational Expenses
Capital Equipment

     Total                 $0            $0             $0

Income

Surplus/Deficit            $0            $0             $0


------------------------------------------------------------------
```

FIGURE 7.10 Template ready for data entry

usually one that contains all of the label or title information and appropriate formulas (figure 7.9). It does not, however, contain any actual numeric information (figure 7.10). Thus, the format of the template, which does not change, can be saved and reused as often as necessary. When the substantive information is entered for a particular iteration of the spreadsheet, it is then saved under another name to preserve the original.

In Lotus, the process of saving a file usually occurs after some work has been performed on the worksheet. If the user wants to preserve the initial worksheet (named, let us say, btemplat), then the file with the changes must be given a different name—say, burx. The command to save the changed file would then be /FILE SAVE burx.

In the application development for the master template, the initial step is to determine what information needs to be included. This information consists of:

- titles and labels needed to identify the information in the template
- specified cells for data entry
- appropriate formulas, formats, and cell protection options

Using Lotus

In the remainder of this case study, we will go through the details necessary to produce templates, fill them in with data from the bureaus, and combine all the bureau requests into a total department request. Once again, for reference, figures 7.9 and 7.10 show the template in two versions: the template with the formulas, and the template as one would see it before data are entered.

Entering labels We start with a title by moving the cursor (or cell pointer) to a suitable location on the spreadsheet and typing in "Budget Request: Bureau Template." Remember, as soon as Lotus sees that a letter has been entered into a cell, it assumes that no math will be done and makes the entry in that cell a label—that is, a word or phrase. Lotus automatically places a single quotation mark (') in front of the word or phrase to designate it as a label.

If the title were something like 1st Budget Request, the entry of a 1 as the first character would signal that some math is to be done. Lotus would balk because 1st is not a legitimate mathematical operation. In this case, the user should insert the ' before 1st, so that the entry reads '1st. Now it is a label.

Column-width adjustments Entering the cell labels for category and year is a fairly straightforward procedure. The only aspect that may not be obvious is resetting column widths for the CATEGORY labels and the YEAR columns. Lotus has a default column width of nine characters. That may not be sufficient for either the categories or the dollar amounts. In setting column widths, it helps to have some idea of the maximum width before starting. The different categories, such as Personnel Services, appear to require at least twenty characters. The command to change the column width is /WORKSHEET COLUMN-WIDTH SET, followed by the number 20 if the desired width is twenty spaces. However, if the categories are entered in column A, and column B is not used, then characters from column A can spill over into the area reserved for column B.

For the dollar amounts to be entered in the spreadsheet, the columns must contain at least seven digits, because the budget requests are in the millions. Setting the column width at seven characters would not work, however, since the formatting used to display dollar signs and commas (e.g., $2,344,074) must also be taken into account. This brings the column width up to ten, or thirteen if decimals are desired ($2,344,074.00). Setting the column width appropriately reduces the possibility of appearing to overwrite part of a cell's content by placing data in the cell to its right.

Lotus allows one to set all the columns at a width greater (or less) than nine characters by using the /W G C, or WORKSHEET GLOBAL COLUMN-WIDTH, command. For example, all the columns could be set at twenty by means of the GLOBAL command. However, in our case we want column A to be twenty characters and columns C through E to be thirteen. Therefore, we will use the command to set one column at a time: / W C S, or WORKSHEET COLUMN-WIDTH SET. As with many Lotus commands, this column-width command permits one to tailor the worksheet to produce an appearance appealing to the eye.

Specifying data-entry locations is also a very simple proposition. Leaving the needed cells empty suffices at this point. One word of caution: A common error relating to "empty" cells is the use of the space bar to "clear" a cell. This procedure should never be used, because it does not actually clear the cell. Instead, it makes the cell contents a blank label, which may later serve to confound calculations. The correct way to clear a cell is to erase its contents. In Lotus, this involves the / R E, or /RANGE ERASE, command. If /R E is used, then nothing should appear in the cell when the cursor is on it.

Formulas   The major effort devoted to the design of this template occurs in the creation of the appropriate *formulas* and *formats*. Both give Lotus and other spreadsheets enormous power. Formulas permit Lotus to take data entries from anywhere on the worksheet and run many different types of calculations. These can be simple calculations, such as adding a row of numbers, or more complex calculations, such as calculating the net present value, which we explore in chapter 8.

The formulas used in this application are of the straightforward variety, primarily employing the @SUM(RANGE) function. The first is used in the row labeled Total in figure 7.9. This formula is used to sum up the three major expenditure categories: @SUM(C9..C11). Once this formula has been entered correctly, Lotus provides a method to copy it to other locations, thereby saving keystrokes and avoiding mistakes. The /COPY FROM TO command is used to replicate this formula for columns D and E. The next formula must subtract total expenditures from income to arrive at a surplus or deficit. In column C, the formula for the prior year surplus or deficit is +C15-C13 (Income - Total, where Total refers to total expenses). Again, this formula is copied across the other two columns.

Formatting   Once the formulas have been entered into the template, the next step is to provide the appropriate formats for the various cells. Lotus has numerous formats, all of which improve the appearance of the worksheet. The formats run the gamut from currency ($) to percentages (%) to dates (which has a number of forms). In this case, the currency format will be used. A /RFC0, which stands for /RANGE FORMAT CURREN-

CY, 0 DECIMAL PLACES, needs to be executed for any cell range with dollars. Figure 7.10 shows the currency designations.

Integrity and cell protection   The final task in defining the template is to restrict data entry to the appropriate cells in the worksheet. This is accomplished using the cell protection function of Lotus. This function allows the user to define a cell or range of cells as *protected* and, therefore, essentially unchangeable. Achieving this restriction involves two basic steps. First, the *entire* worksheet is protected, using the /WGPE, or /WORKSHEET GLOBAL PROTECT ENABLE, command. Once all of the cells in the worksheet have been protected, the /RU (/RANGE UNPROTECT) command is used to disable the protection for selected cells. For this template, it means unprotecting all the cells in which dollar values will be entered.

Using the cell protection feature of Lotus is an excellent way to manage the entry of data into a spreadsheet. By restricting data entry to a specified location, the analyst can reduce the possibility that mislocated data will corrupt the formulas in the spreadsheet.

☐   A number of third-party vendors have taken the concept of cell protection one step further by offering *auditing* or *entry-check* programs that work with Lotus. These programs work by comparing each cell entry against an "acceptability" table to determine whether the value falls within the desired parameters. In a situation where extensive data entry is required, these programs are an invaluable aid to ensuring the integrity of the data.

Completion of the cell protection options fulfills the definition of the master template, which is then saved. The next phase in the development of this application is to duplicate the template and send a copy to each of the units that will use it. In our three-bureau department, this means sending it to bureaus X, Y, and Z, as well as to the central office in the department.

Editing   Before the template is sent, a few modifications must be made. For the bureaus, the only change is to the title. Instead of Bureau Template, the title will reflect the names of the bureaus: X, Y, and Z. This is easily accomplished by using the F2-EDIT key to edit the content of the title cell. Although this F2 key provides only a rudimentary editing capacity, it is adequate when the bulk of the work is quantitative in nature.

Once the modifications have been completed, the template is saved under separate names for the bureaus and the department. Then the templates are distributed to the appropriate analysts or managers for initial data entry. After each bureau template has been completed and saved, the files are brought together to create the completed master spreadsheet.

Aggregating   The process of data aggregation makes use of a Lotus spreadsheet feature that allows one worksheet to be added to or subtracted from another. If the worksheets have the same structure and format, it is possible to create a pseudo-three-dimensional effect by linking multiple worksheets together. For this application, the replication of the master spreadsheet for each bureau means that it is possible to overlay the three bureau worksheets onto the master template to create the final spreadsheet. The command to do this in Lotus is /FCAE, or /FILE COMBINE ADD ENTIRE-FILE.

Chapter 7 Structured Managerial Problems

Some spreadsheets, such as Lotus 1-2-3 Version 3, offer the ability to link spreadsheets dynamically in a true three-dimensional matrix. This form of link means that formulas can reference cells not only in the "host" worksheet but also in any linked worksheets. Using such a spreadsheet program for this application would obviate the need for this last step because the bureau worksheet formulas could be linked dynamically to the master worksheet.

The file-linking procedure is relatively simple. The first step is to open (or, more precisely, to retrieve) the master template. With this template as the active worksheet, each bureau worksheet is then added serially. (Note: for this process to work correctly, the cursor in the master template should be at cell A1.) To add the contents of the first bureau worksheet, the /FCAE command is issued, and the name of the bureau template file is specified. The result is that the data from the bureau worksheet are placed into the data-entry areas of the master template. Figure 7.11 shows the request from Bureau X and the final department request after all the bureau requests have been combined.

Automating with macros It is possible in Lotus to simplify this aggregating process through the use of a *macro* (introduced in chapter 2 under the spreadsheet section). It can be used to aggregate the worksheets automatically. An example of this macro is found at the bottom of figure 7.11. The first line includes two pieces of information. The \0 is the macro name. To the right, the macro contains a simple command {HOME} to ensure that the cursor is placed at cell A1 before the files are combined. The /FCAE command tells Lotus to combine a file by adding its entire contents. The name and location of the file is presented on the next line (budgetx in subdirectory dept). These two instructions are then repeated for the remaining two worksheets. The tilde (~) at the end of the file name is a Lotus macro syntax command for the ENTER key. (Subdirectories are discussed in chapter 2 under operating systems.)

The macro is created in three steps. First an out-of-the-way location in the worksheet is chosen for the macro. This is to prevent the macro from overlapping any formulas or data and causing problems in calculations. Second, the commands for the macro are entered. It is important to be careful when entering commands in a macro because Lotus will try to execute the command as it is being entered if the command is not prefaced with a single quotation mark or apostrophe (e.g., '/FCAE). This is also true for the name of the macro, because the \ is the cell contents repeat command for Lotus. The final step in the macro creation process is the *naming* of the macro. Naming is done with the /RNC (/RANGE NAME CREATE) command. The name for this macro is \0 (no apostrophe required). In specifying the range for a macro name, it is necessary only to include the first cell of the macro since Lotus assumes the macro continues vertically until a blank cell is encountered.

The \0 is a special macro name. When a macro is named with a \0, it is executed automatically every time the worksheet is retrieved. If automatic execution is not desired, simply change the macro name to a letter of the alphabet. The macro is executed then by pressing the ALT key in combination with the chosen letter key (e.g., ALT-A).

Although the application developed in this case is relatively simple, it illustrates the value of approaching even routine, structured problems with the framework presented in chapter 4. Using the framework to develop simple applications enhances the analyst's ability to evolve to more complex tasks because a pattern of effective application development is already well established.

Budget Request: Bureau X

```
                              YEAR
--------------------------------------------------------------------
        CATEGORY          PRIOR         CURRENT         REQUEST

Personnel Services       $95,894       $194,275        $259,795
Operational Expenses     $76,644        $95,194         $50,050
Capital Equipment            $0         $24,600          $8,189

        Total           $172,538       $314,069        $318,034

Income

Surplus/Deficit        ($172,538)     ($314,069)      ($318,034)
```

Department Request

```
                              YEAR
--------------------------------------------------------------------
        CATEGORY          PRIOR         CURRENT         REQUEST

Personnel Services    $2,344,074     $2,760,302      $3,036,847
Operational Expenses  $3,532,359     $4,703,280      $5,286,814
Capital Equipment        $41,026       $103,584         $93,778

        Total        $5,917,459     $7,567,166      $8,417,439

Income                $1,253,879     $1,397,282      $1,422,051

Surplus/Deficit     ($4,663,580)   ($6,169,884)    ($6,995,388)
```

Macro for Combining All Three Budgets

```
\0        {HOME}              Places cursor at A1
          /FCAE               Executes the combine command
          dept\budgetx~       Brings in the values of Bureau X
          /FCAE               Executes the combine command
          dept\budgety~       Brings in the values of Bureau Y
          /FCAE               Executes the combine command
          dept\budgetz~       Brings in the values of Bureau Z
```

FIGURE 7.11

CASE 3: TRACKING CAPITAL EXPENDITURES

Purpose and Background

The purpose of our third case is to explore how to track capital expenditures and intercept any items where the expenditure is significantly above a set limit. This is a common and important problem for management because capital items are often quite expensive. Overexpenditure on just a few items can cause serious deficits. For this task, we will build a microcomputer-based tracking system and then create one report to summarize how well we are doing in controlling expenditures for capital items.

☐ Capital items are usually those that will last at least a year. A microcomputer falls into this class. Often a special budget is set aside for capital items.

This third case is a bit more demanding and complex than the first two. Nonetheless, it still falls in the structured category: there are specific rules, and calculations are made to see if the rules are being followed. For this reason, the operational application remains appropriate.

Using the Spreadsheet

This case illustrates a number of important spreadsheet techniques not covered or only partially covered in prior examples. The main technique explored is the database capacity of spreadsheets. We also continue to discuss the programming, or macro, feature associated with spreadsheets and the use of stepwise refinement and other design techniques.

A spreadsheet, within certain limits, can operate like a database. In this usage, the columns become the fields, and the rows become the records. Each field within a record is "connected" to the other fields; that is, they are manipulated as whole. In ordinary spreadsheet mode, the columns and rows are independent and are linked only by formulas, such as the @SUM(RANGE) used in prior cases.

Figure 7.12 shows the partially completed database we will work with in this case. It contains all the capital items budgeted (under Item description) and information about each item, starting with ID# and going to 10% excess flag. For example, the first capital item is number 1116, it falls in the admin budget category, and it is a micro(computer) with periph(eral equipment). It was budgeted for $5,200 and actually cost $5,300, meaning that it ended up being 1.92% over budget.

With this information entered into the spreadsheet, we can begin to perform a number of operations typically associated with databases. We can make queries of the database to find or extract specific items, such as all those for which the expenditure exceeds $500. We can also utilize special database statistical functions to determine totals and subtotals. For example, with the appropriate database commands, it is possible to read across each record, take note of whether the budget category is admin, and add all the budgeted amounts for the admin category.

General Goals and Mechanics of the Tracking System

As noted previously, special energies are devoted to tracking capital expenditures because of the relatively high dollar value of these expenditures. Any one item can be

```
                         Capital Items Database

       Budget          Item          Amount    Amount     % +/-      $+/-    10% excess
   ID# category     description     budgeted  expended  %imbalanc $imbalance flag
   1116 admin    micro with periph   $5,200    $5,300     1.92%    $100.00  not-10%-over
   1117 admin    micro with periph   $5,200    $5,600     7.69%    $400.00  not-10%-over
   1112 admin    legal file 5d         $300       $0
   1118 admin    micro with periph   $5,200       $0
   1114 admin    exec chair            $235     $300     27.66%     $65.00  yes-10%-over
   1127 admin    dictation machine     $306       $0
   1111 admin    legal file 4d         $214       $0
   1128 admin    bookcase              $408       $0
   1113 admin    exec desk           $1,045       $0
   1126 admin    dictation machine     $306     $500     63.40%    $194.00  yes-10%-over
   1136 operate  cellular phone      $1,000   $1,500     50.00%    $500.00  yes-10%-over
   1119 operate  vcr                   $900     $700    -22.22%  ($200.00)  not-10%-over
   1115 operate  midsize sedan      $11,969       $0
   1135 operate  cellular phone      $1,250       $0
   1134 operate  noise headset         $300       $0
   1125 operate  tractor            $16,300       $0
   1130 operate  power saw             $900     $700    -22.22%  ($200.00)  not-10%-over
   1133 operate  forklift            $2,200       $0
   1120 operate  portable radio      $2,300       $0
   1121 operate  portable radio      $2,300
   1131 operate  pump                $1,800
   1124 train    projector           $1,500
   1123 train    sound system        $2,100
   1129 train    cpr kit             $2,010
   1132 train    code blue kit       $1,020
   1122 train    stand                 $200
   1137 train    camera                $910
```

FIGURE 7.12

rather costly, and as a result, lack of scrutiny can be costly. Thus, the general purpose of the tracking system is to keep purchases in line. What follows is an overview of the purchasing process and type of purchasing control assumed in this case.

At the beginning of the budget period, each item to be purchased is entered into the database. As purchase requisitions are received, the requisition is compared with the authorized amount to determine if special approval is required. This comparison demands that we query the database to find the item in question and see if its cost exceeds the authorized amount by more than 10 percent. If so, then special authorization is needed.

From time to time, reports will be generated to summarize the purchasing activity and status of the capital account. We will prepare one such report. This report will create a list of all items exceeding authorized expenditure by more than 10 percent or falling below the budgeted amount by 10 percent or more.

Divide and Conquer

With any general goal, such as keeping track of and containing capital expenditures, the goal needs to be broken down into clearer, more manageable parts. We have used the term *divide and conquer* to characterize this process. In this case study, we will assume that, over the years, a type of natural divide and conquer has evolved with respect to this general goal. That is to say, people working with the tracking systems have identified the major pieces that go into keeping purchases in line, as follows:

- Provide oversight to intercept individual expenditures that overshoot the budgeted amount by a significant margin.
- Show periodically where overruns or savings are occurring on an item-by-item basis.
- Disclose at any point in time the final budgetary results (surplus or deficit) if all remaining budgeted items are purchased at authorized costs.

Other facets could be added to this tracking system, such as the pace of expenditure (on a quarter-by-quarter basis, for example) and analysis by type of item (vehicles, office furniture, etc.), but for the sake of brevity these issues will not be examined.

Design of the Spreadsheet-Based Capital Tracking Application

The first thing we will do is sketch the general makeup or design of the spreadsheet application. In this case, the initial sketch can be particularly helpful because the spreadsheet is quite large and complex. The sketch helps us visualize what goes into the spreadsheet and where.

Figure 7.13 shows the outline of the spreadsheet. In the upper left-hand corner is a table of contents, showing what is in the spreadsheet and the name of the region or area where each part is located. Below the table of contents is the database. In the next vertical block is an area for the macros that will be used to automate some of the analysis. Next to the macro area start the various reports. These reports provide the actual information or evidence on how well we are doing at keeping capital expenditures in line.

Table of Contents

The table of contents (see figure 7.14) serves as a memory aid and as a way of moving from section to section of the spreadsheet. Specifically, it states the name of the spreadsheet application (TRACKING SYSTEM FOR CAPITAL EXPENDITURES) and identifies the major sections in the spreadsheet: the database, the macros, and the reports. Within the sections are further breakdowns. In addition, one can go quickly to any section by using the range name of the section. For example, the database is called CIB. The note below the table tells how to use the GOTO function (the F5 function key) to reach any range and how to return (via the HOME key) to the table of contents.

The Database

The database represented in figure 7.12 contains the partially completed informational core of the application. Overall, it consists of all the items that are to be purchased and space for data that will be inputted once an item has been bought. More specifically, it consists of eight fields. The ID# is a unique identification number, permitting the analyst to locate any capital item. The budget category allows for three types: administrative, operating, and training. Each item is described briefly in the next field or column. Budgeted or authorized amounts are placed next. Actual cost follows. The remaining fields show whether the actual cost was greater or less than the authorized amount.

PART III Use of the Framework in Developing Applications

```
┌─────────────────────────────────────────────────────────┐
│                      WORKSHEET                          │
├─────────────────────────────────────────────────────────┤
│   Name of           Macros                              │
│   Spreadsheet                                           │
│                       ☐                                 │
│   Table of                                              │
│   Contents                                              │
│                       ☐                                 │
│   ┌──────┐                                              │
│   │      │                                              │
│   └──────┘                                              │
│                                                         │
│                                                         │
│                                                         │
│                                                         │
│                         Report           Report         │
│   Database              ┌──────┐         ┌──────┐       │
│   ┌──────┐              └──────┘         └──────┘       │
│   └──────┘                                              │
└─────────────────────────────────────────────────────────┘
```

FIGURE 7.13

Because items costing more than 10 percent over the authorized amount must be approved, special flags are set for those items. In the database shown in figure 7.12, several such items have already been authorized.

☐ One of the important points to understand about databases in spreadsheets is that ordinarily the database is restricted to one file. Multiple files with the possibility of relating one file to the other, as discussed in the database chapter (chapter 5), are generally not possible. However, more spreadsheets are incorporating the facility to move back and forth quickly between relational database software and spreadsheet software. This way the sophisticated multiple files can be manipulated in the database and then accessed by the spreadsheet.

Beginning the Process: Finding Individual Items

The tracking process starts when a bureau submits a purchase requisition. The purpose of this part of the tracking process is to determine if the cost exceeds the budgeted amount by more than 10 percent and, if so, to obtain approval. Once this initial screening has been satisfied, the cost of the item is inserted into the spreadsheet database record.

For purposes of illustration, the first requisition is for item 1114, an executive chair. Its anticipated cost is $300. We need to locate that item in the database and compare the purchase price with the original budget price to determine if the purchase requires special approval.

Obviously, with such a short list of items, there is little need to use all the programming that follows. However, we will assume that there are 500 to 1,000 items in the database and that we need an automated way of locating them easily.

Stepwise refinement and pseudocode for query As we have noted, it is often best to think through the steps involved in a task before writing the syntax to execute the task.

Chapter 7 Structured Managerial Problems

```
TRACKING SYSTEM FOR CAPITAL EXPENDITURES
          Table of Contents
                19xx

Section                        Range Name
------------------------------------------
Database:
Capital items database         CIB

Macros:                        MAC

Reports:
Budgeted versus expended       BVE
Summary of overruns
  and savings                  SOS
Projected surplus or
  deficit                      PSD


Note: To reach any of the sections,
press the F5(GOTO) function key and
the range name given in the table of
contents. To return to the table of
contents press the HOME key.
```

FIGURE 7.14

The process of building the spreadsheet syntax for this query and purchase approval procedure is listed below. We will start at a general level and refine until we have the correct syntax. Broadly, we want to:

- set up the search criterion for the item we wish to locate
- identify and name the database (input area) where the item is located
- give the instructions to find the item
- determine whether cost exceeds budget by more than 10 percent
- enter the cost if not over budget by more than 10 percent, or if approved
- send it back to the department of origin if not approved

In writing the pseudocode, we "hedged" because we know the syntax of the Lotus query commands. In other words, the pseudocode anticipates the ensuing Lotus code. The more familiar one is with the software, the more likely one is to anticipate the actual code.

With the general logic established, it is now possible to start setting up the actual Lotus code to execute the queries and approval scenario. In Lotus, a query consists of two steps. First, it is necessary to set up a criterion area, telling Lotus what to find or extract. Once the criterion area has been established, then the query command is executed.

Set up and name the criterion area   As just noted, database searches in Lotus (called *Data Queries*) start by setting up a criterion area where the record(s) to be located are identified. This actually entails finding a clear area on the spreadsheet and inserting the proper code. Figure 7.15 shows this, along with a partial view of the database. The criterion area is directly above the database.

Specifically, the phrase (or *label*) Criterion for Query appears at the top. This optional label is used to identify the criterion area. Below the title is the field name used for the search—in this instance, ID#. Below that is the specific value for the ID# that is to be located—1114. In other words, the first requisition that came in was a request to purchase item 1114. If item number 1116 comes in next, we will replace 1114 with 1116.

Input area The next task in the query (or search) is to identify and name the input range where the capital items are located. This is our database. We give it the name CIB, for capital item database.

Naming the criterion area and input area is not required, but it is a good practice. When the query command is being executed, the user is prompted for the criterion and input area. In our case, we would just insert the names, QC and CIB, instead of trying to figure out where on the spreadsheet these areas are located and providing the cell ranges. What is required is the area to be included in the criterion and input ranges. In Lotus, the input range for a query must include the row of field names just above the data and all the data. The criterion range needs to include the field name and the actual data that will be used as the criterion.

Query With the criterion and input range identified and named, we can initiate the Lotus query process. The syntax for setting the input and criterion range is:

```
/DATA QUERY
INPUT RANGE
CRITERION RANGE
QUIT
```

If the input and criterion ranges have been given range names, as we have done, these names can be inserted when the user is prompted for the input and criterion ranges. In this analysis, the input range (our database) is called CIB, and the query criterion range is called QC.

With this setup behind us, the actual syntax for our query—that is, to find item 1114—is:

```
/DATA QUERY
FIND
```

If all the preceding steps have been performed correctly, the row, or record containing item 1114 will be highlighted, and the cursor will move from wherever it was to item 1114.

At this point, we can move the cursor to the appropriate cells, enter the cost, and then call on the math capabilities of Lotus to determine whether the proposed cost of this item is within our 10-percent overage limit. In other words, is the $300 cost for the executive chair acceptable? In the column under %imbalance and in the row for item 1114 (figure 7.15), we calculate the percentage over or under for item 1114. The formula, if we

Chapter 7 Structured Managerial Problems

```
                Criterion for Query
                        ID#
                       1114


        Messages for test of 10% overage/underage
        10% exceeded
        yes-10%-over



        10% not exceeded
        not-10%-over




                    Capital Items Database

      Budget      Item          Amount    Amount    % +/-      $+/-    10% excess
 ID#  category   description    budgeted  expended  %imbalanc $imbalance  flag
 1116 admin      micro with periph $5,200 $5,300.00   1.92%   $100.00 not-10%-over
 1117 admin      micro with periph $5,200 $5,600.00   7.69%   $400.00 not-10%-over
 1112 admin      legal file 5d     $300      $0.00
 1118 admin      micro with periph $5,200    $0.00
 1114 admin      exec chair        $235    $300.00   27.66%    $65.00 yes-10%-over
 1127 admin      dictation machine $306      $0.00
 1111 admin      legal file 4d     $214      $0.00
 1128 admin      bookcase          $408      $0.00
 1113 admin      exec desk       $1,045      $0.00
 1126 admin      dictation machine $306    $500.00   63.40%   $194.00 yes-10%-over
 1136 operate    cellular phone  $1,000  $1,500.00   50.00%   $500.00 yes-10%-over
 1119 operate    vcr               $900    $700.00  -22.22%  ($200.00)not-10%-over
 1115 operate    midsize sedan  $11,969      $0.00
 1135 operate    cellular phone  $1,250      $0.00
 1134 operate    noise headset     $300      $0.00
 1125 operate    tractor        $16,300      $0.00
 1130 operate    power saw         $900    $700.00  -22.22%  ($200.00)not-10%-over
 1133 operate    forklift        $2,200      $0.00
 1120 operate    portable radio  $2,300      $0.00
 1121 operate    portable radio  $2,300
 1131 operate    pump            $1,800
 1124 train      projector       $1,500
 1123 train      sound system    $2,100
 1129 train      cpr kit         $2,010
 1132 train      code blue kit   $1,020
 1122 train      stand             $200
 1137 train      camera            $910
```

FIGURE 7.15

inputted it ourselves, would be: +(300-235)/235, where 300 is the requester's amount and 235, the original amount budgeted. Assuming this cell is formatted for percentage, the result would be 27.66%, or 27.66 percent over the authorized amount. It would then be necessary to obtain approval. If approval is secured, we can fill out the remaining columns for item 1114.

As our system stands, it is essentially unautomated. Every time a requisition arrives, we go through basically the same process (except naming the criterion and input areas, which is done once). If item 1136 came in next, we would place that ID# in the criterion area (top of figure 7.15) and execute the command /DATA QUERY FIND. Lotus would take us to item 1136, and we would have to calculate the percentage by which this request is over or under the budgeted amount.

We will automate much of this process by placing formulas in the database so that the percentage over or under is calculated automatically. In fact, we will place formulas in all three database cells where calculation take place: %imbalance (percentage imbalance), $imbalance (dollar imbalance), and 10% excess flag.

Since we have already shown how to construct formulas with stepwise refinement and pseudocode, we will present the formulas without much explanation and without the pseudocode. The formula for %imbalance is:

```
(COST-BUDGETED)/BUDGETED
```

This formula is shown in figure 7.16. Of course, for this formula to work properly, we would need to name the first budgeted value BUDGETED and the first expended value COST. Then, the formula would need to be copied for all the items in the database. The next formula is for $imbalance. It is simply +COST-BUDGETED. This formula, too, appears in figure 7.16.

☐ In a more exhaustive approach to this spreadsheet database illustration, the %imbalance formula and the two to follow, $imbalance and 10% excess flag, would include the option to signify when no purchase has been made. For example, the letters np (for no purchase) might be placed in the expended column until the item is purchased. The formula for %imbalance might then read: @IF(cost="np","np",(cost-budgeted)/budgeted). That is to say, if there is an np in the expended or cost column, place an np in the %imbalance cell; otherwise, go ahead with the caluclation. Similarly, the other two formulas would need to be adjusted to handle the np situation. Most Lotus manuals give full discussion to the variety of options available with the @IF command.

The formula for placing a message to indicate whether the cost is more than 10 percent over the budgeted amount shows a Lotus function that we have not talked about in previous cases. The formula is:

```
@IF(COST>(1.1*BUDGETED),>10%T,>10%F)
```

The third formula is for the 10% excess flag. This particular formula says: if cost exceeds budgeted by more than 10 percent—that is, if it is more than 110 percent of budgeted (> 1.1*BUDGETED)—go to the message contained in the cell named > 10%T (true) and enter the message; if not, go to the cell named > 10%F (false) and enter the message displayed there. The setup necessary for these two messages is explained shortly.

Chapter 7   Structured Managerial Problems

```
                    Capital Items Database with Formulas

         % +/-                    $+/-         10% excess
%imbalance                    $imbalance       flag
(COST-BUDGETED)/BUDGETE  +COST-BUDGETE  @IF(COST>(BUDGETED*1.1),$>10%T,$>10%F)
(E56-D56)/D56            +E56-D56       @IF(E56>(D56*1.1),$>10%T,$>10%F)


(E59-D59)/D59            +E59-D59       @IF(E59>(D59*1.1),$>10%T,$>10%F)



(E64-D64)/D64            +E64-D64       @IF(E64>(D64*1.1),$>10%T,$>10%F)
(E65-D65)/D65            +E65-D65       @IF(E65>(D65*1.1),$>10%T,$>10%F)
(E66-D66)/D66            +E66-D66       @IF(E66>(D66*1.1),$>10%T,$>10%F)




(E71-D71)/D71            +E71-D71       @IF(E71>(D71*1.1),$>10%T,$>10%F)
```

FIGURE 7.16

Figure 7.16 shows the detailed syntax for the formulas we have just placed in the database. The first line shows the formulas as we have described them, and the remaining cells show the formulas with the cell references. The formulas for %imbalance, $imbalance, and the 10% excess flag are all included.

By way of summary, if we return to figure 7.15, we can see what this part of the spreadsheet for doing the queries and approvals looks like so far. At the top is the criterion area used to specify what item is being sought; below that are the messages for the 10% excess flags. The yes-10%-over and not-10%-over are the actual messages stored in the ranges named >10%T and >10%F. Thus, when the @IF is true, the message in the >10%T is taken; otherwise, the message in >10%F is taken. The last part of figure 7.15 is the database with the calculations for the items approved.

Report: Overage or Savings

After some period of time, perhaps every two weeks, we need to generate reports to see what the current status of purchases is. Are we staying within budget? If there are any specific problems, where are they? We will do one of these reports for illustrative purposes.

This report supplies a detailed picture of all items costing substantially more or less than expected. Ten percent has been set as the critical point. Thus, we will look at all items costing more than 10 percent over, or at least 10 percent under, the authorized amount.

With one or two exceptions, the actual report is not too complicated to prepare. It relies on much of what has already been done. In fact, it takes us back to the DATA

QUERY command, except that now we extract the information from the database rather than just highlighting it, as we did with the FIND command. This extract type of query requires the database as the input range, some criterion, and an output range in which to place the subset of data extracted. The database will stay the same, but we will need a new criterion range and a special area for the output.

Criterion pseudocode The criterion range in this example is a bit more complicated than in the first example. In that example, we had only to specify the item number. Here, the criterion involves what is referred to as Boolean logic—namely, the use of AND and OR to build the criterion expression. To deal with building this more complicated criterion, we will begin with the following pseudocode: select only those items whose cost is more than 10 percent over the budgeted amount or 10 percent or more under the budgeted amount.

Criterion syntax The appropriate syntax for the selection criterion is:

```
%imbalance
%imbal > .1 #OR# %imbal <= -.1
```

Although it may not be immediately apparent, the criterion syntax simply restates the pseudocode. It might be read: is the content of the cell named %imbal greater than 10% or less than or equal to -10%?

With respect to the specifics of the syntax, the %imbalance is the field to be checked. The %imbal is a range name for the cells in the database containing the information on the exact percentage by which the cost exceeds or falls below the budgeted amount. The #OR# is the Boolean operator. (The # before and after the OR is Lotus's way of presenting, or delimiting, the Boolean operator.)

☐ The # signs are sometimes referred to as *delimiters*. They show (or delimit) where a key word, such as OR, starts and ends. As the Lotus program reads each keystroke from left to right, it needs to have a cue that this OR is a special one and not just some range name the analyst is using.

Reading down the %imbalance field (refer back to figure 7.15) shows how the criterion works. The first entry, 1.92%, is neither greater than 10% nor less than or equal to -10%. Therefore, it is not selected. The first one selected is 27.66%.

Output or extract area With the criterion set, we need to designate an output area. For our needs, the output area consists of the names of all the fields (ID#, Budget category, etc.) in the database and space to hold the results.

Figure 7.17 shows the entire setup for this first report. In the upper left is the criterion that will be used to search the database. To the lower right is a title and the output range with all the fields listed. As will be seen, the results are extracted and placed in the space below the field names.

☐ Lotus uses only the bottom row of the field names. The top row is there for readability.

Chapter 7 Structured Managerial Problems

```
     Criterion for
     %imbalance
     +%imbal>0.1#OR#+%imbal<=-0.1

             Date
             Report on Items Costing Over or Under by 10% or More

       Budget    Item         Total              % +/-     $+/-      10% excess
   ID# category descripti budgeted expended  %imbalanc $imbalanc    flag
```

FIGURE 7.17

With everything set—the input range, the criterion, and the output area—the command to produce the report is:

```
/DATA QUERY EXTRACT QUIT
```

As is often the case, the results are more enthralling than the syntax. From this report (figure 7.18), it is apparent that several items far exceed the 10-percent limit; in fact, some costs exceed the budgeted amounts by as much as 50 or 60 percent. Some items are 10 percent or more under the authorized amount, but these do not balance those over the limit. Indeed, perhaps another report should be generated to see if a substantial imbalance is on the horizon.

Automating Printing with Macros

Displaying on the screen the list of items whose costs are substantially over or under the authorized level is fine for the analyst or manager working with the spreadsheet, but it is important to transmit the results to other concerned parties. As in the previous cases, we assume that the report needs to be printed and circulated. We will assume that, in this organization, automation has not extended to permitting electronic messages; that is, there is no way to send the report from one screen to someone else's screen.

Because this report ought to be issued periodically, there should be a way for the analyst to produce it quickly. One way is to program the printing of the report. This entails writing a short program, or macro, that stores all the commands so that it can be run later by pressing just two keys instead of typing an entire set of commands.

In this Lotus spreadsheet, the macro would say: print the range that contains the general report on overage versus savings. We can start by trying the commands that would go into the macro to make sure that the command set we store in the macro will actually work. Basically these are:

```
/PRINT PRINT RANGE sos RETURN GO QUIT
```

This set of commands will print the report stored in sos (summary of overruns and savings). Presumably, at some earlier point we defined the area of the report with the name sos.

```
Date
Report on Items Costing Over or Under by 10% or More


Budget      Item      Total                % +/-     $+/-       10% excess
category    descripti budgeted  expended   %imbalanc $imbalanc  flag
admin       exec chai   $235    $300.00     27.66%   $65.00     yes-10%-over
admin       dictation   $306    $500.00     63.40%   $194.00    yes-10%-over
operate     cellular  $1,000  $1,500.00     50.00%   $500.00    yes-10%-over
operate     vcr         $900    $700.00    -22.22%  ($200.00)   not-10%-over
operate     power saw   $900    $700.00    -22.22%  ($200.00)   not-10%-over
```

FIGURE 7.18

☐ One feature of this set of commands that has value regardless of the computer language (whether Lotus or some other spreadsheet) is naming the range to be printed. Instead of defining the range each time, define it once with a range name and use that range name in the printing command.

The macro, or program, to automate the print command follows these principles:

- Include each keystroke that would normally be used to execute the tasks.
- Use special macro syntax for keystrokes such as the tilde, ~, for pressing the return key.
- Name the entire set of print commands.
- Call on that name whenever you want to print the general report.

The actual macro might read:

```
'/PPRsos~GQ
```

Essentially, it says: send to the printer (PP) whatever is in the range (R) sos. The G is for GO (the command to initiate the actual printing) and the Q is to QUIT the print routine. Those strange marks—namely the ' (single quote) and ~ (tilde)—are part of the special macro language. The ' causes the string of commands (/PPRsos~GQ) to be stored as a label, and the ~ stands for the RETURN (or ENTER) key.

This macro for printing the report can now be executed simply by depressing the ALT key and the name of the macro. We will call this macro g, for general report. The following sidebar provides more details on naming, testing, and executing macros.

☐ Macros need to be named with one character preceded by a backslash (\). To execute, or run, the macro, it is necessary to depress the ALT key and then the single-character name of the macro. There are also ways of debugging mistakes in the macro, including turning on a step-by-step debugging process by depressing the ALT and F2 keys, but we will leave these items for the reader to explore in reference material on Lotus.

■ CONCLUSION

In this chapter, we have examined several everyday problems that require a considerable amount of paperwork and calculations. Microcomputer applications can assist in reducing the tedium of these tasks. The micro does not necessarily enhance the decisions made based on these applications, although more time may be given to thinking about the ramifications of the results. If analysts and managers are freed from some of the time-consuming paperwork, then opportunities are opened for better decision making.

■ EXERCISES

Part 1

A. The data in the partially completed worksheet represent a "generic" budget. The assignment is to complete the worksheet based on the information in the following scenario:

The City of Utter Confusion is attempting to determine its net revenues for the current fiscal year. Information is available for the first three quarters and has already been compiled into the budget format. However, since no actual information is available for the fourth quarter, projections must be made based on the first three quarters' data. In order to simplify matters, all fourth-quarter revenues are assumed to be the average of the previous three quarters. Costs, on the other hand, are increasing by 2.65% from quarter to quarter.

Complete the worksheet by calculating the needed projections. With the projected fourth-quarter data in place, calculate each line-item total, each quarter subtotal, yearly totals, and net revenues (revenues minus costs).

How would the results be different if the fourth-quarter revenues increased 5% from third-quarter levels?

B. Create a worksheet that records your income. The worksheet should track gross income, all taxes and other deductions, and net income. Design the worksheet so that a running total of all categories is presented on the screen at all times. (Note: Since a year's worth of income is likely to exceed the twenty lines typically in view in a spreadsheet, the key is to divide the screen into two parts: a data-entry area and a total presentation area. In Lotus, the WINDOWS command can be used for this purpose.)

C. Using the income worksheet just created, utilize macros or other procedures to produce the following automated features:

- Upon opening the worksheet file, automatic placement of the cursor for data entry.
- A quarterly report of gross income, federal, state, and local taxes.
- Automated entry of a "standard" income line, such as a biweekly paycheck. (How do you handle a raise in the middle of the year?)
- Creation of graphs that offer income comparison by month or by quarter.

Sample Budget

	1ST QTR	2ND QTR	3RD QTR	4TH QTR (PROJ.)	YTD TOTAL (PROJ.)
REVENUES					
Tax Revenues	$185,500	$185,968	$186,436	?	?
Fee Revenues	185,656	186,124	186,592	?	?
Misc. Revenues	185,812	186,280	186,748	?	?
Total Revenues	?	?	?	?	?
COSTS					
Travel	$85,950	$89,736	$93,522	?	?
Personnel	86,581	90,367	94,153	?	?
Training	87,212	90,998	94,784	?	?
Computing	87,843	91,629	95,415	?	?
Operations	88,474	92,260	96,046	?	?
Overhead	89,105	92,891	96,677	?	?
Total Costs	?	?	?	?	?
Net Revenues	?	?	?	?	?

Part 2

A. A frequent analytical task in organizations is the extraction of a subset of information for analysis from a larger data set. To illustrate several of these procedures, this exercise begins with the development of a worksheet containing information related to housing in a community. The first step in this process is the creation of the data set.

   Create a database in a spreadsheet that contains the following information (as column headings or fields):

- Parcel number (consecutive from 1)
- Street address
- Type of dwelling (in the data use the following coding scheme: 1 = single family, 2 = townhouse, 3 = mobile home, 4 = multifamily)
- Total square footage of dwelling
- Assessed valuation
- Property tax (2.5% of assessed valuation)

   Once the headings for the database have been entered on the worksheet, create twenty to twenty-five entries (records) for the data. Create a variety of entries for each of the headings, but make sure that columns such as type of dwelling, square footage, and assessed valuation have several identical values.

B. Using the database just developed, create the following reports based on the data in the database:

- A report that lists each property in order of assessed valuation (highest to lowest)
- A report that lists each property by size (largest to smallest)
- A report that summarizes total assessed valuation, average assessed valuation (using a statistical function such as @AVG), highest and lowest assessed valuation, total property tax revenues, ans average property tax

   (Note: many of these reports are created through the use of DATA commands such as DATA SORT in Lotus.)

C. So far, we have focused on using the entire database to produce reports and summary information. In a real database of this type, there would likely be several hundred to several thousand entries. Often, however, the analyst only needs to deal with information relating to a portion of the total database. Creation of the following reports provides practice in this technique.

   Using data from the housing database, create the following reports:

- A report on the assessed valuation and property tax for all single family dwellings
- A comparison of the average total square footage for each type of dwelling in the database
- A listing of all dwellings, by address, that have an assessed valuation greater than the average assessed valuation
- A report of all dwellings, by type, that have an assessed valuation less than that of the average assessed valuation
- A comparison of the average property tax for townhouses and multifamily dwellings

(Note: There are basically two ways of producing these reports. A crude method is simply to delete unwanted information from a copy of the database. Although this method works, it is tedious and requires a constant reopening of copies of the database to produce other reports. A more sophisticated approach is to use commands such as the DATA QUERY and DATA QUERY EXTRACT commands in Lotus to pull the needed information from the main database and create the report on another area of the worksheet.)

CHAPTER

8

Semistructured and Unstructured Managerial Problems

INTRODUCTION

Purpose and Overview

In this chapter, we move away from the simpler, structured problems of chapter 7 and toward the more complex, semistructured and unstructured types. These problems occur less frequently, are less susceptible to simple decision rules, are affected by multiple factors, and are confounded by political considerations. Sometimes these situations are characterized as choice under uncertainty. Throughout the chapter, we will look at the contribution microcomputer applications can make to dealing with these issues.

As a way of exploring these more complicated problems, we draw on selected topics, specific applications, and certain spreadsheet techniques and functions.

- *Topics:* Planning and financing topics are highlighted because these often involve the difficult choices associated with semistructured and unstructured problems.
- *Applications:* Decision support applications (DSAs) are used because these are designed to handle issues involving choices and options.
- *Spreadsheet techniques and functions:* Macros and menus are used to help automate selection of options and presentation of results. Special formulas related to interest rates, regression analysis, net present value, and cost/benefit are also included because these are frequently involved in complicated decisions.

Topics

The topics of planning and finance frequently cast managers and analysts into areas rife with uncertainty. In planning efforts, managers regularly attempt to project well into the future. Ordinarily, the best that can be done is to rely on past trends and speculation about what will dominate or emerge in years to come. Issues of finance commonly go with planning. For many financial questions, managers must look to the future and try to anticipate the demands that will be placed on government agencies as well as the resources communities and nations will possess to meet these demands.

Decision Support Applications

The framework presented in chapter 4 suggested that decision support applications (DSAs) are most useful in dealing with the type of semistructured and unstructured managerial problems explored in this chapter. In general, DSAs are geared toward examining options and showing at least some of the impacts associated with the choice of one option over another.

Before we proceed to the cases, it will be helpful to provide a short discussion of decision support applications. We will also look at the type of software to be used and how the software can be exploited for these applications.

DSA design requirements Full-fledged decision support applications are formally defined as interactive computer-based systems designed to aid managerial judgment with semistructured and unstructured problems. These extensively developed decision support applications have three major components:

1. models that reflect the interrelations and outcomes associated with the problem or decision under consideration
2. databases that capture the necessary information for the models
3. a user interface that presents the options, choices, and results to the analyst or manager

Because the decision is so prominent in a decision support applications, it provides the starting point. As a result, we ask at the outset: What is the problem or focal point of the decision? What is at stake? What criteria are important? What factors affect and shape the problem? These questions are critical because much of the remaining work will depend on the answers. For example, in one of the cases, the immediate problem is heavily overburdened and congested highways. In this instance, the problem is viewed as one of obtaining ample revenue to improve the road system. The problem could just as well be defined as emanating from too much growth, with the solution focused on growth control.

A related requirement in DSA construction is the reliance on models. Models are used to define and identify what contributes to or explains the problem. Model building revolves around these questions: What are the important elements and factors in the problem? How do these factors interrelate, and what is likely to be most or least important in shaping the problem? Assistance in building such models can come from scanning the professional literature for models already outlined and constructed, tapping the experience of agency staff, and exploring other local experiences. Models can be quite simple or quite complex. We present illustrations of both.

Data also play a special role in the decision support application. No longer are data collected just to keep good records or to keep track of events. Rather, data must reflect the factors that will most likely affect the decision. Those data may very well come from both inside and outside the organization.

The decision support application should also have an easy way of being used. Alternatives important to the decision ought to be readily apparent, and results associated with these alternatives should be displayed prominently.

General design requirements In addition to the specific demands associated with the design of decision support applications, certain general requirements are ever-present in the design of computer applications. Overall, the construction of a decision support application follows the general guidelines laid out in chapter 4: identify the type of problem at hand, divide it into its main components, and proceed toward greater and greater detail (i.e., stepwise refinement) until the application is produced.

DSAs in a micro environment This full-fledged view of decision support applications, with explicit and clearly developed models, databases, and interfaces, may be somewhat compromised in the microcomputer environment. The definition comes primarily from situations in which professional computer analysts are heavily involved in developing the application. With highly trained systems analysts committed to a project, sophisticated applications can be built. In a microcomputer environment, where computer specialists play less of a role, decision support applications will likely begin as partially developed and then perhaps evolve to include all the characteristics of DSAs, strictly defined.

Another term that is used to convey the evolutionary development of decision support applications is *prototyping*. In prototyping, the approach is to develop a working application, experiment with it, and then continue to refine it as time permits. In some cases, a "final" application is never reached. Policy makers and analysts, under the pressures of the moment, take the best they can obtain from the application and weave that information into the decision.

Differences are apparent between the decision support application of this chapter and the operational application of chapter 7. Although both rely on the general design tools of divide and conquer and stepwise refinement to break larger problems into more manageable ones, the operational application is essentially a vehicle for describing, tracking, or summarizing a bureaucratic process. It adds, subtracts, compares, and combines, but it does not give much attention to options and choice among options. The decision support application has at its core the examination of options so that managers can assess the impacts of different courses of action.

DSAs and Spreadsheets

Despite the differences between operational and decision support applications, the spreadsheet is the software of choice for implementing both. The primary value of spreadsheets in building DSAs is their "what if" capacity. In a decision situation, policymakers and analysts wish to examine the outcomes for different alternatives. For example, what happens to a projected deficit if the cost-of-living allowance is reduced from 4 percent to 2 percent, or what happens to traffic congestion if twenty million dollars are cut from the capital improvements budget? Spreadsheets are excellent vehicles for handling these scenarios.

Although the decision support application makes special demands on the way the spreadsheet is used, many of the spreadsheet guidelines discussed in chapter 7 are equally appropriate here. Among these are dividing the spreadsheet into modules and providing a table of contents or menus to usher the user around the spreadsheet.

In addition to the spreadsheet techniques introduced in chapter 7, we will explore several specific spreadsheet capacities that were not discussed in chapter 7. Among these are a technique that allows us to automatically substitute numerous values into what-if calculations, instead of manually changing them one at a time; several new functions, including the calculation of interest payments per period on debt, regression applications for revenue projection, and the calculation of net present value for capital projects; and an automated application in which the user simply enters the values and views the results.

Sophistication of Application Design

Although the decision support applications developed in this chapter are relatively sophisticated, there are always more "bells and whistles" that can be added. In reality, however, managers and analysts, working as end users, simply do not have the time (or sometimes the skill) to elaborate each application to the point where others can use it with little or no knowledge of the software. As a result, some applications will be of the "quick and dirty" type that the analyst uses at his or her desk. Others will be more exhaustive and automated.

What is important, regardless of the level of sophistication, is the soundness of the logic that underlies the application and the use of good design concepts and tools so that applications are valid and flexible enough to accommodate more than one unique decision situation. Without sound logic and good thinking about the problem, the power offered by the spreadsheet application is not fully realized. Without a well-organized and flexible design, the spreadsheet becomes another element of complexity rather than a tool to manage complexity. The cases and spreadsheet applications in this chapter will be designed to show the importance of cogent logic and good organization.

Cases

Three specific cases are examined in this chapter. The first is designed to show how an application can be developed to help with decisions concerning when to sell bonds so that the operating government can maintain adequate cash flow for capital projects. The second case involves examining an array of tax and funding sources to determine the mix of sources that might best fund a road-building effort over a twenty-year period. The last case examines the situation in which a decision needs to be made about the economic viability of a major incinerator project.

■ CASE 1: BUDGETING CASH AND TIMING BOND SALES FOR CAPITAL PROJECTS

Background and Purpose

In this first case, we draw on capital construction projects for our examples. The capital projects could be recreational parks, school buildings, irrigation facilities, or communications towers. Regardless of the nature of the undertaking, these projects are ordinarily sizable in terms of the time it takes to plan, fund, and construct them. Typically, governments (local governments, in this case) authorize large bond issues to fund these projects. For even a small public facility in a congested suburban area, the government may have to authorize ten or fifteen million dollars in bonds to pay for the construction. We are concerned here with one aspect of capital project planning: laying out a plan so

Chapter 8   Semistructured and Unstructured Managerial Problems

that we can see how much cash we will likely have on hand at each stage of the project to pay for the construction. For the most part, this means timing the sale of bonds originally authorized by the governing body so that money is available when needed.

> Governments, often through major banks, sell bonds to investors to finance capital projects. The governments use the money from the bonds to pay for the project. Over a period of time—say ten years—the government will pay the investors back what the investors lent plus interest. Most often, the money to pay back the investors comes from taxes.

This initial case is a decision support application designed to lay out options and help decide on the timing of bond sales to provide and replenish cash for a set of capital projects. In essence, the application is a budgeting and planning exercise. It is done prior to the actual execution of the project. It gives us an idea of what period-by-period borrowing demands we will likely face and how to meet these demands.

The application has several parts. One element is a budget of cash needed for each period the projects run. This period-by-period budgeting of cash is based on experience from prior projects. A second, and main, part of the application is an effort to devise a plan for selling the bonds that will provide the cash. It is usually not fiscally prudent to sell the total amount of bonds authorized prior to the start of the project. Although such action assures that funds will be available, the amount of interest paid will probably be larger than if sales are made closer to the time when the money is needed. Complicating this reasoning, however, is another element that must be incorporated into the application: the variability in interest rates. Even though cash may not need to be replenished at a particular time, prevailing interest rates may be very attractive relative to what the rates are projected to be in future months. Finally, the government needs to watch the size of the total debt as it borrows, so that it does not exceed any of its present debt limits. In our application, we will try to capture all of these dimensions: cash needs, cash flow, interest rate concerns, and debt limit questions.

This is a complex situation that exhibits some of the characteristics of semistructured and unstructured problems. Individuals planning the cash flow and the timing of bond sales face numerous uncertainties. The rate at which cash is used can veer sharply from the expectation. A project may move faster or slower than anticipated and thus throw off the plans set in the original budget. Interest rates can turn up or down very quickly, nullifying the best of schemes. Debt limits can be severe. As a result of the many factors involved and the uncertainty associated with each, the microcomputer application can only act as a decision aid. It cannot substitute totally for the judgment of expert decision makers. In effect, managers siphon information from the application but incorporate other considerations not included in the application.

Using the Spreadsheet

The spreadsheet is an invaluable tool for this problem, with the "what if" capacity being particularly helpful. At numerous intervals, we will want to ask questions such as: what happens to the cash position if we delay borrowing and wait one or two periods before we sell more bonds? The what-if capability permits us to try different strategies and record the results associated with each strategy. In addition, the Lotus spreadsheet that we are using has built-in analytical tools for calculating the impact of several different interest rates on total repayment.

Developing the DSA

Particularly critical in situations where many variables are involved is a specification of what information is desired from the application. Unfortunately, answers to these questions may not be immediately apparent. The complexity of the situation is the first barrier. So much is needed that it is difficult to differentiate between what is important and what can be ignored. Another barrier is misperceptions about the capabilities of microcomputers. Managers and analysts not familiar with computer applications may either over- or underestimate the potential of the microcomputer.

Because of the complexity of the problem, we will approach development of this application iteratively—that is, solidify a few ideas and goals, try them, then move to a more extensive coverage of the problem. Managers and analyst often follow this route. They may not have the time, the computer skills, or the breadth of experience to map out a complete effort.

As a way of adding another element of reality, not only will we take an iterative approach to building this application, but we will also "bungle" one of our first efforts—not to the extent that it does not work, but to the degree that it will represent a poorly constructed and tangled application. Also, in this case, we focus on the flow and ideas involved in building the application. Less attention is given to the syntax used in constructing the application.

First Attempt

The first limited attempt focuses on developing an application that will enable us to assess the impact of different bond sales strategies on the availability of cash for a given project. Specifically, we estimate the amount of money required by a project for each of several periods. Then, we suggest alternative scenarios for bond sales. For each alternative, we look at whether there is too little cash available or too much remaining at the end of each period.

For the purpose of this and subsequent refinements, the general procedure for bond sales is to sell some bonds prior to the start of a project in order to have cash on hand when the project starts and then to sell at the end of each time period if additional funds are necessary.

Rather than belabor all the steps that went into the construction of this application, we will focus on the final product and why it is a clumsy effort.

Figure 8.1 shows the initial version. The first important pieces of information are in the row labeled Budgeted. In this row are the total authorized amount for the project (100 units of cash), the amount borrowed to date (50 units), and the authorized remaining (i.e., not borrowed). Following this information are the budgeted or expected cash needs for the project for each of four time periods. In project 1, 20 units of cash are budgeted for T1, 20 for T2, and 30 each for T3 and T4. The amount budgeted for each of the four time periods (20+20+30+30) equals the total amount authorized for the project (100 units).

Chapter 8   Semistructured and Unstructured Managerial Problems   217

```
              Cash Budget and Bond Sale Analysis


              Total    Borrowed Authorized         Time Periods
Project 1   Authorized to Date  Remaining    T1    T2     T3     T4
---------------------------------------------------------------------
Budgeted       100       50        50        20    20     30     30

Bud. Cum.                                    20    40     70    100

Period Bal.                                  30    10    -20    -50


Props. Sale
```

FIGURE 8.1

    The next row is labeled Bud. Cum., for budget cumulative, and gives the cumulative amount budgeted (or cumulative amounted needed) as we move from period to period. For example, the budget cumulative in T2 is 40, which is the 20 from T2 plus the 20 from T1.

    The Period Bal. (period balance) row represents a critical calculation. It shows how much cash we will have available at the end of each time period. It is calculated by subtracting the budget cumulative amount from the amount borrowed to date. In other words, it tells us how much we will have left after subtracting the cash needed from what we have already borrowed. Scanning the Period Bal. row in figure 8.1 suggests that the project will exhaust the cash borrowed to date sometime during T3 if no new bond sales are undertaken. Specifically, the cash picture in the period balance for T3 falls to -20 units (70, which is the budget cumulative, subtracted from 50, the amount borrowed to date). This, of course, assumes that no new borrowing is initiated.

    The what-if part of the application is contained in the Props. Sale (proposed sale) row. For example, if 50 units of bonds are proposed for sale in T1, that figure is placed in the cell intersected by T1 and Props. Sale (see figure 8.2). The infusion of 50 units of cash then ripples through the relevant parts of the applications—notably, Borrowed to Date and Period Bal. (compare these values in figures 8.1 and 8.2). With a proposed sale to raise 50 units of cash in T1, the period balance changes to 80 in T1 (100-20, or the new Borrowed to Date minus the Bud. Cum.), 60 in T2, 30 in T3, and 0 in at the end of T4. Now the cash picture looks good. At no time is the period balance in a negative, or cash deficient, position.

    Unfortunately, as it stands, this is a clumsy, hard-to-follow application. In particular, the blank space on the left side of the application and the general lack of symmetry make it difficult to read. The titles on the far left (Budgeted, Bud. Cum., etc.) really go with the data under the time periods. Between the titles and the relevant data, however, is other information (Total Authorized, etc.) or blank spaces.

    The application also has a glitch—not a fatal one, but a glitch. If the 50 units were borrowed at the end of T1, the period balance for T1 should not go from 30 units to 80.

PART III Use of the Framework in Developing Applications

```
                 Cash Budget and Bond Sale Analysis

              Total    Borrowed  Authorized        Time Periods
Project 1  Authorized  to Date   Remaining    T1    T2    T3    T4
-----------------------------------------------------------------
Budgeted      100        100         0        20    20    30    30

Bud. Cum.                                     20    40    70   100

Period Bal.                                   80    60    30     0


Props. Sale                                   50
```

FIGURE 8.2

The 50 units sold at the end of T1 should really be reflected in future period balances. That is, we assume that proceeds from the bonds sold at the end of the period go to pay costs in the next or subsequent periods. Worse, even if bonds were sold at the end of T2, the period balance for T1 would increase, given the way the current application is designed.

At this point, we can dismiss the fact that a design flaw exists, or we can go back to the drawing board. Often, the initial inclination is to find a "fix." However, a fix for a flawed application usually makes the application more complex and, therefore, is not worth the time. It takes too long to explain, and errors will creep into the application. In this case, we will go back to the design board.

Second Attempt

This second cut is primarily a redesign to eliminate the glitch encountered in the initial iteration and to make the application easier to follow. The redesign starts by taking a look at the source of the imperfection in the original application. As it turns out, having only one Borrowed to Date (figure 8.2) feeding back into all the period balances is the culprit. Every time an entry is made into Props. Sale, that amount finds its way back to the sole Borrowed to Date amount. Because all the period balances are dependent on that one Borrowed to Date amount, all period balances change, even those that are past. A new design ought to have a separate Borrowed to Date for each time period. This way, additions via proposed sales would not affect the past period balances but only the future ones.

Our new model (see figure 8.3) takes note of the flaws in the original design. For each separate period (T1 through T4), there is a separate Borrowed to Date value. Additionally, we insert both an ending period balance (End. Period Bal.) and a beginning period balance (Beg. Period Bal.) to clarify what we mean by period balance. We also change the layout so that the information is more compactly presented. These changes are shown for a different capital project, project 2.

Chapter 8 Semistructured and Unstructured Managerial Problems

```
                Budgeted Amounts and Bond Sales Analysis
                             Project 2
                               (000)

    Auth. Amt.              400

    Time Period              T1         T2        T3        T4
    ------------------------------------------------------------
    Borrowed to Date        250        250       250       250

    Auth. Remaining         150        150       150       150

    Budgeted                150        100       100        50
    Bud. Cum.               150        250       350       400

    End. Period Bal.        100          0      -100      -150

    Beg. Period Bal.        250        100         0      -100
    Props. Sale
```

FIGURE 8.3

The terminology for the new application is familiar, though arranged differently. For each project, the Auth. Amt. (authorized amount) is located in the upper left corner. The time periods, T1 to T4, are arrayed across the top. Down the left side are the categories or measures that describe the budgeting and status of cash, as well proposed sales of bonds.

The calculations for the various categories are relatively straightforward and can be understood by tracing the values in figure 8.3. However, for completeness, all the definitions are spelled out here:

- Auth. Amt. (authorized amount) is the total amount that can be borrowed, and presumably the total needed to complete the project. In project 2, it is 400 units.
- Borrowed to Date represents how much of the authorized amount has been borrowed. For T1, the Borrowed to Date is the amount of borrowed money we started with, assuming that some money is always borrowed before a project begins. The Borrowed to Date for periods beyond T1 consists of Borrowed to Date from the prior time period plus any new sales from the prior period. (Because we assume that borrowing occurs at the end of a period, the funds from the borrowing are placed only in the next period.)
- Auth. Remaining (authorized remaining) is simply Borrowed to Date subtracted from Auth. Amt.
- Budgeted is the best guess on how much cash will be needed in each period.
- Bud. Cum. (budgeted cumulative) is the accumulation of budgeted dollars from period to period. For example, Bud. Cum. in T2 is 250, or the sum of Budgeted in T1 (150) and Budgeted in T2 (100).
- End. Period Bal. (ending period balance) is Bud. Cum. subtracted from Borrowed to

```
                Budgeted Amounts and Bond Sales Analysis
                              Project 2
                                (000)

Auth. Amt.                  400

Time Period                 T1         T2         T3         T4
-------------------------------------------------------------------
Borrowed to Date            250        350        400        400

Auth. Remaining             150         50          0          0

Budgeted                    150        100        100         50
Bud. Cum.                   150        250        350        400

End. Period Bal.            100        100         50          0

Beg. Period Bal.            250        200        150         50
Props. Sale                 100         50
```

FIGURE 8.4

Date. The ending period balance for T2 is 0 because the Bud. Cum. of 250 subtracted from Borrowed to Date of 250 leaves 0 dollars.
- Beg. Period Bal. (beginning period balance), with the exception of T1, is Borrowed to Date minus the previous Bud. Cum. Thus, for example, the Beg. Period Bal. for T2 (100) is Borrowed to Date for T2 (250) minus Bud. Cum. for T1 (150).
- Props. Sale (proposed sale) is how much we propose to sell in the bond market to raise cash.

Testing alternative strategies With our refurbished application, we can return to assessing strategies for maintaining adequate cash flow in our project. After examining the ending period balances in figure 8.3, it is apparent that some sales will probably be necessary in T1 because without any sales, the ending period balance will drop to 0 in T2 and -100 in T3.

With 150 units of authorized money remaining in T1, we will split that between T1 and T2, selling 100 units in T1 and 50 in T2. Figure 8.4 shows that selling 100 units in T1 and 50 in T2 solves the cash problem. Comparing figure 8.3 with figure 8.4, we can see that the ending period balance for T2 goes from 0 to 100, the -100 in T3 goes to 50, and the -150 in T4 falls to 0. A 0 in the ending balance for T4 is acceptable because T4 is the last period and a 0 means that all the cash has been exhausted.

The what-if in figure 8.4 works in the following manner. The proposed sales in T1 (100) are added to the T2 borrowed to date (250), for a total borrowed to date in T2 of 350. The budget cumulative is then subtracted from the borrowed to date (350 – 250) to give the ending period balance of 100.

☐ The period balances in this application are not designed to go to zero when a period is completed. When the projects are actually being carried out, the application to track the execution of the

Chapter 8 Semistructured and Unstructured Managerial Problems

```
         Budgeted Amounts and Bond Sales Analysis
         Project 2
         (000)

Auth. Amt.                    400

Time Period                   T1        T2        T3        T4
-----------------------------------------------------------------
Borrowed to Date              250       300       375       400

Auth. Remaining               150       100        25         0

Budgeted                      150       100       100        50
Bud. Cum.                     150       250       350       400

End. Period Bal.              100        50        25         0

Beg. Period Bal.              250       150       125        50
Props. Sale                    50        75        25
```

FIGURE 8.5

projects would have to be dynamic in nature, allowing for decrements to zero in any given period with the remaining money carried forward.

With this scenario of sales (100 in T1 and 50 in T2), the cash problem is resolved, but at the cost of heavy borrowing early in the project. Is it possible to string out the borrowing? Because the application is primed for this type of what-if, let us try a sales sequence that spreads the sales over a longer period—for example, selling 50 units in T1, 75 in T2, and 25 in T3. As shown in figure 8.5, the cash problem is not exacerbated; neither the T2 nor T3 ending period balance descends into the minus or zero category. In T2, the ending period balance is 50; in T3, it is 25; and in T4, it is 0. The what-ifs can continue in this trial-and-error fashion.

To provide a more in-depth understanding of the workings of this application, a screen print of the syntax is given in figure 8.6. The screen print displays all the formulas and their exact cell locations. Note, for example, that Borrowed to Date in T2 is the sum of cells C47 plus C57—that is, Borrowed to Date from T1 plus Props. Sale at the end of T1. Using this screen print, the entire application can be reproduced and run.

Displaying all strategies As the application stands, one would need to print each new bond sales trial to compare the results. That is to say, figures 8.4 and 8.5 would both need to be printed to compare the different sales strategies. A preferable route is to transport these alternative sales scenarios and results to another part of the spreadsheet so that they can all be compared at once. This improvement can be accomplished with the aid of Lotus's macro language.

Reliance on pseudocode plus a good knowledge of Lotus syntax will help produce a macro to accomplish the task of creating a table of results. Assuming that a particular

```
37
38
39              Budgeted Amounts and Bond Sales Analysis
40                              Project 2
41                                (000)
42
43  Auth. Amt.                  400
44
45  Time Period                  T1              T2              T3              T4
46  ------------------------------------------------------------------------------------
47  Borrowed to Date            250          +C47+C57        +D47+D57        +E47+E57
48
49  Auth. Remaining         +$C$43-C47      +$C$43-D47      +$C$43-E47      +$C$43-F47
50
51  Budgeted                    150             100             100              50
52  Bud. Cum.                  +C51         +D51+C52        +E51+D52        +F51+E52
53
54  End. Period Bal.    +$C$47-$C$52   +$D$47-$D$52   +$E$47-$E$52   +$F$47-$F$52
55
56  Beg. Period Bal.           +C47         +D47-C52        +E47-D52        +F47-E52
57  Props. Sale                 50              75              25

    A           B              C              D              E              F
```

FIGURE 8.6

sales strategy has already been completed and a transfer of results is in order, the pseudocode would be as follows:

- Go to the Props. Sales row (figure 8.4) and copy that row from its original location to an empty, new location in the spreadsheet. Each time a new proposed sales pattern is tried, that constitutes a new bond sales or timing strategy.
- Go to the End. Period Bal. row and "transport" the results to one row below the copied Props. Sales in the new report area. This shows the results for a given bond sales strategy.
- Go to the output or results area and review the results.
- Repeat as many times as you change the proposed sales strategy.

With a few exceptions, most of the syntax for this pseudocode would not be difficult to find in a Lotus manual. One exception is the command that enables you to "move one row below" the last filled cell (or row) in the results table. This need arises when you wish to add a new row of alternatives and a new row of ending period balances to the results area. The command to move the cell pointer past the last filled row is {END} and, in our case, {DOWN 2}. When the {END} {DOWN 2} sequence is encountered, the cursor goes to the last filled cell (i.e., END) and then down one more to avoid overwriting the contents of the last filled cell.

☐   Reserved words from the Lotus 1-2-3 syntax are capitalized, as with END or DOWN.

Chapter 8   Semistructured and Unstructured Managerial Problems

```
                Macro to Generate Alternative Results
\b      {GOTO}p2alt~
        /Cp2alt~{UP 20}{RIGHT 8}{END}{DOWN 2}~
        {GOTO}p2oc~
        /RVp2oc~{UP 17}{RIGHT 8}{END}{DOWN 2}~
        {GOTO}altocs~
```

FIGURE 8.7

The other bit of syntax that might be difficult to unearth is the command to "transport" the values in the row of cells for ending period balance. The word "transport" is used to differentiate it from copy. With a COPY command, any formulas in the cells are copied. Copying the formulas from the original location to the report area would do us no good. As soon as we made another change in Props. Sale, the copied row of End. Period Bal. in the report would change to reflect the new status of sales.

What we want are the *values* in End. Period Bal. for the Props. Sale with which the balances are associated, not the formulas. The Lotus command that enables us to transport the values only from one part of the worksheet to another is /RANGE VALUE. This command transfers the value from End. Period Bal. (e.g., 100, figure 8.5), not the formula in the cell (e.g., +$C$47 − $C$52, figure 8.6).

With this preliminary discussion on syntax, we can now translate the pseudocode into the macro. Figure 8.7 shows the macro used to generate a table of results. The first line of the macro says to go to the row where the proposed sales are stored (named p2alt, or project 2 alternatives). Next we copy (/C or /COPY) the proposed sales row to a location up 20, right 8, and down to the first clear row. Essentially we are finding a clear area to the right of the project table. The copy command is acceptable in this situation because no formulas are in the Props. Sale row. Once the Props. Sale row has been copied, we go to the End. Period Bal. row (name, p2oc, or project 2 outcomes), then "transport" the values (/RV or /RANGE VALUES) up 17, to the right 8, and finally to the first clear row in the results table. The last thing we do is go to the results table (named altocs, alternative outcomes) to review what we have placed there.

The \b to the left of the macro is the name of the macro. Recall that macros are named with one letter and identified as macro names via the backslash (\).

As it stands, the macro is designed only for the second capital project. The range name, p2alt, is the specific row for proposed sales in project 2. Similarly, the p2oc is the range name for the ending period balance in project 2. The altocs is the report area designated to receive the results from the second project.

The macro could be generalized by inserting the prompt command, {?}, where the range names are for proposed sales, ending period balance, and report table. The {?} command causes the macro to pause and allows the user to make the appropriate input. With this generalization, the macro could be used to construct bond sales results tables for other capital projects.

224   PART III   Use of the Framework in Developing Applications

```
    Macro for Automating Bond Sales Strategies

    \a          {GOTO}p2alt~{RIGHT}
                {GETNUMBER "Amt Sold T1 ",C57}{RIGHT}
                {GETNUMBER "Amt Sold T2 ",D57}{RIGHT}
                {GETNUMBER "Amt Sold T3 ",E57}{RIGHT}
```

FIGURE 8.8

This macro could even be expanded via the {GETNUMBER} command to allow the user to automate the changing of the bond sales strategy. With this expanded macro, the user would be prompted to input the number of units to sell in T1 through T3. With this macro, we get closer to an application that is fully automated.

Figure 8.8 shows this automated macro. It starts by going to the row where the proposed sales (named p2alt) will be entered, then moves one cell to the right so that the cursor is on the cell for entering the proposed sales for T1. Next, with the GETNUMBER command, the user is required to enter the amount of the sales for T1 by responding to the prompt, "Amt Sold T1." The user continues to enter bond sales by depressing the ENTER key and responding to the next prompt for entering the number of units to be sold. The process is repeated until all three entries—T1 through T3—have been made (T4 should always be 0 because we sell at the end of all periods and T4 marks the end of the project).

Integral to a macro such as the one in figure 8.8, but not included in this one, is a check to determine whether the bond sales proposed push the borrowed total beyond the amount authorized. In a free cell to the right of the last cell for entering bond sales could be a statement designed to determine whether the amount authorized has been exceeded. If so, there could be two beeps. If not, then a message such as "Total OK" might appear. We accomplish this with an @IF statement that says, in effect, if the total of the proposed sales exceeds the authorized amount, type the word "beep" and give two beeps; otherwise, type the phrase "Total OK."

Figure 8.9 gives the results table generated by the macro in figure 8.7. It allows us to compare alternative strategies for bond sales. As we have already seen, we can stretch out the sales over three periods—that is, 50 in T1, 75 in T2, and 25 in T3—and perhaps save on interest payments, without encountering any cash flow problems.

Third Iteration

The third embellishment of this bond sales decision aid is adding a table to capture the impact of these bond sales on any debt limits this government has set for itself. Typically, local governments can borrow only so much. What might appear to be a viable bond sales strategy in terms of providing an adequate cash flow may not be acceptable in terms of proscribed debt limits.

For purposes of illustration in this case, two limits are used: debt as a percentage of assessed real property value, and debt per capita. For the first limit, we do not want our

```
    Outcomes for Different Bond Sales Alternatives
Alternatives      T1        T2        T3        T4
Props. Sale      100        50
End. Period      100       100        50         0
Props. Sale       50        75        25
End. Period      100        50        25         0
```

FIGURE 8.9 Third iteration

```
              Debt, Bond Sales, and Debt Limits
                           (000)
Category           T1         T2         T3        T4
------------------------------------------------------
Total
Debt              1075     1139.17    1126.19   1088.65

Retired          35.83      37.97      37.54     36.29

3% of Assessed
  Value?         2.24%      2.37%      2.34%     2.27%

$.015/
  Capita?       0.0134     0.0142     0.0140    0.0136

Total Proposed
Bond Sales         75        100         25         0
```

FIGURE 8.10

total debt to exceed 3 percent of the assessed value of all property. For the second, we are reluctant to see total debt go beyond .015 per capita (however, remember that the figures are in thousands of dollars).

Figure 8.10 outlines our debt limit table. The total proposed sales for each time period for all the capital projects is captured in the last row, Total Proposed Bond Sales. For T1 it is 75, meaning that the combined sales for projects 1 and 2 for time period T1 come to 75 units. That amount is added to Total Debt in the first row. In essence, we are adding the total proposed bond sales to the amount of debt the government is already carrying. To capture the fact that some part of the debt is paid off each period, the calculation of Total Debt is rounded out by retiring 1/30 of the debt in each period. Total Debt is then compared to each of the criterion limits to determine whether the limits have been exceeded. So far, neither of the limits (3% of Assessed Value, $.015/capita) have been exceeded.

Let us take a closer look at the mechanisms in figure 8.10. The 75 in Total Proposed Bond Sales for T1 is added to a preexisting debt of 1000 (in the formula but not shown) to yield a Total Debt for T1 of 1075. Of the 1075, 1/30 or 35.83 is retired in T2, but 100 of new debt is added in, resulting in a new Total Debt of 1139.17. The 1139.17 is compared with the assessed property value (which is in the formula for 3% of Assessed Value) and with the per capita restriction (in the formula for $.015/Capita). Neither restriction is exceeded. The same process can be continued for T3 and T4.

Although we have put a good deal into this table, we need to do more work to complete it. As it stands, the table on debt limits is helpful but not yet realistic. The amount of total proposed bond sales is only part of the amount that goes into total debt. Interest on the bonds must be added. In some cases, it can double the amount originally borrowed. For this reason, we need one more refinement.

Fourth Iteration

The final enhancement to the application is to include interest rates as a consideration in timing bond sales and in calculating the total cost of borrowing. High interest rates mean the bonds will be more costly; low interest rates bring down the cost of financing.

Besides making the application more realistic, the inclusion of interest rates provides an opportunity to demonstrate several capabilities of spreadsheets. Most spreadsheets have built-in functions to calculate the payment for given interest rates. Many spreadsheets also have ways of varying the interest rate in order to show the impact of different rates on payments. Lotus has both these capacities.

To calculate the cost of selling bonds at a given interest rate, we will use a simple formula—principal times interest rate—that assumes that interest is a flat percentage of principal. For example, if the interest rate were 6 percent when the 75 units of bonds were sold, then the interest payment would be 4.5 units per period. Figure 8.11 shows the interest payments at 6 percent. It is assumed that the interest on the 75-unit loan will be paid each period until the loan matures and that the 75 units will then be paid in full.

For simplicity, we will assume that the interest stated is for whatever length of time the period is, although the interest rates are assumed to be per annum. Thus, if our periods were really six months, the annual rate would be 12 percent.

Because we do not know whether we will be able to sell our bonds at the target rate of 6 percent and because rates can change over time, we have extended our analysis of the impact of interest rates to include other possible rates—namely, 6.5 percent, 7 percent, and 8 percent. Lotus permits us to calculate the payments for all these interest rates with one command, DATA TABLE. Essentially, this command replaces the 6-percent interest rate in the principal-times-interest-rate formula with each of the other rates and gives a payment for each rate. In other words, when the rate is 6.5 percent, then .065 is substituted for .06 in the formula, and so on for each interest rate.

To use the /DATA TABLE command, it is necessary first to arrange the data in a way prescribed by Lotus. The range of interest rates to be included in the what-if analysis must be arrayed in a column with an empty column to the right of it. It is in this empty column that Lotus will place the payment per period for each interest rate. Directly above the empty column (in actuality, where the 4.50 is in figure 8.11) goes the formula, principal*interest rate. All that remains is execution of the /DATA TABLE command. The execution is: /DATA TABLE 1 (1 stands for 1 input column), then a prompt for the

```
                    Debt, Bond Sales, and Debt Limits
                            with Interest Rates
                                   (000)

    Category              T1        T2        T3        T4
    ----------------------------------------------------------
    Total
    Debt                1075     1139.17   1126.19   1088.65

    Retired             35.83     37.97     37.54     36.29

    3% of Assessed
      Value?            2.24%     2.37%     2.34%     2.27%
    $.015/
      Capita?           0.0134    0.0142    0.0140    0.0136

    Total Proposed
      Bond Sales          75       100        25         0

    Target Interest Rate
              0.06
         Other
    Interest Rates   Payment
                       4.50
             0.065     4.88
             0.07      5.25
             0.08      6.00
```

FIGURE 8.11

table range. The range includes the column with the interest rates, the empty column to its right, and the cells above the range where the formula is placed. The last prompt from Lotus is for the input cell. The input cell is where your original interest rate is located. In our case, it is the target rate of 6 percent. If all placements and commands have been carried out correctly, each alternative or other interest rate is inserted into the input cell and a payment per period is given for all the interest rates, including the original rate. For T1, the payment for the original rate is given where we placed the formula. The other payments are given in the cells to the right of each rate. For example, the payment at 8 percent is 6.00 units (see figure 8.11).

Because we will be borrowing in other periods, we also want to look at rates in those periods. According to the economic forecast available to us for T2 and T3, interest rates are expected to go down, which reinforces our inclination to hold off on borrowing.

Figure 8.12 shows the interest payments per period assuming different interest rates in T1, T2, and T3. Specifically, at the target rate of 6 percent in T1, the cost of borrowing 75 units is 4.50; at the target rate of 5.75 percent in T2, the cost of borrowing 100 units is 5.75; and at the target rate of 5.5 percent in T3, the cost of borrowing 25 units is 1.38.

```
                    Debt, Bond Sales, and Debt Limits
                            with Interest Rates
                                   (000)

Category                T1         T2         T3         T4
-----------------------------------------------------------------
Total
Debt                   1075      1139.17    1126.19    1088.65

Retired                35.83      37.97      37.54      36.29

3% of Assessed
  Value?               2.24%      2.37%      2.34%      2.27%

$.015/
  Capita?              0.0134     0.0142     0.0140     0.0136

Total Proposed
  Bond Sales           75         100        25         0

Target Interest Rate
              0.06                0.0575                0.055
        Other
  Interest Rates    Payment               Payment               Payment
                     4.50                  5.75                  1.38
           0.065     4.88       0.06       6.00       0.06       1.50
           0.07      5.25       0.07       7.00       0.065      1.63
           0.08      6.00       0.075      7.50       0.07       1.75
```

FIGURE 8.12

With interest rates predicted to decline, we may now want to go back and see if we can spread out the borrowing even more into periods T2 and T3.

Finally, we need to add the interest payments and return to the debt limits. It may be necessary to rethink the borrowing strategy because, now that we have included interest payments as part of the cost of borrowing, one of the two debt limit criteria may be exceeded. In figure 8.13, we see that the per capita amount goes quite close to the $.015 limit in T2 and stays near it for the remaining periods. With higher interest rates or greater borrowing demands, that per capita limit may be exceeded. Given that the decision aid in figure 8.13 has been set up to do any number of what-ifs, it is possible to see at what borrowing level and interest the debt limits might be exceeded.

In a situation this complex and with uncertainty surrounding all the elements, the decision makers may override the data or results of the application. The application provides information, but it does not provide final answers. For example, managers may feel that they will be left too vulnerable by dragging out the sale of bonds over several periods. They may feel that a cash shortfall would be so embarrassing that this possibility outweighs the small savings to be derived by holding off on borrowing. Any number of

Chapter 8 Semistructured and Unstructured Managerial Problems

```
                    Debt, Bond Sales, and Debt Limits
                           with Interest Rates
                                  (000)

Category                  T1       T2       T3       T4
------------------------------------------------------------
Total
Debt                    1079.5  1153.77  1151.93  1125.16

Retired                  35.98    38.46    38.40    37.51

3% of Assessed
  Value?                  2.25%    2.40%    2.40%    2.34%

$.015/
  Capita?                0.0135   0.0144   0.0144   0.0140

Total Proposed
  Bond Sales               75      100       25        0

Target Interest Rate
        0.06                      0.0575             0.055
    Other
    Interest Rates   Payment              Payment             Payment
                       4.50                 5.75                1.38
         0.065         4.88       0.06      6.00      0.06      1.50
         0.07          5.25       0.07      7.00      0.065     1.63
         0.08          6.00       0.075     7.50      0.07      1.75

Cumulative              4.5                10.25               11.63
Interest Payment
for Target Interest Rate
```

FIGURE 8.13

managerial practices or political preference may have priority over the results derived from the application.

CASE 2: FINANCING LOCAL HIGHWAY IMPROVEMENTS

Purpose

In this second case, we set out to build an application that will help find a mix of financial funding sources productive enough to meet the huge dollar demands of an extensive road construction program. The case offers an opportunity to use the capability of spreadsheets (Lotus in particular) to project or extrapolate long-term trends in these funding sources.

PART III   Use of the Framework in Developing Applications

To perform these projections, we will use some fairly sophisticated projection methods, such as regression, and several less complicated methods, such as annual percentage change. Extensive use will be made of the what-if power of Lotus to see how funding projections change under different assumptions.

To a considerable extent, the design of this case will follow what is commonly called a "bottom-up approach." Work will be done within individual modules first, with each module focusing on a set of funding sources. After all the individual modules have been completed, a way will be devised for the modules to work together. This bottom-up approach is quite common in the fast-paced world of government managers and analysis. We will see some of the difficulties and complications this approach entails.

Overall, this case offers an excellent illustration of building a decision support application with a spreadsheet. At almost every step, there are choices and options. Using the what-if power of the spreadsheet, different assumptions can be entered in order to observe the results and examine their viability.

The Problem

The particular problem at hand is finding adequate long-term financing (over a twenty-year period) to construct enough road capacity to ameliorate an areawide traffic congestion problem. The heart of the task consists of:

- developing an overall model that shows how the different parts of the problem affect each other
- estimating total capital (dollars) needed to build sufficient road capacity to reduce the congestion to tolerable levels
- identifying alternative sources of funding to raise the capital
- projecting amounts that can be obtained from these sources
- finding the mix of funding sources considered best (a mix that is both productive and politically feasible) for meeting the total capital needs

Background, Goals, and Constraints

The cause of the congestion in this jurisdiction is the level of economic growth and failure of road construction to keep pace with increased traffic. In the transportation literature, level of service (smooth traffic flow) is measured on a scale of A to F, with A being the least congested and F, the most. In our case, the situation has deteriorated from B and C to D and E, and in some instances, F.

The jurisdiction has a number of options for combating this traffic congestion problem. It can control growth, manage traffic better, or build more roads. Because most of the area's influential leaders, as well as the general population favor continued economic growth and development, the option chosen by policy makers is to add more road capacity rather than halt growth. Adding capacity, however, entails substantial financial strains. In the past, much of the highway funding has come from the state or federal government, but neither has sufficient resources to fund large parts of the current need. In particular, obtaining more aid from the federal government is not a viable option.

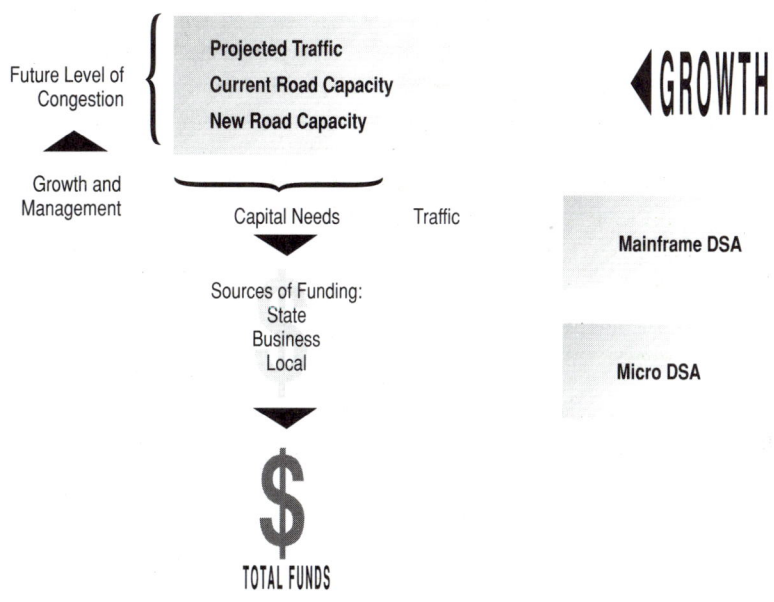

FIGURE 8.14 Transportation model

Model and Elements

Although the decision support application we will build covers only a limited aspect of the entire traffic problem—namely, finding adequate funding—we will outline a more exhaustive model in order to provide a fuller picture of the problem and factors involved. Figure 8.14 depicts the model. The first elements in the model are growth and the impact growth has on projected traffic. In turn, it is these traffic projections overlain on the current road capacity that are used to estimate future congestion. If growth and traffic increase without more roads being added to the current supply, congestion will worsen. Growth management and traffic management are also depicted in figure 8.14 (see left side) and can also have an impact on congestion, but are not among the central variables for reducing congestion.

With a picture of future levels of congestion, the next task is determining how much capital is required to reduce congestion. In this part of the model, new road capacity is added until congestion falls to a tolerable range, which is considered to be at the C level on the scale. The amount of money needed to reduce congestion to this level establishes the capital needs. In short, it is the cost of new road capacity needed to bring congestion to tolerable levels that defines the total capital expenditure required.

Once the total capital requirement has been established, attention turns to possible funding sources and how much of the needed capital they can provide.

Exchange Among Computer Models

In actuality, very few factors in the model in figure 8.14 are covered in the microcomputer-based decision support application. Growth, traffic projections, new road capacity, and needed capital investments are all calculated in a sophisticated simulation model run on a mainframe computer. Growth control and traffic management are also excluded from the microcomputer DSA. The primary focus of the microcomputer DSA is the various sources of funding and the dollars that each can generate over a twenty-year period.

Exchanges among computers take place because different computers have different strengths and weakness. Mainframes are often used when large amounts of data and demanding calculations are involved. In addition, a model may be implemented on a particular computer purely because of the history of computer use in the organization. For example, an organization may have invested heavily in mainframes and used those machines for their modeling. Now, the micros take data from these mainframe programs and do the more focused analysis.

Developing the Microcomputer DSA

The microcomputer decision support application, then, is limited to funding questions: alternative sources of funding, how much can be obtained from each, and whether any reasonable mix of funding sources can produce enough dollars to meet the total capital requirement for new roads.

The point of departure for building the funding decision support application is the total capital needed over a twenty-year period (assumed to be 1986–2005). Using the projections of the mainframe metropolitan simulation model, the total capital investment required for this jurisdiction to maintain reasonable traffic conditions (level C) is about two billion dollars (in 1986 dollars). The model also suggests that a 30-percent higher level of funding would yield a noticeably better road system (level B) and a 30-percent shortfall would have the opposite effect, noticeably worse results (level D).

Beginning the Divide and Conquer: Major Funding Sources

With the capital outlay estimated by the mainframe model to be two billion dollars, the initial broad question in building the micro application is identifying the major sources of funding. This will allow us to concentrate our energies and skills on discrete types of funding. At least in the beginning, we will work within each source to ascertain how much can be derived from that source. We might even have particular individuals focus on each source to speed the work, assigning people with special skills to concentrate on their area of expertise. Later, we will assemble and juggle all the viable funding sources to see how they can be manipulated to meet the total capital requirement.

Assuming that little money can be expected from the federal government, the major categories of funding are:

- state funds—formula-driven transfers from the state to the locality
- business extractions—contributions businesses make above and beyond regular taxes in order to gain the privilege of developing in congested or potentially congested areas
- local funds—typically, taxes and general obligation bonds

Of these sources, the one that is unusual is business extraction (also called exaction). Ordinarily, businesses pay their taxes and fees and contribute no more to finance public services. However, because of the enormous shortfall occurring in road construction and because of the problems created by rapid economic growth across the nation, many communities in areas of rapid growth are imposing various types of surcharges on business to pay for the physical improvements needed to handle the growth.

Building the First Worksheet

Given these three major funding sources, a possible first step in building our decision support application is to develop some estimate of the percentage that ought to be derived from each of the three sources. This estimate is very rough and probably driven by "gut" political feelings and general knowledge of the potential of each source.

Initially, the shares for the three primary funding sources are pegged at one-third each. This is probably high in terms of business extractions (since businesses already pay taxes), but because of the considerable economic development taking place, businesses may have to be pushed for more than what they view as their fair share.

With these targets and assumptions set, it is possible to put together our beginning worksheet for the microcomputer DSA. Shown in figure 8.15, it contains the total capital requirements for good, adequate, and poor traffic movement; the allocation of these totals among the three main sources (state, business, and local); and the assumptions that drive the allocations. We see, for example, that to meet the capital needs for good traffic movement we must obtain $867 million ($866,666,667) from each of the three sources. That figure falls to $467 million if we can (or must) live with poor traffic movement.

The Power of Generalization

This spreadsheet, though simple on the surface, reinforces several of the advantages of spreadsheets as well as a number of lessons discussed earlier in constructing spreadsheets.

Although not directly apparent from the spreadsheet in figure 8.15, this worksheet has what-if power built into it. It is possible to change any of the assumptions in the bottom row and have those changes automatically reflected throughout the worksheet. For example, if elected officials saw the assumption of one-third coming from business extraction as too high, then business extractions could be lowered to 20 percent with state and local splitting the remaining 80 percent. All one needs to do in order to recalculate the contributions is type the new percentages in the appropriate assumption cells: under state contribution, 40% (actually, .4); under business, 20%; and under local, 40%. Figure 8.16 shows the results: business contributions are now $400 million for adequate roads, compared to $667 million when one-third of all contributions came from business.

This what-if capability is achieved through the spreadsheet's built-in power of *generalization*. It is harnessed by employing formulas with cell locations (or range names), instead of actual values (i.e., numbers or constants), in the body of the spreadsheet. If actual values (such as 33.33%) were used in calculations (such as dollars needed from the state), then new calculations could be made only by changing that value wherever it appeared. Instead of the specific value, therefore, it is the cell reference for state contribution that goes into the formulas used in calculating the dollars needed from the state. This use of formulas with cell references is like having a direct pipeline or mechanical arm from the assumption cells to the cells where the dollar values are determined. Change the assumption, and the change is transmitted to the target cells.

```
                    Twenty-Year Highway Program
                           CAPITAL NEEDS
                               and
              Relative Contribution of Major Funding Sources

Traffic
Movement          Total             State           Business           Local
-------------------------------------------------------------------------------
good         $2,600,000,000      $866,666,667     $866,666,667     $866,666,667
adequate     $2,000,000,000      $666,666,667     $666,666,667     $666,666,667
poor         $1,400,000,000      $466,666,667     $466,666,667     $466,666,667
-------------------------------------------------------------------------------

                               Assumptions

                  Capital         State            Business           Local
                   band        contribution      contribution      contribution
              -----------------------------------------------------------------
                  30.00%          33.33%            33.33%            33.33%


Notes: The total needed for adequate traffic
movement comes from the Metropolitan Computer
Simulation. It is based on the road capacity
needed to achieve a C level of service. The
30% band for good versus poor traffic also
comes from the simulation. The allocation of
1/3 to each of the three sources is a starting
estimation. It will be adjusted as empirical
estimates are made for each source.
```

FIGURE 8.15

Figure 8.17 shows the formulas used to generate the results in figures 8.15 and 8.16. For example, the cell where we calculate state funds needed for good traffic movement contains the formula $B$11*C$21. B11 is the reference to the $2.6 billion, which was shown as the total for good traffic movement in figure 8.15; the use of the dollar sign ($) will be explained a little later. Cell 21, from the assumptions area, contains the percentage to be contributed by the state—33.33% in figure 8.15, 40% in figure 8.16. This formula serves to generalize the calculation, enabling us to substitute any value for percentage contribution by the state. In fact, we could name this variable %state and have the formula read $B$11*%state, where * is the multiplication sign and %state refers to the content of cell C21 in the assumptions section.

In actuality, the formulas can be more complex than alluded to in the above paragraph but to convey the idea of generalization, we have presented a simplified version. We will return to these formulas later, after we have seen how much the various sources can produce.

```
                  Twenty-Year Highway Program
                          CAPITAL NEEDS
                              and
              Relative Contribution of Major Funding Sources

  Traffic
  Movement         Total            State          Business           Local
  ---------------------------------------------------------------------------
  good      $2,600,000,000    $1,040,000,000    $520,000,000    $1,040,000,000
  adequate  $2,000,000,000      $800,000,000    $400,000,000      $800,000,000
  poor      $1,400,000,000      $560,000,000    $280,000,000      $560,000,000
  ---------------------------------------------------------------------------

                               Assumptions

                 Capital          State          Business           Local
                  band        contribution     contribution      contribution
                 ---------------------------------------------------------------
                 30.00%           40.00%           20.00%            40.00%


  Notes: The total needed for adequate traffic
  movement comes from the Metropolitan Computer
  Simulation. It is based on the road capacity
  needed to achieve a C level of service. The
  30% band for good versus poor traffic also
  comes from the simulation. The allocation of
  each of the three sources is a starting
  estimation. It will be adjusted as empirical
  estimates are made for each source.
```

FIGURE 8.16

State Contributions Module

The first major funding source for local highway construction is state contributions. The dominant sources of state highway funds have been dedicated fuel taxes, vehicle taxes, and fees. As dedicated revenues, these can be used only for transportation expenditures. Each locality in the state receives a share of these taxes and fees according to a formula.

Our immediate task is to estimate how much can be expected from the state over a two-decade period. In general, this means looking at what has been funneled to the locality in the past and then using a set of assumptions to project into the future. Broadly, those assumptions can be that the situation will stay the same, get better, or grow worse. Ordinarily it is good practice to do at least an optimistic and a pessimistic calculation.

☐ Although data from 1985 are available and included in estimating trends, the two-decade period for calculating funds from the state covers the years 1986 to 2005. The reason for excluding 1985

```
                        Twenty-Year Highway Program
                              CAPITAL NEEDS
                                   and
                 Relative Contribution of Major Funding Sources

          A              B              C              D              E
 1
 2
 3
 4
 5
 6
 7
 8   Traffic
 9   Moveme        Total          State          Business       Local
10   -------------------------------------------------------------------
11   good     (1+$B$21)*B12    +$B$11*C$21    +$B$11*D$21    +$B$11*E$21
12   adequa       2000000000   +$B$12*C$21    +$B$12*D$21    +$B$12*E$21
13   poor     +B12-(($B$21)*B12) +$B$13*C$21  +$B$13*D$21    +$B$13*E$21
14   -------------------------------------------------------------------
15
16                              Assumptions
17
18              Capital         State         Business        Local
19              band         contribution   contribution   contribution
20   -------------------------------------------------------------------
21               0.3             0.4            0.2            0.4
22
```

FIGURE 8.17

from the total projected state contribution is that the study began in 1985. As a result, the interest was in the next two decades.

To start the projection, we look at the revenues targeted for this jurisdiction. The graph in figure 8.18 represents how much this particular locality has received (or will receive) in the period 1985–1990. Without any statistical work, it is clear that the dollars from the state are on a downward trend.

☐   The graph in figure 8.18 was produced using Lotus's /GRAPH command.

In the face of this downward trend, we are going to make two projections. The pessimistic one assumes that the trend will continue on a path very similar to one in the period 1985–1990. The other, more optimistic projection assumes that the trend will continue downward but at a slower, more gradual pace. We can visualize the pessimistic trend as a straight line to zero dollars and the optimistic as a bowed curve with the amounts getting smaller but not hitting zero.

Chapter 8 Semistructured and Unstructured Managerial Problems 237

State Contributions
six-year period

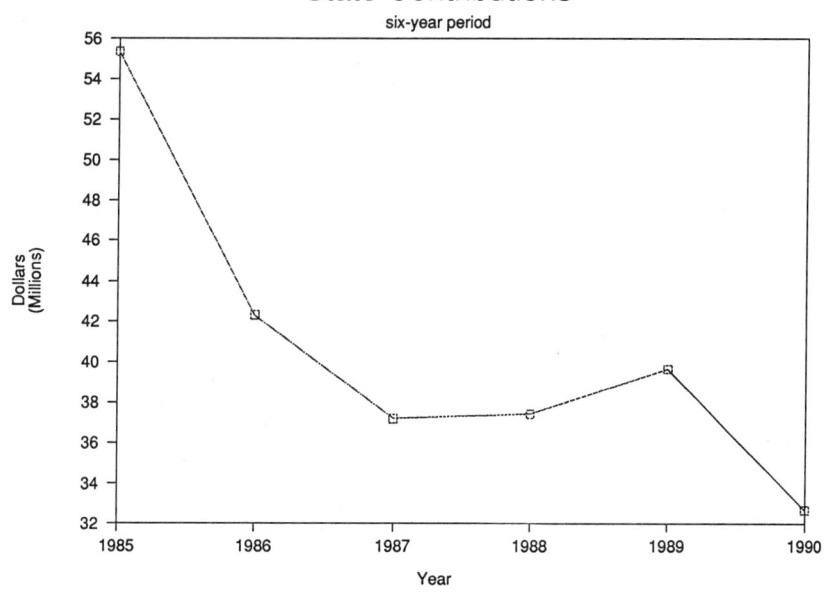

FIGURE 8.18

For both these projections, we will rely on *regression analysis*. Regression analysis, though not necessarily the best tool, does permit projection of future trends from past or current experiences. Additionally, the spreadsheet package we are using, Lotus 1-2-3 version 2.01, has the capability to perform regression analysis.

Pessimistic projection To calculate the funds available under the pessimistic assumption, we do a *straight-line* regression estimate. In other words, we assume that funding will continue to drop in the future just as it has over the six years for which we have data. Although Lotus does much of the statistical work for us, what we are essentially doing is determining the "average" decline (the *slope* or *coefficient*, as it called in the Lotus package) for the six years of data we have. Then, using this estimate, we project the funds expected to be available for the remainder of the two-decade period.

☐ In linear regression, the slope is an estimate of the change in *y* for every unit change in *x*, where in this instant *y* is dollars from the state and *x* is number of years. Although the term *average decline* (or change) is used in the text to convey the general idea of the slope, the actual formula for the slope is more complicated than the arithmetic average. A typical computing formula for the slope is as follows:

$$b = [N\Sigma XY - (\Sigma X)(\Sigma Y)]/N\Sigma X^2 - (\Sigma X)^2$$

where *b* is the slope, *N* is the number of observations, and *x* and *y* are the data or individual observations. In the regression illustration here, we have six observations; the *x*s are all the years, 1985 to 1990; and the *y*s are the dollar amounts for each year.

PART III Use of the Framework in Developing Applications

```
Estimated State Contribution: 1986-2005
1985-1990 Base; 1991-2005 Projected

                       Base and
                       Projected
              Year     Construction
                       Dollars
              ---------------------
              1985     $55,355,500
              1986     $42,317,500
              1987     $37,204,500
              1988     $37,421,500
              1989     $39,660,500
              1990     $32,680,500
              1991     $28,660,433
              1992     $25,199,605
              1993     $21,738,776
              1994     $18,277,948
              1995     $14,817,119
              1996     $11,356,290
              1997      $7,895,462
              1998      $4,434,633
              1999        $973,805
              2000
              2001
              2002
              2003
              2004
              2005

Total, not including 1985...   $377,994,071
```

FIGURE 8.19

What is obtained from this regression analysis is an annual decline (slope, or coefficient) of about $3.5 million per year for the first six years. Projecting a continuation of this decline results in no dollars being available after 1999. That is, if $32.7 million are sent to the locality in 1990 and that amount drops by about $3.5 million a year, in a few years no dollars will be forthcoming. Figure 8.19 shows the results of this pessimistic projection.

Regression with the spreadsheet To conduct the regression analysis, Lotus has a function that is reached via the command /DATA REGRESSION. Once in the regression function, one only needs to define the *x*-range (independent variable), the *y*-range (dependent variable), and an output range where the regression results can be placed. With our six years of data (1985–1990) as the starting point, the years 1985–1990 are the *x*-range and the dollars (55.4 million, 42.3 million . . . 32.7 million) the *y*-range. For the output, we choose an unused part of the spreadsheet not too far from our six years of

Chapter 8 Semistructured and Unstructured Managerial Problems

```
       Regression Analysis: State Contributions
                  (1985 to 1990)
                G            H              I
             Regression Output:
40 Constant Regression Output:     $6,919,170,119
41 Std Err of Y Est                   4902152.3543
42 R Squared                          0.6855882625
43 No. of Observations                           6
44 Degrees of Freedom                            4
45 Degrees of Freedom                            4
46 X Coefficient(s)    ($3,460,829)
47 Std Err of Coef.    1171838.548
```

FIGURE 8.20

information. After all the ranges have been set, we simply depress the G key for GO. Figure 8.20 shows the output of the regression analysis based on the first six years.

The important results of the regression analysis that will be used to project the amounts for the remaining years (1991 on) are the *constant* (the point at which our straight line crosses the y axis where x equals zero) and the X coefficient (the estimated annual increase or decrease). The constant, as shown in figure 8.20, is $6.9 billion, and the X coefficient is $3.5 million (rounded). The equation for estimating funds in figure 8.19, for each year from 1991 to 2005, is:

$y = a + (bk)$

In this equation, y is the estimated dollar amount for each projected year, a is the constant, b is the amount of annual decline or increase in dollars (the coefficient), and k is the year for that particular estimate. For 1991, the equation would essentially look like this, although the actual values from figure 8.20 would have to be used or referenced:

$y = a + (b * k)$
$y = 6.9 \text{ billion} + (-3.5 \text{ million} * 1991)$

Remember, however, we do not want to put actual numbers in the formula for each year. We want to generalize it in case we want to make changes later. To do so, we can use cell references in the formula and then copy the generalized formula to wherever it is needed. Thus, the formula—$y = a + bk$—is simply expressed in terms of the appropriate cell references.

In our spreadsheet, the constant a is in cell I40; the coefficient b is in H46 (see regression output in figure 8.20); and the first year for which we want to predict—1991—is in cell B45. If we create the following formula:

+$I$40 + ($H$46 * B45)

in the cell for estimating 1991 dollars, it will produce the estimate for 1991. Use of the dollar sign ($) in the formula makes the first two cell references *absolute*, permitting a quick copy for the rest of the years. For example, in 1992 and 1993 the equations will be:

$y=\$I\$40+(\$H\$46*B46)$ or $y= 6.9$ billion $+ (-3.5$ million $* 1992)$
$y=\$I\$40+(\$H\$46*B47)$ or $y= 6.9$ billion $+ (-3.5$ million $* 1993)$

As we copy this formula downward to reach the year 2005, I40 (the constant) and H46 (the coefficient) will not be altered because they are *absolute*, whereas the B46 (the year) will change because it is *relative*. If I40 and H46 were not made absolute, then as we copied downward they would change to I41 and so forth. But the constant and coefficient are in cells I40 and H46 and not anywhere else. These must remain the same even though the year changes.

The final bit of work in this pessimistic calculation (figure 8.19) is adding the dollar values to obtain a total. Lotus accomplishes this with the formula @SUM(B40..B53), or the sum of all dollars from 1986 through 1999. Subsequent years (2000 to 2005) are not included because the amount turns negative for these years. The resulting total is slightly less than $378 million dollars.

Optimistic projection This straight-line estimate, while easy to execute in Lotus, may not represent a realistic projection. It is unlikely that the dollars from the state will completely evaporate. What might occur is a more gradual decline and a gradual introduction of other funds.

To capture this assumption of a slow, gradual decline, the dollar amounts for 1985 to 1990 are transformed via a logarithmic (log) function. This transformation essentially lowers the dollar values in the early years and increases the dollar values in later years to produce that more elongated, smooth decline. In Lotus, the log transformation is performed by a function @LN(dollar value), where LN stands for the natural log.

The graph in figure 8.21 shows the difference between the pessimistic and optimistic assumptions. The regression results for the log-transformed data are very different from the results under the straight-line statistical procedure. With the transformed results, there is a smooth, gradual decline, and the dollars in the later years never go to zero.

> Most statistics books show how to perform log transformations. Essentially it involves taking the log, then taking the exponential to get the results back to their original unit, which in this case is dollars.

We have taken one liberty with the log-transformed regression to achieve our optimistic result. The log transformation is achieved by taking dollars away from the beginning years and adding them to the end years. The total dollars remain essentially the same. However, what we want is a larger allocation. To get this, we put back the original dollar amounts for the first five years of the two-decade projection (1986–1990), since that is what the locality will in fact receive, and further, we add $10 million to each successive year (starting with 1991) on the assumption that the state will somehow find additional funds. The result under this optimistic assumption is a total of $476 million for the twenty-year period, as opposed to less than $378 million in the pessimistic projection.

We now have enough information to use the results of this detailed analysis to see whether the dollars estimated are adequate to meet the total needed from the state, which we calculated in our first worksheet in figure 8.15. Unfortunately, not even the optimistic

Chapter 8 Semistructured and Unstructured Managerial Problems 241

Optimistic versus Pessimistic

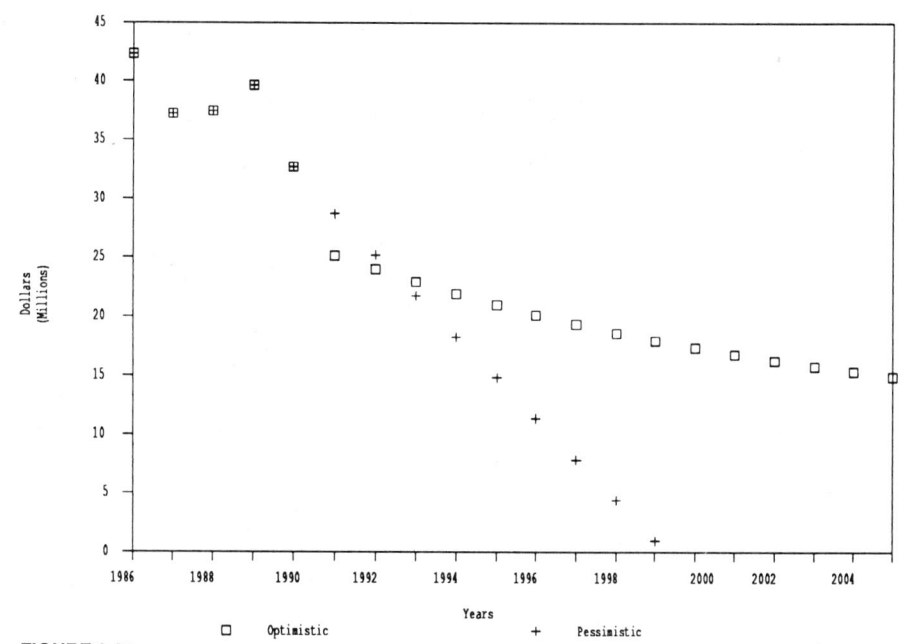

FIGURE 8.21

estimate of $476 million provides sufficient funds to cover the $667 million required from the state for adequate roads. In fact, it is almost $200 million shy of the target, although it would just cover the state contribution for poor traffic movement if that is any consolation. At this point, it is apparent that either more state funds are required or the expectation for state contributions must be reduced. As we will see later (figure 8.27), we will add $20 million per year instead of just $10 million for 1991 to 2005. This will push the potential state contribution to over $626 million.

Business Extractions Module

Our second major funding source is business extraction. Although a number of taxes or assessments could be used to obtain these extra revenues or extractions from business, here we will look only at one: impact fees.

Impact fees are designed to collect revenue directly from developers whose projects are causing increased use of facilities (roads, schools, etc.) or whose projects are increasing pressure for new facilities. These impact fees are usually above whatever taxes are normally collected. Fees can be levied on the number of units constructed (e.g., housing units), on square footage, or on the amount of traffic generated.

In this jurisdiction, we will assume that impact fees could be levied on two types of development: residential dwelling units and commercial structures. To simplify the estimate of revenue produced, residential fees are based on the number of residential dwelling units built, and commercial fees are based on the square footage of commercial space constructed. We ignore size of residential units, income produced by commercial property, and traffic generated by new development.

Impact fees for new housing For our estimate of fees generated from new housing, we need to make several projections and assumptions. We need to estimate how many new houses will be built each year for the next twenty years, what percentage of these will fall under the impact fee, and what the actual impact fee will be in dollars and cents. All these critical decisions are independent of the power of the spreadsheet, although, as we have seen, we can change the assumptions almost at will to assess the effect of different decisions on revenues generated.

For the estimate of the number of new units, we simply go to the experts who deal with housing. If their estimates seem reasonable, we will use those estimates. For this case study, our sense is that new housing will be robust for at least the next decade and then fall off a bit. The jurisdiction is a maturing one with limits on how much more it can grow. Indeed, the experts confirm this assessment. New construction is predicted to fall from a high of more than 6,000 units at the beginning of the period (1986) to a low of 3,200 by the end of the period (2005).

To estimate the portion of housing falling under the fee we need to do some political second-guessing because the local council will exert a considerable influence on this decision. Our guess is that most units will fall under the fee, perhaps with exclusions for housing for low- and moderate-income families and housing for the elderly. There is a good deal of pressure for more revenues, and the council will likely try to be "fair" to all parties by taxing most of them. On the basis of these factors, we estimate that 90 percent of the units will be covered by the fee.

For the dollar amount of the fee, we will look around the local region and the country to see what the prevailing rate is. We will also do some work to see how much roadway can be built for different fee levels. Based on these factors, we arrive at a fee of $1,200 per unit.

Algorithm With all this information, it is now possible to move to more detailed levels, including the algorithm for estimating the revenue from the fees and the spreadsheet implementation.

In this case, the algorithm for calculating the annual dollars collected from the impact fee is quite simple: the number of new units times the portion covered by the fee times the fee itself. The pseudocode might read:

New_units times %covered times house_fee

Notwithstanding the simple nature of the calculations, it is still important to construct an attractive, easy-to-manipulate spreadsheet (see figure 8.22). First, the worksheet is laid out so that the more general information on assumptions and total revenue is placed at the top and the more detailed year-by-year estimates are near the bottom. Specifically, the introductory section notes that 90 percent of new units will be covered by the fee, that the fee is $1,200 per unit, and that developers pay the fee. Next comes the estimated revenue generated, which in this case is in excess of $98 million. Finally, the year-by-year details show how many housing units are expected to be produced and the resulting annual revenue from the fee. For example, in 1990, 6,100 new residential units are

Chapter 8 Semistructured and Unstructured Managerial Problems

```
                PROJECTED FEES FROM NEW HOUSING UNITS
                             1986-2005

         The fees for housing units are based on the
         following assumptions:

   a.     90% of all new housing will be covered by the fee
   b.     $1,200 will be the fee levied for each new housing unit
   c.            The fees are to be paid by the developers


         ------------------------------------------------
      I  Total fees                                      I
      I  from housing:                   $98,496,000     I
         ------------------------------------------------

                     Jurisdiction Detailed Analysis

                     Estimated           Projected dollars
                      annual                 assuming
                       new                       90%
             Year     units         of new units affected at
                                              $1,200
                                             per unit
         ---------------------------------------------------------
             1985
             1986     6,100                $6,588,000
             1987     6,100                $6,588,000
             1988     6,100                $6,588,000
             1989     6,100                $6,588,000
             1990     6,100                $6,588,000
             1991     5,020                $5,421,600
             1992     5,020                $5,421,600
             1993     5,020                $5,421,600
             1994     5,020                $5,421,600
             1995     5,020                $5,421,600
             1996     3,920                $4,233,600
             1997     3,920                $4,233,600
             1998     3,920                $4,233,600
             1999     3,920                $4,233,600
             2000     3,920                $4,233,600
             2001     3,200                $3,456,000
             2002     3,200                $3,456,000
             2003     3,200                $3,456,000
             2004     3,200                $3,456,000
             2005     3,200                $3,456,000
                    ---------------------------------------------
             Sum     91,200                $98,496,000
```

FIGURE 8.22

projected. Fees collected on 90 percent of these units, at $1,200 each, will yield more than $6.5 million.

In addition to the attention given to layout and appearance, the worksheet is also set up to enhance the what-if capability. Remember, we can utilize the what-if power by "generalizing" the content of the spreadsheet. In this spreadsheet, it is the two key assumptions that are generalized: the percentage of dwelling units covered by the impact fee, and the fee itself. Either the 90-percent coverage or the $1,200 fee in the assumption section could be changed to determine the effect on revenues. The projections for number of housing units could also be generalized, but are not. These numbers came from a regional agency that did not give any ranges for the forecast. As a result, the analyst simply took the data as prepared by the experts.

In this case, the generalization is achieved by a slightly different technique than simple cell references. It is possible to assign a name to a value and use that name in the formulas. In the impact fee spreadsheet, we will use %Covered rather than a cell reference to refer to the percentage of development covered by fees and the name Housefee for the dollar fee per unit. One advantage of using a naming convention is that it provides a memory aid, helping the user read and keep track of what is taking place in the formula.

☐ To tag or name a value in a single cell, Lotus requires the following command: /RANGE NAME CREATE, followed by whatever name you wish to give and, finally, the cell where the value is located. If .9 is in cell B8, the command to name it %Covered is: /RNC %Covered B8.

Figure 8.23 shows what is behind the numbers in figure 8.22 and illustrates the use of the naming convention. As noted, the percentage of development covered by fees is called %Covered, and the impact fee for each housing unit is called Housefee. In the formulas to calculate the estimated fees, these names are used in place of the actual values. For example, in cell D28, the formula to estimate revenues for 1986 is:

+C28 * $%Covered * $Housefee

☐ Again, the $ in front of $%Covered and $Housefee is needed to make the cell location in the formula absolute. Thus, when copied, the reference will remain 90% for %Covered and 1200 for Housefee.

This translates into 6,100 housing units completed in 1986 multiplied by 90%, with the product then being multiplied by $1,200. The result, as we saw in figure 8.22, is more than $6.5 million.

Just as with cell references, the what-if analysis can be handled easily when the naming convention is used. Simply replace the values in cells B8 and B9. For example, the fee could be raised to $1,500 by inserting 1500 in cell B9. Later, when we seek to extract more from business contributions, we will conduct a what-if with both %Covered and Housefee.

As another element of automation, the spreadsheet in figure 8.23 is set up to link the sum of each year @SUM(D28..D47) in cell D49 to the upper section of the spreadsheet under Total fees from housing. This is achieved by placing the cell location +D49 in one of the cells in the block designated Total fees from housing. The + sign is needed in front of D49 so that Lotus interprets it as a cell location and not a label. Whenever a new sum is calculated it is transferred to the upper part of the worksheet.

```
                    PROJECTED FEES FROM NEW HOUSING UNITS
                                 1986-2005

              The fees for housing units are based on the
                 following assumptions:

    a.      90% of all new housing will be covered by the fee
    b.   1,200   will be the fee levied for each new housing unit
    c.         The fees are to be paid by the developers


         ------------------------------------------------
       I  Total fees                                      I
       I  from housing:       +D49                        I
         ------------------------------------------------

                   Jurisdiction Detailed Analysis

                    Estimated           Projected dollars
                    annual                        assuming
                    new            +%COVERED
         Year       units           of new units affected at
                                   +HOUSEFEE
                                                per unit
         ---------------------------------------------------------
         1985
         1986       6100   +C28*$%COVERED*$HOUSEFEE
         1987       6100   +C29*$%COVERED*$HOUSEFEE
         1988       6100   +C30*$%COVERED*$HOUSEFEE
         1989       6100   +C31*$%COVERED*$HOUSEFEE
         1990       6100   +C32*$%COVERED*$HOUSEFEE
         1991       5020   +C33*$%COVERED*$HOUSEFEE
         1992       5020   +C34*$%COVERED*$HOUSEFEE
         1993       5020   +C35*$%COVERED*$HOUSEFEE
         1994       5020   +C36*$%COVERED*$HOUSEFEE
         1995       5020   +C37*$%COVERED*$HOUSEFEE
         1996       3920   +C38*$%COVERED*$HOUSEFEE
         1997       3920   +C39*$%COVERED*$HOUSEFEE
         1998       3920   +C40*$%COVERED*$HOUSEFEE
         1999       3920   +C41*$%COVERED*$HOUSEFEE
         2000       3920   +C42*$%COVERED*$HOUSEFEE
         2001       3200   +C43*$%COVERED*$HOUSEFEE
         2002       3200   +C44*$%COVERED*$HOUSEFEE
         2003       3200   +C45*$%COVERED*$HOUSEFEE
         2004       3200   +C46*$%COVERED*$HOUSEFEE
         2005       3200   +C47*$%COVERED*$HOUSEFEE
         ---------------------------------------------------------
         Sum  @SUM(C28..C47)  @SUM(D28..D47)
```

FIGURE 8.23

Impact fee on commercial development The process for calculating revenue from commercial impact fees is virtually the same as the procedure for the residential fees, and is not shown here. We start at a general level, mapping out the amount of commercial square footage expected over the next twenty years, then estimate the percentage we expect the council to place under the fee, and finally set the fee itself. These decisions are refined into the spreadsheet where the actual calculations are made. The amount estimated from these fees over a twenty-year period is in excess of $159 million.

The final task in this module on business extractions is to total all the estimated revenues (fees on new residential units plus fees on new commercial square footage) and determine how close they come to the dollars needed from business sources. The total is slightly more than $258 million ($98.5 million from housing fees plus $159.5 million from commercial fees). With these results, it is obvious that either more must be extracted from business or the expected business contribution must be reduced from the $667 million targeted from business in our initial worksheet (figure 8.15).

Local Government Contribution Module

The last module, local government contributions, is virtually a repeat of techniques already used. Estimates are made for specific local government funding sources and combined to assess how close they come to the needed dollars. For local contributions, we look at sales tax and general obligation bonds.

Only the results are presented here because the spreadsheet application parallels those developed for estimating revenue from impact fees. As it turns out, the sales tax is projected to produce sizable revenues, totaling almost $600 million. This large amount is a function of the huge and growing economic base in our case study jurisdiction. Growth is taking its toll on the highways, but it is also producing a vigorous economy.

Like the sales tax, general obligation bonds could be large producers of funds. In fact, nearly $1.1 billion could be raised from bonds. This is a function of the affluence of the community, for bonding capacity is based on factors such as assessed property value and per capita income. With a nearly $30-billion real property base that is increasing at a rate of 10 percent a year, the bonding capacity is quite high. We used the assumption that the community could raise bonds up to 3 percent of its total assessed real estate value and that 33 percent of that total would go to roads.

The projections from local government (in contrast to the state and business projections) greatly exceed the dollars needed to meet our initial assumption of one-third of the total capital from each sector. Local government could raise more than $1.6 billion compared with its targeted goal of .67 billion.

Integrative Module

At this point, we have three separate modules—one for state contributions, one for business, and one for local. However, we have no way of tying them together. What we want now is an integrative module. This final module must pull all three together and set up a worksheet to integrate the individual estimates into a grand worksheet. With such a worksheet, it is possible to do what-ifs on the individual assumptions and see the results

Funding Capital Needs for Road Building

Table of Contents	Summary Section	Critical Assumptions

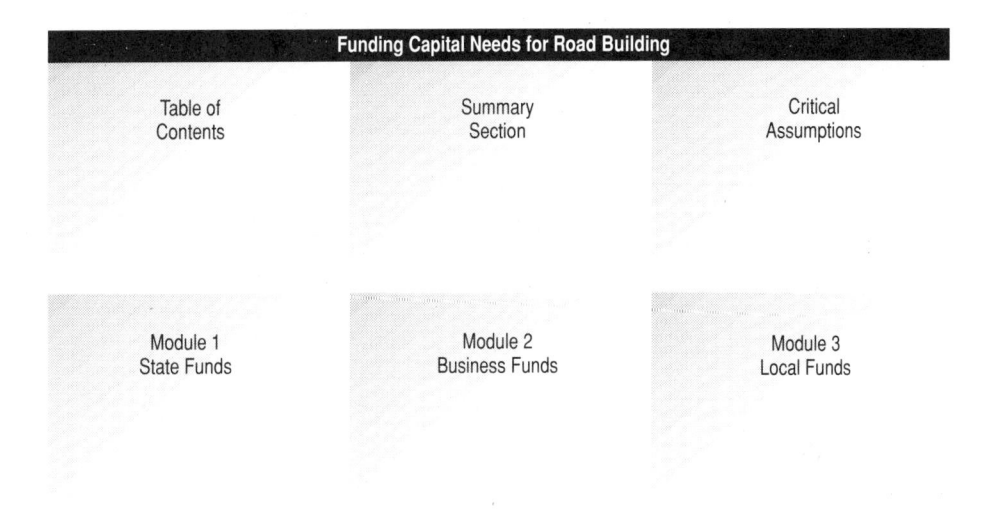

Module 1 State Funds	Module 2 Business Funds	Module 3 Local Funds

FIGURE 8.24 Master worksheet

in the same worksheet. In particular, we are interested in changing the assumptions to increase the contributions of the state and the business community.

All worksheets in one approach For this exercise, we will take a very simple approach to creating an integrative module. We will literally bring all three worksheets together in one grand worksheet. In Lotus, the command /FILE COMBINE COPY ENTIRE-FILE can be used to transfer files to a new worksheet. First, however, we should sketch the outlines of this master worksheet—particularly, where the main components will be placed.

The outline in figure 8.24 shows the three contribution modules—state, business, and local government—arranged in a row below a set of sections or modules that have not yet been discussed. These sections will enable us to perform, simply and directly, the what-if analysis needed to manipulate all three funding modules.

Although this "grand worksheet" approach is simple to carry out, we need to make a few comments about this approach of integrating everything into one large spreadsheet. Although this master worksheet is commonplace to spreadsheet manipulation in the mid- and late 1980s, it is cumbersome and will gradually be supplanted by the ability to link spreadsheets. Instead of replicating each individual worksheet in one large spreadsheet, more advanced spreadsheet packages will be able to take cell references from one worksheet and place them in another worksheet. For example, it would be possible to change the assumptions in all the individual worksheets and see the results in the central worksheet, or vice versa.

Making the master worksheet easy to use The master spreadsheet, built by combining all three funding worksheets into one, encompasses all the financial data we need but is not fashioned to allow us to perform what-if analysis easily. There is no single place to go to make a change. If we want to change the assumption for state contributions, for

```
            Integrative Spreadsheet for Highway Capital Needs
                        and Funding Sources

                           Table of Contents


The several modules available in this master spreadsheet are listed
below. Reach them by pressing the F5 function key and the letters
beneath Range Name. Return to the Table of Contents by pressing HOME.

Area of the Worksheet                       Range Name
-----------------------------------------------------------
Table of Contents                           Home Key

Summary Tables:
------------------------------
Total Capital Needs                         TC
Bottom Line—Dollars Available               BL
Surplus or Deficiency by Source             SD

Critical Assumptions:                       CA
------------------------------

Individual Modules:
------------------------------
State Contributions                         SC
Business Contributions                      BC
Local Contributions                         LC
```

FIGURE 8.25

example, we will need to hunt through the entire worksheet to find the cell where that assumption is located. There is also no element in the master worksheet to receive the results of changes in the assumptions.

To make the master sheet easier to operate, we have added three new elements (figure 8.24): a table of contents to outline what is in the worksheet and where; a single area to show the pertinent results (summary section); and a single area from which all the assumptions can be manipulated (critical assumptions).

The table of contents (figure 8.25) identifies the important areas of the spreadsheet and the names of those areas: Summary Tables, Critical Assumptions, and Individual Modules.

Getting to these areas is quite easy. First, each area is given a range name. For example, the SC in the table of contents is a range name for the state contribution module. Once the range has been named, moving to that area involves pressing the F5 function key (the GOTO key) and the name of the area where one wishes to go. Thus, pressing F5 and SC (capitalization not necessary) moves one immediately to the state contribution area.

Next, we need summary tables to receive the results of any what-if manipulations.

```
                    Total Capital Needs
         Ideal Relative Contribution of Major Sources

Traffic
Movement         Total           State          Business          Local
---------------------------------------------------------------------------
good          $2,600,000,000   $866,666,667    $866,666,667    $866,666,667
adequate      $2,000,000,000   $666,666,667    $666,666,667    $666,666,667
poor          $1,400,000,000   $466,666,667    $466,666,667    $466,666,667



                       Total Dollars Available
                             All Sources
             (adjusted for more state and business contributions)

Goals           Total            State          Business          Local
---------------------------------------------------------------------------
             $2,401,720,232   $476,553,616   $258,012,000   $1,667,154,615

Actual %        120.09%          19.84%          10.74%          69.42%
Desired %       100.00%          33.33%          33.33%          33.33%



                       Capital Surplus/(Deficiency)
                              by Source
Traffic
Movement         Total           State          Business          Local
---------------------------------------------------------------------------
good          ($198,279,768)  ($390,113,050) ($608,654,667)   $800,487,949
adequate       $401,720,232   ($190,113,050) ($408,654,667) $1,000,487,949
poor         $1,001,720,232      $9,886,950  ($208,654,667) $1,200,487,949
```

FIGURE 8.26 Summary tables

This section contains three tables: a repeat of the original worksheet in figure 8.15, showing the contributions needed from each source for different levels of traffic movement; a "bottom line" segment that shows whether the $2 billion can be met, and from which sources; and a third segment that points out the surplus or deficiency for each source, given our one-third required contribution from each source.

Figure 8.26 displays these summary tables, along with the initial results from integrating all three modules. They reaffirm what we already know. Looking at the middle section, Total Dollars Available, we see that the $2 billion for adequate traffic movement can be easily raised, but that most of the money comes from local contributions.

Building this summary section does not present any serious difficulties. The table on total capital needed and relative contributions can be transported from the original files where it resides. The bottom line table—total dollars available—can be created by referencing the cells where the appropriate results are located. For example, the dollars realized under state contributions ($476,553,616) is simply a reference to the cell in the state module where total state dollars from the optimistic option are calculated. In this case, it is +M184 or the range name Tstaterv, for total state revenues. The last table is a comparison of what is needed from each source against what can be produced. For example, comparing the $667 million needed from the state for adequate traffic movement with the $476 million available yields a deficiency of about $190 million.

The final element essential to managing this large worksheet is to have one area with all the critical assumptions, so that any assumption can be changed easily without hunting through the detailed modules. Recall that the initial assumptions to produce the results in figure 8.26 were as follows:

Source	Critical Assumption
State Contribution	Original amount for first five years and add $10 million for each year, 1991 to 2005
Fee from Housing	$1200/house and 90% covered
Fee for Commercial sq ft	$3/sq ft and 90% covered
Local General Obligation Bonds	3% of assessed value and 33% to transportation

These assumptions, when plugged into all the formulas, generated enough to cover the $2 billion needed for adequate traffic movement. However, most of the money comes from the local government. Thus, we may want to change the assumptions. If we had one area on the worksheet in which these assumptions could be changed easily, we could try alternatives, particularly to obtain more from the state and from business. Figure 8.27 depicts such an assumptions section. The contribution from the state is raised from $10 million for each year between 1991 and 2005 to $20 million for each of these years. Fees from new housing have been increased from $1,200 to $1,500. The cap on assessed value of real property has been lowered from 3 percent to 2 percent, meaning that local borrowing for general obligation bonds can now go up to only 2 percent of assessed value. These new assumptions will all be transferred to the appropriate module (state, business, and local contributions) to generate new results that will then be transferred back to the Bottom Line section to give a summary of how much could be obtained under the revised assumptions. There is, in fact, a substantial change in amount from each source. The state contribution is now $626.5 million compared with $476.5 million; business contribution is $396.5 million compared with $258 million; and the local share is $1.3 billion instead of $1.67 billion.

For this critical assumptions section to work properly, the assumptions in it must be tied to the individual modules. A simple way is to find the cell where the assumption is located in the individual module and place that cell reference in the appropriate cell in the assumptions section. For example, if B125 is the location for housing unit fees, place +B125 in the cell where the $1,500 appear in figure 8.27.

With this setup, it is easy to make changes and observe the results. Pressing the Home key takes us back to the table of contents. Here it is possible see all the modules available.

```
          Critical Assumptions: Name and Current Value

Relative contribution from major sources:   Range Name     Current Value
           State                             statepc              40.00%
           Business                          buspc                20.00%
           Local                             localpc              40.00%

Major assumptions for state contributions:
           Amount of dollars added           addstate        $20,000,000

Major assumptions for business contributions:
           Fee for each housing unit         housefee             $1,500
           Fee for each sq ft commercial     sqftfee                  $4
           Percent new development covered   %covered             90.00%

Major assumptions for local contributions:
           Borrowing as a percent of
             assessed value                  borrowpc              2.00%
           Percent to transportation         %2trans              33.00%

Depress the F5 function then the range name of the critical
 assumption to get to and change the assumption.
```

FIGURE 8.27

Then we can move around and make our changes. Pressing the function key F5 followed by CA takes us to the critical assumption area. Here a change can be made. For example, add $20,000,000 to the state contribution instead of $10,000,000. Pressing F5 BL then takes us to the "bottom line" range to see the results of the change.

Manipulating the grand worksheet At this point, the what-if analysis can be easily iterated. The hard work of the individual modules is finished. All the work is in one spreadsheet, set up in a way that allows quick changes and quick observation of the results of those changes.

The "only" problem now is convincing the state and the business sector to contribute more money to this grand road project. Here again, we see the decision support application as an aid to decision making. The application provides information, allows us to manipulate that information, and gives us a potentially powerful analytical tool. However, we still realize that many assumptions have gone into the DSA and that the results must be politically acceptable to be implemented.

CASE 3: MENU-DRIVEN COST/BENEFIT APPLICATION

Background and Purpose

One goal in this case is to develop a decision support application that is more extensively automated than the prior two applications. By automated we mean that the analysts or managers are placed immediately into the decision support application as soon as they enter the system (accessing Lotus, in this instance). Once into the application, they are presented with a menu of options that allows them to make selections and use the application. At no time does the user need to do any of the work of building the application, which has already been programmed into the software. All the user does is enter the critical data about the problem or concern and view the results.

The topic used to illustrate this case is a cost/benefit analysis (C/B) for a particular project. Cost/benefit is a technique that permits us to examine the desirability of a project using economic criteria. Essentially, if the economic return calculated in dollars is attractive relative to the investment, then we have grounds for proceeding with the project.

Before we get into the application, it is important to make a brief detour to discuss several of the concepts central to cost/benefit analysis. We will cover these concepts by looking at the same project that we will examine in the application.

Determining costs and benefits: A first step The sample project for which we will conduct the C/B analysis is an incinerator designed to generate energy. In turn, the energy can be sold to a power company. The initial task in the C/B decision process is to lay out the costs and the benefits of the project. The costs include the original investment and the annual operating costs. These, we assume, are not too onerous to estimate. Engineering studies have been conducted and compared to past experience. Calculation of the benefits present a more subjective task, however. Not only do we want to include fees paid by users and the income from the energy we sell, but we also want to include several indirect benefits. One of these is the benefit derived from shutting down the landfill that was endangering the water supply. With these factors in mind, figure 8.28 shows the resulting costs and benefits used for this exercise—although, as we will see, costs and benefits for any project can be entered, as long as they remain within the present constraint of twenty years of data.

In looking at the costs and benefits, we see a large initial investment of $6,000,000. Operating costs, too, are sizable at the outset—$1,000,000 in year 1—but taper off after the project has been operated for a few years. In contrast, benefits start small ($500,000 in year 1) and increase as the project continues ($1,700,000 in year 15).

For the purpose of this exercise, the actual task of estimating these costs and benefits is not a part of the microcomputer application. That estimation is completed separately but is a critical input. If either costs or benefits are drastically inflated or deflated, then the application, regardless of how sophisticated, will be working with invalid data. Such situations are not uncommon in decision support applications. Poor data often make the system useless. For the DSA to be of value, the assumptions and data that go into the application must be reasonable.

If the cost and benefit data are reasonably accurate, one can proceed with the remainder of the analysis. However, the next step is not a simple comparison of the total costs with the total benefits. The process of comparison is more complicated. Fortunately, Lotus and other spreadsheets possess powerful tools for doing most of these complicated comparisons. Nonetheless, it is important to have a basic appreciation of the complexities in order to use the computer tools wisely.

```
Costs and Benefits for Incinerator Project

YEAR
START (0)   6,000,000           0
       1    1,000,000     500,000
       2      500,000     600,000
       3      400,000     700,000
       4      300,000     800,000
       5      200,000     900,000
       6      100,000   1,000,000
       7      100,000   1,300,000
       8      100,000   1,400,000
       9      100,000   1,500,000
      10      100,000   1,600,000
      11      100,000   1,700,000
      12      100,000   1,700,000
      13      100,000   1,700,000
      14      100,000   1,700,000
      15      100,000   1,700,000
      16
      17
      18
      19
      20
```

FIGURE 8.28

Dealing with future monetary value One reason for the complexity is that the dollars of benefit in future years cannot be taken at face value. For example, the $6 million spent in the initial year cannot be assumed to be of less value than the $6.8 million dollars earned in the last four years of the project, because the initial $6 million could be invested and collect, perhaps, 10-percent interest. By the time we reach the point where the $6.8 million is collected, the original $6 million would have grown to about three times the original amount. In short, money spent or earned early on could be invested at this earlier date and thus be worth more than an equal amount of money earned later.

Discounting We incorporate the effect of time on value by discounting all future dollars back to their present value. This way all dollars are on the same plane. If we believe that we could earn 10 percent on today's investment, we take 10 percent as the discount rate. It turns out that the present value of the $6.8 million earned in the last four years, discounted at 10 percent, is only slightly more than $2 million—quite a reduction! But now these values from future years can be compared with present values.

It should now be quite apparent that those estimates of costs and benefits for each year are important. A $1.7 million return or benefit in year 5 will be worth more than a $1.7 million payoff in year 11. It should also be apparent that the discount factor is critical. If a high discount factor is used, the benefits or value of future dollars will be reduced considerably. That means it will be hard to justify a project because heavily discounted future dollars will look inconsequential when compared with high initial costs.

Internal rate of return (IRR)   Oftentimes a discount rate can be selected simply by taking the going interest rate for creditworthy borrowers (commonly referred to as the prime rate). For this exercise, we will pursue a somewhat complicated route in choosing a discount rate for assisting with the cost/benefit comparisons. It is usually possible to find a discount rate such that the discounted value of the net benefits (i.e., benefits minus any costs and investments) is made to equal zero. In other words, we keep trying different discount rates until one discounts the net benefits to zero. This way costs and benefits are in equilibrium. Called the *internal rate of return* (IRR), this is the highest discount rate we can accept and still rationalize the project on economic grounds; that is, economic gains are at least equal to expenses. If the discount rate that must be used is higher than the IRR, then the project will not produce a net benefit. In short, we like to find high IRRs so that projects can be discounted a good deal and still show a net benefit. If the current interest rate on bank deposits is higher than the IRR, then it is more profitable just to put the money in the bank than to undertake the project under review. Admittedly, government projects stand or fall on more than purely economic criteria, but the IRR is still a consideration.

As a supplement to the IRR, we will also compute the benefit ratio, or percentage return expected from the project (benefits/costs). The higher the ratio of benefits to costs, the greater the "profit" ratio, and the more attractive the project is on economic criteria.

☐ In government projects, these economic criteria of net present value and benefit ratio provide only a guide for determining whether projects should be undertaken. If voters or interest groups demand certain projects, the economic criteria may be negated. In addition, many public projects do not have a clearly defined set of monetary benefits. In our case, fees can be charged for use of an incinerator, but what about projects such as recreation centers or new schools? We tend not to see many of these as income-producing. In these cases, sheer public demand may be the most viable criterion.

Using the Application

At this point, we have all that is needed to try out the C/B application. We have the cost and benefit data for the incinerator; we know that we are going to examine several discount rates, some which should be higher than current interest rates; and we know that we will eventually use IRR to make judgments about the economic attractiveness of the project.

In the C/B application built to illustrate our more extensively automated DSA, the application loads as soon as we start up the Lotus spreadsheet. That is, immediately after typing 123 or Lotus, the application becomes available to the user. What the user sees is a main menu and description for using the menu (figure 8.29). Five choices are listed in the main menu: C/B Data Entry, D.R. Entry (for discount rate), Results, Print, and Graph Choices. Following these five choices are a set of more detailed instructions on what each choice means and how to use the spreadsheet application.

Assuming no cost/benefit data have been entered, the first thing to do is select the

Chapter 8   Semistructured and Unstructured Managerial Problems   255

```
                                                          MENU

   C/B DATA ENTRY   D.R. ENTRY   RESULTS   PRINT   GRAPH CHOICES
   ENTER YEARLY COST/BENEFIT DATA

   ABOVE IS THE MENU FOR THE COST/BENEFIT ANALYSIS. YOU
   CAN MOVE FROM OPTION TO OPTION BY PRESSING THE LEFT
   ARROW KEY <- OR THE RIGHT ARROW KEY ->. IF STARTING
   A NEW COST/BENEFIT ANALYSIS, MAKE SURE THE C/B DATA
   ENTRY OPTION IS HIGHLIGHTED AND THEN SELECT THE C/B
   DATA ENTRY OPTION BY PRESSING THE ENTER KEY. FINISH
   THE WORK IN THAT OPTION, AND THEN SELECT THE D.R.
   ENTRY FOR DISCOUNT RATE. ONCE BOTH OF THESE ARE
   FINISHED, YOU CAN EXAMINE THE RESULTS, EITHER FROM
   THE RESULTS, PRINT OR GRAPH CHOICES OPTION. RETURN TO
   THE MENU IF NECESSARY BY HOLDING DOWN THE ALT KEY AND
   AT THE SAME TIME DEPRESSING THE M KEY.



                                                          CMD
```

FIGURE 8.29

C/B Data Entry option. Selecting this option takes us to an area where we can input the data. Figure 8.30 shows the blank data-entry screen, some simple instructions on how to enter the data, and the necessary instructions to return to the main menu. After all the data have been inserted, the application is restarted according to the instructions in the upper right of the data-entry screen. Simply, an ALT-M will get us back to the main menu.

Following the instructions in the main menu, the next step (again assuming this is a new C/B analysis) is to select D.R. Entry. Three discount rates can be entered (figure 8.31). In contrast to the method of entering the cost/benefit data, where the user had to move the cursor from cell to cell, as soon as the first discount rate has been inserted and the ENTER key depressed, the cursor automatically moves down one row enabling us to enter the second discount rate. When the third and last entry has been made, we are automatically taken back to the menu. A similar technique could have been used in entering the cost/benefit data, but was not done in order to show different degrees of automation.

In actuality, the programming to automate the data entry for costs and benefits would be more involved than for discount rates. Since up to twenty years of data could be inputted for costs and benefits, any automation scheme would need to first ask the user how many years of data, keep track as the data were entered, and take the user out of data entry as soon as the number of years had been reached.

After the cost/benefit data and discount rates have been entered, the main menu offers three ways of reviewing the results. Choosing the Results option produces a numeric display (figure 8.32). This display includes the discount rates originally entered, the dollar

```
         A          B          C          D       E
    1
    2
    3
    4
    5   TEMPLATE FOR NET PRESENT VALUE ANALYSIS    (PRESS ALT-M FOR MENU)
    6   ====================================================================
    7   DATA ENTRY FOR YEARLY COSTS AND BENEFITS: MOVE THE CURSOR
    8   TO B13 AND ENTER THE COST DATA. THEN MOVE CURSOR TO C13 TO
    9   ENTER THE BENEFIT DATA. UP TO 20 YEARS CAN BE INPUTTED.
   10
   11  YEAR       TOTAL COSTS TOTAL BENEFITS
   12  ------------------------------------------------------------------
   13  START (0)
   14         1
   15         2
   16         3
   17         4
   18         5
   19         6
   20         7
   21         8
   22         9
   23        10
   24        11
   25        12
   26        13
   27        14
   28        15
   29        16
   30        17
   31        18
   32        19
   33        20
```

FIGURE 8.30 Data entry screen for cost/benefit input

return, the percentage return, and the IRR. As might be expected from the initial discussion of C/B concepts, the lower the discount rate, the more viable is the project. At a discount rate of 7.5%, the project shows a positive net present value (NPV) of more than $1.2 million. The percentage return is also positive: 15.94%. According to the IRR, it is possible to have a discount rate as high as 9.75% before the project turns sour.

It is the Results part of the spreadsheet that provides the analyst with the what-if capability that is so important to the ultimate selection of a discount rate. If a 7.5% discount rate is justifiable in terms of current interest rates (e.g., current interest rates are in the 6.0% to 7.0% range), then the project can definitely go forward on economic grounds. If this 7.5% is deemed too low compared to current interest rates, we can push

```
================================================================
SELECTION OF DISCOUNT RATES

SELECT UP TO THREE DISCOUNT RATES FOR
NET PRESENT VALUE CALCULATIONS
                                      Type as decimal
DISCOUNT RATE #1:                     (e.g., .075) and
DISCOUNT RATE #2:                     depress ENTER key
DISCOUNT RATE #3:                     after each number.
```

FIGURE 8.31 Screen for entry of discount rates

```
    ================================================================
    SELECTION OF DISCOUNT RATES

    SELECT UP TO THREE DISCOUNT RATES FOR
    NET PRESENT VALUE CALCULATIONS
                                              Type as decimal
    DISCOUNT RATE #1:              7.50%      (e.g., .075) and
    DISCOUNT RATE #2:             11.00%      depress ENTER key
    DISCOUNT RATE #3:             14.00%      after each number.



    ================================================================
    TEMPLATE FOR NET PRESENT VALUE ANALYSIS    (PRESS ALT-M FOR MENU)
    NET PRESENT VALUE RESULTS                  PERCENT RETURN

    DISCOUNT RATE #1:             $1,264,326        15.94%
    DISCOUNT RATE #2:              ($561,880)       -7.55%
    DISCOUNT RATE #3:            ($1,611,781)      -22.73%

    INTERNAL RATE OF
    RETURN:                            9.75%
    (Discount rate where benefits = costs)
```

FIGURE 8.32

the discount rate as high as 9.75%. If we started the application over and substituted discount rates of 9.0%, 9.5%, and 10.0% for the three rates initially entered, we would then see the present value and return for these discount rates.

Returning to the main menu (via ALT M), we are offered two other ways of viewing the results. The PRINT command permits us to obtain a hard copy printout, and the GRAPH CHOICES lets us see the results in graph form (figure 8.33).

Now that we have seen the C/B application at work, several comments are in order about the degree of automation in this application. Although the menu makes the application easier to use, the application is not totally automated. In a more fully automated system, the user would be completely controlled by the application. For

INVESTMENT RETURN ANALYSIS

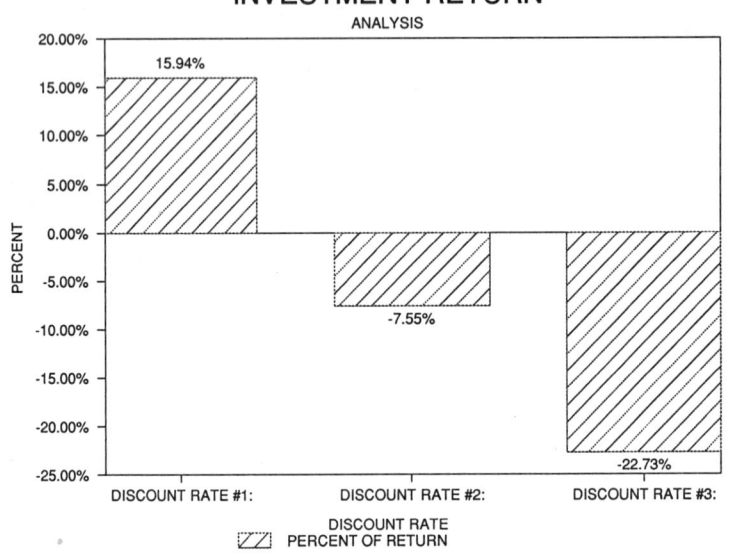

[Bar chart showing:
- DISCOUNT RATE #1: 15.94%
- DISCOUNT RATE #2: -7.55%
- DISCOUNT RATE #3: -22.73%
Y-axis: PERCENT, ranging from -25.00% to 20.00%
Legend: PERCENT OF RETURN]

FIGURE 8.33

example, the program would send the user to an input area, move the user from input item to input item, and then send the user back to the menu. Here we show variations on this theme. One part of the application—the screen for discount rates—is fully automated; the other parts, only partially so. Thus, the reader can see the difference between partially and fully automated systems.

Other options or techniques could very well be added to the application. For example, one extra option might include erasing all the inputs—that is, the cost/benefit data and the discounts—so the application would be ready for the next project. However, the options offered here show enough variety to suggest how an automated decision support system works.

Describing the Application

Having seen how to use this C/B application, it is now important to describe what is behind the various menus and screens and to show how to build the application.

The application to help determine the economic viability of this incinerator project (or other projects) is built with a spreadsheet. The spreadsheet application is divided into two major parts or sectors. One part includes all the areas where the data are entered and the results calculated and displayed. The other major part of the spreadsheet application consists of the macros (or programs) that automate the use of the application. In other words, instead of the user navigating from one part of the spreadsheet to another, the macros automate the process. The macro, in a sense, asks us where we want to go via the menu, takes us there, and brings us back to make another selection. This is a step beyond the previous case, where we had to look at a table of contents and use the GOTO (F5) key to move to a particular part of the worksheet.

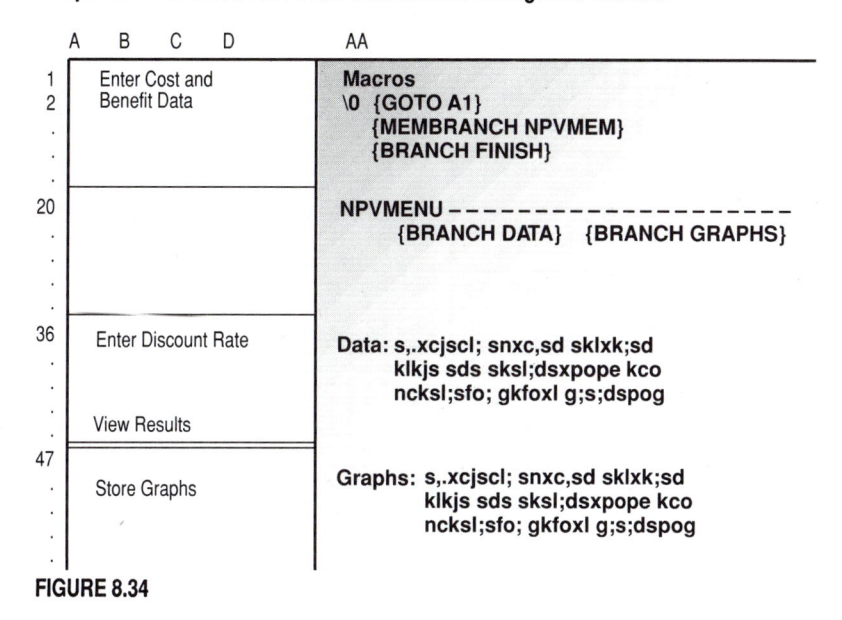

Chapter 8   Semistructured and Unstructured Managerial Problems   259

	A	B	C	D	AA

1	Enter Cost and Benefit Data				Macros
					\0 {GOTO A1}
					    {MEMBRANCH NPVMEM}
					    {BRANCH FINISH}

20					NPVMENU ------------------- {BRANCH DATA} {BRANCH GRAPHS}

36	Enter Discount Rate
	
	View Results
					Data: s,.xcjscl; snxc,sd sklxk;sd
					    klkjs sds sksl;dsxpope kco
					    ncksl;sfo; gkfoxl g;s;dspog

47	Store Graphs				Graphs: s,.xcjscl; snxc,sd sklxk;sd
					    klkjs sds sksl;dsxpope kco
					    ncksl;sfo; gkfoxl g;s;dspog

FIGURE 8.34

Figure 8.34 shows the layout of the entire spreadsheet. On the left side of the figure we see the work areas where the cost/benefit data are entered, where the discount rates are entered, where the results are viewed (i.e., net present value, internal rate of return, and gross profits), and where the graphs are stored. On the right side are the macros that automate the application by automatically sending us to one of the work areas instead of forcing us to maneuver around the spreadsheet on our own.

The Heart of the Automation: The Macros

The heart of this interactive interface between the user and the application is a series of macros, or programs, controlled by the menu that appears whenever the spreadsheet is opened or the key sequence ALT-M is pressed. The use of a menu-driven interface (see chapter 6) reduces the complexity of the task confronting the user. In this case, the analyst simply selects the appropriate task from the main menu, and the macros in the application carry out many of the necessary operations.

This menu-driven, macro-based approach to a decision support application follows a top-down, modular approach. Figure 8.35 represents the macro used to control the menu. The initial macro, replicated in order to be both an auto-executing macro (\0) and a keyboard-command macro (ALT-M), makes use of a Lotus command called MENUBRANCH that invokes the Npvmenu macro. This macro controls the initial menu (C/B Data Entry, etc.) that the user sees. A modular approach is taken in the rest of the macros, each executing a particular function (e.g., BRANCH Data). These macros (Data, Rates, etc.), along with the flow of the program, will be examined in some detail.

When the program is initiated, the cursor (and the user) is sent to a clear area of the spreadsheet called Menuarea so that the menu can be displayed without clashing with other working parts of the spreadsheet application. Next, the program branches to the

```
Macro for Menu Drive Net Present Value Cost Benefit Analysis

\0       {GOTO}Menuarea~
         {MENUBRANCH Npvmenu}
         {BRANCH Finish}

\M       {GOTO}Menuarea~
         {MENUBRANCH Npvmenu}
         {BRANCH Finish}

Npvmenu  C/B DATA ENTRY      D.R. ENTRY           RESULTS          PRINT              GRAPH CHO
         ENTER YEARLY COST/B SELECT DISCOUNT VIEW RESULTS          PRINT RESULTS      SELECT GR
         {BRANCH Data}       {BRANCH Rates}       {BRANCH Res}     {BRANCH Prt}       {BRANCH V

Finish   {QUIT}

Data     {GOTO}A1~
         {QUIT}

Rates    {GOTO}C41~
         {?}{DOWN 1}~
         {?}{DOWN 1}~
         {?}~
         {GOTO}Menuarea~
         {MENUBRANCH Npvmenu}

Res      {GOTO}A47~
         {QUIT}
```

FIGURE 8.35

```
Prt       /PP~
          RA36..G66~
          AGQ~
          {QUIT}

View      {GOTO}GRPHNote~
          {MENUBRANCH Grphs}
          {BRANCH Finish}

Grphs     COST-BENEFIT ANALYSN.P.V. ANALYSISRETURN ON INVESTMENT
          LINE GRAPH OF YEARLLINE GRAPH OF TBAR CHART OF THE RETURN ON INVESTMENT
          /GNUB-C~         /GNUNetval~       /GNUReturn~
          {ESC}Q~          {ESC}Q~           {ESC}Q~
          {GOTO}Menuarea~  {GOTO}Menuarea~{GOTO}Menuarea~
          {MENUBRANCH Npvmenu{MENUBRANCH Npv{MENUBRANCH Npvmenu}
          {BRANCH Finish}  {BRANCH Finish}{BRANCH Finish}

Note: Some of the commands or selections are not readable because
the cell width for many of the cells is only 9 characters in length.
```

FIGURE 8.35 *(Continued)*

PART III Use of the Framework in Developing Applications

menu controlled by the program Npvmenu. The menu is displayed in the clear area of the spreadsheet where the cursor is, and we can select one of the options.

In more involved programs such as this one, it is important to distinguish between program flow and cursor control. The program starts with the first instruction, {GOTO}Menuarea~, and then proceeds to the next instruction, {MENUBRANCH Npvmenu}. This is the program flow. It is the cursor (and the user) that goes to the locations on the spreadsheet where the work is done. While the cursor is at Menuarea, program flow or control might be moving down the C/B Data Entry path taking the program flow to the program Data. In Data, the cursor gets sent from Menuarea to the cell location A1 (figure 8.35). Program control continues its sequential flow, moving to the command QUIT, which takes the user out of the macro.

Each of the options (C/B Data Entry, D.R. Entry, etc.) is eventually controlled by a branch to a new macro outside the Npvmenu program. Three of these macros—Data, Rates, and Res—are designed to direct the user to specific portions of the application. Data (figure 8.35) takes the user to the area ({GOTO} A1) where the cost/benefit data are entered. As noted, this particular part of the macro is not highly automated. It takes the user to the appropriate area, but the user must know enough (or be able to follow instructions) to input the data and then depress the ALT-M key sequence to return to the menu.

Rates (figure 8.35) is more completely automated. It carries the user to the sector ({GOTO} C41) where the discount rates are entered via the question mark prompt, {?}. The {?} pauses the program until the user enters some data. However, in this macro, the macro puts the user in the exact cell where the first discount rate should be entered. Once the user enters the first discount rate, the macro automatically takes the user (actually the cursor) one cell down ({DOWN 1}) to enter the next discount rate. Finally, the macro takes the user back to the clear area ({GOTO}Menuarea) and the menu display ({MENUBRANCH Npvmenu}).

Recall that the tilde (~) is equivalent to the ENTER key. Thus, {GOTO}A1~ is equivalent to pressing the F5 function key (which is the GOTO key), then pressing A1, and finally pressing the ENTER key.

Res, like Data, is a simple "get you to the right area" macro that is not automated to return you to the menu. In short, it puts the user in the area ({GOTO} A47) where the results are shown. After the observations have been made by the user, the user must restart the menu by pressing the ALT and M keys.

The Prt macro (near lower left of figure 8.35) is designed to produce a printout (/PP) of the results section of the application. The macro selects the appropriate range (RA36..G66), aligns the paper, prints, and quits the program (AGQ, where the A stands for align, G stands for go ahead with the actual printing, and Q stands for quit). After printing has been completed, the macro returns to the application. If this last command (Q) is omitted, the user remains in the print command menu of Lotus.

The View macro is an example of how one macro can be used to call another. In this case, the View macro is used to call another menu system macro called Grphs. The Grphs macro is similar to the Npvmenu macro in that it allows branching to the three target graphs (see bottom of figure 8.35). In order for this macro to work, each graph must be created and named (and the spreadsheet resaved) *before* the macro can be invoked. The commands in the macro simply make an existing graph active. For example, if the user wants to see the C/B analysis graph, the command /GNUb-c gets, names, uses and displays b-c, the cost/benefit graph. When the user is finished viewing the graph, pressing the ENTER key terminates the graph command menu and returns to the application. Because the graphs are dynamically linked to the spreadsheet, each change in a cost or benefit value or selected discount rate is automatically reflected in the graph. An additional feature of this approach is that the last selected graph remains current. This means that it can be selected at any time by using the F10 function key, without the need to go through either the graph menu or the macro system.

The Finish macro is the simplest of the options. It serves as a command termination macro that exits the program. It would also be possible to include a Finish option in the original main menu (C/B Data Entry, D.R. Entry, etc.), allowing the user to quit the application at any time. A more involved Finish, taking you back out of Lotus, would include a /QUIT YES, or /QY, sequence.

Formulas in the Application

Earlier in the discussion, we noted that some of the complexities of cost/benefit analysis can be handled by powerful formulas available in Lotus. Several of the formulas used in this application will now be presented and explained. In general, they help maximize the use of the built-in financial functions of Lotus to reduce the need for user-defined computations.

Essentially, this application makes use of just four formulas. The first, used to calculate the difference between annual net benefits and net costs, is a simple subtraction (see figure 8.36). This formula subtracts costs from benefits. For example, +C12-B12 subtracts the content of cell B12 (6,000,000) from the content of cell C12, (0). The importance of this formula is that it provides the annual net value used in calculating both the net present value and the internal rate of return.

Returning to figure 8.28, where the analysts actually entered the costs and benefits, the column (D) containing these formulas appears to be missing. This column has been hidden by means of the /WORKSHEET COLUMN HIDE command to simplify the visible worksheet. Since the user does not make direct use of this information, there is no reason to clutter the screen with it. As an aside, this procedure can also be used to hide intervening columns when printing noncontiguous columns.

The second set of formulas (see figure 8.37) calculates the net present value (@NPV) and the percentage return for each discount rate provided by the user. In these formulas, Netval is the range name for net benefits, calculated in figure 8.36. Note the use of mixed-addressing (use of $ for absolute copy) to simplify the copying of the formula while holding the row numbers for the data range consistent.

The third formula, @IRR(0.1,Netval), found in cell C54 (figure 8.37), is used to calculate the internal rate of return for the project. For this formula to work, Lotus requires that a "guess" be entered into the formula to serve as a starting point for the IRR calculations. The program then goes through a series of iterations in an attempt to find the IRR. If the initial guess is too high or too low, the program will not find the IRR and

```
TEMPLATE FOR NET PRESENT VALUE ANALYSIS      (PRESS ALT-M FOR MENU)
================================================================
DATA ENTRY FOR YEARLY COSTS AND BENEFITS

YEAR          TOTAL COSTS TOTAL BENEFITS              NET BENEFITS
-----------------------------------------------------------------
   START (0)    6,000,000              0             +C12-B12
           1    1,000,000        500,000             +C13-B13
           2      500,000        600,000             +C14-B14
           3      400,000        700,000             +C15-B15
           4      300,000        800,000             +C16-B16
           5      200,000        900,000             +C17-B17
           6      100,000      1,000,000             +C18-B18
           7      100,000      1,300,000             +C19-B19
           8      100,000      1,400,000             +C20-B20
           9      100,000      1,500,000             +C21-B21
          10      100,000      1,600,000             +C22-B22
          11      100,000      1,700,000             +C23-B23
          12      100,000      1,700,000             +C24-B24
          13      100,000      1,700,000             +C25-B25
          14      100,000      1,700,000             +C26-B26
          15      100,000      1,700,000             +C27-B27
          16                                         +C28-B28
          17                                         +C29-B29
          18                                         +C30-B30
          19                                         +C31-B31
          20                                         +C32-B32
```

FIGURE 8.36 Formulas to calculate net benefits

will report an ERR in the cell. This means that the initial guess should fall approximately halfway between the highest and lowest possible realistic discount rates. At the writing of this book, 10 percent is a reasonable compromise.

☐ A desirable extension to this application would be the inclusion of a "goal-seeking" function that would allow the user to specify a target rate of return. The program would then calculate (if possible) the discount rate needed to produce the desired return. Unfortunately, the version of Lotus used to construct this application (Version 2.01) does not offer a built-in goal-seeking option. Production of a goal-seeking subprogram for this application requires that an extensive set of macros be developed. An example of this form of macro programming can be found in Darien Fenn's book 1-2-3 Command Language, Release 2, published by Que Corporation, 1986, on pages 386 to 389. For those who do not aspire to the development of complex command language programs, several third-party vendors offer Lotus add-ins to carry out a number of financial functions, including goal seeking.

The principal value of this application lies in the use of macros and menus to illustrate how a decision-aid tool can be simplified. Clearly, a non-computer-oriented analyst or

```
              Formulas for Net Present Value, Percent Return,
                   and Internal Rate of Return

================================================================================
SELECTION OF DISCOUNT RATES

SELECT UP TO THREE DISCOUNT RATES FOR
NET PRESENT VALUE CALCULATIONS
                                        Type as decimal
DISCOUNT RATE #1:           0.075       (e.g., .075) and
DISCOUNT RATE #2:           0.11        depress ENTER key
DISCOUNT RATE #3:           0.14        after each number.


================================================================================
TEMPLATE FOR NET PRESENT VALUE ANALYSIS    (PRESS ALT-M FOR MENU)
NET PRESENT VALUE RESULTS            PERCENT RETURN

DISCOUNT RATE #1:@NPV(C41,NETVAL)   (@NPV(C41,$NETVAL))/(@NPV(C41,$COSTS))
DISCOUNT RATE #2:@NPV(C42,NETVAL)   (@NPV(C42,$NETVAL))/(@NPV(C42,$COSTS))
DISCOUNT RATE #3:@NPV(C43,NETVAL)   (@NPV(C43,$NETVAL))/(@NPV(C43,$COSTS))

INTERNAL RATE OF
RETURN:             @IRR(0.1,NETVAL)
(Discount rate where benefits = costs)
```

FIGURE 8.37

manager is more likely to make use of a problem-solving tool if it is easy to use, fast, and provides the needed results without excessive and complicated manipulations. The net present value application reduces a tedious and time-consuming task to one that is simple and fast. At the same time, the application is not so restrictive in its construction as to exclude the human element. As indicated earlier in this case, most cost/benefit analyses involve some negotiation and compromise, both in the selection of included costs and benefits and in the selection of the discount rate. An NPV application that did not permit the analyst to easily construct what-if scenarios would likely remain unused.

CONCLUSION

Chapter 8 focuses on more complicated managerial problems, often referred to in the literature as semistructured and unstructured. Typically, finance and planning problems fall into these categories. When managers are confronted with these problems, decision support applications can be helpful as a decision aid. The decision support application sets up the problem so that the analyst or manager can work through some of the realistic options in order to see the impacts of these options. Three cases—one on cash flow, one on financing new roads, and one on cost/benefit analysis—have been presented to illustrate these more complex problems and the use of decision support applications. Throughout, the spreadsheet has been employed to build these applications. A number of lessons have been conveyed on alternative techniques and methods for building decision support applications with spreadsheets.

EXERCISES

Part 1

A. For this exercise, a partially completed appropriation worksheet is presented (see next page, FY 1991 Appropriation Worksheet). This worksheet is used to determine a total appropriation based on the current year approved budget and carryover from previous years. Note that the carryover may represent either a surplus or a deficit.

Complete the worksheet by providing the appropriate subtotals, totals, and percentages.

One of the perceived values of a spreadsheet is the ability to perform what-if calculations. Recalculate the worksheet based on the following:

- What if the FY 1990 ADD-ON were increased by 7.5% for all *funded* characters?
- What if the OMB CARRYOVER ADMIN. ADJUSTMENT were reduced by 6% for all noncharacter categories?

B. Using the worksheet provided for the previous exercise, design a master worksheet that would allow the information from four agencies to be tallied for an overall appropriation/carryover analysis. As part of the design process, create a sketch of the location of the worksheet components and write a pseudocode description of how the elements will fit together. As a final step, create the worksheet.

C. Design a macro-driven menu system for the worksheet created in B that will allow the user to select a specific agency or overall tally without having to search the entire worksheet manually.

Part 2

A. For this exercise, we provide a partially developed decision support application, with some of the formulas and some of the results given. This particular decision support application is designed to examine alternative funding levels for functions that might make up the major functions of a government. Your task is to complete the application so that different percentage changes (increases or decreases) can be used to propose budget amounts for next year. One change will be an across-the-board change; that is, the percentage change is the same for all functions. The other change will be divided into a high and low change to reflect policy preferences. Important results of the application will be the ending percentage allocated to each function and the amount for each function.

The Lotus application in this worksheet (see page 269, Alternative Budget Allocation) has two major parts. In the top half of the application are given last year's

FY 1991 APPROPRIATION WORKSHEET
AGENCY:
FUND:
ANALYST:

	CHARACTER 20	CHARACTER 30	CHARACTER 40	CHARACTER 50	CAPITAL PROJECTS	GRANT PROJECTS	TOTAL	FRINGE BENEFITS	INCOME
FY 1990 ADVERTISED BUDGET	850000	1000000	0	1500000	1350000	275000	?	88950	325000
FY 1990 ADD-ON	150000	0	50000	250000	500000	0	?	45000	
FY 1990 APPROVED BUDGET									
1ST HALF YEAR APPROPRIATION	400000	650000	35000	875000	1000000	100000	?	75000	175000
ADJUSTMENTS	25000	0	0	55000	0	0	?	15000	
TOTAL PRE-CARRYOVER APPROP.	?	?	?	?	?	?	?	?	?

--CARRYOVER--   --CARRYOVER--   --CARRYOVER--

-CARRYOVER APPROP. ADJ.	-75000	0	-15000	-45000	-45000	0	?	-10500	-52000
-OMB CARRYOVER ADMIN. ADJ.	-15000	-200000	-20000	-100000	-100000	0	?	-3000	-2200
-BO5 ADJUSTMENTS	0	50000	-4000	-10000	-25750	0			
TOTAL CARRYOVER APPROP.	?	?	?	?	?	?	?	?	?
TOTAL APPROPRIATION TO DATE	?	?	?	?	?	?	?	?	?
TOTAL APPROPRIATION TO DATE	?	?	?	?	?	?	?	?	?
CARRYOVER AS % OF TOTAL	?	?	?	?	?	?	?	?	?

and next year's budget amounts for the four major functions of this government. These functions, shown in the first column, range from administration to social services. In the second column is the budget amount from last year for each function. The third column is designed to give the percentage allocated (% alloc.) to each function for last year. For example, public housing received 26.32% of all dollars. Starting in the fourth column are proposed percentage changes and amounts for next year. Specifically, column 4 shows the amount for next year given an across-the-board increase of 5%. In column 5 is the amount for next year given either a high or a low percentage change. This version of the application assigns 8% as high and 2% as low. The last column is the percentage allocated when either a high or a low percentage change is given. These percentage allocations can be compared with those for last year to find any reallocations.

The second part of the application allows the application to be generalized; that is, essentially any percentage change can be used to propose next year's amounts. As we have seen, two types of percentage changes are used: across-the-board, where the same percentage change is assigned to each government function; and a high–low change, where a larger change is assigned to some functions and a smaller change to others.

The way the two parts of the application work to achieve this generalization is that cell locations, not specific percentages, are placed in the formulas that generate the amounts for next year. Notice in the top half of the application, column 4, that the cell location ($E$17), not the percentage (5%), is put in the formula +B9*(1+$E$17) to calculate next year's amount for administration. To obtain another set of results, only the 5% in cell E17 needs to be adjusted. (Remember that the dollar signs in a cell reference in Lotus make that location absolute, so that when the formula is copied the cell references do not change.)

The various cases in this chapter, especially the case on funding the transportation system, provide other illustrations of how to generalize decision support applications.

Your first task in completing this application is to reproduce what is in columns 1 and 2 of the top half, as well as the percentage changes shown in the bottom half. Then, complete columns 3, 4, 5, and 6 with the appropriate formulas—that is, formulas to calculate percentage allocated, amount for across-the-board changes, and amount for categories of changes. Sample formulas are given for columns 3 (% alloc.) and 4 (across-the-board amt). Changes for column 5 are high for Administration, then low, high, and finally low for Social Service. After using the percentage changes given (.05, .08, and .02) try different ones.

Finally, in setting the high and low percentage changes for the four government functions, consider what might constitute a "liberal" versus a "conservative" policy. For example, part of a liberal agenda might be to give a high percentage increase to public housing. A conservative agenda might emphasize public safety or, alternatively, cutting back by assigning negative percentages (such as −.03).

B. As described in this chapter, fully developed decision support applications have interfaces whereby users can easily enter data and review results, extensive databases from which to draw information, and models to manipulate the data. What factors

Chapter 8 Semistructured and Unstructured Managerial Problems

```
                  ALTERNATIVE BUDGET ALLOCATION, NEXT YEAR (000)
       (1)           (2)         (3)           (4)            (5)          (6)
                  Last Year                 Next Year
                                %        Across the     Categories         %
    Function       Amount     Alloc.     Board Amt.     of Changes       Alloc.
    -----------------------------------------------------------------------------
    Administration $125.00  +B9/$B$13   +B9*(1+$E$17)    $135.00         13.49%
    Public Housing $250.00    26.32%      $262.50                        25.49%
    Public Safety  $400.00                $420.00
    Social Service $175.00                $183.75
    Total          $950.00   100.00%      $997.50       $1,000.50       100.00%


                              Percent Changes:                %
                              Across the board              0.05
                              Categories
                                High                        0.08
                                Low                         0.02
```

work against the development of full-fledged, sophisticated decision support applications in an environment where microcomputers are used not by professional data personnel, but rather by day-to-day program or staff managers and analysts?

C. List the factors that might work against using the results of a microcomputer decision support application in government policy making.

D. The revenue figures that follow are for a six-year period, 1986 to 1991. Using linear regression, project the revenue for the next two years in the sequence, 1992 and 1993.

Year	Revenue
1986	1698332
1987	1723223
1988	1745632
1989	1897230
1990	1910987
1991	1990192

E. Investments of dollars in different program elements are often assumed to have differential impacts on program results. The worksheet that follows (Analyzing Alternative Strategies) shows a partially completed Lotus application for such an analysis.

The purpose of the worksheet is to determine the increase in arrests for an additional investment in a given input (such as foot patrol). The impact, or increase in arrests, depends on the amount invested, an impact factor, and the probability of that impact factor exerting its entire effect. The amount invested is simply the additional dollars given to carry out the particular function (theoretically, negative

```
                    ANALYZING ALTERNATIVE STRATEGIES
      (1)         (2)         (3)       (4)     (5)       (6)         (7)
                Investment Investment Impact  Impact  Probability  Increased
    Input         Range      Amount   Range   Factor    Factor      Arrests

    Foot patr    10-20K       11000  .02-.06   0.03      0.1          33
    Computers    5-10K               .01-.07
    Training     7.5-12.5K           .03-.05
    Weapons      2.5-5K              .01-.06
    Vehicles     8-12K               .02-.06
    Education    3-7K                .04-.05

    Actual Total              11000            0.03                   33
    Total for
       Mid-Range Value         50750           0.235

                           Probability Factor Matrix
                    .01       .02      .03      .04        .05    .06&.07  Total
    Foot patrol               0.8      0.1      0.06       0.02    0.02      1
    Computers       0.7       0.2
    Training
    Weapons
    Vehicles
    Education
```

amounts could also be used). The impact factor translates or develops a relationship between dollars invested and arrests. That is, for every dollar invested, there will be some arrests generated. In the present application, the impact factor selected for foot patrol is .03, or .03 arrests for every dollar invested in this function. If $1,000 were invested, then 30 arrests (1000*.03) would be generated. However, the impact factor is moderated by a probability that the particular level of impact will occur. For some impact factors, the probability of occurrence is high; for others, it is low. If the probability were 1, then the impact factor would have its total effect. The logic used in this application is that the higher the impact, the lower the probability. For example, one might get a .07 impact for an input of more computer power, but it is not highly likely.

In the top half of the worksheet, the first column lists the various inputs that can affect arrests, ranging from foot patrol to education. The second column shows the range of investments permitted (with the K referring to thousands of dollars). In the third column, the desired investment is inserted by the user. Column 4, Impact Range, shows the low and high impact that can be expected for that input. Column 5 gives the user an opportunity to select an impact factor from the given range. Column 6, Probability Factor, requires that the user look down to the Probability Factor Matrix to find what probability goes with the impact factor selected. For example, a .03 impact factor for foot patrol has a .1 (10%) probability. The last column (7) in the top half of the application gives the number of additional arrests that can be expected for a given combination of investment, impact factor, and probability factor.

The assignment for this problem is to complete the worksheet and then use it to project increased arrests. Completion of the worksheet will entail four tasks. First, reproduce the application as it stands, except for Increased Arrests and Total; formulas, not the numbers shown, will go into these. Second, produce the formula that goes in the cells for increased arrests. This formula needs to multiply the invested amount by the impact factor by the probability factor. Third, finish the Probability Factor Matrix for computers, training, weapons, vehicles, and education. In doing this, it is important to recognize that for each input, the individual probabilities must add to 1, because the probability of an event cannot exceed 1. Thus, under total for the Probability Factor Matrix, there needs to be a formula to sum individual probabilities. Also, probabilities only go into cells for which there is an impact factor for that input. As mentioned, the logic used in the current matrix is that low impact factors have a high probability of occurring, whereas high impact factors have a low probability. Finally, formulas will be needed to total investment amount, impact factors, and increased arrests.

Of course, as far as results are concerned, the higher the number of arrests, the better the set of choices is.

CHAPTER

9

Data-Intensive Structured and Semistructured Problems

■ INTRODUCTION

Purpose and Scope

In developing microcomputer applications for this chapter, we will identify the relevant types of managerial problems, the topics that convey the essence of these problems, the microcomputer applications that can be used to solve these problems, general guidelines for building these applications, and the software that can be used. Following this introductory material, we will present several case studies to illustrate the main points of the chapter.

Type of Problem

In chapter 9 we move to a different type of structured and semistructured problem. For the most part, these problems are not quite as routine as those in chapter 7 (e.g., summing and comparing revenues), but are not as fraught with uncertainty as those in chapter 8 (e.g., projecting two decades into the future). The problems in chapter 9 are distinguished by the fact that they involve organizing and manipulating large amounts of data. As a result, what complexity does exist emanates not from clashes of political values or sheer uncertainty about outcomes, but from the sheer volume of data. We refer to these managerial problems as *data-intensive* structured and semistructured problems.

Topics

The task of managing organizational resources and programs is typical of these data-intensive structured and semistructured problems. For these tasks, the more value-laden issue of choice of major direction has been considered and, to a large extent, decided. The task at hand is to make effective use of resources and programs. What resources are available, what are their costs, and how are the resources currently being used? What is the intended purpose of a particular program, how close are program results to the stated

Chapter 9   Data Intensive Structured and Semistructured Problems   273

goals, and what are the reasons for success or failure? Answering these questions often means organizing, sifting through, and manipulating large pools of data.

General and Specific Design Elements

In building computer applications, as we have seen, there is usually a general logic as well as a more specific set of guidelines. In chapter 8, for example, the general logic derived largely from the divide-and-conquer approach, whereas specific guidelines emanated from decision support applications. In this chapter, the general logic again borrows from the framework of designing microcomputer applications, including divide and conquer, stepwise refinement, algorithms, and pseudocode.

Management Information Applications

The specific direction for developing computer assistance for managing data-intensive resource and programmatic problems comes from management information applications (MINAs). Like the operational application (OPA) of chapter 7 and the decision support applications (DSA) described and used in parts of chapter 8, these management information applications have special features and guidelines.

The usual process of building a management information application breaks into three major endeavors. One is the analysis of the resource or program objectives and the data needed to assess progress toward these objectives. Another is the organization of the data, because data on resources and programs can be voluminous. A third is the preparation of the actual microcomputer application. These three major components, and the steps within each, can be summarized as follows:

1. Analysis of objectives or problems
    a. Problem to be solved or objectives to be reached
    b. Methods of identifying problems or objectives and assessing progress
2. Data organization and relational databases
    a. Collection of relevant data
    b. Normalization of databases
3. Development and operation of application
    a. Design of overall application and associated menus
    b. Data structure and description of data
    c. Data entry and checking
    d. Queries and reports
    e. Updates

The management information application has a close relative in an application referred to as *transaction processing* (TPA). TPA is used to collect and organize data, primarily to reduce paperwork and keep good records. The management information application does this and adds the dimension of orienting the effort toward the needs of management. In the case studies, we will be including elements of TPA because it is closely related to the management information application.

Analysis

The analysis facet of building a management information application is the reflective part of the process. During this stage, one tries to determine what resource or program problems are to be addressed or what objectives are to be pursued. Typical problems are overburdened agencies, low productivity, low morale, high turnover, and failure to improve services. Common goals and objectives include improved safety, better productivity, and faster service delivery.

In some quarters, goals and objectives are assigned separate meanings, with goals referring to broad statements of purpose and objectives referring to specific accomplishments that can be measured. Here, the two will be used interchangeably.

The usual modes for exploring problems or setting objectives include interviewing, surveys, review of past decisions or documents, and observation. These methods are used to unearth problems and formulate goals. Traditionally, in the mainframe computer environment, the analysis has been time-consuming. Those involved in the task were professional systems analysts working out of a central office. First, they needed to become familiar with the operation of the project in question; then, the analyst and the user had to agree on the definition of the problem and type of computer application that would be most worthwhile.

The limitations associated with the long time horizon and high cost of collecting information on problems and goals are somewhat mitigated when developing microcomputer applications, because the user takes over much of the task of analyzing the problem and developing the application. The user, acting to a significant extent as the application developer, has immediate access to relevant documents, can rely on his or her own knowledge about problems and goals, and can easily query his or her colleagues on matters related to defining the problem or goal.

In some respects, the mainframe and microcomputer worlds are coming closer together because the software for both is becoming more user friendly. As a result, users are able to play a larger role in both spheres.

Much of this involvement by the user is a function of the the fact that the software for microcomputers is easy to learn and to develop into applications. Samples, or prototypes, of the application can be generated quickly so that the user sees a quick preview of how the application performs.

Notwithstanding the advantage of having the analyst or manager, as the knowledge source about the problems, also play a key role in translating that knowledge into the application, the job of defining problems and goals is still a difficult one. Goals are often unclear, sometimes too abstract to measure, or even in conflict with one another. As a result, statements about objectives can be unclear.

The user is not alone in this process of translating problems into microcomputer applications. Users can obtain assistance from Information Centers and from central Management Information Centers. Although Information Centers are usually more geared to questions from users, both type of centers can help users.

Data Organization and Relational Databases

The next step in the development of the management information application is to begin assembling the data that can help track the objectives or problems. The data for these objectives or problems can be assembled in a variety of ways. In at least some cases, the data have already been collected as a routine part of the everyday transactions of the government. Calls that come in for services are recorded, responses to the calls are part of the record, and the results of the effort are also included in the files. In other cases, the relevant data have never been collected systematically and must be gathered from scratch. In still other cases, the data task is not to collect more data but to reduce the volume of data to make it more manageable. Overall, the key is to collect and automate those data that will give the best picture of problems, goal achievement, or progress without overburdening the automated systems.

After the relevant data have been identified and assembled, it is then necessary to organize them into the database. For now, not much discussion will be devoted to the issue of data organization and relational databases, since the core concept for organization of the data—normalization—was presented in chapter 5. However, by way of summary, it is important to remember that normalization seeks to ensure flexibility and efficiency in organization of the data. *Flexibility* refers to being able to extract almost any type of information from the database; *efficiency* refers to avoiding waste or redundancy. Care should be taken to avoid the three "data traps": repeating fields, insertion anomalies, and deletion anomalies. The case studies in this chapter will provide ample illustration of how to organize large pools of data and avoid the data traps.

Development and Operation of the MINA

The analysis and the data organization provide the foundation for developing the actual microcomputer management information application. It is the application that provides a system for entering and checking the data, for making changes or updates in the data, and for producing the answers to managerial questions.

There are myriad ways of developing a microcomputer-based MINA, and myriad levels of sophistication. We will examine some very simple applications, with just one data file and only the most rudimentary modes of reporting and querying, as well as much more sophisticated ones, involving menu systems to walk the user through the application, special checking routines to make sure the data are accurate, elaborate reporting schemes, and expert systems to mine the richness of the database.

Software

For the most part, our software tool for implementing the management information application will be the database management system (DBMS). This software has the capacity to work with and manage large pools of data. It can be used to facilitate data entry, conduct routine validity checks, generate simple and complex reports, and develop rudimentary expert systems.

Differences Among Applications

One of the differences between the applications in this chapter and those in the prior two chapters is the amount of programming involved. Unlike the spreadsheet, which served as the basis for chapters 7 and 8, the DBMS often requires more programming right from the start. Many of the general design concepts are still the same, however. Large problems should be broken into smaller, more manageable ones (divide and conquer); similar tasks should be grouped (modularity); and difficult processes or problems should be thought out in English (algorithms and pseudocode) before any programming or coding is undertaken.

Case Studies

Subject matter The specific cases selected for this chapter are designed to reflect resource and program management. The initial case falls in the telecommunications area and involves tracking requests for installing or changing computerized telephone services. For purposes of presentation, this task is divided into two cases, one showing a simple system and one showing a more complex effort. The next set of case materials comes from the public safety area. It, too, is a tracking system, designed to organize records on the amount and type of training and certification fire prevention personnel have received. For the last case, we return to the telecommunications function. However, the focus turns from mere tracking of records to determining the effectiveness and efficiency of service delivery.

Approaches Although the careful process of first analyzing the problem, then organizing the data, and finally developing the application is a valuable aid in constructing the microcomputer applications for these cases, the reality of the management world is such that this ideal approach is often compromised. For this reason, we offer two contrasting styles of developing microcomputer applications for resource and program management. In one, a bottom-up approach is used. Here, the designers and users launch an application as quickly as possible. Some attention is given to goals and objectives and the data organization needed to assess progress, but scant attention is paid to optimal organization of data files or to form and operation of the application. Only after the limitations of this approach appear do we move on to build a more fully developed application. To illustrate the bottom-up approach, we will develop two applications for tracking the delivery of selected telephone services. One will be rather simple, the other more comprehensive, but still bottom-up.

The contrasting approach is a top-down effort, wherein the designers and users spend a good deal of time considering the goals and objectives, the data needed, the organization of the data, and the overall appearance of the application. For the top-down approach, we will look at a system for training and certification records of public safety personnel. In this effort, we will be much more systematic about identifying goals, structuring the necessary data files, and building an application that is easy to use. The last case will also follow the top-down style.

CASE 1: A BARE-BONES TELEPHONE SERVICE APPLICATION

Background and Purpose

The first case, building a tracking system for adding to or making changes in office telephones, shows a simple management information application that will be turned into a more sophisticated one. Such an evolution is quite common. Oftentimes, after users learn the basic tools for developing a management information application, they rush into implementing a rudimentary application. However, they then become frustrated with the limitations of these basic tools and search for more powerful techniques to build the management information application.

The telephone service request system In this telephone service request system, the major services that can be requested are: installing a new telephone, moving existing telephones to new locations, removing old telephones, and changing the software on current telephones to obtain either simpler or more sophisticated answering capabilities. A request for any of these services initiates a paper flow. First, the department or operating unit wishing to acquire a particular service fills out a request form and sends it to the telecommunications coordinator. With this form, and any other clarifying information, the coordinator completes a work order and sends it both to the vendor who will perform the actual work and to the department that requested the job. When the vendor completes the job, the vendor notifies the coordinator by sending a bill. The coordinator contacts the requesting unit to determine if the work has been completed and submits the invoice for payment if the requesting party is satisfied. If not, there is a round of calls to iron out any problems.

As with most of the cases portrayed, this one does not assume a highly automated, interdepartmental computer system. The forms discussed here represent part of the paper component of the telephone service request system. Although the form itself could be developed with a microcomputer software package, we assume that the movement of forms is still done the old-fashioned way—hand-carried interdepartmental mail. Electronic communication of these requests would add another, and very exciting, dimension to the computerization of this system.

The telephone service request MINA The general purpose of the microcomputer-based management information application for this telephone service delivery function is to keep track of and report on all the requests. With a large number of requests, volumes of paper files can build up over time. Queries, searches, summaries, and reports are much easier if the materials are stored in computer files. In this case study, we describe the first effort to build the management information application, moving from the preliminary analysis of the problem, to development of a simple MINA, to use of this MINA, and finally to recognition of the limitations of these efforts.

Preliminary Analysis

The analysis for this initial application is brief and simple. The telecommunications coordinator is overwhelmed by the amount of paper in his files. He is experiencing difficulty in organizing, locating, and determining the status of requests. When requesters or vendors call about a particular order, the telecommunications officer must go to his paper files to find that request. When the status of a request is changed (completed, for example), the telecommunications officer, must find the original document and add the new information. When managers ask for summary data on telephone service requests, the telecommunications officer must compile the results manually by thumbing through all the paper-based request forms. As a result, a microcomputer-based management information application using a database management system (DBMS) is recommended to perform the following functions:

- entering a request to the management information application and sending a summary copy to the vendor and requester
- answering inquiries about the status of a request
- processing the vendor's invoice
- recording the date of the completed task
- generating reports on the number and type of requests as well as on the requesting agencies

Data Organization

With the functions and requirements of the management information application identified, the next step is to build a database. At this point, only one data file will be constructed. Because only one file is involved, the basic task consists of listing the fields that will constitute the file. Fields represent the items that go into the data file. It is these fields that are needed to answer the questions and meet the requirements laid out in the analysis. The fields for this MINA are:

- a unique order number that identifies each request
- a billing code that is part of the accounting system and identifies whose account is to be charged
- a department or unit name that identifies the unit making the request
- the contact person for the requesting unit
- the address of the contact person
- the phone number of the contact person
- the date the request is received
- a short description of the work requested
- the vendor selected to perform the work
- the vendor contact person
- the vendor's address
- the phone number of the vendor contact person
- the date the job is completed

Several of the fields are simplified for the purpose of this illustration. For example, in a more thorough setup, the contact person's name might be separated into two fields, last name and first name. Additionally, as we proceed with the application, we will see the limitations of using only one data file. For at least some of these limitations, we will make design improvements.

Listing the fields only tells what information ought to go into the database; it does not show how to actually set up the database. The way the database is set up depends, in

Chapter 9   Data Intensive Structured and Semistructured Problems   279

```
Structure for database: C:phonedb.dbf
Number of data records:       1
Date of last update   :
Field   Field Name   Type        Width    Dec
    1   PHORDERNUM   Numeric         5
    2   BILLCODE     Character       5
    3   UNITNAME     Character      25
    4   CONTACTPER   Character      25
    5   CONADDRESS   Character      25
    6   CONPHONE     Character       8
    7   DATEREQUES   Date            8
    8   WORKDESCR    Character      50
    9   VENDOR       Character      25
   10   VENCONTACT   Character      25
   11   VENPHONE     Character       8
   12   VENCHARGE    Numeric         5     2
   13   DATEFINISH   Date            8
** Total **                        223
```

FIGURE 9.1 Database structure for original phone service file PHONEDB.DBF

part, on the DBMS selected. With dBASE III Plus, which is the DBMS vehicle in this case, it is necessary to give each field a name (the name needs to comply with several rules, such as not being longer than ten characters), to decide on a data type (character, numeric, etc.), to establish a maximum length for the data that will be put into the field, and to designate the number of decimal places if the field is numeric.

In dBASE III Plus, the database (or file) is initiated with the CREATE command. CREATE is followed by the name of the file—for example, CREATE Phonedb. All the data elements together (field name, type, etc.) constitute what is commonly called the *data structure* for the file (or database). After the CREATE command is issued, a blank data structure for field name, type of data, width of data, and decimal spaces (if any) is presented to the user.

For field names (such as Phordernum) and files names (such as Phonedb), only the first letter is capitalized in the text but not in the dBASE programs. In the dBASE programs, field names and file names are entered in all lowercase letters. dBASE reserved words (such as CLEAR) are capitalized, both in the text and in the programs. Reserved words are dBASE commands. Occasionally, a field name will appear entirely in caps. This occurs if dBASE capitalizes everything, as is the case in figure 9.1.

The completed data structure is shown in figure 9.1. There are thirteen fields in all (numbered on the far left side of the figure). Each field has a name, a data type, a width, and an option for decimal places if the data type is numeric.

The first field is called Phordernum, for phone request order number. It is assigned a numeric data type, which means it can contain only numbers—no letters or special characters. Phordernum is designated numeric because later a system will be devised to calculate the order number for each request automatically. If no calculations were to be

```
Record No.         1
PHORDERNUM         1
BILLCODE           de001
UNITNAME           department of energy
CONTACTPER         stevens ron
CONADDRESS         777 w. 7th street
CONPHONE           797-3345
DATEREQUES         03/23/89
WORKDESCR          install 5 new phones, room 321
VENDOR             phone-x
VENCONTACT         robbins jean
VENPHONE           797-8788
VENCHARGE          0.00
DATEFINISH          /  /
```

FIGURE 9.2

made, the data type could have been made character. Looking at the other defining features of the field Phordernum, we see that it can hold up to five characters, which means the designers do not expect order numbers to exceed 99999. It needs no decimal places, because the order numbers will be whole numbers.

Several other fields are of interest because of their data type. Datereques refers to the date the request was made. It is "date" type. In dBASE III Plus, one date type format is mm/dd/yy, or month/day/year. Thus, if the first request is received on January 7, 1990, then the input is 01/07/90. Workdescr, designated character type, is given a length of fifty characters so that a short description of the work requested can be included in the file. Vencharge refers to the vendor's charge or bill for service rendered. It is numeric, with a width of eight digits, including two decimal places for cents. In assigning eight digits (including the decimal point but not the dollar sign and comma), the designers assume that the charge will never exceed $99,999.00.

Default Data-Entry Screen

Once the data structure has been established, data can be entered. In dBASE III Plus, that can easily be accomplished with the *default data-entry facility*. If the database is already in use (USE Phonedb), then the APPEND command brings up the default data-entry screen. The screen is very basic, but adequate for the job.

Figure 9.2 shows an example of the default data entry for the Phonedb database. Note that the names of the fields are listed on the left. Beside each field is a highlighted space (not visible on the printout) equal to the width declared when the data structure was established. For example, a width of five characters is set for Phordernum and also for Billcode. In both these cases, no more than five pieces of data can be put into each field. Notice, however, that Phordernum has only one space filled, whereas Billcode has all five filled (de001).

For a person who is very familiar with the data, the default input screen is sufficient. That person will know the next order number, the correct names of departments, and

Chapter 9 Data Intensive Structured and Semistructured Problems

```
phordernum billcode contactper         conphone  vendor
         1 de001    stevens ron        797-3345  phone-x
         3 de001    stevens ron        797-3345  phone-x
        10 de002    stevens ron        797-3345  all-tron
         2 dt001    author jean        797-3344  phone-x
         4 ds       rogers joe         733-2344  tele-comm
         5 ds       peterson jim       453-3451  all-tron
         6 dt002    peters mary        453-9812  all-tron
         7 da       miller paul        453-8723  tele-comm
         8 da       miller paul        453-8723  all-tron
        13 da       miller paul        453-8723  tele-comm
         9 df       stewart barbara    797-9987  phone-x
        12 dpw01    montone vic        797-2317  all-tron
        12 dpw      montone vic        797-2317  tele-comm
        14 dp&r     vines jeanne       733-2934  all-tron
        15 dp&r     vines jeanne       733-2934  tele-comm
        16 dt001    willis steve       797-2391  tele-comm
```

FIGURE 9.3 Selected data from Phonedb file

other specifics needed to enter the data. For example, the order number for this first record is 1, the Billcode is de001, and all the data in this file are to be entered in small letters, not capitals. A written guide should also be prepared to standardize these guidelines.

☐ As we proceed with this rudimentary management information application, we will see that we fail to follow a number of the guidelines suggested in chapter 6 for system access. Thus, if one person developed this system, then access to and use of the system would depend on that person's remaining with the office. In case 2, we will make some changes and improvements to avoid such dependencies.

With this default data-entry form, it is possible to see the strengths and weaknesses of such formats. In terms of strengths, almost no setup time is involved. As soon as the data structure has been established, the default form is ready. Default data-entry screens also have rudimentary guides and editing features. In this DBMS, dBASE III Plus, the screen shows the width of information that can go into each field. Further, if one tries to place a character in a numeric field, the DBMS system will not allow it. Similarly, characters could not be put in fields that are date type.

The main weakness of default screens is the lack of instructions on the screen. How does the data-entry person know what the next order number should be? How does the person know whether all input should be in small letters? Moreover, if a person does not follow the rules for how the data should be entered and the mistakes are not caught, the database will be compromised. For example, the same order number may be entered more than once. The same vendor's name may be spelled differently, resulting in faulty reports about the total business given to each vendor. Later, methods will be presented for avoiding or minimizing these problems.

After all the data have been entered via the default data-entry screen, the data are ready for analysis. Figure 9.3 gives some of the data—namely, the Phordernum,

Billcode, Contactper, Conphone, and Vendor. In the first record, we have Phordernum 1, Billcode de001, Contactper stevens ron, Conphone 797-3345, and Vendor phone-x. Next we will look into ways of analyzing the data.

DBMS Query Commands

Just as default data-entry screens are serviceable for simple data input, so too are query commands for simple searches. With the data now inputted, it is possible to engage the query facilities of the DBMS. In one query, or search of the file, the user may wish to see which vendors are working with which units. The command in dBASE III Plus would be:

```
LIST unitname,vendor
```

Another request might be to find which orders are not being done by a particular vendor. That could be expressed:

```
LIST phordernum for vendor # 'all-tron'
```

where the pound sign (#) means "not equal to." If someone has a suspicious streak, he or she might look for all the orders that one contact person has with one vendor:

```
LIST phordernum for contactper='vines jeanne'.AND. vendor='phone-x'
```

Suppose one wants to print out a particular phone order request. Though more involved than necessary, the following set of commands, requesting a printout of phone order request 10, shows more of the commands available in dBASE III Plus:

```
USE phonedb
INDEX ON phordernum TO phoneidx
SET INDEX TO phoneidx
FIND 10
DISPLAY TO PRINT
```

☐ The same results could be obtained with DISPLAY FOR phordernum = 10 TO PRINT.

These commands open (USE) the data file Phonedb, INDEX the file from the lowest order number to highest, place the index file in use via the SET INDEX command, FIND Phordernum 10, and PRINT the desired record. The results would be similar to figure 9.3, except that only Phordernum 10 would be printed, and all thirteen fields would be included.

In actuality, the last command, DISPLAY TO PRINT, would need to be more sophisticated; otherwise, the printout would not be appealing. Because the PRINT command does not work like a word processor, in terms of spacing and layout, the

DISPLAY command would need to be modified to obtain an appealing printout. For example, several DISPLAY commands could be used and a TRIM function incorporated to control the spacing:

```
DISPLAY TRIM(contactper)+' '+TRIM(conaddress)+' '+TRIM(conphone)
```

This command would trim, or remove, any trailing spaces between the fields (notice all the blank spaces in figure 9.3) and place only the number of spaces or blanks enclosed between the quotation marks. The plus sign (+) concatenates, or combines, one field after another. In short, a somewhat complicated DISPLAY statement is needed to produce an attractive printout.

☐ Queries like the one to find information on a particular service order can be done through the use of menus provided by dBASE III Plus. The menus remove the burden of having to remember or having to look up all the syntax such as SET INDEX TO phoneidx. Of course, if the user does any extensive programming, then learning the syntax is necessary.

Other requests can be enacted in the same way. Decide on what needs to be done, outline the logic, decide on the proper syntax, and try it until correct.

Report Generators

Attractive reports can also be generated from the data in the files. The sample report in figure 9.4 shows which offices have requested service, who the contact person is, and the date of each request. Any combination of the thirteen fields could be used in creating this type of report.

Report generators in dBASE III Plus and other DBMS are quite easy to use. For the most part, they are menu-driven. Usually, the initial menus ask for titles with later menus requesting the fields to be used and any special calculations.

Limitations

Everything suggested so far has been relatively straightforward. Useful work can be accomplished with elemental tools such as the default data-entry screen, queries, and report generators. However, a user will likely become frustrated with the present system. Three limitations quickly become apparent: the single data file, the default data-entry screen, and the need to enter each command every time a special query request is made.

Single data file When inputting data in the single file setup, one quickly notices the redundancy of repeatedly entering the same address and phone number when the same contact person appears for a second or subsequent time. For example, if "stevens ron" is the contact person for the department of energy and makes a second or subsequent request (see figure 9.3), his address and phone number will (likely) be the same. It does not make much sense to repeatedly reenter the data on "stevens ron." Some of this redundancy can be eliminated by having a separate file for contact people. With a separate file, the address and telephone number are taken out of the order file and placed in a separate contact file.

```
Page No.      1
Date
                       List by Requesting Office

Requesting              Contact                    Date
Office                  Person                     Requested


department  public works  montone vic              03/08/88
department  public works  montone vic              07/07/88
department of admin       miller paul              09/08/88
department of admin       miller paul              04/04/88
department of admin       miller paul              10/09/88
department of corrections willis steve             09/11/92
department of energy      stevens ron              03/23/88
department of energy      stevens ron              09/01/88
department of energy      stevens ron              05/09/88
department of finance     stewart barbara          08/08/88
department of sanitation  rogers joe               02/17/88
department of sanitation  peterson jim             08/21/88
department of traffic     author jean              08/23/88
department of traffic     peters mary              01/03/88
parks and recreation      vines jeanne             11/02/88
parks and recreation      vines jeanne             12/09/88
```

FIGURE 9.4 Sample report, using a report generator

Now, the order file has only the contact's name; the contact file has the contact's name, address, and telephone number. Once the address and telephone number have been entered into the contact file for a given contact person, they do not need to be reentered every time that person makes a new request (unless, of course, there is a change). If information must be obtained from both files, the two files can be related. A method for relating two files will be shown later.

The same logic for developing multiple files on contact persons can be extended to vendors. A separate file on vendors might include the vendor's address, telephone number, and perhaps the name of the billing agent. Then, the order file need have only the name of the vendor, with more detailed information on vendors being located in the separate vendor file.

Also frustrating with this single file database is the difficulty of including information on the progress of or subsequent questions (or complaints) about, an order. What if the database user wanted to log all calls from the requester and include these in the file? How many new fields would be needed? It is indeterminant. Guessing is of little value because some orders may have no subsequent questions and others, twenty or thirty. The solution is a separate file for subsequent questions. That file would include the order number, the nature of the inquiry, and the date of the question. Each time a question came in, it would be added to this file.

With these changes, there now exists a richer, multifile system. Much more information is available, many more agency objectives can be handled, and the data are not all cluttered in one file. Details on a multifile system and how to create one will be given later.

Data entry The next limitation, the problems with the default data-entry screen, has already been discussed. In general, default screens do not provide sufficient guidance for entering and checking the validity of data.

Queries and reports The other major frustration with our current approach is typing in all the commands every time a query is needed or a printout is requested. Would it not be timesaving to put these commands in a program and generalize the program so that any order could be printed? Would it not also be inviting to have a menu for selecting this and other programs that run all the queries and reports? In case 2, we describe how to build at least part of such an easy-to-use system.

☐ So far in this case, we have not explicitly proceeded through the framework logic of divide and conquer, stepwise refinement, and pseudocode. What we are doing is showing the bottom-up, or inductive, process one might use in "discovering" a sophisticated system. Although the discovery process is useful, it should not be the main method for systems development. If a designer does not "discover" a weakness and correct it, that flaw can create serious inefficiencies.

■ CASE 2: ENHANCING THE TELEPHONE SERVICE SYSTEM

Overall, several improvements can be incorporated into this initial telephone service application to make it more powerful:

- developing multiple files rather than trying to place all information in one file
- learning how to link files, once there are multiple files in the database
- replacing the rudimentary default data-entry screen with customized screens that are easier to use
- building menus to ease access into and maneuverability around the application
- developing generalizable programs that can respond to a variety of user questions about the data

Taken together, these improvements will yield a more comprehensive management information application. The menus will be the gateway to the application. The customized data-entry screens will enhance the data-entry function. The multiple files will reduce the problem of entering the same data repeatedly and will allow the designer to incorporate more goals.

Although the improvements will make for a better and more comprehensive system, we will introduce them piece by piece to stay with the bottom-up approach. Once we are finished with all the changes, we will try to tie them together.

In this second case study, we show how these several improvements might be made. Although this involves quite a bit of programming, one can see the logic behind the programming. If the user understands the general parameters of the application and the logic, then he or she can obtain assistance with any of the knotty programming problems.

```
Structure for database:  C:phonedb1.dbf
Number of data records:
Date of last update     :
Field   Field Name    Type          Width      Dec
    1   PHORDERNUM    Numeric           5
    2   BILLCODE      Character         5
    3   UNITNAME      Character        25
    4   CONTACTPER    Character        25
    5   DATEREQUES    Date              8
    6   WORKDESCR     Character        50
    7   VENDOR        Character        25
    8   VENCONTACT    Character        25
    9   VENPHONE      Character         8
   10   VENCHARGE     Numeric           6         2
   11   DATEFINISH    Date              8
   12   DURATION      Numeric           3
** Total **                           194

Structure for database:  C:contactd.dbf
Number of data records:
Date of last update     :
Field   Field Name    Type          Width      Dec
    1   CONTACTPER    Character        25
    2   CONADDRESS    Character        25
    3   CONPHONE      Character         8
** Total **                            59
```

FIGURE 9.5 Two-file database: Phonedbl and Contactd

Multifile Databases

The first task in the redesign is to move away from the single file database. For this case, one more file will be added to illustrate the process.

In the analysis of the original single file design, we mentioned that repeating the information on the contacts' addresses and telephone numbers was redundant. Such redundancy could be avoided by creating a separate file on contact persons. The new database would then have two files: a telephone service order file (Phonedb1) and a contact file (Contactd). These two files are represented in figure 9.5. Note that the first file, Phonedb1, only has one field for the contact person, Contacterer. The second file, Contactd, has all the information on the contact person: name (Contactper), address (Conaddress), and telephone number (Conphone).

Compare the original design that had only one file (figure 9.1) and the current design with two files (figure 9.5). With this two-file design, if "stevens ron" makes a second or subsequent request, only his name will be entered in the file called Phonedb1. All the other information about him (address, telephone number) is entered in the other file called Contactd, but it is entered only once. If the trailing data about him are voluminous, then quite a bit of time is saved with this two-file system.

Chapter 9 Data Intensive Structured and Semistructured Problems

Creating these new files is relatively easy. In fact, the two files can be created by partitioning the single file with which we started (Phonedb in figure 9.1). The original Phonedb file can be copied to a new file (called Phonedb1) but without the fields Conaddress and Conphone. Similarly, the Phonedb file can be copied to another new file (called Contactd), but taking only Contactper, Conaddress, and Conphone, and setting certain conditions so that only one record for each Contactper is copied. The result is two new files: one has everything the original had except Conaddress and Conphone; the other has only the three fields for the contact person—Contactper, Conaddress, and Conphone.

The work involved in creating these two new files from the original file can be facilitated by means of several tools commonly found in the DBMS, including dBASE III Plus. These tools, though somewhat sophisticated, do illustrate the many facilities available in DBMS.

Because several commands are necessary for all this copying and rearranging, it is wise to put them into a program. If the program does not work properly, all one need do is get back into the program (e.g., MODIFY COMMAND copy2ph1) and make the necessary changes. Without a program, it might be necessary to retype many of the commands just to correct one mistake. Figure 9.6 shows two programs that could be used to partition the original file in figure 9.1 into the two files shown in figure 9.5.

Figure 9.6 shows the syntax for creating the new file Phonedb1 from the original file Phonedb. After some comments, indicated by asterisks (*), the first command, USE Phonedb, makes the original file active and ready for use. The next command is the heart of the program. Specifically, it is the FIELDS option in the COPY TO command that allows one to select which fields to carry from the old file to the new. Note that all the fields except Conaddress and Conphone are listed, signaling that those fields should not be copied to the new file, called Phonedb1. The remaining commands simply display the fields or the structure for the new file.

☐ To create and store a program in dBASE III Plus, all one need do is type the command MODIFY COMMAND (or MODI COMM, for short) followed by the name of the program—MODI COMM copy2ph1, for example. The MODI COMM takes the user into an editor, where the program is typed by the user. Pressing the key sequence CTRL END saves the program. The command DO followed by the program name (e.g., DO copy2ph1) executes the program. If the program has any errors, just reenter the edit mode (again using MODI COMM), find the error, correct it, and rerun the program (DO and whatever the program name is).

The syntax in the second program is somewhat different from the first. The reason is to make sure that each contact person is copied only once. Note the SET UNIQUE ON command. With this command and the subsequent INDEX commands, the conditions are set so that only one record is copied for each contact person. For example, if there were sixteen records in the original Phonedb file, but in fact only ten different contact people, then the new contact file, Contactd, would contain ten records. Most DBMS have this option for copying only unique records for some given field. Thus, it is important to make sure what type of copy is intended and what syntax is appropriate.

Notice also that there are quite a few comments in both programs. These comments are set off from the rest of the program (i.e., the statements that actually cause the program

```
*Named copy2ph1, this program creates a new database,  *
*phonedb1, with selected fields from the first database,*
*phonedb.                                                *
USE phonedb
COPY TO phonedb1 FIELDS phordernum,billcode,unitname,contactper,;
 datereques,workdescr,vendor,vencontact,venphone,vencharge,;
 datefinish
*The next several statements pause the program, then    *
*display the fields for the newly created database file *
*phonedb1.                                               *
WAIT
? 'New database has the following structure'
USE phonedb1
LIST STRU

*Named copy2cdb, this program creates a new database,   *
*contactd, with three selected fields from the first    *
*database, phonedb, and only one record for each contact*
*person.                                                *
USE phonedb
*The next three commands make it possible to copy each  *
*contact persons record only once. Recall that a contact*
*person's name may be listed more than once in the      *
*original file.                                         *
SET UNIQUE ON
INDEX ON contactper TO onerec
SET INDEX TO onerec
COPY TO contactdb FIELDS contactper,conaddress,conphone
*After a pause generated by the WAIT, the fields from   *
*the new database file, contactd, are listed via the    *
*LIST STRUCTURE command.                                *
WAIT
? 'New database has the following structure'
USE contactdb
LIST STRU
WAIT
? 'Check to see if the unique worked'
LIST
```

FIGURE 9.6 Copy programs for creating new database files from an original file

to execute, or carry out, its function) by the asterisk. The comments tell what the program is doing.

Relating Files

Although the two-file system has its advantages, it creates a need to link, or relate, the two files when information is required from both files. For example, the user may want to see the request number, the name of the contact person, and the contact person's telephone number. Such a request can be filled by linking two files because both files share a common field—the name of the contact person (Contactper).

Ordinarily the logic for linking two files involves opening both files, ordering (technically, sorting or indexing) both files on the common variable so that it is easier for a record in one file to find its parallel record in the other file, and finally establishing the link from one file to another by identifying the common variable. Thus, in this case, we get our two files (Phonedb1 and Contactd), order or INDEX them on the variable that will serve as the link (Contactper), and then activate the link

☐ Care must be taken in deciding which file is the anchor file when two files are linked. In this case, we want to see the requests from the orders file, Phonedb1, and attach phone numbers from the Contactd file to see the telephone number of the requester. Thus, each record (order request) in Phonedb1 will search out its parallel record (using Contactper as the link) in Contactd. If Phonedb1 had twenty records, then the results would have twenty records, each showing the requester and the requester's phone number. Using Contactd as the anchor file and linking it to Phonedb1 would give different results. Remember, Contactd has each person listed only once. If there were only five different contact persons for all twenty requests, then a link with Contactd would generate only five records.

The dBASE III Plus syntax for relating the files is shown in figure 9.7. Again, the coding is placed in a program (Relonctp, for relate on contact person) so that it can be edited for mistakes if errors occur. Remembering that the asterisk simply allows for comments, the syntax translates into the following steps:

1. Clear any files out before starting (CLEAR ALL).
2. Get (USE) and index (INDEX) both files on the field to be linked—namely, Contactper.
3. Open two work areas (via the SELECT command) for the files to be linked.
4. Activate the indexes (INDEX).
5. SELECT the file from the first work area by its alias name, Phones. (dBASE uses a second-name, or alias, convention when joining files.)
6. Link, via the SET RELATION command, the Phones file with the Contactd file on the field Contactper.

With this program relating the two files, it is possible to draw information from both. Figure 9.8 shows only partial results of such an effort (i.e., not all records shown) using a simple LIST command. Notice that fields from both files (Phonedb1 and Contactd) are contained in the list. The syntax for that LIST command is:

```
LIST phordernum,contactper,contactd->conphone
```

To distinguish fields in the linked file (Contactd is linked to the active file, Phonedb1 or its alias Phones), it is necessary to prefix the linked fields with the file name—for example, Contactd-Conphone. Fields, such as Phordernum, from the main file do not need a prefix.

```
*This program, named relonctp, is designed to allow      *
* the file  phonedb1 to be related to the file contactd  *
* on the field contactper.                               *
*See text for discussion of program.                     *
CLEAR ALL
USE phonedb1
INDEX ON contactper TO phcontix
USE contactd
INDEX ON contactper TO contix
SELECT 1
USE phonedb1 index phcontix ALIAS phones
SELECT 2
USE contactd INDEX contix
SELECT phones
SET RELATION TO contactper INTO contactd
LIST phordernum,contactper,contactd->conphone
```

FIGURE 9.7 Program to relate two files

```
Record#   phordernum contactper        contactd->conphone
     2             2 author jean       797-3344
     4             4 rogers joe        733-2344
     1             1 stevens ron       797-3345
     3             3 stevens ron       797-3345
```

FIGURE 9.8 Results of list command using access to two files

As microcomputer software progresses, all these details of linking files are receding into the background. All the user need do is identity which files to link and be careful to identify which file is the anchor and which is linked. Both dBASE III Plus and dBASE IV have the capacity to walk the user through a simple set of menus to link two files without all the programming employed in figure 9.7. For example, dBASE III Plus offers a CREATE VIEW command that walks the user through what is called the set up of the files and associated indexes; the relate, which indicates the file that will initiate the relation; the field that will link the files; and finally a set of fields to select the fields to LIST or DISPLAY. This is all done in what is referred to as the ASSIST mode, which is dBASE's menu system for guiding the user through prompts rather than having the user write programs as in figure 9.7.

Customizing Screens

The next enhancement to the telephone service management information application is to build a customized data-entry screen to replace the default data-entry screen (see figure 9.2). In doing so, we want to achieve these improvements:

- offer a more attractive appearance
- assist the data-entry person with hard-to-remember details

Chapter 9 Data Intensive Structured and Semistructured Problems

```
Last phone order number was:          1
The next phone order number is:       2
Press any key to continue . . .


        ORDER INFORMATION FOR PHONE SERVICE DATA
      • Press ENTER once you have completed a field
      • Press CTRL END to save and return to menu
      • Pres ESC to abort and return to menu
      • You can use the arrow keys to go from cell to cell

Phone Order Number
Billing Code
[de,dt,ds, and da are valid code prefixes]

Contact Person
[last name first and all small letters]

Date Request Made      /  /

Describe the Work Order
[be specific and brief]

Vendor's Name
[phone-x, tele-comm, and all-tron are valid]

                                            Ins

Give name of vendor contact person
Enter phone number of vendor
Enter the vendor's total bill
When the job is completed, enter that date   /  /



Do you want to enter another order? Y/N
```

FIGURE 9.9

- use more descriptive phrases for the fields
- provide instructions on what to enter for several of the fields

The customized data-entry screen is pictured in figure 9.9. (Note that this is a screen to handle the file Phonedb1, where conaddress and conphone were eliminated.) The very first piece of information is what the last phone order number was and what the next should be. With this information, the data-entry person will not be confused about numbering the orders.

With this custom screen, the data-entry person simply needs to read the instructions and follow the fields presented on the screen. Phone Order Number is the first field to enter and, in contrast to the default screen, is spelled out completely. With the default screen, only the dBASE III Plus field name (Phordernum) is given. The same elaboration is carried out for each field, although different techniques are used to show some of the variations possible. For example, for some fields, more explicit instructions are given, such as entering the last name first and typing in all small letters for the contact person's name. Slightly different wording is also used. In an actual entry screen, consistency in approach is desired to reduce confusion.

Customized data-entry screens can have other features that are worth noting. Many DBMS permit interactive, or on-line, data editing and checking. With these features, a criterion is set for a given field, and the data-entry person cannot continue if that criterion is not met. For example, if the phone order number (Phordernum) has to be unique, the program will check every time a number is entered to see if that number already exists. If it does, the person needs to choose another. Spelling can also be checked, as well as proper categories and ranges.

The programs to execute this screen are presented in figure 9.10. The main program has several parts, or blocks. Overall, these are designed to keep track of the order number, delete any stray blank records, place you in a loop so you can keep entering records as long as you want, present you with the data-entry screen, wipe clean (or refresh) the filled data screens so you can start on new ones, and store inputted records into the appropriate database file. In addition, the database would have to be in use.

In the initial block, one of the first things this program does is to call another small program, DO Whatspon (what is the next phone order number?). This small program keeps track of the order number (see the latter part of figure 9.10). It starts by going to the bottom of the file (GO BOTTOM) to locate the last record. If this record happens to be the first (if RECNO()=1), then the order number (Phordernum) is set to 0 to indicate that the user is starting a new file and then increments by 1 to assign number 1 to the first record. If it is not the first record, the ELSE path is taken and we do some "house cleaning" before we do any incrementing. In particular, there is some coding to get rid of blank records that might have been added accidentally (namely, DELE, which stands for DELETE, and PACK to complete the Delete). The actual deleting is done inside the DO WHILE ... ENDDO segment. The DO WHILE part of the program searches for any such records at the bottom of the file. It keeps deleting them until all are eliminated. Once all the blank records have been disposed of, then the number is increased by 1 and displayed.

When the program Whatspon is finished executing, it takes the user back to the main program (via the RETURN) and begins to execute the command following the call to Whatspon.

In this second block of the main customized data-entry program is a loop controlled by the DO WHILE ... ENDDO command (specifically DO WHILE UPPER(order)="Y"). The loop allows the data-entry person to continue adding records as long as the control or temporary variable Order, is set to Y for yes. Just before the ENDDO is a sequence of code giving the person a chance to decide whether to add another record or not. It starts with an @ 13,5 SAY command, asking whether the data-entry person wants to add another record. If the answer is Y, then we continue with the programs and enter more data, but first going to the program DO Whatspon to show

```
*Named fonorder, this program produces a custom screen *
*for entering all the items for a given phone order    *
*request.                                              *
*Housekeeping to clear the screen and suppress         *
*certain feedback from appearing on the screen.        *
*Needed files are already in use.                      *
CLEAR
SET TALK OFF
*Block or part one of the program, which calls on the  *
*program whatspon, which determines the next order     *
*number.                                               *
DO whatspon
*Start of the custom screen.                           *
APPEND BLANK
*Start of the loop to allow the data-entry person to   *
*keep entering orders until a "N" for no is given.     *
STORE 'y' TO order
DO WHILE UPPER(order)="Y"
CLEAR
*The commands for arranging the display for the        *
*custom screen.                                        *
@ 1,10 SAY 'ORDER INFORMATION FOR PHONE SERVICE DATA'
@ 3,12 SAY 'o Press ENTER once you have completed a field'
@ 4,12 SAY 'o Press CTRL END to save and return to menu'
@ 5,12 SAY 'o Press ESC to abort and return to menu'
@ 6,12 SAY 'o You can use the arrow keys to go from cell to cell'
@ 9,5 SAY 'Phone Order Number           'get phordernum
@ 11,5 SAY 'Billing Code           ' get billcode
@ 12,5 SAY '[de,dt,ds, and da are valid code prefixes]'
@ 14,5 SAY 'Contact Person              ' get contactper
@ 15,5 SAY '[last name first and all small letters]'
@ 17,5 SAY 'Date Request Made       ' get datereques
@ 19,5 SAY 'Describe the Work Order   ' get workdescr
@ 20,5 SAY '[be specific and brief]'
@ 22,5 SAY "Vendor's Name           " get vendor
@ 23,5 SAY '[phone-x, tele-comm, and all-tron are valid]'
READ
*Clears the above material from the screen and displays*
*a second screen.                                      *
CLEAR
@5,5 SAY 'Give name of vendor contact person' get vencontact
@7,5 SAY 'Enter phone number of vendor ' get venphone
@9,5 SAY "Enter the vendor's total bill " get vencharge
@11,5 SAY 'When the job is completed, enter that date ' get;
 datefinish
READ
SKIP
```

FIGURE 9.10 Program for customized data-entry screen

```
    STORE ' ' TO order
    @ 13, 5 SAY 'Do you want to enter another order? Y/N? ' get order
    READ
    IF UPPER(order)='Y'
        DO whatspon
        APPEND BLANK
    ENDIF
ENDDO

*For this program, whatspon, syntax is explained in*
*the text.                                         *
SET TALK OFF
CLEAR
GO BOTTOM
IF RECNO()=1
    STORE 0 TO phordernum
    ? 'Last phone order number was:           ',phordernum
    newpon = phordernum+1
ELSE
    DO WHILE EOF() .OR. phordernum=0
        DELE
        PACK
        GO BOTTOM
    ENDDO
    ? 'Last phone order number was:           ',phordernum
    newpon=phordernum+1
ENDIF
? 'The next phone order number is: ', newpon
WAIT
RETURN
```

FIGURE 9.10 *(Continued)*

what the next record number should be and then adding more data. If an N for no, or anything other than a Y, is entered by the user, we leave the data-entry screen program.

Much of the remainder of the main customized data-entry program—specifically, the commands within the DO WHILE . . . ENDDO—consists of statements denoting where information should be placed on the screen. For example, the statement @1,10 SAY 'ORDER INFORMATION FOR PHONE SERVICE DATA' places that title in the first row, tenth column. With these @ SAYs, it is possible to display text or variables anywhere on the screen.

☐ dBASE divides the screen into 25 rows and 80 columns. Thus, to put something in row 5, column 20, the @ SAY would read: @5,20 SAY '....'.

Another element of the program starts with the READ after the @23,5 line. Because not all the fields can be placed on the screen at one time, we first put the fields from

Phordernum to Vendor on the screen, then READ them into the database. Next, we CLEAR the screen, put Vencontact and the rest of the fields on the screen and READ those once those data have been entered.

Numerous methods are available for building these custom screens. This particular screen was built by actually writing a program. Many DBMS (including dBASE III Plus and dBASE IV) offer alternative "paint" programs. With these paint tools, no actual programming is needed. The designer decides which fields to place on the screen, where to put the fields, what to call or label them, and what graphic features (boxes, circles, underlines) to employ for highlights or emphasis. The designer literally moves to a particular part of the screen and designates what will be there. These paint programs are generally easier and more fun to use than the program-writing approach presented here. For example, instead of trying to determine how something will look at grid position 16,5 on the screen, just move the cursor of the screen paint program to the desired part of the screen, place what is needed, and "step back" to see how it looks. If it is unsatisfactory, move it to another location.

In dBASE III Plus, using the screen paint program is a matter of the CREATE FORMAT command, which is part of the ASSIST mode mentioned earlier. Once this command is selected and a name given to the (screen) format, the user then moves through a set of menus and painting procedures. First, the user selects the file that will provide the fields, then loads the desired fields on to what is called a blackboard. At this point the painting process enters. All the fields are on the blackboard and the user can name or rename anything simply by typing it. No more @ SAY commands. Borders and boxes can also be added by calling on a graphics option.

Screen paint programs become even more attractive when one considers that the programming code is generated as the user places the objects on the screen. Thus, once the data-entry screen has been painted, the user can go into the program and modify individual parts of it to obtain more precise control over screen appearance.

☐ Also important to helping users fully understand the content of a database is a data dictionary. The data dictionary defines each field. Some DBMS have dictionary facilities. Even if a DBMS does not have a specific facility, a data dictionary can be created simply by designating a file for definitions. For example, there can be a file to define exactly what is meant by Billcode, Unitname, or any other variables in figure 9.1. The memo capacity of dBASE III Plus, whereby long notes can be stored after a field name, gives one opportunity for data dictionaries. The data dictionary can also be printed out and used as a reference manual.

Menus

Continuing with the enhancements, we move next to using menus to facilitate operation of the management information application. (These are user designated menus, not menus in the assist mode.) The principal idea behind menus is to allow people not familiar with the DBMS to use the system easily. Figure 9.11 shows the opening menu for this telephone order system. According to the menu options, the user can choose one of five activities, including quitting the system. Each of these options probably opens to another menu that provides further, more specific options. For example, the data-entry option might open to a menu that presents the option of inputting data to the telephone order

```
PHONE ORDER TRACKING SYSTEM
1. Data Entry
2. Print Out Orders
3. Queries
4. Reports
5. Quit


Enter Choice =>
```

FIGURE 9.11

service file, the contact person file, or whatever other files exist. Nested within these data-entry menus would be the program for the customized data-entry screen.

Menus such as the one portrayed in figure 9.11 are nothing more than programs written in the DBMS language. Figure 9.12 lists the program that controls the opening menu displayed in figure 9.11. After a few introductory comments and commands, it uses the @ SAY commands to position the messages and options on the screen. The first of the @ SAYs (@ 2,15 SAY 'PHONE ORDER TRACKING SYSTEM') positions the title, and the remainder of the @ SAYs position the several options (Data Entry, etc.). The DO WHILE loop allows the user to continue using the menu until he or she decides to quit. Within the DO WHILE . . . ENDDO loop, it is the DO CASE . . . ENDCASE command that executes the options selected from the menu.

Ordinarily it is the DO CASE command (DO CASE . . . ENDCASE) that lies at the heart of menu programs. For each menu option, there is a CASE statement (e.g., CASE choice=1) to execute that option. For example, if the user selects option 1 (Data Entry) from the menu, the CASE command executes the choice=1 element and calls the program Entrmenu. Entrmenu is a program that probably offers a menu for the various files that can receive data. As noted, one of the programs called by these submenus would be the data-entry programs in figure 9.10.

Specialized Programs

The last enhancement is to write a program that produces one of the queries alluded to in the menu. Specifically, in figure 9.11, one of the options is Queries. Selecting this option would likely lead to a menu of queries, with each query option backed by a program to execute that query. In fact, there would be programs and subprograms for all the options listed in the opening menu. These programs, in effect, make the system more fully automated. One need only select options from the menus; no actual programming is performed by the user.

Suppose the Query option in the main menu leads to a Query Menu with three options: display orders by date requested, show orders by vendor, and pull out any specific order. Each of these might require a separate program. We will demonstrate one of these programs.

For purposes of illustration, we will look at a program to print out information for a

```
*Named fonemenu, this program displays the various*
*options open for the phone order system.         *
*Necessary database files selected elsewhere.     *
*Housekeeping.                                    *
CLEAR
SET TALK OFF
*Set loop criterion and start loop.               *
choice=0
DO WHILE choice < 6
CLEAR
@ 2,15 SAY 'PHONE ORDER TRACKING SYSTEM'
@ 5,10 SAY '1. Data Entry'
@ 6,10 SAY '2. Print Out Orders'
@ 7,10 SAY '3. Queries'
@ 8,10 SAY '4. Reports '
@ 9,10 SAY '5. Quit'
@ 12,10
INPUT 'Enter Choice ' TO choice
    DO CASE
    CASE choice=1
        DO entrmenu
    CASE choice=2
        DO printout
    CASE choice=3
        DO conquery
    CASE choice=4
        DO conrpts
    CASE choice=5
        CLEAR
        RETURN
    OTHERWISE
        @ 14,10
        ? 'Must enter 1, 2, 3, 4 or 5'
        WAIT 'Press any key and please restart program.'
        choice=0
    ENDCASE
ENDDO
CLEAR
```

FIGURE 9.12 Program for opening menu of telephone order system

specific phone order. Part of this program has already been created in a prior example. It is listed once again here:

```
USE phonedb
INDEX ON phordernum TO phoneidx
SET INDEX TO phoneidx
FIND 10
DISPLAY TO PRINT
```

Although this program prints out order information, it is too inflexible. Every time one wanted to execute the program for a different order, one would have to edit the program and change the order number. For example, if the order number desired were 22, the 10 in the program would have to be changed to 22. Fortunately, there is a generalizing tool sometimes called *replaceable parameters*. By using this tool, it is possible to transfer the desired order number at the time the program is executed. The resulting program might read:

```
USE phonedb
CLEAR
INDEX ON phordernum TO phoneidx
SET INDEX TO phoneidx
ACCEPT "What phone order do you wish to print? " TO wish
FIND &wish
DISPLAY TO PRINT
CLEAR
RETURN
```

In this program, we are asked (or prompted) via the ACCEPT statement to specify which order we want to print. If we enter 17, for example, then 17 is placed in the variable Wish and the program FINDs order number 17. The program will then print order number 17 (assuming, of course, that the printer is turned on).

This program would probably be called from a DO CASE statement in a Query Menu program. For example, if the option to find a specific phone order were number 3 in the Query Menu, then a CASE choice=3 is included and a program is called to execute choice 3.

☐ The query program described here could be enhanced in a variety of ways. One would be to add an "error trap." If a person asks for an order number that does not exist, the program would catch (trap) this mistake, let the user know, and ask if the request is to be repeated. A more attractive PRINT command could also be written.

Summary

By way of summary, these first two cases show a typical bottom-up approach for designing a management information application. Using this approach, a simple application is developed in case 1 and operated on a "quick and dirty" basis. Although this application allows the user to begin and take advantage of the DBMS, it is rudimentary. Improving the application requires a number of enhancements, which are presented in case 2. These include multiple files, development of custom data-entry screens, use of menus, and preparation of specialized programs.

With all these improvements, we have a fairly comprehensive system. The menu in figure 9.11 offers access to the system. For example, by opting for number 1, we would eventually see the attractive data-entry screen in figure 9.9. Once the data have been entered, we can then probe the data for useful information. The section of case 3 on specialized programs provides an illustration of the type of program that would help probe the database.

Although the effort in cases 1 and 2 has now produced a broad-based application, it was not accomplished in the most systematic fashion. As a result, the pieces do not immediately appear to constitute an integrated application. Quite frankly, this piece-by-piece approach is common in application development. A user develops part of the application, uses that facet, then adds pieces as he or she learns more or has the time to continue the development process.

In the next case, a top-down approach guides the development. It will provide a contrasting scenario for developing a microcomputer application.

■ CASE 3: AN APPLICATION FOR FIRE AND RESCUE TRAINING RECORDS

Purpose and Background

This case, which focuses on tracking the training records of a fire and rescue agency, covers several ways of using a management information application and the attendant DBMS. However, in contrast to the prior case, the design follows a top-down approach. With such an approach, we try to lay out most of what we want to accomplish at the outset rather than start with a narrow focus and add elements as we go along. In pursuing this top-down approach, we cover the following points:

- conducting a system analysis to determine goals, objectives, or problems
- identifying the data relevant to these goals or problems
- setting up, via normalization, the multiple files that permit us to handle large numbers of fields
- using hierarchy charts to identify the major tasks and their place in a menu-driven management information application
- laying out an extensive set of menus to guide the user through the system
- using the tools of algorithms, stepwise refinement, and pseudocode to develop the programs to execute the tasks in the management information application
- providing the flexibility within the programs to make wide-ranging searches of the database
- integrating some special features, such as simple expert system capabilities, to automate certain routine decisions

Identifying Objectives and Problems

This third case, as noted, involves building a microcomputer application for organizing and analyzing the training records of a fire and rescue agency. In developing such an application, it is important to appreciate how critical these training records are to the agency. In fire and rescue agencies and other such units involved in public safety, employees of the unit often cannot take part in a particular operation unless the appropriate training has been received and all requisites for certification have been met. Mistakes in sending uncertified personnel invite poor performance and lawsuits.

Thus, the objective of this management information application is clear: to provide quick and accurate information on the status of training and certification. For example, who has it, what kind, when is recertification necessary, and what requirements remain before certification is reached?

National organizations establish the requirements for training and certification, along with a standardized career ladder from beginning firefighter to fire officer and inspector. States and localities also have requirements, but these rely heavily on the national standards.

In addition to timely and accurate information on the training and certification of personnel, agencies seek to relate certification to performance, both at the individual level and at the operating unit level. For assessment of individual performance, managers want to know if training results (courses, scores, certification, etc.) are related to awards, disciplinary action, or personnel performance rating. For operating units, managers want to know how the training relates to response time, extent of property losses and damages, and cost and efficiency measures such as equipment breakdown. Of course, for any thorough evaluation, it would be necessary to include considerations other than training because other factors, such as the availability of equipment and type of geographic area protected, also influence performance.

For this particular case, the focus is mainly on setting up a management information application for producing timely and accurate data on training and certification. We assume that the agency has only a rudimentary automated system and wants to develop a better one. Any consideration of relating training and certification to performance must wait until the basics are under control.

Identifying and Assembling Data

Once the objectives and problems are understood, the next step is to identify and assemble the data. For this case, it turns out that much of the data identification and collection has already occurred. At two or three points in the past few years, the agency was forced to make a formal assessment of data and information needs for tracking training and certification. In one case, the chief wanted a summary of all training and certification (only to find out that most of the records were in paper files). In another situation, a suit over an employee's performance emphasized how important it is to have ready access to information rather than having many of the records in paper files that must be hand searched. Both of these situations spurred the agency to consider systematically what data were needed to track training and certification.

Taking advantage of the benefits of prior data collection efforts, the following data fields are considered integral to answering the questions raised about certification and training:

- date of training
- instructor's name(s)
- course identification
- number of hours for the course
- enrollee identification
- enrollee's demographic characteristics
- enrollee's score in the course
- enrollee's rating of the course
- instructor's qualifications
- employee's certification status in each certification area

Along with the questions of what data to collect and how to organize these data into a flexible and efficient database, there is also the practical question of what forms are needed to collect the data.

```
Employee Records

EMPLID   LASTNAME   AGE  FFIA FFIB FFII FOI FOIIA FOIIB
-----------------------------------------------------------
I 176    xxx        30    y    y
I 198    yyy        40    y    y    y    y   y
I 433    zzz        20    y
```

FIGURE 9.13

For the information sought here, there might be four forms: one for each course that is offered, one for all the enrollees in each course, one for each instructor that is filled out for all the courses the instructor teaches, and one to capture the employee's background. In designing these forms, it is important to keep in mind that the data in the forms will eventually be entered into the computerized database. The more attuned the form is to use by employees and data-entry people, the better the form.

Normalization

With all the fields identified, we move to the process of establishing files (i.e., the database) to hold the data. The goal is to achieve a database that is flexible and efficient. This can be accomplished by avoiding several of the common dangers and traps discussed in chapter 5.

A common danger, when faced with volumes of data about people, is to build one file with all the data fields in it. A typical example is taking enrollee ID and making one record for each enrollee. That record would include the enrollee's demographic characteristics and all the courses she or he could take. Figure 9.13 shows a file with these repeating fields for all the courses (FFIA, FFIB, etc.). Although this is a simple solution to organization of the data, it is not an efficient one. Some employees may have taken just a few courses, whereas others may have taken many. For example, employee 433 has taken only one course while employee 198 has taken five courses.

☐ Recall that files consist of several fields and many records. The fields are equated with the variables covered, such as enrollee ID, date of training, etc. The records are the actual data put into the files. In a given record, there is one piece of data for each field. For the file in figure 9.13, the record is the employee's record, and the fields are Emplid, Lastname, etc.

The careful normalization process spelled out in chapter 5 is a preferred route for organizing this set of data. Recall that a well-organized database is flexible and efficient. It enables users to access, manipulate, and extract information in ways relevant to their concerns. Little waste and redundancy in the data setup is an added benefit.

A critical step in normalization is to think about what major groupings might exist for all the fields previously listed. These groupings are defined by identifying the main, or dominant, fields in the data. Using this guiding criterion, four topical groupings are:

- employee background
- training records

```
Employee Background

EMPLID  LASTNAME   FIRSTNAME   DOB GENDER OFFICE PHONE
-----------------------------------------------------
I 176              xxx
I 198              yyy
I 433              zzz
```

FIGURE 9.14

- certificate status
- instructor information

Employee background is a logical first group. We need to have information on such factors as age, gender, starting date, and home address. There is a constant call for information on each individual and for aggregate or categorical summaries of the employees in the agency. This file serves to answer those queries.

Training records also constitute a main theme. We need to know exactly what course each individual took, when, and how well she or he did. Likewise, certification is presented as a distinct theme because there will be many questions on certification.

Finally, maintaining records on the instructors and their qualifications is important. This file can be used to find who can offer which course.

Once the main groupings are set, the next step is to identify the fields related to each grouping. Putting each main category and its related items together constitutes a single file (sometimes called a *table*). As the files are built, it is necessary to check for the various data traps so that flexibility and efficiency are maintained. Three of these traps are repeating fields, insertion anomalies, and deletion anomalies (all discussed in chapter 5).

We will skip any critical perusal of the employee background file because it is fairly easy to construct and turns out to have no serious problems. The resulting file is shown in figure 9.14.

For the training records file, we will delve into the details of its design. As shown in figure 9.15, training records are organized around each class taken by an employee. That is, each class taken becomes a unique record. For example, emplid 176 took two classes, FFIA and FFIIA, and there is a separate record for each class. The fields in this file are Emplid, Class, Section, Date, Score, and Instructor. All these fields seem to relate to Class, thus making for a well-constructed file.

Files are also suppose to have keys. The key consists of the combination of fields needed to make that record unique. Class alone will not do because many people will take the same class. Emplid will not suffice either because a person may take many classes. Emplid and Class are adequate only if repeats do not occur. Because repeats do happen (people fail or drop out), a Date is added to distinguish the same class taken at different times. Section may even need to be included to get a unique record, if there is more than one section. Although Emplid does not constitute a key, its presence is important. At some time, it will be necessary to link the employee background file and training records file. Since both files have Emplid as a field, the two files can be related on this field.

Chapter 9   Data Intensive Structured and Semistructured Problems

```
Training Records

  EMPLID     CLASS    SECTION   DATE      SCORE    INSTRUCTOR
  ------------------------------------------------------------
  I 176      FFIA        1      5/12/89    79      Johnson, B
  I 198      FOIIB       1      7/13/90
  I 433      INVIIC
  I 176      FFIIA
```

FIGURE 9.15

With the file laid out, it is necessary to check for the several traps. Repeating fields do not present a problem. Unlike the early version given in figure 9.13, there is only one class per record. In other words, instead of stringing out all the classes taken by each employee, we add a record every time an employee takes a class. Notice that the second time employee 176 takes a class (FFIIA), we simply add a new record for 176. Although this negates the ability to pull out one record and see all the classes taken by a given employee, it eliminates the inefficiency of having many blank fields for the people who did not take a particular class. In addition, there is almost no problem in summarizing the file to see all the classes taken by a particular employee (e.g., 176). dBASE has a SET FILTER TO command that can be set to the Emplid of interest. Then a LIST command will pick only those particular Emplids. Another quick query for a particular employee might be LIST FOR Emplid = '176' (assuming Emplid is character data). The commands SORT or INDEX can also be used in conjunction with the report generator to produce lists arranged by Emplid.

Although repeating fields are not a problem in the training records file, there are other possible problems with this file. Unless separate files for class and instructor exist, this database may be vulnerable to insertion and deletion anomalies. For example, if the class PEOII (public education officer II) has not been offered, it will never appear in the database. Not only will it not appear, but neither will the information about it.

Thus, with this file organization, there is no generic information on type of class in the database. To capture such information, we add a separate file called Curriculum. In it, we list every class that is available, along with the length of the class in hours (Hours), the type of person qualified to teach it (Qualify), and a brief description of the class (Descript). Figure 9.16 shows this file.

There is one other problem with the training file in figure 9.15. We know that a certain person took a class and we now have generic information on the type of class, but what is missing is information on each class actually offered. We know that FOIIB was given on 7/13/90, but we do not have information on the class as a whole. For example, how many people took it? To fill this void, we will add a class file. In fact, we can place the instructor's name in the class file, instead of listing it for every individual who took that particular offering of that class. Figure 9.17 shows the class file.

With all this work, we have cleaned up several serious problems associated with the

```
Curriculum

CLASS         HOURS    QUALIFY   DESCRIPT
---------------------------------------------
I FFIA
I FFIIA
I FOIA
I FOIIB
I INVIIC
I PEO I
I PEO II
```

FIGURE 9.16

```
Class

CLASS    INSTRUCTOR    NUMSTUDENT   HOURS   DATE
-------------------------------------------------
I FFIA   Johnson, B        25         1.5
I FFIA
I FFIIA
I FOIA
I FOIA
I INVIIC
```

FIGURE 9.17

training records file. Additionally, the curriculum and class files we added have no serious problems.

Now let us examine the certification file (see figure 9.18). It is set up in a manner that appears to violate one of the cautions noted earlier—namely, repeating fields. A long string of certifications is enumerated for each employee. In this case, one could get away with this approach if the certifications are not too numerous or if few are expected to be added. Additionally, there is the simplicity of having all the certifications for each employee in one record.

An alternative to stringing all the certifications in one record for each employee is to construct this file just as the training record file was designed. In this case, certifications are added only when attained (see figure 9.19). Moreover, other fields (RECERTIFICATION DATE, etc.) are added to give a more exhaustive file.

Any type of information that can be obtained from the first version of the certification file can be obtained from the second. The second is more parsimonious in that data are entered only upon certification. In the first, all certifications are enumerated and then filled in when the event occurs.

We could add one more file—a generic one on certification. It would cover each

Chapter 9 Data Intensive Structured and Semistructured Problems   305

```
Certification

EMPLID FFI FFII FFIII FOI FOII INVI INVII HAZ EMT
-----------------------------------------------------
I 433   Y    Y
I
I
```

FIGURE 9.18

```
Certification (without repeating fields)

EMPLID    CERTIFICATION    DATE      RECERTIFICATION DATE
---------------------------------------------------------
I 176        FFII         8/13/82
I 433        FFI
```

FIGURE 9.19

type of certification and what is necessary to achieve it. Finally, we could have a file on instructor information, which we identified earlier as a valuable file.

Building the Application

With the systems analysis and database design behind us, it is now possible to develop the microcomputer application to enter and then tap the information in the database.

In essence, the application will be constructed to input data on training and to answer the range of questions managers and employees have about the information in the database—primarily what training individuals have acquired and who is certified for which specialties.

Hierarchy charts One way to start producing the application is to sketch a hierarchy chart. The hierarchy chart contains the main application areas to be developed and the specific tasks within each of the major areas. It is a divide-and-conquer technique, but with the added appeal of showing the modules and relationships among the modules.

Drawing on certain functions integral to most applications plus the questions just listed, figure 9.20 shows the hierarchy chart.

At the top of the chart are four functions and tasks:

- enter data
- training records
- certification status
- performance reports

MAIN MODULE

Enter Data
Training Records
Certification Status
Performance Reports

▼

Enter Data	Training	Certification	Performance
Employee Background	Summary by Station	Types of Certification	
Training Records	Summary by Rank	Report by Station	
Classes	Individuals by Year		
Curriculum			
Certification			
Instructors			

FIGURE 9.20 Hierarchy chart

Each of these functions is then linked to a module below it. With the hierarchy chart, the developer can see the overall picture and the parts that constitute that picture.

Data entry The first of the main functions in the top box of the hierarchy chart is data entry. The data-entry function links to a module on the second rung that provides the opportunity to enter data for any of the files. In all there are six files (employee background, training records, etc.), so there are six options in this module. These were the files that were developed (via the normalization process) in the prior section.

This data-entry module will be carried out by preparing a menu that lists each of the options and then takes the data-entry person to the screens for actual input of the data. Other than listing the data-entry option for this module, however, no more will be said about it because data-entry routines were covered in case 2 (see figures 9.9 and 9.10).

Other functions Of the remaining functions in the main module—training, certification, and performance—we will take a closer look at two: training records and certification status. The purpose of the training records module is to provide information on who has taken what kind of training. It is also possible to ask questions about different groupings of people and the training experience by grouping. Certification status is similar. We should be able to obtain information about individuals and about different categories of individuals. The performance module, which will not be explored, offers information on how well individuals are doing and how well different groups are doing.

Menus and programs The chart in figure 9.20 outlines what functions or topics are to be covered and certain details about the organization of the overall system. It is, in

```
              WELCOME TO THE TRAINING
              AND CERTIFICATION SYSTEM
        Choose one of the 5 options

           1. Enter Data
           2. Training Records
           3. Certification Status
           4. Performance Reports
           5. Quit

        Which choice do you want?
```

FIGURE 9.21

essence, a design tool. The chart is implemented, or translated into applications, through a series of menus and programs. Generally, there is at least one menu for each module. For example, the first module would be implemented with a menu (similar to the one in figure 9.11 for case 2) showing that the application has four major functions. If a user wants to enter data, he or she selects that option from the menu. Once the enter data option has been selected, the user gets into another menu, this one being the options for entering data. Probably at this point the user would select a particular file or files for the actual data entry.

It is important to appreciate that programs drive all the menus and the work done by the menus. We will examine at least some of the programs.

The main or opening menu that the user sees implements the main module in figure 9.20. The main menu could be accessed by executing the program (e.g., DO Mainmenu), or it could be displayed as soon as the user enters the system. Most DBMS offer a way to execute a program as soon as the DBMS software is started. Figure 9.21 shows the type of menu the user might see to start off the system in figure 9.20.

The program for this opening menu is similar to that in figure 9.12. It is shown in figure 9.22.

For each of the first four options in the main menu, there would be a follow-up set of menus to permit the user to execute any of the capabilities of the application. These menus would be executed by the DO statements in the CASE part of the the DO CASE section of the program (see figure 9.22).

Most of the implementation in case 3 revolves around queries and a simple expert system for determining certification.

Queries: Training Records

One interest in this case is tracking the training records. In the training records module (see figure 9.20), there are three options for querying or reporting on the files in the database. The first two are for groupings of employees: one summarizes training experience by fire station, the other by rank. The third permits us to look at individual training records. These options would be presented to us via a menu.

PART III   Use of the Framework in Developing Applications

```
SET TALK OFF
STORE 0 TO choice
DO WHILE choice <=4
CLEAR
@5,15 SAY "WELCOME TO THE TRAINING"
@6,14 SAY "AND CERTIFICATION SYSTEM"
@9,3 SAY "Choose one of the 5 options"
@12,3 SAY "1. Enter Data"
@13,3 SAY "2. Training Records"
@14,3 SAY "3. Certification Status"
@15,3 SAY "4. Performance Reports"
@16,3 SAY "5. Quit"
@18,3 INPUT "Which choice do you want? " TO choice
DO CASE
   CASE choice=1
      DO datatry
   CASE choice=2
      DO traintry
   CASE choice=3
      DO certtry
   CASE choice=4
      DO perftry
   CASE choice=5
      DO quitprg
   OTHERWISE
      CLEAR
      ? 'Next time please enter a 1,2,3,4, or 5'
      wait
      choice=0
ENDCASE
ENDDO
```

FIGURE 9.22

An alternative to having specific reports or queries is to make the format more general or flexible. In such a format, the user could choose any field on which to summarize or group the training data. For example, the user might be presented with a list of fields (age, rank, fire station, starting date, gender, etc.) and then asked on which of these to summarize. Statistical packages are generally very good at presenting data in different aggregate forms. If this type of flexibility were desired, then the database files could be converted (or directly imported) to be made available to a statistical package such as PC SAS, SPSS/PC, Statgraph, or Statpac.

Of the three options in the training module, it is this third effort—querying the database to look at individual records—that we will highlight. We will write a short dBASE program to execute it.

Objectives   The purpose of this program is to enable the user to display or print all the training records for any single employee and, further, to specify whether the display or printout should show all years or just one particular year.

Chapter 9   Data Intensive Structured and Semi-Structured Problems   **309**

Pseudocode   The place to start building this program is not with the coding of the actual DBMS commands (dBASE III Plus is used here), but rather with the more English-like pseudocode. Pseudocode, as we have seen, allows one to concentrate more exclusively on the logic or solution, without getting sidetracked by the specifics of the coding. A simple pseudocode listing for this program might read:

- Make sure the right file or files are in use.
- Obtain the Emplid number from the user.
- Index the file on Emplid so that all the desired Emplids are in one place in the file.
- Find out if the user wants a specific year or all years. If the user wants one year, what is it? If not, then note that all years are acceptable.
- Display the records that meet the conditions specified.
- Give an option to print the results.
- Give an option to loop through the process again.

Once the application developer or development team is satisfied with the pseudocode for a particular task, then programming can commence or the pseudocode for other modules can be prepared. In this case, we will go directly from the pseudocode to the programming.

Program coding   Figure 9.23 presents a rudimentary program in dBASE III Plus for this query task. A walk-through will highlight some of the features of moving from pseudocode to programming, as well as some of the programming features of dBASE III Plus.

In this very simple effort, there are about forty lines of code and comments. An * in the first space of a line makes the line a comment line. It is not part of the "executable" program; in other words, it is not integral to finding the particular employee and displaying his or her training records. The comment lines are notes to the programmer or to others reading the program. In some respects, the comments are like the pseudocode; they tell in English what is taking place in the executable program.

☐   It is possible to have the pseudocode serve a double role, pseudocode and comment statements. If the pseudocode is written inside the same editor as is used for the program, then one can easily insert the programming below the pseudocode statements. In this manner, the pseudocode becomes the comments for the program. In dBASE, this means writing the pseudocode inside the modify command mode, which is the default editor for composing dBASE programs.

The initial comment lines give the name of the program and tell what the program does. Following are some comments about housekeeping and what could be done to elaborate the program. Housekeeping tasks are typical in programming; they provide ways of making the program neat and appealing. For example, the SET TALK OFF prevents certain responses from appearing on the screen and thus gives the program a cleaner look. A subsequent executable line—USE—complies with our pseudocode and gets the file we need for this part of the program. The CLEAR command clears the screen so that the program has a neat, uncluttered screen with which to work.

The initialization is the next important code. Initialization simply gets some of the variables ready for use in the program by assigning them an initial value. In this program three variables—Choice, Choice1, and Year—are initialized. These are variables that are

```
*This program, called querynum, allows the user to query  *
*any employee's training record by the employee's         *
*ID number. However, the program only permits one query at*
*a time. The program must be reentered to do              *
*subsequent queries.                                      *
*Housekeeping.                                            *
SET TALK OFF
SET SAFETY OFF
USE Training
*A DO (DO WHILE) loop could be placed here to permit      *
*the user to repeat this query.                           *
CLEAR
*Initialize memory variables to blank.                    *
STORE ' ' TO choice,choice1,year
@3,19 SAY 'PROGRAM TO FIND EMPLOYEE TRAINING RECORDS'
?
*This section of the program finds the particular         *
*employee.                                                *
ACCEPT "Enter the employee's ID number " TO choice
INDEX TO training ON emplid
FIND &choice
WAIT
CLEAR
*In this part of the program, the user has a chance to    *
*obtain the records for any one year.                     *
ACCEPT 'Do you want a specific year of records? (y/n) ' TO;
 choice1
*The indentations in the IF THEN ELSE ENDIF statement     *
*are not necessary. They make the program more            *
*readable.                                                *
IF UPPER(choice1)='Y'
    ACCEPT 'Which year, for example, 87 or 88: ' to year
    SET DATE ANSI
    CLEAR
    LIST FOR emplid='&choice' .AND. DTOC(date)='&year'
ELSE
    CLEAR
    LIST for emplid='&choice'
    WAIT
ENDIF
```

FIGURE 9.23 Simple query program—no repeat requests

not in the database but are necessary to run the program. We use these to store our requests, such as which Emplid or which Date to find.

All of these variables (Choice, Choice1, and Year) are initialized to blanks with the STORE ' ' TO command. The variables are initialized to blanks because they are character type, not numeric, data. STORE 0 (zero) TO the three variables would indicate that they were numeric.

Chapter 9 Data Intensive Structured and Semi-Structured Problems 311

The @ SAY is a way of putting a title on the screen, and the ? with nothing after it skips a line (i.e., prints a blank line) on the screen. Specifically, the @ 3,19 SAY places the title at row 3, column 19. After the title, the next thing seen on the screen is the statement "Enter the employee's ID number." This prompt is produced by the ACCEPT statement. When the user enters the number, the number is "accepted" to the variable Choice, which holds whatever ID number was entered.

Much of the rest of the program nicely parallels the pseudocode. With the INDEX, we put the file in ascending order so that the several instances of the ID number we want are all located together. The FIND locates (or places a pointer at) the first instance of that employee number.

One item in the FIND statement needs explanation. The ampersand (&) is used here and in a few other places. This gives flexibility to the program. It means use whatever is stored in the variable that follows the ampersand. For example, FIND &choice means find the first instance of whatever is stored in Choice. If we store Emplid 176 in Choice, the FIND &choice would read FIND 176. Without the &, the computer might try to find something *called* Choice rather the *contents* of Choice. With the &, it is possible to place anything in Choice, change it if necessary, and use the contents of what is stored in Choice. Again, it makes programming more flexible.

The WAIT statement simply causes a pause, giving the message: "Press any key to continue." The CLEAR clears the screen.

The last important set of statements are those directed toward determining whether the user wants one year of training records for that particular person, or all years. An IF..ELSE..ENDIF statement handles this chore just as we indicated in the pseudocode. If the user wants a specific year of records (ACCEPT 'Do you . . . ' to choice1), that year is chosen (ACCEPT 'Which year . . . ' to year) and listed with the LIST FOR command that specifies the employee ID number and year. If a single year is not wanted, then the ELSE clause is followed, and all records for that employee are displayed.

A slightly more elaborate version of this program is shown in figure 9.24. It includes a loop (DO WHILE cont ='y' . . . ENDDO) so that the user can go through the program any number of times and find the training records for many different employee ID numbers. Notice how the DO WHILE . . . ENDDO "brackets" the body of the program. The beginning of the DO WHILE loop follows the twelfth line of the program. Everything inside the loop can be repeated as long as the user continues to respond "y" to "Do you wish to continue?" The bottom of the loop is the last statement, ENDDO. Control of the program loops from top (DO WHILE) to bottom (ENDDO) as long as Y is entered in response to the call to continue. The comments in figure 9.24 are also more elaborate. Thus, a reading of the comments helps explain the syntax.

Many more elaborations can be added to this program. For example, it is possible to provide an option to print the results. It would also be wise to have some "error trapping" capability in the program. What if the user inserted an ID number not in the database? There should be some message and a way to help the user correct the mistake.

A Simple Expert System: Certification Status

The second module that we examine is the certification module. The general purpose of this module is to determine whether an employee has met certification requirements in a

```
*This program, called querylop, allows the user to query*
*any employee's training records by the employee's     *
*ID number (emplid) and then loop                      *
*through to query another.                             *
*Housekeeping: these two SET commands keep             *
*certain messages from appearing on the screen.        *
SET TALK OFF
SET SAFETY OFF
USE Training
STORE 'y' TO cont
*This program has no error trapping to catch emplids   *
*that do not exist.                                    *
DO WHILE cont='y'
CLEAR
*Initialize memory variables to blank.                 *
STORE ' ' TO choice,choice1,year
@3,19 SAY 'PROGRAM TO FIND EMPLOYEE TRAINING RECORDS'
?
*This section of the program finds the particular     *
*employee.                                             *
ACCEPT "Enter the employee's ID number " TO choice
INDEX TO training ON emplid
FIND &choice
*If SET TALK is switched to ON at this point and the   *
*the emplid does not exist, the message no find will   *
*be given.                                             *
WAIT
CLEAR
*In this part of the program, the user has a chance to *
*obtain the records for any one year.                  *
ACCEPT 'Do you want a specific year of records? (y/n) ';
 TO choice1
*The indentations in the IF THEN ELSE ENDIF statement  *
*are not necessary. They make the program more         *
*readable.                                             *
If UPPER(choice1)='Y'
    ACCEPT 'Which year, for example, 87 or 88: ' TO year
*SET DATE ANSI place date in form of yy/mm/dd, which   *
*facilitates searching on year.                        *
    SET DATE ANSI
    CLEAR
*The DTOC() changes the date type to character so that *
*the date can be searched like a character string.     *
*The .AND. is part of the Boolean logic which allows   *
*one to set the search criterion to find something when*
*both things are true (.AND.); when either is          *
```

FIGURE 9.24 Query program to find and display records of any one employee

```
*true (.OR.); and when something is not true       *
*(.NOT.). The periods around .AND. are delimiters  *
*which prevent dBASE from thinking that AND is a field *
*name.                                             *
    LIST FOR emplid='&choice' .AND. DTOC(date)='&year'
ELSE
    CLEAR
    LIST FOR emplid='&choice'
ENDIF
WAIT
CLEAR
ACCEPT 'Do you wish to continue? (y/n)   ' to cont
ENDDO
```

FIGURE 9.24 *(Continued)*

given area. One can imagine that this request would be made quite often. After taking the necessary courses or training, employees will be eager to know whether they have successfully fulfilled the stipulations. Given the likely volume of requests, designing a computer application to make the decision will be more efficient than having a staff member shuffle through all of someone's paper records.

Since this part of the application will peruse the data and use several rules to reach a conclusion about certification, we will view this as a rudimentary expert system. It would be possible to expand the system so that a periodic scan is made of all records to see who is certified and the information printed in a report. For this exercise, we will do the more basic task of designing a system to review someone's record only when a request is made.

Because there are many types of certification, it would be advantageous to write one or a few programs to handle the decisions for all the certifications. Such a strategy would certainly reduce the amount of programming, especially if there were twenty or thirty types of certification.

For purposes of illustration, we will take one type of certification as an example rather than taking the more elegant route of writing one program that can handle inquiries about many types or levels of certification. Our illustration will be limited to the fictitious category Ff2 (short for FFII, or firefighter II). We want to be able to identify those who can now be certified at Ff2.

Analysis As with the query program on training records, it is best to start this programming effort at a general level. What are the requirements for certification at Ff2? What files will be needed? What is the logic for making the certification determination?

For this fictitious Ff2, the certification requirements are:

- must be certified at Ff1 and not at Ff2
- must have taken two courses, Ff2a and Ff2b
- must have passed both with a score of at least 70

Our general logic starts by finding out the status of the employee's current certification. We want to know whether the person is certified at Ff1. We also want to check whether our candidate is already certified at Ff2. After these checks, there are four possible outcomes:

	Certified			
Ff1	no	yes	no	yes
Ff2	no	no	yes	yes

Of the four outcomes, only the second combination is valid for our current concerns: yes at Ff1 and no at Ff2. The other outcomes are either not relevant or might indicate inaccuracies in the data. If a person is recorded as not certified at Ff1 but certified at Ff2, there is a mistake somewhere. A person who has a no for both Ff1 and Ff2 simply is not a candidate. Someone who has passed both already is certified at Ff2.

Pseudocode The pseudocode for judging whether a person can be certified at Ff2 is as follows:

- Get or make sure the appropriate file is ready.
- Obtain the employee ID number for the targeted employee.
- Index the file on Emplid and type of certification so that the desired Emplid and certifications are in one place in the file and in ascending order.
- Go to the start of that Emplid in the file.
- Because the file is indexed on type of certification, elements of the career ladder such as Ff1 and Ff2 will be in ascending order.
- Initialize both Ff1 and Ff2 to "no" or "false" in order to begin the test to determine if the candidate can be certified at Ff2.
- Start a loop that will continue as long as we are scanning the target Emplid and as long as we have not found a true Ff1; store a "yes" when a Ff1 is found, otherwise leave it as "no."
- Do the same for Ff2, except continue the loop as long as we have not found a true Ff2; store "yes" if a true Ff2 is found, otherwise leave it at "no" or "false."
- Determine the outcome and take the appropriate action; only if the outcome is "yes" for Ff1 and "no" for Ff2 should the determination be continued.
- For those who are certified at Ff1 but not at Ff2, call the program to determine if that person has taken and passed all the requisite course or training work.
- For other outcomes, print the appropriate response, such as already certified at Ff1 and Ff2.

Program coding Two programs are needed to implement this pseudocode. Figure 9.25 shows the dBASE III Plus code for the program Whoscert, the part that determines if the person meets the criterion: certified at Ff1 and not at Ff2. Since it has no new syntax beyond what has already been presented, it will be discussed only in general terms.

After initializing both certifications, Ff1 and Ff2 (via the STORE command), to no, we get the employee's ID number and index the file so we can take a close look at the

Chapter 9   Data Intensive Structured and Semi-Structured Problems

```
*The name of this program is whoscert. It is designed to *
*determine whether a person can be certified for FF2.    *
*This program tests one set of criteria—                 *
*namely, at what level is the employee certified?        *
*If the employee is certified at FF1 but not at          *
*FF2, then a second program, certff2, is called to see   *
*whether the employee has passed the requirements for    *
*FF2.                                                    *
*Housekeeping: SET TALK OFF and other commands to control*
*what goes to the screen could go here.                  *
CLEAR
*Title:                                                  *
@3,15 SAY 'PROGRAM TO DETERMINE CERTIFICATION AT FF2'
*Get the certification file, certify.                    *
USE certify
*At a minimum, certify would have an ID number and a     *
*certification field.                                    *
*Initializes the certification to no                     *
STORE 'no' to ff1
STORE 'no' to ff2
?
*For whom are we looking?                                *
ACCEPT "Enter the employee's ID number " to select
*Index on both ID number and whether the person is       *
certified and find the target ID number                  *
INDEX on emplid+certificat to certidx
SET INDEX TO certidx
FIND &select
*Proceed with a set of loops to see if target ID number  *
*is certified at ff1 and/or at ff2.                      *
DO WHILE emplid='&select' .AND. ff1='no'
    IF certificat='ff1'
        STORE 'yes' to ff1
        ? 'ID number ',&select, 'is certified at ff1'
        ? "It's necessary to see if s(he) is certified at ff2"
        WAIT
    ELSE
*Check for inaccurate data; if no ff1, no ff2            *
IF certificate='ff2'
    STORE 'yes' to ff2
ENDIF
        SKIP
    ENDIF
ENDDO
DO WHILE emplid='&select' .AND. ff2='no'
    IF certificat='ff2'
        STORE 'yes' to ff2
        ? 'ID number ',&select, 'already certified at ff2'
```

FIGURE 9.25 Program designed to illustrate simple expert system, part 1

```
            WAIT
            RETURN
      ELSE
            STORE 'no' TO ff2
      ENDIF
SKIP
ENDO
*Display a message for the various outcomes          *
IF ff1='yes' .AND. ff2='no'
      ? 'ID number ',&select, 'is certified at ff1, but not at ff2'
      ? 'He or she is eligible for certification at ff2'
      WAIT
*Pass the ID number to the certff2 program via a WITH    *
*statement in this program and a PARAMETERS statement in *
*the certff2 program. Most programming books discuss the *
*topic of passing parameters from one program to another.*
*The topics of global and local variables are also       *
*integral to the topic of passing parameters.            *
DO certff2 WITH select
ENDIF
IF ff1='no' .AND. ff2='no'
      ? 'ID number ',&select, ' not eligible for ff2'
      WAIT
ENDIF
IF ff1='no' .and. ff2='yes'
      ? 'Problem: ID number ',&select, 'improperly certified at ff2'
      WAIT
ENDIF
IF ff1='yes' .AND. ff2='yes'
      ? "ID number ',&slect, ' already qualified at ff2.'
ENDIF
```

FIGURE 9.25 *(Continued)*

person's certification status (inside the two DO WHILE . . . ENDDO loops). If the employee exhibits the preliminary qualities, we go to a new program (DO certff2 WITH select) to check for course and training work. If the person meets these later qualifications, we display the appropriate message. We have an assortment of other displays for those falling outside our present concerns.

For a more detailed picture of the program, the comment statements (indicated by asterisks) lay out the flow and mechanisms of the program.

Those candidates who pass the first qualification (certified at Ff1 but not at Ff2) must be run through a second program to see if they have taken and passed (with a score of 70 or better) two courses, Ff2a and Ff2b.

The dBASE III Plus program Certff2, shown in figure 9.26, handles this part of the determination. In essence, this program is called from the first program, Whoscert. One item that needs explanation is the dBASE III Plus reserved word PARAMETERS. The command PARAMETERS gives the program more power for generalizing. When the program is executed or called, any employee number can be given. It is then stored in

Chapter 9 Data Intensive Structured and Semi-Structured Problems

```
PARAMETERS who
*This program, called certff2, determines whether an      *
*employee can be certified at ff2.                        *
*Housekeeping.                                            *
*Get the training file.                                   *
STORE 0 to yesff2
USE training
*At a minimum, training would have three fields, an       *
*ID number, class taken, and class score.                 *
CLEAR
*Who will be certified?                                   *
? 'The employee in question is: ',&who
WAIT
INDEX ON emplid+class TO trainidi
SET INDEX TO trainidi
FIND &who
DO WHILE emplid='&who'
    IF class='ff2a' .AND. score > 70
        STORE 1/2 TO yesff2
*yesff2=yesff2+1/2 could also be used instead of the      *
*STORE command.                                           *
        ? yesff2
    ENDIF
    IF class='ff2b' .AND. score > 70
        yesff2=yesff2+1/2
        ? yesff2
    ENDIF
*SKIP to the next record.                                 *
SKIP
ENDDO
DO CASE
    CASE yesff2=1
    ? 'ID number ',&who,' should be certified at ff2'
    WAIT
    CASE yesff2<1
    ? 'ID number ',&who,' should not be certified at ff2'
    CASE yesff2>1
    ? 'There is an error in ID number ',&who,' records'
ENDCASE
*RETURN to the program that called this one.              *
RETURN
```

FIGURE 9.26 Program designed to illustrate simple expert system, part 2

the temporary variable Who. For example, when the program is called by the command DO Certff2 WITH select, an employee ID number is passed to the parameter Who. The next time the program Whoscert is run, another employee number can be used. Then the employee ID number is placed wherever the temporary variable Who appears in the program Certff2.

Another new item in the code for Certff2 is the use of an accumulator (Yesff2) to see if the person has met all the requirements. Because the person needs to pass two tests, we add ½ to the accumulator when a passing score is encountered. Thus, a pass on both Ff2a and Ff2b would amount to 1 in the accumulator and mean certification at Ff2.

In the code, we loop (DO WHILE Emplid=&who) through the records of our target person, searching to see whether the person has taken Ff2a and Ff2b. The first time the loop encounters Ff2a, the accumulator is incremented by the following code: STORE 1/2 TO Yesff2 if the score is > 70. For the second course, Ff2b, the dBASE code is a bit different. It is: Yesff2=Yesff2+1/2. In the second step, we need to take what is already in the accumulator (that is, Yesff2), add 1/2 (Yesff2+1/2), and then replace the old value in the accumulator with the new one. The = in the code Yesff2=Yesff2+1 means replace what is on the left side with the result of what is on the right side.

With these two programs working together, it is possible to determine whether a person not previously certified at Ff2 is now certified at Ff2. Other enhancements could be added to these programs, but the fundamentals have been demonstrated.

■ CASE 4: USING DATABASE INFORMATION FOR DECISION MAKING

Background and Purpose

In this last case, we want to examine how and to what extent the information in a database can be used to aid decision making. So far, the databases have been used primarily to keep good records. For example, the purpose of cases 1 and 2 was to automate the recordkeeping process of organizing and tracking requests for telephone services. Beyond this recordkeeping function, the telephone service database was extended only to simple queries, such as finding information on the contact person requesting a particular service.

When we move from recordkeeping and simple queries to more involved items, such as questions about the efficiency and effectiveness of a particular service, we move from structured to semistructured problems. These semistructured problems are less routine, and their solution is not totally dependent on the information in the database. More creativity, discretion, and judgment are necessary.

To examine a less structured situation, we take a problem that draws on the telephone service database in cases 1 and 2. In this extension, we address the issue of whether services are being deployed too slowly. We will assume that the telecommunications officer has received a number of complaints about delayed and drawn out delivery of services.

A First Step: Calculating Time Taken

Initially, the telecommunications officer might want to get a quick ranking of requests from those taking the most time to those taking the least. He or she might also want to see what the average time is and whether differences exist by type of request. The steps necessary for performing this analysis and making it readily available will be described. First, we look at the individual elements that go into completing the analysis, then we place these into a program and test the program.

With the existing telephone service database, it is possible to calculate the time elapsed for all requests that have been completed. The database has both the date of request (Datereques) and the date a service was completed (Datefinish). In addition, dBASE III Plus has the capability to do "date arithmetic"—that is, determine the number of days between two dates. For example, request number 3 was made on 09/01/88 and finished by 10/09/88; dBASE III Plus can determine the number of days between the two dates.

In order to generate a report showing all the requests, from those taking the least to those taking the most time, several programming and modifying tasks are necessary. First, we must calculate the time taken to complete those requests that have already been finished. The expression below is sufficient to make the calculation:

```
Numdays = Datefinish-Datereques
```

If 04/24/88 were stored in the first record for Datefinish (date the work was finished) and 03/23/88 in the first record for Datereques (date the work was requested), the total number of days (Numdays) between the finish and beginning would be 32 days.

Once the number of days taken to complete a service request has been determined, that result must be stored in the database to make it available for further analysis. However, as the database stands, it has no field to receive these results. Fortunately, with dBASE III Plus and many other DBMS, new fields can be added to the database. In dBASE III Plus, the command is MODIFY STRUCTURE. A new field called Duration is added to the appropriate file.

With this new field added to the file, the results of the date arithmetic (Numdays = Datefinish − Datereques) can be easily inserted into the database using a REPLACE command. The command for this situation is:

```
REPLACE Duration WITH Numdays
```

The command takes whatever is in Duration (which is nothing right now) and replaces it with the value in Numdays, which is the number of days taken to complete a given request.

Building a Test Program

All the commands discussed so far can be placed in a short program, shown in figure 9.27. This preliminary, or test, program is designed to show the results at various stages on the screen. A test program like this (where values are changed or updated) should be tried initially only on a sample database, not the actual database. If the program does not work properly, only the sample database will be compromised.

> Testing is something that should be performed on all programs. In essence, it means checking a program for accuracy of the answers given. Ordinarily, a program is tested by exposing it to a range of situations to see whether the program gives accurate answers. Small sample or test sets of data can be used, but these should incorporate the range of data that will be used in the program. Often, the computer results are compared to hand-calculated results, using the small sample data set.

In this test program (figure 9.27), we do some preliminary initializing (STORE 0 TO Numdays), go to the top of the file (i.e., the first record), and then loop (via a DO WHILE

PART III   Use of the Framework in Developing Applications

```
*Calcudur is the name of this program. It determines *
*the number of days from the start to  the finish of *
*a telephone service order. Once the number of days has been   *
*calculated, that number is placed in a new field,    *
*duration, via a REPLACE command.                     *
*Screen control commands could be placed here.        *
*Would need the appropriate database.                 *
STORE 0 to numdays
GO TOP
*Do until the end of the file is reached.             *
DO WHILE .NOT. EOF()
    numdays=datefinish-datereques
*Calculations are displayed as a check. These will    *
*be removed once the program is running properly.     *
    ? 'Record number ',recno()
    ? 'Finish ',datefinish
    ? 'Begin ',datereques
    ? 'Number of Days ',numdays
    WAIT
        IF numdays > 0
            REPLACE duration WITH numdays
        ENDIF
    ? 'Duration ',duration
    WAIT
    SKIP
ENDDO
*Short report to show the time it took to complete    *
*all service orders that were completed.              *
INDEX ON duration TO duridx
LIST phordernum,duration FOR duration > 0
?
AVER duration FOR duration > 0
```

FIGURE 9.27 Time it takes to complete a service and storage of that time

.NOT. EOF(), not end of file) through all the records. Within the loop, we calculate the time elapsed for each project, then replace the field Duration with the number of days (Numdays) it took for the service to be completed.

More specifically, in the first statement we initialize the value of Numdays to 0 (STORE 0 to Numdays). The second statement takes us to the top of the file before we start to loop through all the records. The loop statement starts with the DO WHILE .NOT. EOF() and ends with ENDDO. It allows us to go through all the records in the file. In between the beginning and end of the loop, we calculate the number of days elapsed for each service, display the finish and beginning dates (?Datefinish, ?Datereques) and the number of days to complete the service (? Numdays), then pause (WAIT) while we examine the input dates and the number of days taken. Next, if the number of days (Numdays) is greater than 0, we do the replacement. The Numdays must exceed 0 to be a valid result. If Numdays is 0, that means no date was in the Datefinish field, or more generally, no date appeared in one or both of the date fields. More data are displayed to check these results visually.

The final part of the program is a quick listing of the results, including the average number of days taken. A more elaborate report will be done shortly.

For purposes of testing the program, the sample database should have records that have no date in both the Datefinish and Datereques fields, as well as other possible combinations. The test data and screen display of results offer several opportunities to check the veracity of the program.

Generating a Report

The quick listing of results is adequate for the analysts working with the data, but for sharing the results a more formal report is needed. As we noted in case 1, dBASE III Plus, like other DBMS, has what is called a *report generator*. It permits attractive presentation of results with minimal programming.

In order to generate a report showing the service requests from those taking the shortest to those taking the longest time, it is necessary first to index the file on the field Duration. This means, in effect, putting it in ascending order from least to most time. As soon as the indexing is finished, a report can be created using the report generator. We will start by showing the finished report with selected records in it, then discuss briefly how the report generator is used.

Figure 9.28 shows the report on the time it took to finish all completed services. At the top is a title, nicely centered. Below the title are four columns: one for the type of service requested (Phone Service), one for the number of days needed to finish the request (Number Days), one to identify the agency contact person (Agency Contact), and one to note the vendor (Vendor Name). Below the column headings are the results, which will be discussed later.

Figure 9.29 shows the program used to produce the report in figure 9.28. Actually, it is a program within a program—or, more precisely, a report within a program. The main program—Timestdy—starts with some housekeeping (e.g., SET TALK OFF). It then sets up the index (SET INDEX TO Duridx) so the file is ordered from lowest Duration to highest. Next, the report is called via the REPORT FORM statement (REPORT FORM Timetofn FOR Duration > 0). The report is contained in Timetofn. This is the report inside-of-a-program concept: Timetofn is inside Timestdy. After the report has been executed, we return to the program, Timestdy, and calculate the average number of days it takes to complete a service request (AVERAGE Duration FOR Duration > 0 to Timeavg). The last thing done in the program Timestdy is listing (?) the average number of days stored in the temporary variable Timeavg.

The report generator that lies inside the program is easy to use. However, it is important to know that the report was built first, then inserted into the program.

In dBASE III Plus, a report is initiated with a CREATE REPORT command. For our purposes, it would be CREATE REPORT Timetofn (the name of the report). The rest is straightforward. It operates from pull-down windows. For example, to identify the fields that go into the report, one selects "Columns," then enters the name of the field

PART III   Use of the Framework in Developing Applications

```
Page No.      1
Date
                  Number of Days Needed to Complete
                        Phone Service Requests

Phone                   Number    Agency              Vendor
Service                 Days      Contact             Name


install 5 new p         32        stevens ron         phone-x
move phone in r         38        stevens ron         phone-x
install 2 new p         41        rogers joe          tele-comm
move 4 phones f         45        miller paul         tele-com
place 2 new pho         52        stewart barbara     phone-x
place 4 new pho         54        montone vic         all-tron
install softwar         56        montone vic         tele-comm
change software         70        author jean         phone-x
install softwar         78        stevens ron         all-tron
add software to         90        peters mary         all-tron
remove software        110        miller paul         all-tron

The average number of days to complete a service is:          61
```

FIGURE 9.28 Report on time taken to complete service

```
*Called timestdy, this program shows how various *
*types of database management tools can be placed*
*in one program and run at one time. First, a    *
*report that was constructed using the report    *
*generator is run. Then a simple function—in this *
*case, the average—is used to complement the     *
*results of the report.                          *
*Having the appropriate database and doing the   *
*indexing would be necessary.                    *
SET TALK OFF
CLEAR
SET INDEX TO duridx
REPORT FORM timetofn FOR duration  > 0
?
AVERAGE duration FOR duration > 0 to timeavg
? 'The average number of days to complete a service is: ',timeavg
```

FIGURE 9.29 Program for report on time taken to complete service

(e.g., Duration) and heading (e.g., Number Days) in a windowed area that drops down from the Columns designation. This process is repeated until all the fields needed for the report have been selected. Additionally, report generators often preview or show what the report looks like while you are building it so that you can make changes before actually executing the report.

Interpreting and Using the Report Results

Once the report is finished, we can use the report results in two ways. First, the report in and of itself provides insight into the problem, or possible problem. Second, we will draw a small sample of service requests from the report and conduct a brief study on the particular agencies involved.

Just a quick glance at the report reveals a pattern in how long it takes to complete a request. Almost all those at the bottom of the list—that is, with the longest duration—are requests to change software. Most of those involve one vendor (all-tron), but any vendor tackling a software change would presumably take a long time.

To gain more insight into the situation, it is probably wise to visit three or four agencies and ask about the nature of work on their telephone service. A sample that includes all types of service requests (new phones, move phones, and software) would be appropriate. In this case, the sample might include the request from Miller to move phones, the request from Montone to place new phones in service, and the request from Stevens to install software. Choosing the requests from Miller might be particularly good, because he has had experience with all three types of requests: new phones, moving phones, and software changes, although not all the jobs are completed and thus not all are shown in figure 9.28.

Based on the interviews and discussions with the contact persons, it may very well turn out that the software changes are indeed at the center of the delays, perhaps because this task is new to the technicians. Time-tested tasks, such as installing or moving phones, may not present a problem.

After taking the sample of service requests and having these discussions with the agency contact personnel, the telecommunications officer would have several difficult decisions to make. If this software-related problem is the type of problem that will gradually work itself out as the technicians gain more experience, this may or may not show in an analysis by date of request. For example, if the more recent requests for software changes are finished sooner, then a simple call to the vendors might be sufficient to expedite or encourage the improvements that appear to be taking place. If an analysis by date of request exhibits no improvement over time, then the telecommunications officer needs to decide whether this is a general problem, independent of the company doing the software work, or if the one company doing most of the software work does not have the skill to provide the service. The data may not help answer this question, because only two software jobs have been completed by a vendor other than All-tron. If, after reviewing all the available information, the telecommunications officer makes the judgment that it is a general problem independent of company, what action does the telecommunications officer take? Bring the task in-house? Negotiate a penalty clause with contractors? All these actions go beyond the data in the file, putting the decision maker in uncertain territory. These uncertainties are characteristic of semistructured problems. The data go only so far in assisting the decision maker. Decision makers need to add their judgments to the information analyzed.

Before closing this case, one more data item needs attention. In the analysis, we judged from the work description field (Workdescr) whether the job involved installing new phones, moving phones, or changing software. However, we actually had to read the description to determine the type of service. The database would probably benefit from a set of codes designating the type of job (including multiple services). This would mean adding another field to the database, perhaps called Typereques. In the field Typereques, we might enter N for new, M for move, S for software, and other codes for combinations if work orders could include combinations.

In many DBMS, it would be possible to create another field, such as Typereques, from the content of the present Workdescr field. First, it would be necessary to modify (i.e., use the MODIFY STRUCTURE command in dBASE III Plus) the database in order to add and name the complementary field. Once this is done, it is possible to read what is contained in the field Workdescr, determine the type of service, and place a code in the complementary field. dBASE III Plus has a command that looks for and identifies words from longer phrases. For example, in the phrase "install three new phones," the dBASE III Plus dollar sign ($) command can determine whether any of the words *new, move,* or *software* is contained in that phrase.

```
IF 'software' $ workdescr
    ? 'software was found in record number ',RECNO()
ENDIF
```

This particular command displays a message if the word *software* is contained in the record read. RECNO() tells the record number.

The sample program in figure 9.30 illustrates the use of the $ command. The program assumes that multiple requests (e.g., *new* and *move*) can occur. The program also encompasses the possibility that none of the words (*new, move, software*) will be found. This option is incorporated by setting a "switch" to "f" and turning it to "t" whenever a true case (*new, move,* or *software*) is found. If no true case is found, then the "f" prevails, and a statement is displayed saying that none of the key words was found in a particular record.

CONCLUSION

Management information applications and their attendant DBMS can assist the analyst and manager in a variety of functional areas and in solving problems of differing degrees of difficulty. This chapter draws examples from resource and program management. Within these functional areas, structured and semistructured problems have been covered.

The logic for developing management information applications should not be unfamiliar to analysts and managers. In many cases, the thinking that goes into solving problems in general can go into building microcomputer applications. However, there is a technological element. Normalization of the data is important, and the syntax for the programming is not without its trials. Fortunately, advances in software will reduce the technological burden. So-called CASE (computer-aided systems engineering) software is being developed to assist with the design of multiple-file databases. Newer DBMS have tools that can help generate the syntax of programs by expressing, in English-like statements similar to pseudocode, what needs to be done. Each advance in software should make the technology less imposing. Nonetheless, for semistructured and unstruc-

```
*Called convert, this program searches for words in*
*longer phrases. When the target word is located,  *
*a message to that effect is given.                *
SET TALK OFF
STORE 'f' TO found
GO TOP
DO WHILE .NOT. EOF()
    IF 'new' $ workdescr
        ? 'new was found in recno ',RECNO()
        WAIT
        STORE 't' TO found
    ENDIF
    IF 'software' $ workdescr
        ? 'software found in recno ',RECNO()
        WAIT
        STORE 't' TO found
    ENDIF
    IF 'move' $ workdescr
        ? 'move found in recno ',RECNO()
        WAIT
        STORE 't' TO found
    ENDIF
    IF found = 'f'
        ? 'none of the key words found in recno() ',RECNO()
        WAIT
    ENDIF
    STORE 'f' TO  found
CLEAR
SKIP
ENDDO
```

FIGURE 9.30 Finding a word contained in a phrase

tured problems, decision makers will still need to rely on their own experience and judgment.

Finally, we saw that for certain types of managerial problems in the structured or semistructured category, large volumes of data are involved. Management information applications, using relational database management software (DBMS), are often built to deal with these types of problems. In this chapter, four cases have been developed to show many of the techniques used in building the management information application.

The initial application was quite rudimentary, relying mainly on the default features of the DBMS. The second case enhanced these basic features, with the purpose of building a more comprehensive application. Multiple files, customized data-entry screen, menus, and a generalized program were all used to make the application a broader and easier one to use. Although the end result of these first two cases was a broad-based system, it was built bottom-up: one piece was added onto another. The third case, which involved record tracking for safety personnel, took a top-down approach to building the management information application. In the top-down approach, the entire system is sketched before the application is built. Here we saw many of the same techniques used in case 2, but used in a more systematic fashion. The last case added another dimension to management information systems, going beyond tracking to examine program performance.

In general, a management information application will have both a tracking and a performance element to it. It may also have expert elements, such as the one in case 3 designed to determine who should be certified at certain levels.

EXERCISES

The exercises for this chapter are of two types. One type allows the user to develop a relatively broad information system. Data are provided for this exercise. The other type of exercise focuses on discrete issues in database design and use. No data are provided.

Part 1

The first exercise is designed to provide experience with building and using a management information application (MINA) for routine as well as relatively complex managerial problems. Recall from this and other chapters that routine problems are referred to as structured, and complex problems as semistructured or unstructured.

To assist with this exercise, a set of data is provided. The data consist of eleven fields and fifty records. Fewer than fifty records can be used. The eleven fields are:

- Employ(ee) ID: a unique identification for each employee
- Job description: essentially a generic title
- Date of birth
- Salary
- Overhead: fringe and other costs needed to support the position
- Year started: year started with the agency
- Perform(ance) rating: rating assigned on a scale from 1 (poorest) to 5 (best)
- Sick leave: number of days taken in the current year
- Department: the number of the department for which the employee works
- Education: c=college, h=high school, g=graduate school, s=grade school or some secondary schooling
- Award: whether the employee received an award in the current year

The exercise can be done by normalizing the database (breaking the eleven fields into two or more files with attention given to avoiding the several data traps) or by placing all eleven fields into one file. Both chapter 5 and this chapter cover the steps for normalization.

The main purpose of the exercise is to set up a database to keep track of employee records, including employee performance. A manager or analyst might undertake this effort if he or she had some discretion in tracking employee effort, or if he or she is experimenting with an employee tracking system.

A. The initial task in the exercise is to set up a hierarchy chart similar to the one in figure 9.20. The purpose of the hierarchy chart is to identify the major components of the database, or major jobs that the database system should accomplish. One obvious job is to enter the data accurately. A perusal of the eleven data fields should help identify the major jobs the database could accomplish.
B. The second task is to build a transaction-processing system by actually setting up the database and entering the data. Most database management software allows either a rudimentary system or one that can be customized to include extra features considered important in achieving an accurate, easy-to-use system. Case 1 offers an example of a simple data-entry system; case 2, a customized one.
C. The third task is to query the database. For each of the following questions, generate one or a set of queries to answer the question.

1. Give the employee ID and department for all employees.
2. Give the employee ID and age for each employee. Repeat this, ordering the employees from youngest to oldest.
3. Who are the employees with a high school education? What is the problem with trying to order this file from those with the lowest formal education to those with the highest?
4. Who are the employees in department 2, and what are their dates of birth?
5. Who are the people in department 2 who have a high school education?
6. Which employees have not received an award?
7. What is the performance rating of employees in the salary range $20,000–$30,000?
8. Which employees have a performance rating of 5 or have received an award?
9. What is the educational level for people born after 1965?
10. Change the data in educational level from s, h, c, and g, as follows:
    a. For s, use gs, where gs means grade school or some secondary.
    b. For h, use hs, where hs means high school.
    c. For c, use ug, where ug means undergraduate.
    d. For g, use zg, where zg refers to graduate school.

D. Most DBMS have a report generator that produces attractive-looking results. Do the following reports, remembering that it is often necessary to index on the variable that will be used for grouping the data in the report.

1. Do a report on educational level of employees by department.
2. Which departments have the most sick leave?
3. Show salary and year started for each employee, and get salary subtotals for each department.
4. Which job descriptions are costing the agency the most, and what type of performance rating are we seeing in these job categories? Hint: index, or order, on salary.

E. As the next part of this exercise, put together a menu-driven program. The menu should permit the user to select and do all the data tasks done so far in this exercise. In other words, it should let the user enter data, make queries, and generate reports. As such, it will capture aspects of both transaction processing and management information processing.

The menu could have the following appearance:

```
                        MENU FOR EMPLOYEE DATA
        Data Entry and Information Management Functions

        1. Add records
        2. Delete records (by employee number)
        3. Selected queries
        4. Selected reports
        5. Quit

        Enter Choice =>
```

Here are some examples of what the program should be able to handle:

1. A new employee joins the agency and has these data for the current year: employee number 51, department 4, date of birth 12/11/64, college education, job description Outreach, salary 27000, overhead 15000, year started 1990, performance rating 3, no awards, and sick leave 3 days.
2. Employee 21 has resigned; delete that record.
3. Be able to do a query showing educational level and department for any employee.
4. Be able to run a report specified in D.2 or D.3 of this exercise.

To design the entire menu structure, it is necessary to use stepwise refinement, modularity, and pseudocode to make the project manageable. Notice that some of what is assigned in the menu-driven program has already been done in earlier parts of the exercise.

F. As the final task in this exercise, decide on a raise for each employee. Assume first that the total money available is 8 percent of the total salaries for all employees. Decide on what criteria to use for the raises, then develop an algorithm to translate these criteria into a programmable set of instructions that will generate the raise for each employee, yet not exceed the total money set aside for raises.

Employ ID	Job Description	Date of Birth	Salary	Over- head	Year Started	Perform Rate	Sick Leave	Depart- ment	Educat- ion	Awar
1	executive	02/03/47	57000	50000	82	4	3	1	c	T
2	executive	06/01/39	32000	38000	85	4	9	1	h	F
3	clerical	12/11/57	19000	11000	79	3	11	1	h	F
4	manager	08/21/30	41000	45000	81	5	2	1	g	T
5	clerical	04/01/64	15000	9000	83	3	12	2	h	F
6	manager	08/25/35	35000	32000	76	4	5	2	c	F
7	adm assist	11/30/57	21000	23000	81	4	7	2	g	F
8	manager	01/01/25	31000	45000	73	3	12	2	c	F
9	adm assist	06/17/42	27000	32000	74	3	7	2	c	F
10	clerical	10/29/53	16000	23000	82	5	2	2	h	F
11	adm assist	09/13/63	18000	21000	78	3	2	2	c	F

```
12  clerical      05/19/33  21000  24000    80    4    10    2   h   F
13  outreach      01/29/57  25000  42000    81    3    11    3   h   F
14  maintenance   08/03/64  18000  27000    83    3     0    3   h   F
15  secretary     07/25/32  29000  41000    72    5     0    3   h   F
16  outreach      02/22/61  24000  34000    84    2    12    3   c   F
17  manager       12/05/32  33000  45000    77    5     0    3   c   F
18  outreach      06/15/23  39000  48000    76    3    13    3   h   T
19  outreach      08/12/59  27000  32000    80    4     0    3   c   F
20  outreach      08/30/65  19000  29000    86    3     0    3   h   F
21  outreach      06/07/27  40000  43000    65    4     4    3   h   F
22  outreach      07/09/47  32000  45000    74    2    10    3   h   F
23  outreach      11/07/55  28000  39000    79    3     4    3   c   T
24  outreach      07/24/60  23000  37000    80    3     0    3   h   F
25  outreach      08/22/53  31000  39000    78    5     4    3   h   T
26  adm assist    08/08/59  23000  30000    83    3     0    3   c   F
27  secretary     11/22/29  39000  46000    66    3    12    3   h   F
28  clerical      06/12/59  19000  31000    84    5     0    3   h   F
29  manager       08/09/44  39000  33000    81    4     3    4   c   F
30  clerical      02/27/67  15000  11000    85    2     9    4   h   F
31  outreach      03/05/52  18000  19000    79    4     4    4   c   T
32  adm assist    07/29/57  23000  21000    83    3     8    4   c   F
33  outreach      08/18/41  22000  18000    73    3     9    4   h   F
34  outreach      12/09/59  22000  23000    82    0     0    4   c   F
35  outreach      04/24/64  17000  11000    84    2     2    4   c   T
36  outreach      11/30/26  31000  29000    70    5     0    4   g   F
37  maintenance   10/21/41  16000  19000    66    2     9    4   h   F
38  secretary     11/10/30  32000  30000    67    5     0    4   g   T
39  maintenance   01/23/63  12000   9000    84    3     0    5   s   F
40  manager       05/15/36  45000   4000    66    3    11    5   g   T
41  maintenance   02/03/42  19000  26000    74    5     7    5   h   F
42  secretary     05/15/63  36000  39000    86    4    13    5   h   F
43  maintenance   09/21/64  16000  19000    84    3     0    5   g   T
44  adm assist    03/17/57  28000  30000    83    4     1    5   g   F
45  adm assist    09/23/54  30000  27000    77    2     9    5   c   F
46  maintenance   08/11/25  23000  19000    63    5     0    5   s   F
47  adm assist    03/27/45  35000  34000    79    5     0    5   g   T
48  maintenance   12/12/30  27000  23000    68    2     0    5   h   F
49  maintenance   11/22/61  17000  12000    84    3     3    5   c   F
50  maintenance   03/03/51  21000  18000    77    5    12    5   h   F
```

Part 2

A. Take a problem of interest to you and go through the process of developing a set of microcomputer application programs to manage the relevant data. Start with the analysis of the problem, then move to data organization, and finally to development of the microcomputer application. For example, suppose an office has an extensive set of paper files on hazardous waste sites in the state and wants to set up a microcomputer system for the files. Doing a case study of an actual office or problem might be the best way to carry out this particular assignment.

PART III   Use of the Framework in Developing Applications

B. For a problem of your choice (or a problem assigned to you), sketch a customized data-entry system. Be particularly careful about including features that will make the system easy to use and accurate. For example, how might you be sure that the entry for a certain data item never exceeds 3000? Material in chapter 5 will also be helpful in building this data-entry system.
C. Following is a data file that has some of the data traps that should be avoided. Identify the repeating fields data trap and improve on the design of the file.

   In this file, a field is added every time a client makes a visit.
D. For any given or assigned problem, show how a hierarchy chart and menu system reinforce each other and go together in developing a microcomputer management

```
Client data file

ClientID   Date of Birth   Category   Visit 1   Visit 2   Visit 3
----------------------------------------------------------------
111        08/08/56        A          xxx       yyy
222        10/22/66        B          aaa       bbb       ccc
333        01/11/67        A          ddd

----------------------------------------------------------------
```

information application.
E. If it takes a grade better than 70 on each of three tests to get an average rating and a grade of 90 or better on one of these tests (plus better than 70 on the other two) to receive a rating of superior, present the pseudocode to determine if a person is rated below average, average, or superior.
F. Using a DBMS assigned to you, list the steps necessary to join or relate two files.

CHAPTER

10

Specialized Software and Applications

■ OVERVIEW

Although the previous chapters have demonstrated the flexibility and diversity of applications based on spreadsheet and database software, there are some applications that require capabilities not possible with even the most sophisticated database or spreadsheet programs. These applications require the use of specialized programs designed to facilitate specific (though perhaps still very complex) tasks. This chapter explores four of these specialized programs and surveys their use in developing special-purpose applications. The four types of programs are: project management, expert systems, presentation graphics, and desktop publishing.

Before discussing these programs, it is worth noting why they are termed *specialized programs.* It seems at least once a year a software company or developer touts its product as the next Lotus or dBASE, in an attempt to convince the user population that it is a truly significant program that will revolutionize the way work is done. Unfortunately, most of these new software packages, though very useful, fail to live up to the initial hype about them. The reasons for these limited successes may be as varied as the software, but there is usually an underlying common thread that ties them together. The common thread is that the programs are designed to address specific, technical problems and not the broad categories of applications possible with a database or spreadsheet.

Because of their specialized nature, most of these programs also have three common characteristics: a requirement of preknowledge of the subject area, limited applicability, and long or steep learning or use curves.

Applications developed using software packages for project management or expert systems, for example, require that the user not only learn the syntax of the specific package, but also have a good working knowledge of the substantive concepts upon which the software package is based. This means that users must be facile in the use of the *technique* before they can employ a computer-based software package that utilizes it. In obviously technical areas such as computer-aided design (CAD), this expectation is readily apparent and acknowledged. Unfortunately, in areas such as project management, which are closer to the mainstream of managerial endeavors, users tend to assume that mastery of the commands and syntax of a particular package also brings with it a knowledge of how to use it. This is far from true. In fact, one of the most difficult aspects of developing an application based on specialized software is mastering the concepts and techniques used in the package.

Specialized software packages are designed for users who already possess a basic knowledge of the substantive tools and techniques involved. Buying an expert systems development package does not automatically bring with it an education in the theory, design, or application of an expert system. Nor does a graphics package mystically imbue the user with artistic or design capabilities. Perhaps one of the greatest stumbling blocks to the development of successful applications based on specialized software packages is the failure to recognize the level of substantive knowledge required for successful use. Failing such recognition, the novice user is often confronted with a bewildering array of concepts (e.g., PERT, CPM, forward-chaining, kerning, picas) that instantly raise frustration with the package to intolerable levels.

Specialized applications, by their nature, have limited applicability. Designed to facilitate solutions to specific categories of problems, the specialized software package is far less flexible than a generalized package such as a spreadsheet. Managerial and operational difficulties arise when users attempt to fit the problem to a solution (the software package).

Understandably, users want to use a package with which they are already familiar to solve whatever problems arise. In many cases, however, the specialized package is simply not appropriate and offers neither the logic nor the techniques to solve the problem at hand. For example, although project management software often contains tools such as calendars and timelines that produce a project schedule, they are not designed to produce daily appointment calendars or appointment schedules. Yet users frequently attempt to produce such applications, blaming the software when the application fails to achieve its desired goal. A corollary to this dilemma is the belief that the true value of a package is its ability to solve a wide spectrum of the organization's problems and that, therefore, the package must be used to justify its acquisition. Instead of using the package only on those problems clearly applicable to its strengths, attempt after attempt is made to force the package to analyze problems and provide solutions that are far outside its designer's intent. Both of these perceptions ignore the fundamental reasoning behind a specialized package: to solve specific, technical problems. When properly applied to the right category of problem, the specialized package can serve to reduce problem-solving time dramatically, enhance productivity, and expand capacity. Applied improperly, the package, like any other misapplied problem-solving technique, not only will fail to solve the problem but may create additional difficulties.

Given the technical nature of specialized software packages, it should not be surprising to discover that these packages generally have long or steep (or both) learning curves and require extensive amounts of time for proper use. The length and difficulty of learning and using a specialized package is directly related to the complexity of the task it seeks to facilitate. This is just as true of a complex spreadsheet model as it is of a complex graphics presentation or an expert system.

The length and steepness of the learning curve for a specialized software package is a function of two related factors: the complexity of the task and the complexity of the solution. Complexity of the task refers to the number of possible variables that must be analyzed to produce a viable solution. For example, in an expert system, the complexity of the task takes two forms: the number of *rules* (logic chains) required to cover possible options, and the number of database *elements* that the rules must manipulate. Consider that increases in these numbers do not result in a linear increase in complexity. Rather, complexity of the system increases geometrically with element and rule size.

Complexity of the solution refers to the number of different techniques needed to complete the development of an application and produce a useful product. A successful desktop publishing project, for example, requires text entry, text formatting, graphics design, font selection, page layout, and page formatting. Each of these techniques requires the user to gain mastery of a formidable set of commands and procedures. Learning this volume of commands is obviously going to require a substantial commitment of both time and effort. Additionally, even once mastered, the time required to implement the complex series of procedures needed to produce a finished product is considerable. Dramatic time savings are not a guaranteed by-product of specialized applications.

Clearly, applications based on specialized software packages are not designed for the casual or novice user. Specialized applications almost always involve trade-offs: increased power and sophistication in exchange for extended personnel commitments and organizational support. Clear examples of this kind of trade-off can be found in graphics and desktop publishing applications. There is no question that the products of these applications, when done carefully and appropriately, rival the products of expensive design and publication companies. However, production of these applications requires an organizational commitment to train at least one employee in both the substantive (design) and procedural (software) aspects of the application, provide that employee with justly compensated time to both develop and use the application, and supply the resources (e.g., specialized hardware) necessary for the continued use of the application. A brochure-publishing application that was once farmed out to a commercial design and printing company may save the organization money on production of the brochure, but it will also cost the organization in terms of substantial employee time and additional resources. Obviously, this is not a simple undertaking. Too often, the organization management simply imposes the development of a specialized application upon unsuspecting employees (or the employees self-select themselves) without concern for additional training, work load, or resource commitment requirements. This state of affairs seldom makes for a successful application.

The reader is cautioned to keep these conditions and limitations in mind when considering the development of specialized applications. The prudent organization exercises caution by conducting a cost/benefit or cost-effectiveness analysis before making the decision to proceed with a potentially resource-intensive application.

In the sections that follow, each of the four specialized software applications mentioned at the outset of this chapter is examined. The purpose of these brief explanations, it must be noted, is not to produce experts in the tools and techniques, but to survey the requirements and components of the various program areas.

PROJECT MANAGEMENT

Project Management (PM) refers to a series of techniques used by managers to plan and track projects. PM is based on two techniques: program evaluation and review technique

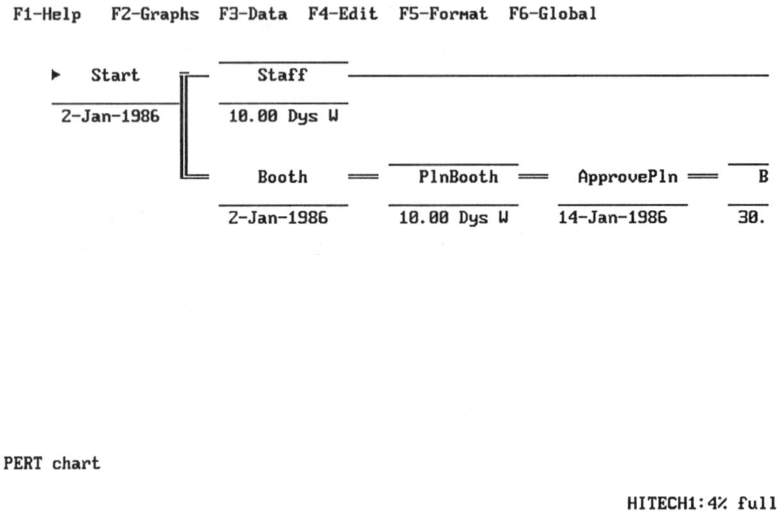

PART III   Use of the Framework in Developing Applications

```
F1-Help    F2-Graphs  F3-Data  F4-Edit  F5-Format  F6-Global
```

```
     ▶  Start   ┬─────    Staff   ──────────────────────────────────────
        2-Jan-1986│       10.00 Dys W
                  │
                  └─────    Booth   ═════  PlnBooth  ═════  ApprovePln  ═════  B
                           2-Jan-1986      10.00 Dys W     14-Jan-1986         30.
```

```
PERT chart
                                                                    HITECH1:4% full
```

FIGURE 10.1 Sample PERT chart

(PERT) and critical path method (CPM). Developed to keep track of such complex projects as the building of nuclear submarines, PM has become a mainstream management technique commonly used in capital (building) projects or where the allocation of time and resources is complex.

PM is a visually oriented methodology that makes use of a PERT diagram to show the relationship among the various components of a project (often referred to as *tasks* and *milestones*) and a Gantt chart to illustrate the time relationships among project elements. Tasks that cannot be delayed without delaying completion of the entire project are said to be on the *critical path*; tasks that may be delayed or extended are said to have *slack* or *float* time. (For a more extensive discussion of PM and its application to public sector projects, see Levine, 1986.)

Applications developed based on project management software generally fall into one or more of these three categories:

- project planning
- project control and tracking
- resource allocation and administration

To accommodate the variety of analytical techniques needed for each category, most top-line microcomputer-based PM software packages offer several modules that permit the user to custom-tailor the final application to the specific project needs. Typically, PM packages such as Harvard Total Project Manager II, which is used for the examples in this section, as well as Promis, Microsoft Project, Project Workbench, and others include techniques such as those that follow.

PERT charts represent diagrammatically the relationships among the various elements of a projects (see figure 10.1). In PM, the PERT chart is the technique used to develop the overall project structure through the use of *milestones* (goals) and *tasks* (objectives). The value of the PERT chart lies in providing information both on the

Chapter 10 Specialized Software and Applications

```
F1-Help   F2-Graphs   F3-Data   F4-Edit   F5-Format   F6-Global

                          Jan                    Feb
                   30      6     13     20   27   3      10     17
  ► Start          ◆
    2-Jan-1986

    Booth          ◆
    2-Jan-1986

    PlnBooth      ━━━━━━━━
    10.00 Dys W

    Staff                 ━━━━━━━━━━━━━━━━━━━━━━━━━━━
    10.00 Dys W

    ApprovePln             ◆
    14-Jan-1986

    BldBooth              ━━━━━━━━━━━━━━━━━━━━━━━━━━━
 Gantt chart
 PERT chart   ━━━━━━━━━━━━━━━━━━━━━━━━━━━━━━━━━━━━━━━━
                                                         HITECH1: 4% full
```

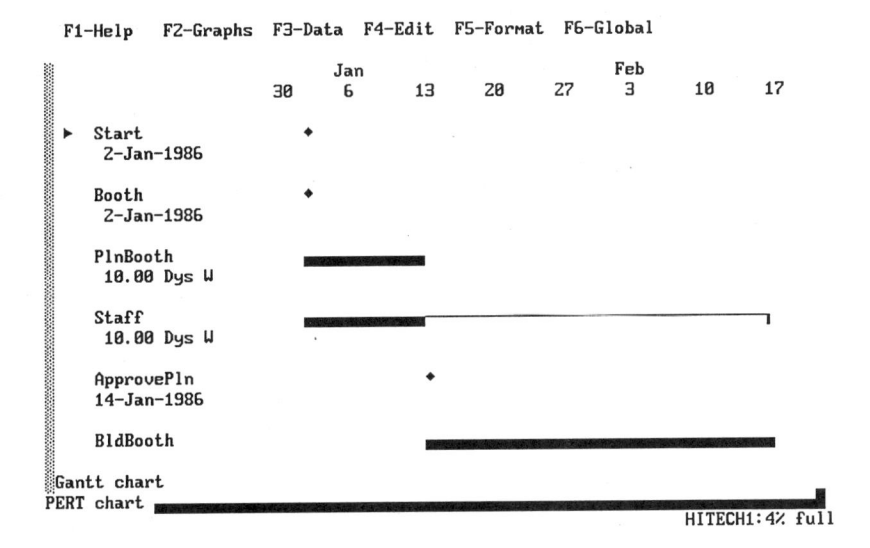

FIGURE 10.2 Sample Gantt chart

duration of each task, facilitating the development of time estimates for completion of interdependent tasks, and on the dependency of tasks. The *dependency network,* as it is sometimes called, clearly delineates sequenced tasks, or *paths,* throughout the project. Essentially, the PERT chart acts as a road map of the project, guiding managers in the planning of the project and in the tracking of tasks completed, tasks current, and tasks to be undertaken forthwith. The PERT chart is a technical device that is very useful in reducing the perceived complexity of a project. By dividing all of a project's elements into tasks and milestones, PERT introduces a set of common units that facilitates understanding of the processes at work in the project.

Gantt charts are graphic representations of project element sequencing, time relationships, critical path, and slack time (see figure 10.2). The Gantt chart is the most widely used aspect of PM, often as a stand-alone technique. The primary value of the Gantt chart is that it presents the user with a schedule that also depicts the time relationships among the project tasks. As a planning tool, the Gantt chart is valuable in establishing projected start and completion times for tasks, offering the user a ready view of overlapping or double-scheduled elements. As a tracking tool, the Gantt chart enables the user to compare projected versus actual task times and to revise the project schedule if needed.

Calendar forms are used to specify the length of the workday, workweek, and holiday or nonwork periods (see figure 10.3). The calendar function is important in PM because work usually occurs during a set workday and does not typically continue during weekend or holiday periods. A PM calendar allows the user to specify the length of the workday, the number of workdays in a week, and the duration of weekends and any nonwork holidays. Nonworkdays are then correctly figured into elapsed time calculations for task duration.

Work breakdown hierarchy charts graphically illustrate task priority and sequence (see figure 10.4). The work breakdown chart is primarily a planning device that allows

PART III Use of the Framework in Developing Applications

```
F1-Help    F2-Graphs  F3-Data   F4-Edit   F5-Format  F6-Global
                              1986
             January         February                  March

                  1  2  3  4                    1                        1
         5  6  7  8  9 10 11      2  3  4  5  6  7  8      2  3  4  5  6  7  8
        12 13 14 15 16 17 18      9 10 11 12 13 14 15      9 10 11 12 13 14 15
        19 20 21 22 23 24 25     16 17 18 19 20 21 22     16 17 18 19 20 21 22
        26 27 28 29 30 31        23 24 25 26 27 28        23 24 25 26 27 28 29
                                                          30 31
                                       1986
              April             May                       June

               1  2  3  4  5              1  2  3      1  2  3  4  5  6  7
         6  7  8  9 10 11 12      4  5  6  7  8  9 10      8  9 10 11 12 13 14
        13 14 15 16 17 18 19     11 12 13 14 15 16 17     15 16 17 18 19 20 21
        20 21 22 23 24 25 26     18 19 20 21 22 23 24     22 23 24 25 26 27 28
        27 28 29 30              25 26 27 28 29 30 31     29 30
Calendar wallchart
                                                                HITECH1:4% full
```

FIGURE 10.3 Sample calendar form

```
F1-Help    F2-Graphs  F3-Data   F4-Edit   F5-Format  F6-Global
```

                                        ▶   Goal
                                      ├──────────┤
                              Booth   Staff

                    ├──────────┤
            PlnBooth   BldBooth

Work breakdown
PERT chart
                                                                HITECH1:4% full

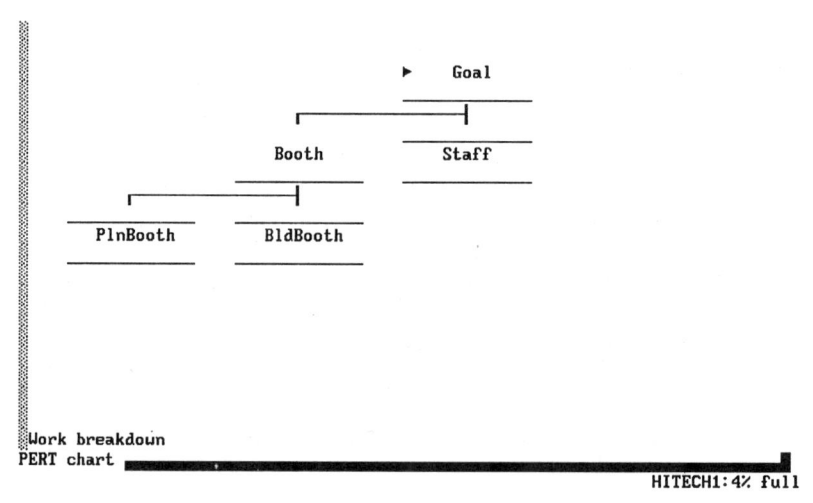

FIGURE 10.4 Sample work breakdown hierarchy chart

the user to think of the organization of a project in terms of priorities. By representing priorities in a classic tree diagram, the chart makes it easier to discern relationships. Project elements derived from the priority structure form the basis for the PERT chart and the Gantt chart.

Cost breakdown reports (see figure 10.5), usually by both resource and task, indicate both projected and actual costs, highlighting any cost overruns. The inclusion of cost information in microcomputer-based PM software is a fairly recent addition that brings

Chapter 10 Specialized Software and Applications

```
F1-Help   F2-Graphs   F3-Data   F4-Edit   F5-Format   F6-Global
```

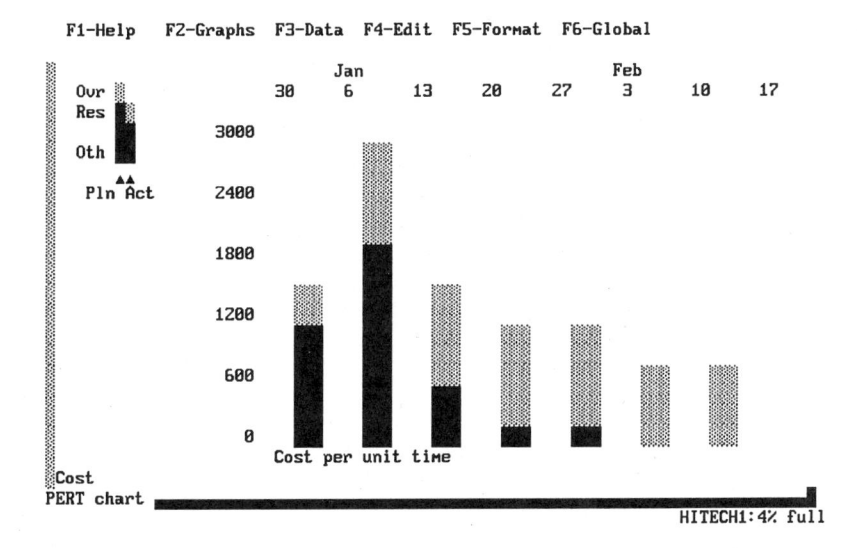

```
                         Jan                      Feb
   Ovr              30    6    13    20    27     3    10    17
   Res
                3000
   Oth
   ▲▲
   Pln Act      2400

                1800

                1200

                 600

                   0
                        Cost per unit time
 Cost
 PERT chart
                                                    HITECH1:4% full
```

FIGURE 10.5 Sample cost breakdown report

```
F1-Help   F2-Graphs   F3-Data   F4-Edit   F5-Format   F6-Global
```

						More →
		Time		Working	Maximum	Overt
Resource	Quantity	Units	Cost/unit	hrs/day	hrs/day	rate
CarpentrAsst	1.000	Dys	8.00	7.50	11.50	12.00
MaintAsst	1.000	Hrs	8.00	7.50	11.50	12.00
MaintMgr	1.000	Dys	150.00	7.50	7.50	0.00
SalesAsst	1.000	Hrs	12.00	7.50	11.50	18.00
SalesMgr	1.000	Dys	250.00	7.50	7.50	0.00
	1.000	Dys	0.00	7.50	7.50	0.00

```
 Resource list
 PERT chart
                                                    HITECH1:7% full
```

FIGURE 10.6 Sample resource chart

the micro-based package significantly closer to the capability of mainframe computer PM systems. Cost breakdowns provide the user with an additional dimension of control. Frequently, the resources of time and money can be traded off in a project, depending on the availability of each. Having the information available on both time requirements and task costs, the user can employ additional available money to reduce excessive task time or extend or delay a task to accommodate a monetary shortfall.

Resource charts (see figure 10.6) and *reports* (see figure 10.7) provide information on resource availability, allocation, and loading (percentage of total available used).

338   PART III   Use of the Framework in Developing Applications

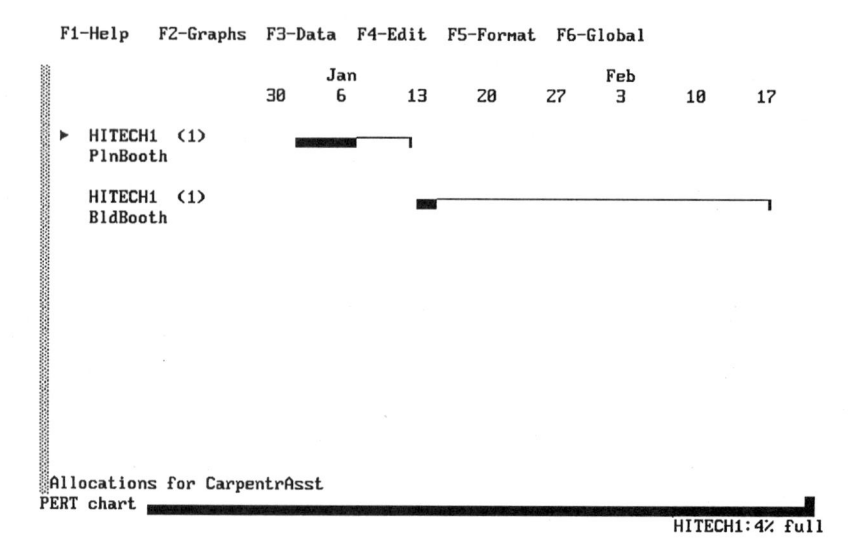

```
F1-Help    F2-Graphs   F3-Data   F4-Edit   F5-Format   F6-Global

                        Jan                        Feb
                 30      6      13      20     27   3      10      17

►  HITECH1  (1)
   PlnBooth        ▬▬▬▬▬▬▬▬▬▐

   HITECH1  (1)
   BldBooth                        ▬▬▬▬▬▬▬▬▬▬▬▬▬▬▬▬▬▬▬▬▐




Allocations for CarpentrAsst
PERT chart  ▬▬▬▬▬▬▬▬▬▬▬▬▬▬▬▬▬▬▬▬▬▬▬▬▬▬▬▬▬▬▬▬▬▬▬▬▬▬▬▬▬▬▐
                                                        HITECH1: 4% full
```

FIGURE 10.7 Sample resource report

Because all projects make use of resources and projects must often compete for limited resources, having the capacity both to define the available resources and to track their allocation provides the manager with an effective mechanism for ensuring that waste, duplication, and overlap are kept to a minimum. In some PM programs, the user is allowed to define a resource inventory that may be allocated across more than one project. The software keeps track of cross-project allocations and can indicate overallocation of any resource (e.g., assigning the same person to two projects at the same time).

It is interesting to note that the approach followed in many PM software packages is functionally equivalent to the analytical framework developed for problem analysis presented in chapter 2. A PM application often begins with a work breakdown that proceeds deductively from the desired goal through the detailing of the tasks needed to achieve that goal. This is an example of the top-down problem definition strategy suggested in chapter 2.

The modular nature of the PM package permits incorporation of only those aspects that are relevant to the particular project under consideration. In addition, the theory and technique of PERT encourage the division of complex projects into subprojects for which the needed level of information detail can be maintained without engendering overwhelming complexity. For example, in the design of a project to sponsor a conference, there would be several tasks relating to the production of publicity materials. These publicity tasks constitute a subset of the entire project. In the PERT chart for the overall project, all of the related publicity tasks could be represented as a single task (with a total elapsed time for all the constituent publicity tasks). A more detailed view of the publicity tasks could be created through a separate PERT chart. In fact, some of the high-end PM packages offer a dynamic-link function that carries changes made in the subproject automatically to the main project. Thus, the modular approach of PM corresponds to the modular structuring and divide-and-conquer strategy suggested in earlier chapters.

As the foregoing discussion implies, one of the real strengths of PM techniques is their ability to assist in making sense of complexity. The complexity of a project however, is an organized complexity that is at least semistructured. For example, a project to build a new city hall is certainly appropriate for a PM application. It can also be viewed as a semistructured problem because certain actions must occur in a specific order (e.g., the foundation must be laid before the walls are built) while other actions may be scheduled in a variety of ways to accommodate uncertainties in weather, materials availability, or other factors.

PM applications are appropriate in those circumstances in which there is a specific goal or target to be achieved, a need to allocate specific resources to accomplish the project, a limited and specific time frame for project completion, a number of interrelated and dependent tasks, and an overall project focus that is essentially progressive (i.e., does not involve repetitive loops that interact with one another) toward a specific conclusion. Examples in which these conditions are met include capital projects (such as buildings), report generation, conference scheduling, and program design. Each of these examples meets the requirement of being a semistructured problem that can take advantage of the specific tools offered in a PM application.

Development of PM-based applications is not appropriate in situations in which one or more of the critical variables of *time, resources*, or *task dependency* are missing. It is important to keep in mind that PM is not designed as an appointment-scheduling technique. Nor is it appropriate for open-ended, ongoing tasks that are addressed on an ad hoc or variable time schedule.

To develop an effective application based on a PM program, then, requires that several diverse elements coalesce. First, a specific set of conditions must exist in the problem that requires the scheduling of tasks, allocation of resources, and management of time. Second, the user must possess adequate knowledge of the specialized techniques, such as PERT, CPM, and Gantt charting, needed to operationalize the application. Third, the problem must be at least semistructured, with a clear logic of action and reasonable criteria (e.g., time savings) for making decisions. Only when all three of these conditions are met will the PM application function effectively.

EXPERT SYSTEMS

Expert systems (ES) are one of the first practical outgrowths of the field of artificial intelligence. Basically, an ES consists of three parts: logic algorithms (called a *knowledge base*), a database, and an inference engine that ties the other two components together. The ES is used to answer questions or solve problems by applying the rules of logic developed for the system to the information database and drawing conclusions.

The ES is usually developed in an area in which an existing body of technical knowledge can be aggregated into a database and a series of logic rules developed for the use of that information. For example, a fire department might develop an ES to assist in the handling of hazardous materials. In this case, the ES would consist of a database containing all of the available material on hazardous materials and rules of logic concerning materials interaction, containment, handling, and disposal. Essentially, the

ES acts as a computer-based consultant to assist the user in solving a complex problem. (Additional information on expert systems can be found in Harmon, Maus, & Morrissey, 1988.)

Unlike the project management application, which must fit a specific and limited format for effective use, the expert system is driven more by the *processes* involved in the application than by the absolute nature of the subject matter. An ES may be used for a variety of purposes, including resource allocation, problems diagnosis, scheduling, management of complexity, and decision support. In addition, Robert Blanning (in Silverman,1987) suggests several more general ways that expert systems may be classified:

- by the technology employed, such as the structure of the knowledge base
- by the level of organization (strategic, tactical, operational) at which the ES is implemented
- by the functional area of the organization (e.g., planning, finance, transportation) where the system is used
- by the type of problem for which the ES provides support

Until fairly recently, the construction of an ES required the use of a "knowledge engineer" who had the expertise to design the system elements and facilitate development of the knowledge base (rules) and database. Frequently requiring the use of specialized computer programming languages such as LISP or Prolog, construction of an ES was a daunting task far beyond the capabilities of the typical public sector analyst or manager. With the advent of microcomputer software packages such as ExSys, First Class, and VP-Expert, the level of basic ES theory required to construct a useful ES system has been greatly reduced. It has not, however, been eliminated.

To develop a useful ES, the analyst or manager must still possess a reasonable level of knowledge about both the structure and process of the ES. Knowledge of the structure of an expert system rests on a clear understanding of the information (elicited from the appropriate experts and reliable sources) needed to construct both the knowledge base and the database that will be used by the system. In essence, this means that the ES developer must be familiar enough with the *substance* of the problem area to be able to determine what constitutes a sufficient aggregation of knowledge for the ES. For example, to develop an ES to assist planners in evaluating zoning variances, it is necessary to have enough of an understanding of the zoning permit process to judge what information is relevant for the knowledge base and the database and at what point information collection is sufficient to permit use of the ES.

Knowledge of the process of an ES includes a basic understanding of the nature of the inference engine used, as well as the logic-chaining process. For example, there are two logic approaches to designing an ES: forward chaining and backward chaining. Forward chaining is essentially inductive in nature, making use of a number of symptoms or other pieces of evidence to select from the knowledge base a relevant hypothesis that explains the symptoms. Figure 10.8 offers an illustration of inductive queries in an ES covering commercial insurance policies. The classic ES for pharmaceutical analysis, MYCIN, is an example of a system based on symptom search.

A backward-chaining ES proceeds with an exhaustive testing of the hypotheses stored in the knowledge base. This type of ES is useful in selection situations in which the user wishes to select an optimum solution from among a number of alternatives. An

```
┌─────────────────────────────────────────────────────────────────────┐
│  Is any occupant of the building other than Office, Apartment or Mercantile? │
│  Yes                      No ◄                                      │
│                                                                     │
│  Do Apartment/Mercantile occupancies exceed 25% of total floor Area? │
│  Yes                      No ◄                                      │
│                                                                     │
│  Is the Actual Cash Value of the building less than 75% of Replacement Cost? │
│  Yes                      No ◄                                      │
│                                                                     │
│  Is there a restaurant or cafeteria located in the building?       │
│  **Yes**                  No                                        │
│                                                                     │
│                                                                     │
│                                                                     │
│                                                                     │
│                                                                     │
│                                                                     │
└─────────────────────────────────────────────────────────────────────┘
  ↑ ↓ → ←   Enter to select   END to complete   /Q to Quit   ? for Unknown
```

FIGURE 10.8 ES inductive queries (forward chaining)

example of this type of system would be an ES that helped determine an optimum municipal investment strategy based on available resources and market conditions.

An additional consideration that overlaps both the substance and the process aspects of ES construction is the need to select *confidence factors* for expressions in the knowledge base. A confidence factor is a value, from 0 to 100, that represents the belief of the expert contributing the expression that it is true. Confidence factors are critical to the ES because they allow the inference engine to accommodate uncertainty. Confidence factors are used by the inference engine in analyzing inquiries to the ES. The logic of confidence factor use is illustrated in figure 10.9.

In applying the analytical framework developed in chapter 2 to expert systems, it is readily apparent that the ES offers the best possibility for using the computer to analyze unstructured problems. This category of problem is reasonably suitable for analysis using an ES because of the capacity of the ES to incorporate "soft" information based on value judgments and educated guesses. The only real limit encountered in this kind of application is that ES results based on logical reasoning chains may not reflect the "logic" actually used by a political decision maker. The logical structure of the ES is exemplified by the tree diagram in figure 10.10.

The ES is even more appropriate for problems of a semistructured nature, where the increased reliance on rational reasoning fits well with the knowledge base requirements. For example, many local governments find that an ES application designed to recommend actions in toxic chemical situations offers significant benefits. This type of problem clearly fits into the semistructured category because it requires logical conclusions under varying and indefinite conditions (e.g., how rain would affect a spill involving two normally nonreactive chemicals).

In summary, ES applications offer the user the potential for a very powerful, flexible decision-aid tool, but one that requires a considerable front-end investment of time, knowledge, and information to produce. However valuable the concept of an ES may seem, one must not forget that developing an ES is a time-consuming proposition that

```
                                              Editing: Old File insuranc.trc

          first_time◄
          !   (= No CNF 100 )◄
          Client_info◄
          !   Testing Client_Info◄
          !   !   First_time◄
          Client_Name◄
          !   Testing Client_Info◄
          !   !   First_time◄
          !   (= Scranton CNF 100 )◄
          info_client◄
          !   Testing Client_Info◄
          !   !   First_time◄
          !   Testing 1e◄
          !   !   Info1◄
          !   !   !   Testing 1b◄
          !   !   !   !   Info◄
          !   !   !   !   !   Testing 1a◄
          !   !   !   !   !   !   First_time◄
          +    ▲     ▲           ▲   ▲   ▲   ▲   ▲        ▲           ▲
          Insert On  Document Off                Boldface Off Underline Off
             1       2GbRfmt 3       4InsFil 5Update 6Save   7Dir  8Abandn 9       10
```

FIGURE 10.9 ES confidence factors

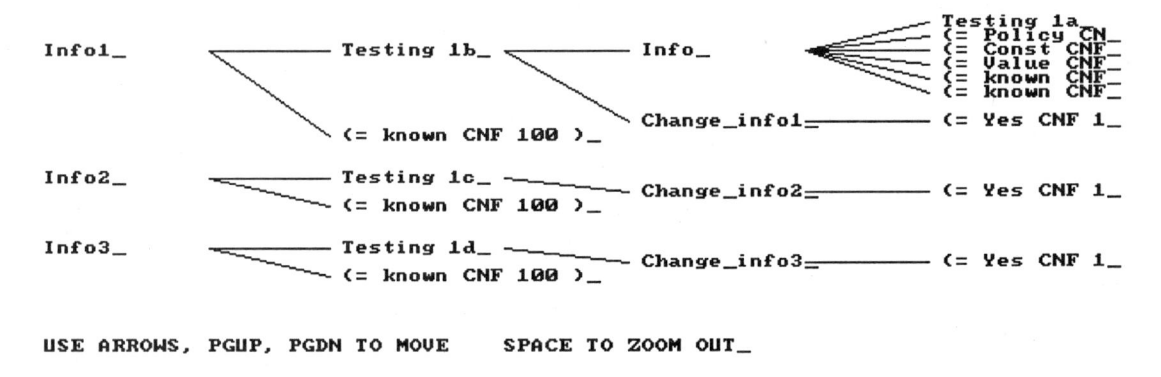

```
Info1_  ─────── Testing 1b_ ─────── Info_ ─────< Testing 1a_
                                                 (= Policy CN_
                                                 (= Const CNF_
                                                 (= Value CNF_
                                                 (= known CNF_
                                                 (= known CNF_
                (= known CNF 100 )_
                                    Change_info1═══════ (= Yes CNF 1_

Info2_  ─────── Testing 1c_ ───────
                (= known CNF 100 )_ Change_info2═══════ (= Yes CNF 1_

Info3_  ─────── Testing 1d_ ───────
                (= known CNF 100 )_ Change_info3═══════ (= Yes CNF 1_
```

USE ARROWS, PGUP, PGDN TO MOVE   SPACE TO ZOOM OUT_

FIGURE 10.10 ES logical structure

exacts a high price in required knowledge and resource commitments. As the technology of ES development progresses, the sophistication required of the user will undoubtedly decline. For now, however, care should be exercised in deciding to proceed with an ES application.

■ PRESENTATION GRAPHICS

The old adage about one picture being worth a thousand words has certainly gained a staunch following among microcomputer users. Continuing advances in monitor screen resolution and color, plus improved resolution (and even color) in hard copy, enable the micro user to produce, with relative ease, graphic images that rival those produced by

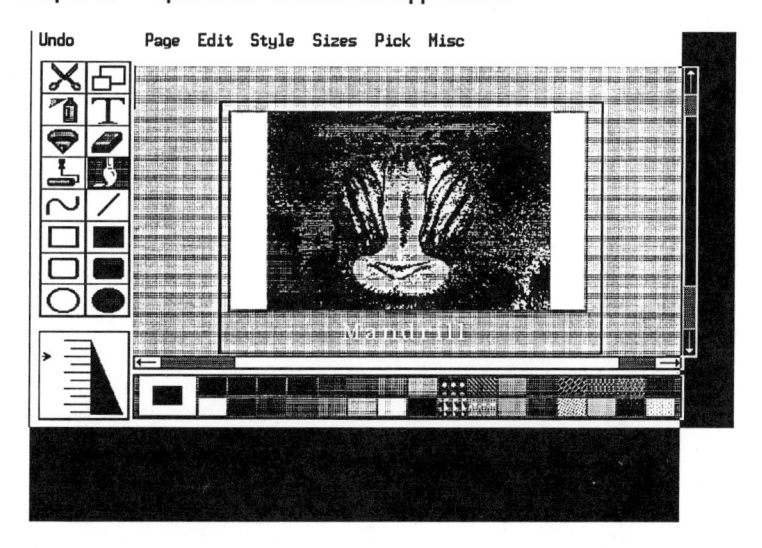

Chapter 10   Specialized Software and Applications   343

FIGURE 10.11   PC Paintbrush

professional designers. As a result, many users are finding that the inclusion of graphics in reports and presentations enhances both the impact and understanding of information.

The term *presentation graphics* is used to cover a variety of tools and techniques used to produce graphic output for publication or audiovisual presentation. Though not strictly a problem-solving approach, presentation graphics have a direct impact on the *communication* of information to the desired audience. The best analysis in the world means very little if the results of that analysis are submerged in a tangled mass of indecipherable data. The use of graphics allows the key information components to be distilled from the supporting information and presented in a visual manner that emphasizes their importance. (A general discussion of the use of presentation graphics can be found in White, 1988.)

Presentation graphics are generally divided into two types:

- *Free-form graphics* may represent any form of artwork from line drawings to full-color, painting-type renditions.
- *Structured graphics* use predefined forms to create specific graphs, such as pie charts, bar charts, or flow diagrams.

Free-Form Graphics

Free-form presentation graphics are usually used to enhance a presentation with images designed to reinforce the information being presented. This form of presentation graphics is the domain of the free-style "paint" programs such as Dr. Halo, PC Paint, PC Paintbrush, and EGA Paint. These programs allow the user to create just about any conceivable image through the use of various "tools" such as pencils, paint rollers or spray cans, circle and box images, and paint patterns. A typical screen for one of these programs (PC Paintbrush) is shown in figure 10.11.

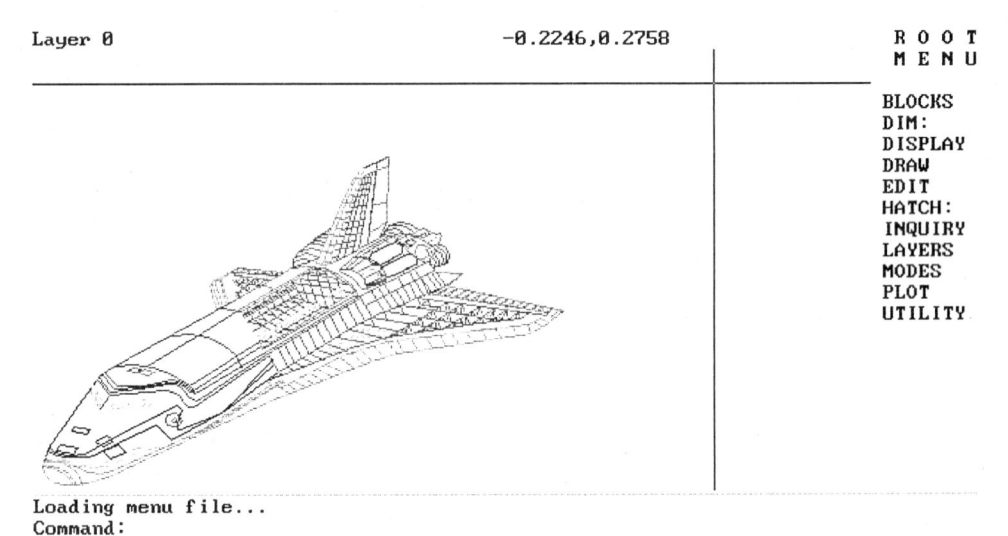

FIGURE 10.12 CAD-generated graphics *(AutoCAD drawing courtesy of Autodesk, Inc.)*

Common applications for free-form graphics programs include the creation of logos, artwork, and technical diagrams. Actually, the last of these applications is usually produced using a special form of graphics package: the computer-aided design, or CAD, program.

Computer-aided design CAD programs, such as AutoCad, enable users to translate very technical design specifications into computer graphics. Rather than simply drawing the image, the user enters the specific coordinates and shapes used in creating the design. In this way, the CAD program can be used to create everything from a bolt to an entire shopping mall complex. For example, figure 10.12 shows a CAD-generated wire-frame model of the space shuttle *Columbia*. There is a substantial catch to the use of such a powerful program, however. CAD programs require the user to possess a *significant* amount of knowledge about engineering, design, and drafting techniques.

In public organizations, CAD applications are being developed by engineering staffs in areas such as public works and planning. By substantially reducing the time required to produce technical specifications for a project, the CAD application facilitates planning, decision making, and resource allocation. For example, consider a project to design a bicycle path system for a local park. Use of a CAD program to create a topographical map of the park and locate the path system offers the analyst opportunities to judge project elements such as the amount of paving material needed, possible interference with existing park structures, precise path locations (which can be translated to direct markings by a survey crew), and overall path distances. Alternate path configurations can be rapidly evaluated and unexpected problems (such as substandard soil for support) figured into required changes.

As the bike path example clearly demonstrates, CAD programs can offer a wealth of information to planners and decision makers beyond the obvious graphic products. Because the CAD graphics are based on technical engineering specifications, calculations of resources needed to complete the project can be derived from the CAD product. This makes costing out the project and determining specific resource demands much easier and faster than traditional methods. Thus, the graphics application, though not a decision-enhancing application in itself, has substantial value in augmenting the development and communication of vital information that does bear directly on the decisions needed to plan and carry out the overall project. As an aside, it might be noted that the CAD product could work well in aiding the development of a project management application to plan and track the project.

The kind of application just presented illustrates how a graphics application fits into the application development framework discussed in chapter 2. In this case, the CAD application allows a complex project to be designed in phases (top-down) and quickly refined to deal with unanticipated demands or problems (stepwise refinement). Of course, the kind of problem amenable to this sort of application is likely to be quite structured because the application developer must know very precise technical specifications before CAD can be used.

Other free-form graphics applications, not using a CAD program, may be more or less complex. The key to success in free-form graphics applications is often creativity more than anything else. Perhaps this is why computer-based graphics are being adopted by many artists and designers. In a sense, the central role of creativity in free-form graphics frequently moves the applications based on these programs into the unstructured category. At the outset, the end product of the application may be fuzzy at best, slowly coming into focus as the computer images take form and are manipulated.

Enhancement of structured images A less exotic use of free-form graphics is the enhancement of structured images such as charts and graphs. Programs such as Freelance and Harvard Graphics enable the user to manipulate graphics by incorporating annotations, adding predefined images, or enhancing the basic graphic image. Many high-end graphics programs now include two features that permit sophisticated manipulation of graphic images: image libraries, and image capture utilities.

Image libraries, also known as *clip art*, consist of a series of predefined images that can be added to graphic drawings. A sample image library from Harvard Graphics is presented in figure 10.13. These images may range from simple line drawing representations of symbols to sophisticated images scanned from photographs with a resolution approaching that of a good halftone. The key to successful graphics is effective communication of the idea represented by the graphic, and inclusion of these images can serve to reinforce the basic idea. Care must be exercised, however, because inappropriate or overly complex images can detract from rather than enhance the graphic's message.

Image capture utilities make it possible to use an image from one program in another. These programs "grab" a screen image and store it in a format that can be used by the graphics program. One of the most sophisticated of these programs, Hot Shot Graphics, is frequently used to create the screen-shot illustrations that appear in many computer books (including this one). For example, a graph created in Lotus can be captured and then edited in the graphics program to add clip art, emphasize some aspect of the graph, or refine the image, as illustrated in figure 10.14. The flexibility offered by screen capture utilities means that a user is not limited to producing only those images possible within a single program.

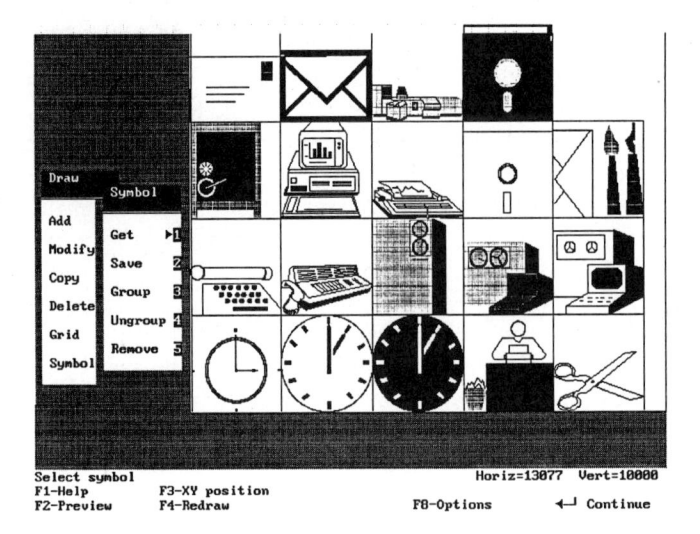

FIGURE 10.13 Image library (Harvard Graphics)

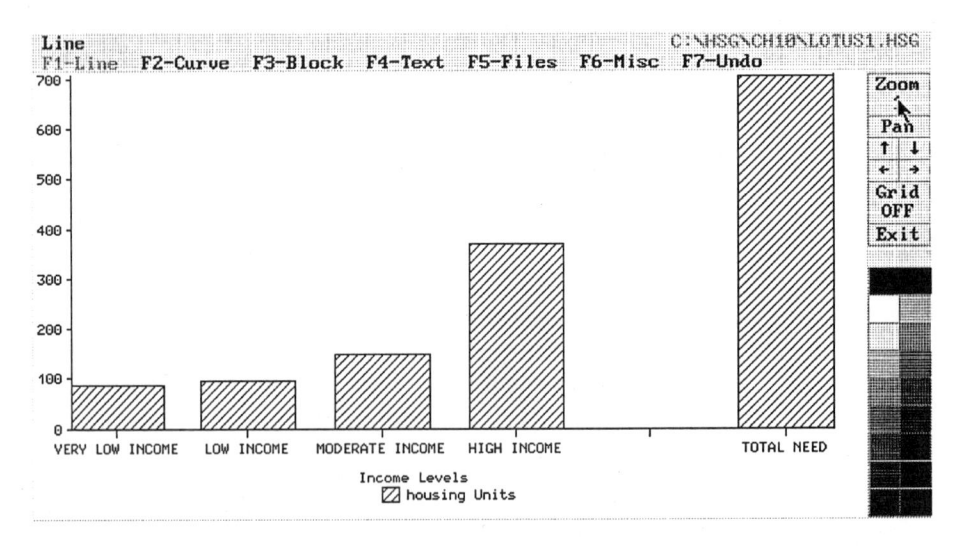

FIGURE 10.14 Graph refinement editing screen (Hot Shot Graphics)

An interesting and useful development of these capture programs is the scanner. *Scanners* are devices that capture hard copy and translate it into an image that can be manipulated on the computer screen. Sophisticated, high-end scanners offer resolution and gray-scale or color rendition comparable to that of a high-resolution television image. The combination of scanned images with a graphics program allows all manner of sophisticated manipulations. For example, the traditional police artist's sketch pad used in identifying suspects can be supplanted by a computer graphics program capable of blending scanned feature images to produce a composite picture of photographic quality.

Another outgrowth of this technology is the photobase, in which scanned photographs are combined with a database program to produce a visual and data record that offers the user vastly more information than could be produced in a traditional database format. Photobases are used in areas from missing child identification to real estate to employee personnel files. Whatever the formal application, the inclusion of the scanned image dramatically improves communication of the information.

Cautions Free-form graphics applications are not without potential liabilities, however. A common problem with graphic design is the time required to produce the desired output. There is an all-too-common tendency to continually refine or "tweak" the graphic in an attempt to improve its attractiveness or sophistication. The time spent in this activity may be substantial, and the consequent payoff relatively small. Care must be exercised in developing graphics-based applications that form does not exceed substance. Image design is an activity that requires both technological expertise and an artist's eye. Poorly designed graphics can reduce the communication of information rather than enhance it.

Structured Graphics

Structured presentation graphics differ from the free-form variety in their use of predefined structures for data display. The structured programs are used to produce charts and graphs based on standard formats, such as bar or pie charts, organizational charts, or flow diagrams. Packages such as ChartMaster, Harvard Graphics, Freelance, Energraphics, and even spreadsheets such as Lotus, Excel, and Quattro offer the user a number of standard graph types for data display. Data may be either entered directly into the program or imported from another file, such as a spreadsheet or database. Use of predefined graphic forms frees the user from the need to draw the graph and allows the user to concentrate instead on selecting the appropriate data for use.

In fact, selecting the data and choosing the form of presentation constitute the key elements of application construction in structured presentation graphics. These key elements can be expressed as three phases of graphic application development: data selection, graph type selection, and graph construction.

Data selection Data selection for graphic application development involves choosing both the type of data to be used and the format. As with any data-based analytical procedure, the analyst must identify the appropriate *level of measurement* for data inclusion. Use of *nominal* data (simple disjunctiveness) in a graph requires that the nominal categories (e.g., sex or race) be represented in a way that makes counting category members possible. For example, a graph representing the ethnicity of a community's population must include both the ethnic categories and some measure, either raw numbers or percentages, of the number of individuals in each category (see figure 10.15). Purely nominal data are not usually sufficient to construct a graph. Use of *ordinal* (capable of being ordered or ranked) or *interval/ratio* (precise and consistent measurements between data points) data enhances the communicative power of the graph as well as opening up greater options for graph presentation.

Once the appropriate type of data has been selected, consideration must be given to the format of the information. Although quantitative data can be represented in a wide

PART III   Use of the Framework in Developing Applications

```
                    Pie Chart 1 Data   Page 1 of 2                    ▼
─────────────────────────────────────────────────────────────────────────
Title:     Ethnic Characteristics
Subtitle:  of Fountain Valley Population
Footnote:  Numbers expressed are percentages

Slice          Label           Value          Cut Slice    Color   Pattern
               Name            Series 1       Yes   No

  1         Caucasian           83                  No       2        1
  2         Black                1                  No       3        2
  3         Hispanic             7                  No       4        3
  4         Asian                8                  No       5        4
  5         Am. Indian           1                  No       6        5
  6                                                 No       7        6
  7                                                 No       8        7
  8                                                 No       9        8
  9                                                 No      10        9
 10                                                 No      11       10
 11                                                 No      12       11
 12                                                 No      13       12


F1-Help                                                         F9-More series
F2-Draw chart              F6-Colors        F8-Options          F10-Continue
```

FIGURE 10.15 Percentage data for graph construction

variety of formats, the two most commonly used in graphs are raw number values and percentages. Raw numbers are used to communicate *absolute* differences among the data. For example, a graph representing the population of cities within a state would use raw population numbers to illustrate absolute size differences. A secondary consideration when using raw numbers is how the magnitude of the numbers should be expressed. Is it more effective to use a large numeral such as 3,500,000 or 3.5 labeled as millions? Large numbers are more difficult to read and may detract from the clarity of the overall representation. Use of representational or abstract numbers presents a cleaner graph but may diminish the impact of the actual number. With some graphic packages, this consideration is moot because the package automatically chooses both the scale of the graph and the format of the numbers.

Percentages are more appropriate when the *proportional* relationships among the data are to be represented. In a graph on ethnicity, use of percentages would be appropriate because one is usually seeking to communicate the proportion of each ethnic group relative to the total population. Because percentages represent a portion of the whole, however, they suppress the magnitude of the numbers they represent. This means that percentages are not appropriate in instances where it important to convey the absolute size of the data being reported. For example, using a graph showing that 33 percent of an organization's employees tested positive for drugs to call for an extensive antidrug campaign is inappropriate if the total number of employees in the organization is three!

Graph type selection   Once the suitable data and format have been selected, the second phase of graphic application development is selection of the graph type. A sample of graph types available in Harvard Graphics is presented in figure 10.16.

The key to this phase is recognizing that not all graph types are appropriate for all types of data. Essentially, there are two types of data that can be represented in a graph:

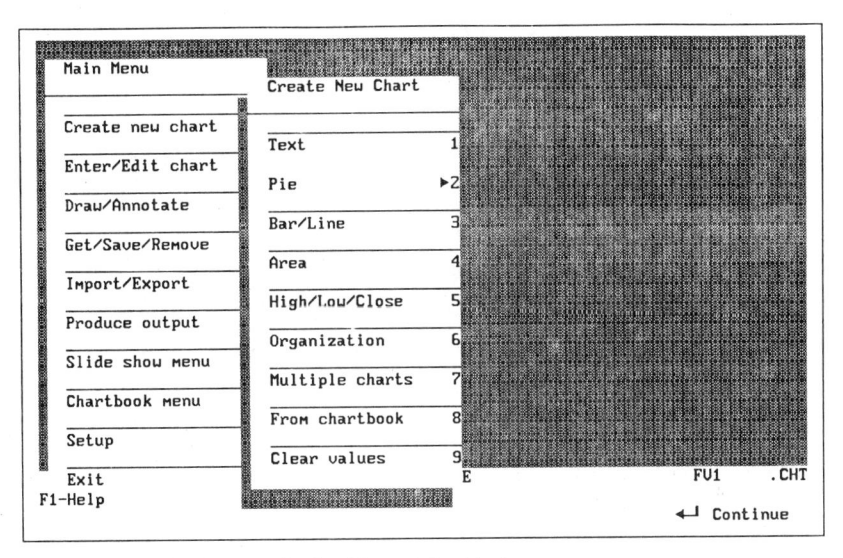

FIGURE 10.16 Graph type selection (Harvard Graphics)

cross-sectional and longitudinal. Cross-sectional data represent two or more categories of information taken at a single point in time. For example, a graph showing average expenditures for road maintenance in each city of a county is cross-sectional. Longitudinal graphs present data over time. Thus, a longitudinal graph might portray average city expenditures for road maintenance over the past ten years.

Common graphs appropriate for use with cross-sectional data are pie charts and bar graphs. Line graphs are generally more appropriate for longitudinal data. It is important to note, however, that any graph capable of illustrating trends (bar and line graphs) can be used for both cross-sectional and longitudinal data.

In a case where either a bar or line graph may technically be used, consideration should be given to the information to be communicated. Bar charts suggest static or disjunctive elements. If the principal intention is to communicate a comparison, then this type of graph serves best. Line graphs imply flow or motion; they better represent information that occurs over time or has a relational pattern.

Graph construction Identification of the graph type to be used brings the user to the third phase of successful graph development: graph construction. A finished graph—in this case, a pie chart—is shown in figure 10.17.

The key concern in this phase is selecting the appropriate data for display. A common fault in graph construction is attempting to include too much data. Excessive data representation in a graph only serves to confuse the information being communicated. It is important to note that certain types of graphs are more amenable to extensive data representation. For example, a line graph can effectively support far more data points than a bar chart can bars. Points on a line are communicated far more easily than are individual bar options.

Although there are no hard-and-fast rules for determining how much information is

Ethnic Characteristics
of Fountain Valley Population

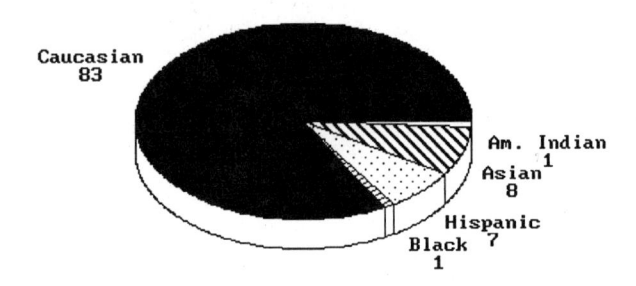

```
Caucasian
    83
            Am. Indian
              1
            Asian
              8
            Hispanic
    Black     7
      1
```

Numbers expressed are percentages

FIGURE 10.17 Finished graph: pie chart

too much, a good approach is to be parsimonious. Remember that one graph should express one concept. Although the graph may be designed to compare data, it should not incorporate so many comparisons as to be rendered unintelligible.

A secondary consideration in graph construction results from the increasing sophistication of graphics packages. With programs such as Freelance or Harvard Graphics, it is now easy to modify the standard graph representations with annotations, overlaid images, or other enhancements. Once again, the user must be careful not to clutter the graph with these add-ons to such an extent that the original information is lost in the confusion. Simple and direct is almost always better when presenting information graphically.

As the foregoing discussion implies, successful development of graphics applications is more complex than it appears at first. Although the ease of current graphics programs makes development of the graphs a relatively easy proposition, the programs are not capable of imbuing the user with any artistic or design sense. As with the other specialized applications discussed in this chapter, construction of presentation graphics requires both a knowledge of process (the mechanics of graph selection and construction) and skill in design to produce effective graphs.

■ DESKTOP PUBLISHING

Desktop Publishing (DTP) is a fairly new field that seeks to bring page layout, design, and publication quality output to the microcomputer user. DTP can be thought of as a combination of word processing, graphic design, and page composition that enables the user to produce output that gives the appearance of professional creation and almost typeset quality. Though not a problem-solving tool in the classic sense, DTP is seen by users as a way of reducing the production cycle for sophisticated publications and enhancing the professional appearance of their end product. (Further information on the subject of desktop publishing can be found in Barry, Davis, & Robinson, 1988.)

Essentially, DTP applications involve three elements:

1. A base document, usually created in a word-processing program, that contains the text to be incorporated into the final product.
2. Graphic images created by scanning or through the use of a presentation graphics program.
3. Page design and layout carried out in the DTP program, combining the first two elements. Text is formatted, graphics are placed and scaled, and additional formatting features such as text sizes and styles, lines and boxes, or columns are specified.

At the present time, the DTP market is dominated by two software packages: Aldus PageMaker, available for both IBM PC/AT–class machines and the Apple Macintosh, and Xerox Ventura Publisher which is for IBM-type micros. In addition to these two packages, there are a wide range of DTP programs, from PFS's First Publisher at the low end to Interleaf's InterPress for Sun and Apollo workstations. For all but the most basic programs, the hardware required to make effective use of the DTP program includes the following components (for IBM-type micros):

1. A fast 80286 or 80386 microcomputer with a large hard disk system. The complexity of the DTP programs requires a fast computer to handle the sophisticated text manipulations within a reasonable time, and the large size of DTP files requires substantial disk storage capacity.

2. A high-resolution graphics card and monitor. Although it is possible to make use of a standard EGA or VGA monitor system, to see an entire DTP page at a resolution that allows fully formed characters (characters too small to be seen at screen resolution are called *greeked*) requires a special DTP full-page monitor and specialized graphics adapter.

3. A mouse or other pointing device. Given the intensely graphic nature of the DTP process, the user must be able to move quickly around the screen, select icons, specify blocks of text, and scale graphics. All of these actions require a greater degree of flexibility than is available using just the keyboard.

4. A high-resolution laser printer. Printers such as the HP LaserJet can be augmented with additional fonts and RAM to support high-resolution graphics and produce very effective output. However, to gain the maximum impact from the DTP package, a laser printer equipped with the PostScript page description language is required. PostScript allows fonts to be scaled in an almost unlimited fashion; text can also be rotated and other special effects added. Built-in graphics "primitives" significantly enhance graphic images and reduce the jagged edges often found in circles and other curves.

As this list suggests, the technical requirements for DTP are substantial. In addition, DTP demands specialized knowledge about page layout, design, and typesetting in order to produce quality products. Terms such as *picas, kerning, ems*, and *greeking* are common in the vocabulary of DTP. Lack of knowledge about effective page layout often results in cluttered documents that use too many fonts on a page, integrate graphics poorly, and generally detract from rather than enhance effective communication. It is for these reasons that DTP falls into the classification of specialized applications. It should also be pointed out that most DTP programs are extremely complex and require both a steep and lengthy learning curve before even a modicum of mastery is possible.

One way of dealing with the inherent complexity and sophistication of the DTP application is to use group processing to produce the final document. This approach relies on several individuals to produce the various components (e.g., text, graphics, page layout) of the product. Each individual specializes in only one aspect of the process, so that only the individual responsible for assembling the components into the final document need be knowledgeable in the details of page composition and construction.

This group processing approach illustrates the value of our analytical framework in relation to DTP applications. Each of the elements of top-down development—divide and conquer, modularity, and stepwise refinement—is present in the process of DTP. Consider a typical example of how the group processing approach might be used to produce a DTP report application.

The first step in the report's production involves all group members in planning the report. In this planning session, group members define the contents of the report and determine individual responsibilities. Using this top-down approach is important in a group-based activity because the various components of the report must fit together appropriately. In this example, the group must clearly define three initial tasks:

1. Data production and analysis. This task might involve the extraction of data from an organization database, transfer to a spreadsheet, and development of specific projections.

2. Text creation. The heart of the report, the narrative text expands on the findings of the data analysis. Note that most of the text development must follow the analysis, although some background and "boilerplate" could be created concurrently with the data analysis.

3. Graphic design. Because it is usually more effective to present data in a graphic manner whenever possible, the data from the initial analysis are examined to determine what graphs would be appropriate for the report. This information, as well as a first cut of the graphs, must be made available to the group member(s) responsible for text creation.

Although these three tasks are relatively straightforward, there are a number of technical points that must also be addressed in order to facilitate assembly of a DTP document. The effective use of computer support in text creation requires that the analytical output from the spreadsheet analysis be made available to the group member(s) involved in text composition. To avoid retyping, the spreadsheet output should be produced in a format (such as ASCII) that can be read by the DTP program in use. Consideration should also be given to the importation of spreadsheet data into the graphics program being used to produce the report graphs. Even though the initial tasks seem to be mostly self-contained, the imprint of a divide-and-conquer modular strategy is clear.

Another advantage of the group approach is apparent in the previous listing of the tasks. With several people participating in application development, tasks that are not serially dependent can be carried out concurrently. Thus, the overall time required to complete the project can be reduced over what is possible with one individual working in a linear fashion. Of course, the group approach also requires considerable cooperation

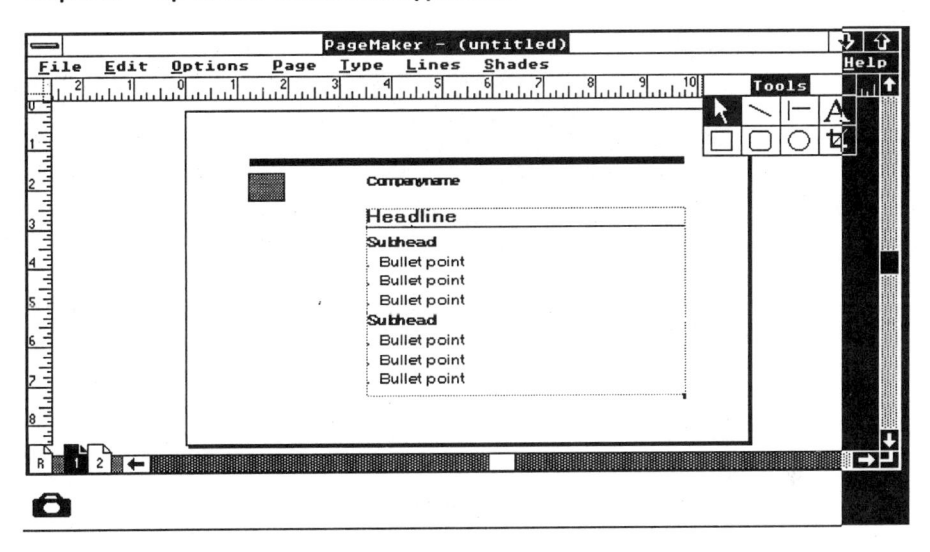

Chapter 10 Specialized Software and Applications

FIGURE 10.18 Style sheet (PageMaker)

among group members to ensure that the sequential tasks are accomplished in a timely fashion.

Assuming that the initial tasks outlined earlier have been completed, the next step is to integrate the component parts. This is the first step in which DTP software comes into direct play, which suggests the overall complexity of the DTP process. Component integration is a multistep procedure that begins with the group's deciding on an overall report format.

Most high-end DTP programs offer the user a series of predefined page and document formats called *style sheets*. An example is shown in figure 10.18. Style sheets define format aspects such as text width or columns, fonts used for headings and text body, pagination, margins, and any continuing features such as highlighted or boxed areas. If the group chooses to make use of one of the predefined style sheets, the task of formatting is reduced to deciding the location and size of graphs and charts that will be incorporated into the document. If the choice is made to develop a customized format, the group must generate a set of clear and consistent instructions on page style, fonts, and element placement for the group member(s) who will actually do the electronic paste-up of the report components.

Paste-up, or the actual creation of the DTP publication, is technically the most complex aspect of the entire DTP process. It is in this step that the format decided upon is implemented in the text. Initially, a *base page* (or pages, for documents with facing pages) is created (figure 10.19). The base page contains instructions for placement of any running headers or footers, page number style and location, and any consistent formatting choices such as base text font, margins, columns, and line spacing. The format established for the base page becomes the default format for the entire document.

With a completed format and base page, the next step is to place the desired text into the document. Most DTP packages support direct importation of text from most word-processing packages, such as WordPerfect, Microsoft Word, WordStar, and Display-

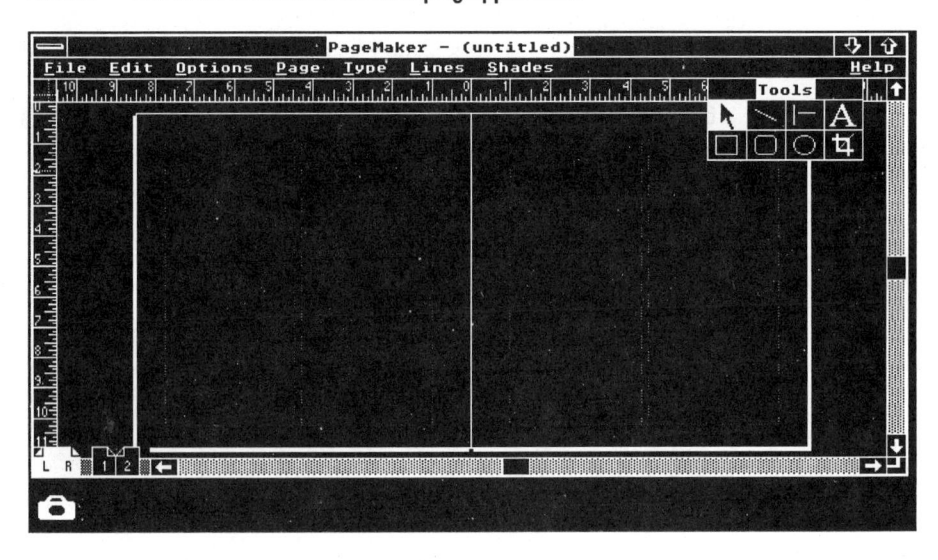

FIGURE 10.19 Sample base pages (PageMaker)

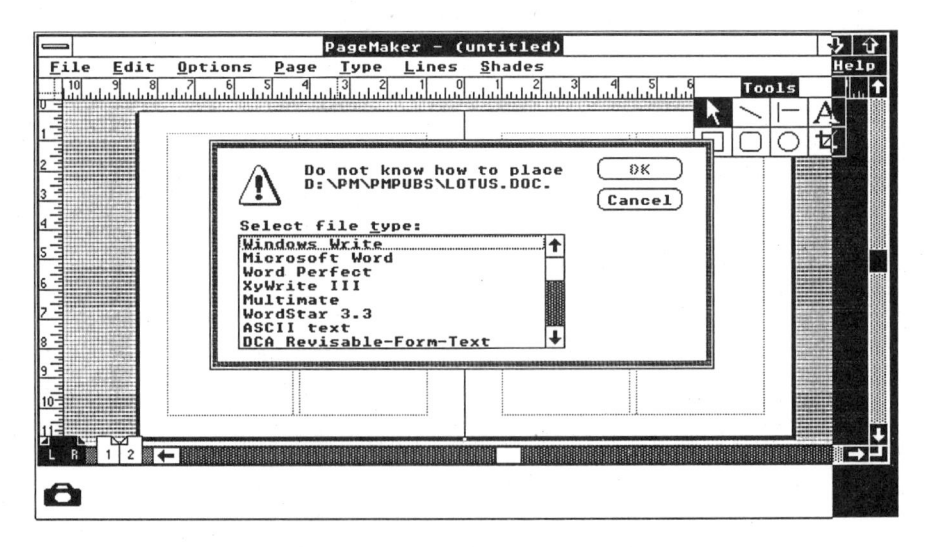

FIGURE 10.20 Importing text from word-processing programs (PageMaker)

Write. An illustration of how PageMaker handles text importation is depicted in figure 10.20. Imported text *usually* retains commands for boldfacing, italics, and underlining. The most common problem areas are columns and indentations, particularly if a proportional font is chosen. This is another case in which it is important for the originator of the text to be aware of the limits and requirements of the DTP package that will be used, because foreknowledge of the text placement approach used by the DTP package can prevent many indentation and columnar problems.

The third phase of DTP document creation is the placement of any supplemental material in the text. In our example, this would include both spreadsheet excerpts and graphs. Placement of material in a document requires selection of the location in the document, preferably as close as possible to the referencing text, and scaling of the imported material to fit the defined margins. Care must be taken not to split a graph or table over two pages, and graphic images must not be scaled so small that they become illegible. This approach, by the way, is a clear illustration of stepwise refinement, because each item must be appropriately located and scaled before progressing to the next. Fortunately, most DTP programs have a feature that "flows" text around inserted material without the need to reformat each page location.

The final step in the preparation of the document is to add any special modifications to text fonts or formats, line drawings, boxes, or higlighted areas of text. Care must be exercised not to clutter the document with unnecessary highlighting or multiple fonts. Overuse of the style tricks available in DTP makes for a confusing document that obscures more than explains.

The process of creating a report detailed (and greatly oversimplified) in this example is the common approach required by most DTP applications. Although not all DTP projects are undertaken through group processing, the functional production steps remain the same.

Many organizations initially find DTP an attractive option to professional design and printing of reports and newsletters. Few, however, give serious consideration to the substantial investment in resources, especially time, required to produce professional-looking results. Both presentation graphics and DTP are phenomenally seductive techniques. It is very easy to get so caught up in the "prettification" of graphs or documents that the balance between time and product is thrown far out of whack. Care must always be exercised that the effort being expended in the production of a graph or document is justified by its utility. All too frequently, this is not the case. Following the application development framework presented in chapter 2 is no guarantee that excessive time will not be devoted to the application. It does, however, offer the user a viable guide that may reduce wasted time.

■ CONCLUSION

In addition to the four techniques discussed in this chapter, there are an increasing number of specialized software programs for technical applications. Programs termed personal productivity managers offer the user a way to schedule activity, record random bits of information and later organize and reference them. Applications based on "hyper-text" free-format database programs facilitate development of complex ideas or organization of complex issues. Decision-aid programs provide a logical format for considering the dimensions of difficult decisions and help the user "think through" an effective decision. Undoubtedly, other specialized programs and applications are on the horizon.

As suggested throughout this chapter, however, each of these specialized programs brings with it a requirement of a certain degree of technical knowledge and sophistication. There is little doubt that, used properly and with sufficient expertise, applications based on project management, expert systems, presentation graphics, and desktop publishing have a proper and valuable place in many organizations. The key to their use is in the proper understanding of their value, planning for the application and use of the applications development framework presented early in this book.

The microcomputer has a tremendous capacity for producing "geewiz" reactions to its possible uses. In the final analysis though, the goal for any user is not to be entranced by technology but to make use of it as a new *tool*. That is what this book has been all about.

REFERENCES AND ADDITIONAL READING

Desktop Publishing

Books:

Barry, John A., Davis, Fredrick E., and Robinson, Phillip. *Desktop Publishing: IBM Edition.* Homewood, IL: Dow Jones–Irwin, 1988.

Felici, James, and Nace, Ted. *Desktop Publishing Skills: A Primer for Typesetting with Computers and Laser Printers.* Reading, MA: Addison-Wesley, 1987.

Grout, William, Athanasopoulos, Irene, and Kutlin, Rebecca. *Desktop Publishing from A to Z.* Berkeley, CA: Osborne McGraw-Hill, 1986.

Parker, Roger C. *Looking Good in Print: A Guide to Basic Design for Desktop Publishing.* Chapel Hill, NC: Ventana Press, 1988.

Waite Group, Inc. (James Stockford, ed.) *Desktop Publishing Bible.* Indianapolis: Howard W. Sams, 1987.

Articles:

Brown, Alex. "Desktop Publishing: A Guide for Skeptics," *Folio: The Magazine for Magazine Management* 17 (January 1988): 121.

Christopher, Abigail. "Desktop Publishing Comes of Age," *High Technology* 7 (July 1987): 51.

Friedman, Rick. "Desktop Publishing: What It Is and What It Is Not," *The Office* 10 (February 1987): 68.

Kelley, Joseph T. "Desktop Publishing in the Finance Office," *Government Finance Review* 3 (August 1987): 39.

Expert Systems

Books:

Harmon, Paul, Maus, Rex, and Morrissey, William. *Expert Systems: Tools and Applications.* New York: Wiley, 1988.

Levine, Robert I., Drang, Diane E., and Eddleson, Barry. *A Comprehensive Guide to AI and Expert Systems.* New York: McGraw-Hill, 1986.

Naylor, Chris. *Build Your Own Expert System: For the IBM PC and Compatibles.* 2nd ed. New York: Halstead Press, 1987.

Siegel, Paul. *Expert Systems: A Non-Programmer's Guide to Development and Applications.* Blue Ridge Summit, PA: TAB Books, 1986.

Silverman, Barry (Ed.). *Expert Systems for Business.* Reading, MA: Addison-Wesley, 1987.

Articles:

Bauer, Richard J., Jr., and Griffiths, Mark D. "The 'Why' of Expert Systems," *Business Quarterly* 52 (Winter 1987): 86.

Corbett, Christopher. "Expert Systems: The Pros and Cons," *Canadian Public Administration* 29 (Winter 1986): 588.

Fordyce, Kenneth, Norden, Peter, and Sullivan, Gerald. "Review of Expert Systems for the Management Practitioner," *Interfaces* 17 (March/April 1987): 64.

Martorelli, William P. "PC-Based Expert Systems Arrive," *Datamation* 34 (April 1, 1988): 56.

Nadkarni, Ashok, and Kenny, Graham K. "Expert Systems and Organizational Decision Making," *Journal of General Management* 13 (Autumn 1987): 60.

Spain, Tom. "Using Expert Systems," *D & B Reports* 35 (November/December 1987): 52.

Tamer, Faud G., and Slocum, Alexander H., "Issues in Development and Application of Conventional and Knowledge-Based Software Systems," *Idea* 29 (Summer 1988): 19.

Presentation Graphics

Books:

Lambert, Steve. *Presentation Graphics on the IBM PC and Compatibles.* Bellevue, WA: Microsoft Press, 1986.

White, Jan V., *Graphic Design for the Electronic Age.* New York: Watson-Guptill, 1988.

Articles:

Brown, Lauren. "Managing Corporate Graphics: In Search of a Strategy," *PC Week* 5 (June 21, 1988): 61.

Dickson, Gary, and Lehman, John A. "Quality Graphics Design Supports Quality Decisions," *Computerworld* 21 (March 16, 1987) 57.

Makley, William. "What's New in Business Graphics? Microcomputers," *The Office* 11 (June 1988): 90.

Rosenthal, Steve. "Choosing Analytical vs. Presentation Graphics," *PC Week* 5 (March 15, 1988): 104.

Shultz, Brad. "Workstation Graphics: Blossoming for Business," *Datamation* 34 (March 1, 1988): 81.

Project Management

Books:

Awani, Alfred O. *Project Management Techniques.* Princeton, NJ: Petrocelli Books, 1983.

Kerzner, Harold. *Project Management: A Systems Approach to Planning, Scheduling, and Controlling.* New York: Van Nostrand Reinhold, 1984.

Krakow, Ira H. *Project Management with the IBM PC.* Bowie, MD: Brady Communications, 1985.

Levine, Harvey A. *Project Manaement Using Microcomputers.* Berkeley, CA: Osborne/McGraw-Hill, 1986.

Articles:

Assad, Arjang A., and Wasil, Edward A. "Project Management Using a Microcomputer," *Computers and Operations Research* 13 (April 1986): 231.

Bermant, Charles. "Project Management Under $200," *PC Magazine* 5 (June 10, 1986): 191.

Leibson, Steven H. "Project Management Software for PCs Helps You Map Out a Plan for Your Project," *Education* 32 (February 5, 1987): 57.

Poor, Alfred, and Brown, Bruce. "Project Management Software: The Top Sellers," *PC Magazine* 5 (February 11, 1986): 155.

Sullivan, Kristina B. "City Planners Meet Budget with Project Software," *PC Week* 5 (May 31, 1988): 84.

Williamson, Mickey, "Project Management Software: PCs Taking Over from Mainframes," *Computerworld* 20 (December 8, 1986): 57.

Glossary

Absolute (Address) Copy Indicated by a dollar sign ($) in Lotus, it ensures that the cell location and content of that cell do not change when a formula is copied. For example, if the formula +$F$2*C14 is copied to the D column, F2 remains F2, while C14 changes to D14. *See also* relative (address) copy.

Access System An application designed to provide the user with access to data and the means to manipulate it.

Algorithm The actual crafting and specification of the solution to a problem. The algorithm comprises the steps one follows to produce a workable answer. In the computer world, it is a set of instructions for carrying out information-processing or analysis tasks.

Application The development of commands and strategies in one or more computer programs to solve a problem or carry out a specific series of tasks. An application is tailored to solve one or a set of problems. It is molded or crafted from software, such as spreadsheets, database management systems, and statistical packages, and can take on a character that does not resemble the underlying software. The microcomputer software is integrated into the application through its capacity to manipulate data, provide specific analytical methods, or facilitate access to both information and analytical procedures.

Archive or Archival Backup Copy of data created for storage in a safe location. Important data files should be archived routinely to guard against possible data loss.

Artificial Intelligence Computer programming that enables the computer to "learn" from its past actions and make choices based on incomplete information.

ASCII (American Standard Code for Information Interchange) The coding used to represent characters and numbers in a microcomputer system. Each letter and number is assigned a unique ASCII code number.

Aspect Ratio Height-to-width ratio of a computer screen. Determines whether circles appear round and squares square.

Auditor A person or program that examines an application to ensure data integrity and command correctness.

Autoexecute A program or macro that runs automatically whenever a program is accessed.

Back Up To make a duplicate copy of information. Backing up should be a routine process for all important data. Also called archiving.

Backslash (\)   Serves different purposes in different software. In DOS, it refers to the change of directories and subdirectories, starting with the root directory. In Lotus, it can be the repeat key or part of the name of a macro (e.g., '\k) if preceded by a single quote.

Bat or Batch   A way of designating a DOS file as a program that can be executed. Inside the batch file, or program, is a set of commands, or instructions to the computer. Running the batch program automatically executes the sequence of commands instead of requiring each command to be typed individually.

BAUD Rate   Unit of measurement of electronic data communication, similar to (but not always exactly like) the number of bits per second transmitted. Useful as a measure of speed of communication.

BCD (Binary-Coded Decimal)   A data structure format used on mainframe computers.

Binary Data Transmission   Electronic transmission of computer data between computing systems in its native machine-code format.

Bit   Shorthand for binary digit. Basic operational unit of a microcomputer. Corresponds to the two possible electronic states: on and off (represented as 1 and 0). How a microprocessor manipulates information.

Boolean   A logical combinatorial system that represents symbolically relationships as those implied by AND, OR, and NOT. For example, if two entities are connected by AND, then both need to have true values to proceed.

Boot   To start or get all the parts of a microcomputer ready for use. Booting occurs when the disk operating system is loaded into the memory of the computer. The term comes from the phrase "pulling yourself up by your own bootstraps," because the disk operating system loads itself into memory where it waits for your commands.

Bottom-Up Approach   Method of application development in which designers and users launch an application as quickly as possible. Some attention is given to goals and objectives and the data needed to assess progress, but scant attention is paid to optimal organization of data files or to form and operation of the application. Only after the limitations of this approach appear does one move on to build a more fully developed application.

Bulletin Board   A computer system application enabling telephone contact with another computer for the purpose of exchanging information, reviewing news, or acquiring software. Frequently operated by individual computer enthusiasts and increasingly by organizations as a method of enhancing access to important organizational information.

Bus   A method of connecting electronic devices to a computer. The term refers to the way in which the electronic signals are carried from one device to another, like passengers on a bus.

Byte   Combination of bits (usually eight for a microcomputer) that forms one character. Thus, 8 bits = 1 byte = 1 character.

CAD (Computer-Aided Design)   Process of using sophisticated computer hardware and software to enhance engineering design.

Catalog   A listing of related files and/or programs.

Cell Protection   Function of Lotus that allows the user to define a cell or range of cells as protected and, therefore, essentially unchangeable.

Character (Alphanumeric, String) Data Type   Character data, such as the name of a department, can be categorized, segmented into parts or ranked in ascending or descending order. *See also* date data type, logical data type, numeric data type.

Command Program A program designed to carry out commands, similar to a batch program. Used to automate a sequence of command instructions.

Conditional Control Structure If a condition is met, do one alternative; if not, do another alternative.

Control Center Interface for dBASE IV that provides greatly expanded access to dBASE functions through a menu system. Replacing and enhancing the dBASE III Plus Assistant, it facilitates basic database commands and allows easy manipulation of more sophisticated programming and report generation capabilities.

CPU (Central Processor Unit) The basic component of a microcomputer containing the microprocessor, RAM, and ROM.

Criterion Area Place where the record(s) to be located are identified when using Lotus database and statistical function.

Critical Path Method (CPM) A set of mathematical formulas used to indicate expected completion dates, likely completion dates, and actual completion dates for project tasks and how those times affect the overall completion date for the project. CPM gets it name from the fact that one chain of dependencies throughout the project will always consume the greatest amount of time.

Critical Success Factors (CSF) A type of analysis that concentrates almost exclusively on what is most essential in solving a problem or taking advantage of an opportunity. Secondary factors excluded.

CRT (Cathode Ray Tube) Technical description of a television picture tube, frequently misapplied to a computer video monitor. *See* VDT (video display terminal).

Cursor or Cursor Control A visual reference point on a computer screen that indicates where activity will take place when the keyboard or other entry device is used. Ordinarily it is represented by an easily seen blinking light, which the user can move to any part of the screen by means of commands or the arrow keys on the keyboard.

Customized Screen A screen that goes beyond the default screen that comes with software, usually requiring some programming to develop. Customized data-entry screens (a) offer a more attractive appearance, (b) assist the data-entry person with hard-to-remember details, (c) use more descriptive phrases for the fields, and (d) provide instructions on what to enter for several of the fields.

Data Dictionary/Data Directory (DD) The tool traditionally used to describe the contents of a database; a listing of relevant data files, their location, structure, and associated programs; similar to a catalog. The data dictionary/data directory does not incorporate the actual data or any of the ancillary material (such as an index or report); rather, it itemizes the names of what is contained in the database and information about or descriptions of the data. Sometimes referred to as metadata—that is, data about data.

Data Flow Diagram (DFD) The result of an elaborate process designed to capture both general and detailed facets of the origin, flow, storage, and processing of information in an organization or for a particular task. Used in information requirements analysis, a full set of data flow diagrams for even a small project may require as much as twenty to fifty pages to cover all the details of the process.

Data Type Establishes what the user can and cannot do with the data—that is, what operations can be carried out with the data. *See* character data type, date data type, logical data type, numeric data type.

Database Large system of files that can operate as an integrated whole. Databases enable one to take a "data picture" of the important aspects of an agency and its environment.

Database Design The process whereby the individual data fields identified in the information requirements analysis are grouped or organized into separate data files that will eventually make up the database. The goal of grouping fields into files is to ensure flexibility and efficiency in the way the data are organized and accessed. Flexibility refers to the ability to rearrange and access the data and data files according to the needs of the user. Efficiency represents a guard against waste and unintended data loss.

Database Management System (DBMS) The DBMS is the software used to create, store, and manipulate the database. Modern DBMS are powerful tools that can distinguish among types of data (character, numeric, logical, and date), keep track of where the data are stored in the computer, add data to the database, alter or summarize it, and produce complex queries, reports, and applications.

Date Data Type Represents day, month, year, or some combination; enables calendar-related calculations. The first of December in the year 1990 can be stored as 12/01/90 in date type data.

DBMS *See* database management system.

Decision Support Application (DSA) A type of application consisting of carefully crafted or selected analytical tools that fit the novel dimensions of less structured managerial tasks, including access to databases with information from both inside and outside the organization.

Default Data-Entry Screen The data-entry screen that comes with the software, requiring no programming or customizing for use. Ordinarily, the screen is basic but adequate to the job. For example, the name of each field may be listed with a highlighted space directly after it to guide entry of the data.

Deletion Anomaly One of the traps to be avoided in database design. It occurs when the sole instance of a data value is unintentionally lost. For example, deleting the record of a resident who moves is acceptable, but if the parcel number or address is stored only in that record, then there is no longer any record that the land parcel exists.

Delimited Format A data file structure in which each data element is separated from other data elements by a particular character, such as a comma or slash.

Desktop Publishing (DTP) Use of sophisticated editing, page layout, and graphic design software, plus a high-quality laser printer, to produce formal documents that would normally be typeset professionally.

DIF (Data Interchange Format) A data file format based on a row and column structure. Used for transferring data between programs that use different data structure formats.

Directories and subdirectories A system commonly used to organize files on a hard disk, consisting of a top, main, or root directory with subdirectories below and tied to the root directory. Similar in concept to a file cabinet, with each file drawer corresponding to a directory and file folders in a drawer corresponding to subdirectories.

Disk Formatting (or Initializing) Process that enables a disk to be used by blocking off any unusable parts of the disk and preparing the remaining good areas (sectors) to receive files.

Divide and Conquer A strategy that encourages or enables the application developer to break down the intricacies inherent in managerial problems into separate modules. Reducing the complexity of problems also reduces the complexity of and resources

Glossary

needed for solutions. A hierarchy chart, with the main tasks listed at the top and individual tasks portrayed at lower levels of the hierarchy, is a physical implementation of divide and conquer.

DOS (Disk Operating System) A collection of commands and programs that provide basic instructions to the computer. Usually used in reference to IBM-compatible computers.

Download To transfer information electronically from another computer to your computer.

EBCDIC (Extended Binary-Coded Decimal Interchange Code) A data structure used on mainframe systems.

Edit Check A means of catching inadvertent errors when data are being entered. Several types of acceptability criteria, or edit checks, can be built into the screen as a way of alerting the data-entry person that an entry error has occurred. Edit checks include proper designation and spelling, proper range, forced input (an entry must be made for a given data input), and uniqueness (each entry for a data field must be different from any other).

Electronic Communications Communication between two computers, whether side by side or over long distances, micro to micro or micro to mainframe.

Electronic Mail Transmission of information such as memos, letters, or reports via electronic connections between computer systems. Involves use of communication software and a number of electronically linked computers to exchange information without production of actual printed material.

End User The primary user of a microcomputer system; the person responsible for making productive use of the microcomputer system.

Ergonomics Scientific study of the relationship of the human body to its surroundings. Used in designing appropriate workspaces.

Error Trapping In interactive programs or applications, a technique for catching any errors in data entry whereby the person inputting the data is alerted to the error and given a suggested list of correct entries. Generally must be programmed in, but more software is offering easy-to-incorporate error-trapping programs.

Expansion Device Piece of equipment connected to a computer that enhances its capability—for example, providing additional RAM.

F2 Function Key In Lotus, key used to edit or change the contents of a cell, whether a label (such as the name of a month) or a value (such as someone's salary).

F5 Function or GOTO Key In Lotus, key used to move the cursor to a particular part of the worksheet.

Field An individual variable or item, such as date of birth or number of employees. The field is the data name and description, not the data themselves. Several fields taken together make up a record.

File A named repository of data or information, generally saved or stored for later use. A file can be a large, complicated spreadsheet or a simple memo.

File Locking Technique that prevents more than one person at a time from accessing a file on a network.

File Management Software used to organize, search, and retrieve information in a database. Also refers to the need to organize data on a hard disk for optimum access.

Find-and-Replace Command Command, available in many word-processing and database management packages, that automates the process of locating a particular item and changing or altering it.

Format In Lotus, the form in which the content of a cell is displayed, such as currency (e.g., $X,XXX,XXX.00) or percent (e.g., XX.X%).

Forms Software Software packages used to design attractive menus. Often driven by a hand-held mouse, these products allow one to easily draw boxes, triangles, or other shapes. Forms software can also be used to design the paper forms used to collect the data to be entered into the computer.

Fourth Generation Language (4GL) As computer languages become more like human communication, they are given a higher generation number. With 4GLs, the user can tell the computer what to do rather than having to spell out in detail each step. Most of the languages software in this book approach the 4GL character.

Framework Commonly used in the information sciences, frameworks are less rigorous and less well tested than theories in the better-developed disciplines. Ordinarily they are derived from related disciplines. The framework presented in this book encompasses the general guidelines and tools for moving from the rough-edged, poorly defined managerial problem to a productive microcomputer application. It suggests where to start with the development, what concepts are important in the problem-solving effort, and what tools can be beneficial for dealing with complexity and assuring accuracy.

Function or Formula In Lotus and other spreadsheets, a statement that allows the user to perform calculations or manipulations with a minimum of typing and analysis. Functions may be mathematical, financial, statistical, string (or character), date, or informational. Straight-line depreciation, for example, can be calculated in Lotus with the function @SLD(COST,SALVAGE VALUE, LIFE).

Gantt Chart A special type of bar chart showing the beginning–end time relationships of project tasks, making it easier to track task completion and view whether a particular task is ahead of, on, or behind schedule.

Generalization Feature of a computer program that enables on to assign different values to a variable. In a generalized computer program, values are stored in a name and that name is used wherever the value should appear. To reanalyze the situation with different values, one need only assign a different value to the named variable.

Gigabyte One billion bytes. Used as a measure of memory or computer storage capacity.

Hardware The physical components of a computer system.

Hierarchy Chart Summary representation of a computer application, showing the main functions at the top of the chart and subsidiary functions on lower rungs of the chart. Resembles the organizational chart of a company or agency.

Hierarchy Rules Order in which mathematical operations are performed: first exponentiation, then division and multiplication, then addition and subtraction. Parentheses ( ) can be used to override the order; operations inside the parentheses are performed as a unit and then combined with work not in parentheses. Thus $3 - 2 = 1$; whereas $(3 - 4)/2 = -\frac{1}{2}$.

Host A computing system used as the main hub in a network. The host controls communication among all the computers on the system.

Information Center (IC) Office responsible for assisting with the development of microcomputer applications. Individuals bring problems or partly finished products and work closely with the information center to develop the application. Frequently, centralizes all microcomputer support in a single entity or staff; can also provide a link between end users and the data-processing staff.

Information Requirements Analysis (IFRA) Analysis designed to generate a list of data fields providing information relevant and pertinent to the goals, problems, and tasks of the division or bureau creating the database. Without relevant information, it is difficult to define the scope and nature of the problem, track projects and programs, and advance or evaluate agency goals.

Input-Output (I-O) Device Physical components of a computer, such as a keyboard and monitor, used for entering or displaying information.

Insertion Anomaly One of the traps to be avoided in database design. It arises when no one engages in an activity or event, even though it is available. With insertion anomalies, the data value never gets into the file. A jurisdiction may have a particular activity with a given rate structure but if no one partakes, then the activity is not captured in the database.

K Kilo, used in reference to number of bytes. Technically represents 1,024 bytes, usually rounded off to 1,000.

Kernel The essential part of a program required for execution. The kernel is the no-frills version of the program.

Key Generally, the dominant or main item in a file. Technically, the key is the unique identifier of each record in a file. The key may include one, two, or more fields depending on how many fields it takes to uniquely identify a record.

Label In Lotus, all character or string data, such as titles and headings, are referred to as labels.

Life Cycle Development A systems analysis and design technique that engenders a very elaborate process for developing computer applications, including an initial investigation and feasibility study, an extensive statement of requirements for the new computer-based system, and a detailed design followed by testing and implementation. All these steps are usually performed by professional systems analysts who work with the user. The user is important in describing needs, but passive in setting up the computer application. Life cycle systems development is generally associated with large mainframe projects geared to heavy amounts of data processing.

Linking Multiple Spreadsheets The ability to create three-dimensional worksheets that pass information from one worksheet to another, dramatically expanding the power of the spreadsheet.

Logging Entering something into a computer.

Logging On Entering a sequence of commands and responses required to gain access to a computer system. Usually involves a user code and password system. Used primarily on mainframe and network systems.

Logic The general problem-solving approach, independent of which specific software or hardware is used.

Logical Data Type Data representing something that is either true or false.

Looping Command Typically a DO WHILE ... ENDDO command structure. In such a structure, whatever falls within the DO WHILE ... ENDDO can be repeated over and over again as long as the DO WHILE condition is true.

Macros A shorthand code that executes multiple commands with a few keystrokes. Individual instructions or commands are packaged into one larger macro, or program, and executed by calling the name of the macro. Most software packages, such as Lotus, WordStar, and DOS, have macro languages.

Mainframe A large, multi-user computer such as an IBM 3090. Also sometimes referred to as a corporate computer. Used for very large and complex tasks.

Management Information Application (MINA) Type of application most useful for middle managers working directly with databases to summarize and check the status of programs, projects, and personnel. Oriented toward semistructured and unstructured managerial problems, but with much less emphasis on major, goal-setting decisions or critical agency choices than is the case with decision support applications.

Megabyte (mb) One million bytes.

Menu A display of options providing easy access to applications and software.

Modem Device for sending computer information over telephone lines. Contraction of MOdulation–DEModulation.

Modularity Part of the general design logic for developing computer applications. Encourages the breakdown of larger problems into smaller, compact modules where the work is similar and at a manageable level. *See also* divide and conquer, stepwise refinement, top-down approach.

Multifile Database A database that consists of more than one file. Requires use of normalization techniques to ensure that data can be easily extracted and combined and the same data are consistently placed in each file.

Multitasking The ability of the computer to execute more than one program (task) at a time.

Network The electronic linking together of two or more computer systems for the purpose of sharing programs, information, or devices such as printers.

Normalization Consists of three stages or steps: identifying and listing all the data fields important to the objectives of the project; grouping all the fields into files; refining the initial groupings so that any serious flaws (namely repeating fields, deletion anomalies, and insertion anomalies) that would detract from achieving a flexible and efficient organization of the data are removed.

Numeric Data Type Type of data (such as salary) on which mathematical calculations can be performed.

Office Automation (OA) Use of computing systems (usually microcomputers) to automate office functions such as document production, filing, and communication.

Office Guru An individual who knows the ins and outs of the microcomputer and takes full advantage of its power to craft an application that is often the marvel of other users or even disciples. Known more formally as a functional support person.

Operating System (OS) A series of commands and programs that enable a computer to function. The OS locates the resources of the personal computer—data, CPU, memory, keyboard, and printer—and tells them where to proceed and what operations to perform.

Operation Processing Application (OPA) A type of application, directed toward structured managerial decisions, that incorporates well-defined statistical, mathematical, or rule-based models for taking input data and calculating or determining optimal solutions.

Glossary

Operator An indicator or symbol for some type of operation. Arithmetic operations are addition (+), subtraction (-), multiplication (*), division (/), and exponentiation (** or ^). Relational operators are equal to (=), greater than (>), less than (<), and not equal to (# or <>). Logical operators are and, or, and not. Operations can also be performed on character or string data. Finding or identifying a part of a string—such as taking the first five letters of a person's last name—might be termed a substring operation.

Ordering, Ranking, or Sequencing Putting a list of items in ascending or descending order or some other specified arrangement. The commands SORT or INDEX are often used for ordering.

Paint Program A type of software package that makes it relatively easy to create pictures of flows and structures or arrange data attractively. The user simply selects an object, such as a box, adjusts its shape and appearance, and places it anywhere on the screen.

Parallel Port Method of electronic transfer of information in which several bits are transmitted simultaneously. Used to connect printers to a computer system.

Peripheral Any physical component, such as a printer, attached to a computer CPU.

PERT (Program Evaluation and Review Technique) A type of analysis that shows how the length of time necessary for completing a task will impact on the time it takes to complete subsequent tasks and the project as a whole.

Pixel A dot of light, the basic component of all characters and designs on a computer screen. A good state-of-the-art computer screen will have 640 pixel columns and 480 pixel rows.

Point and Click Use of a pointing device, such as a mouse, to replace cursor keys and to select items from a menu on the screen.

Pointing Method In Lotus, method of entering information by moving the cursor to the cell where the information is stored and pressing the ENTER key. In fact, once you start moving the cursor—after initiating a formula—for example, the panel or mode indicator in the upper right-hand corner of the Lotus worksheet will read "point."

Power User A professional or managerial computer user who makes extensive use of sophisticated commands and programs to analyze information.

Processor The "brain" of a computer. In a microcomputer, the microprocessor chip (e.g., 80286) that permits the computer to function.

Programming Devising a set of instructions, usually operating on data, to produce a desired result. Similar to giving someone detailed directions for getting from point A to point B, but with the ability to handle very complicated and intriguing paths between A and B.

Project Management A collection of analytical techniques used to plan the details of carrying out large, complex projects.

Protocol Communication standards required in order for communication to occur between computing systems.

Prototyping Quick, partial development of a microcomputer application, often done with the aid of fourth generation languages. At some point, when the participants think the prototype has provided as much information and experience as possible, either a full-scale application or another smaller-scale application is built.

Pseudocode Writing out the solution (i.e., the algorithm) in an English-like language before attempting to construct the actual software code or format for the application. Pseudocode is a combination of English and the language, or syntax, of the software (e.g., Lotus 1-2-3 or dBASE) that will be used in developing the application.

QBE (Query by Example) A software feature that enables the novice user to develop sophisticated queries quickly. The user simply checks or points to the type of information desired (e.g., mortgages in arrears for three months).

Query To obtain, using appropriate commands, relevant information about the organization and its environment by accessing and searching data files. Literally, how one asks questions of the database.

RAM (Random Access Memory) Electronic storage in a computer system of information that is used by the processor. Also called volatile memory because the information stored in it is erased when power to the computer is shut off. RAM is the workhorse of the computer system.

RAM-Resident Program A program that remains in random access memory as long as the computer is turned on. These programs reduce the amount of RAM available for running applications.

Range In Lotus, can be one cell or several cells. The contents of ranges can be moved, copied, edited, summed, or given a different appearance, such as currency or dates.

Record Means of storing pieces of information in a larger file, may contain several items of information related to a single individual, transaction, etc. The individual items, or fields, within a record may be of different data types.

Record Locking Technique that prevents more than one user from accessing the same record in a database at the same time. More specific and sophisticated than file locking because it permits access to other records in the same file.

Redundancy One of the traps to be avoided in database design. When a new record is placed in the data file, redundant data value must be added simply to maintain the symmetry of the file, even though it has nothing to do with the new information and is already present elsewhere in the file.

Relating Files When there are two or more files in a database, a way of relating, joining, or combining the data from different files. The usual method is for both files to contain one field that is the same.

Relational Databases A database consisting of numerous data files with the facility to extract, combine, or relate data from any of these files. Built largely on relational algebra and set theory, its relational logic provides a powerful conceptual tool for dealing with tables of data.

Relative (Address) Copy Feature of Lotus and other spreadsheets that allows one to copy a formula from one location to another and to adjust the formula so that it is correct for its new location. For example, if a column of numbers is summed in column A, then that formula can be copied to sum an equal set of numbers in column B without manually changing the formula. *See also* absolute (address) copy.

Remote Link Electronic connection between two or more computers that are in physically separate locations.

Repeating Fields One of the traps to be avoided in database design. It occurs when an event takes place over and over again, usually for an unknown or highly variable number of times, and the designer tries to allow enough fields (or space) in each record to

Glossary

accommodate the estimated maximum number of events. One solution is to remove the repeating fields and add a new record each time the event actually occurs.

Report Generators A feature of many software packages, including database management systems, that enables one to produce detailed and attractive output (reports), usually without extensive programming.

ROM (Read-Only Memory) One or more computer chips that have a series of electronic instructions permanently encoded in them. Used to provide the most basic instructions to the computer.

SAA (Systems Application Architecture) An IBM effort designed to create a common user interface for all IBM computer systems.

Script A series of commands or responses used to log onto a computer system. Usually an automated procedure that removes the need for the user to enter a user code and password.

SDF (System Data Format) A data structure format similar to ASCII.

Serial Port Method of electronic transfer of information in which one bit is transmitted at a time. Also referred to an asynchronous method of communication.

Shell A program that acts as an interpreter between basic operating system commands and the user. It makes the computer easier to use by overlaying the native commands of a program with a user interface that simplifies commands and syntax.

Smart Statistics Statistical packages that include expert statistician input. For example, instead of the user having to be fully aware of the normal distribution requirement for certain statistics, the statistical package looks at the distribution and provides a message to the user recommending what action to take.

Software Package One or more related programs sold for a specific purpose (e.g., Lotus 1-2-3).

Spreadsheet Software with columns and rows for easy data entry and manipulation. Spreadsheets offer two important tools: quantitative analysis of large or small pools of data, and what-if analysis for any variety of changes in the data.

SQL (Structured Query Language) A set of common commands used to create database queries. Developed for IBM mainframe computers but becoming more common on microcomputer systems in programs such as dBASE IV.

Stepwise Refinement An effective means for avoiding the trap of overly hasty applications development. It means accepting that each subpart of a problem may be at a level of complexity requiring further subdivision (refinement).

Syntax The grammar of commands; the specific rules required for a program or software package to execute properly. Includes spelling, spacing, and word order necessary for the computer to understand what has been entered.

Telecommunications Communication over long distances.

Template A partially completed spreadsheet, usually containing all the label or title information and appropriate formulas but no actual data. Thus, the template, which does not change, can be saved and reused as often as necessary. When the substantive information is entered for a particular iteration of the spreadsheet, it is then saved under another name to preserve the original.

Tilde (~) The Lotus character for the ENTER key, when the Lotus macro language is being used.

Top-Down Approach A general design technique that involves defining goals of the application before trying to build or put any data into the application. The design begins with the general purpose of the application and proceeds to development of more and more specific instructions until the application is complete.

Transaction-Processing Application (TPA) Data recording systems, useful for structured managerial problems that keep track of important events and transactions between the organization and its environment, or within the organization.

Transaction Program Use of a small database and controlling application programs to update a large database. Changes are made to the transaction database and later transferred to the main database.

Transport Values In Lotus, to move the values in a cell or range to a new location, using the command /RANGE VALUE. Differentiate from the copy command (/COPY), which also copies any formulas in the cells to the new location.

Tree Diagram Method of representing the directory structure of a hard disk. Directories are represented as branches extending out from a main (root) directory.

Upload To transfer information electronically from your computer to another.

User Interface The way in which options, choices, and results are presented to analysts or managers, preferably easy to read and use. Includes the commands and syntax that allow the user to interact with the computer program.

User-Friendly Connotes that the software, program, or application is easy to use, generally through menus or very simple commands, and does not require extensive knowledge of a detailed programming language (syntax).

Utilities Programs that enhance the user's ability to perform tedious or routine tasks in a program or operating system. A program that allows one to search many files to determine which contain certain information would be a utility.

VDT (Video Display Terminal) Another term for a computer monitor or screen.

Virus A computer program designed to attach itself secretly to other program code, usually to cause damage or mischief. Viruses are frequently self-replicating and designed to be very difficult to detect.

What-If Analysis Changing a set of assumptions or data to see how the outcome changes. Can be integrated into most software. Spreadsheets are noted for their what-if capacity.

Work Group Processing Organization of workers into groups that share responsibility for a final product. Each group member contributes to the final product. Group members use computers that are networked together to facilitate exchange of data.

Wraparound Feature of word processors that automatically advances the cursor from the end of one line to the beginning of the next line. Facilitates typing by eliminating the need to strike the return key at the end of each line.

WYSIWYG (What You See Is What You Get) Approach taken by graphics programs that provides a true representation on the screen of what will be printed out.

4GL *See* Fourth Generation Language (4GL).

+ In Lotus, when placed in front of a formula (e.g., +B25*100), it means that a custom-built formula is being prepared. Lotus functions or built-in formulas are designated by @.

Index

Absolute copying of spreadsheet formulas, 35, 239–240
Absolute graphics data, 348
ACCEPT command (dBASE), 298, 311
Access systems, 87–88, 143
  familiarity for, 145
  system-external mechanisms for, 163–169
  system-internal mechanisms for, 152–162
  theory and guidelines for, 144–151
ADA programming language, 6
Adding of spreadsheets, 192
Addressing of memory, 59
Administrators:
  data, 126–127
  database, 126
  network, 69
Aggregation of spreadsheet files, 192–193
Algorithms, 50
  development of, 96, 97, 101
  for highway financing case, 242–244
  with MINAs, 276
Alternate database field names, 128
Alternative strategies, testing of, 220–221
Amber screens, 61
Ampersands (&) with database variables, 311
Analyses:
  access to tools for, 87–88
  for database design, 110–112, 132–133
  of information, 10
  for MINAs, 274
  for programming, 50
  for telephone service case, 277–278
  for training records case, 313–314
Anchor database files, 289, 290

AND operator, 52, 204
ANSI standards, 54
Appearance of spreadsheets, 33, 181–182, 191–192
APPEND command (dBASE), 280
Apple computers, 7, 36, 55
Applications:
  access to, 157–162, 165
  cost/benefit, 251–265
  databases with, 131
  decision support, 10–12, 90, 212–214
  development of, *see* Development of applications
  management information, 90, 273–276
  operation-processing, 174–175, 177–182
  vs. software, 86
  specialized, *see* Specialized software
  spreadsheet templates for, 188–190
  for training records case, 305–307
  types of, 10, 94–95
Applications connection, 150, 168
Appropriateness of tasks, 73–74 (*see also* System configurations)
Archival disk backups, 64–65
Arrays, 51
Artificial intelligence (*see also* Expert systems):
  programming languages for, 6, 340
  with querying, 161–162
ASCII format, 70, 150
Aspect ratios for desktop publishing, 76
Assessment of tasks, 15, 73 (*see also* System configurations)
ASSIST mode (dBASE), 290, 295
Assumptions for DSAs, 252
Asterisks (*):
  for database comments, 287, 309
  as file wild card character, 23
Asynchronous communications, 70

AutoCad program, 61, 344
Autoexecute macro, 159–160, 193
Automation (*see also* Macros):
  of DSAs, 251–265
  office, 10–11, 74–76
  of writing with word processors, 42–43
Averages with statistical packages, 38
@AVG command (Lotus), 33

Bachman Charts (BC), 123–124
BACKUP command (DOS), 23
Backup files, 23, 64–65, 129, 151
Backward chaining with expert systems, 340–341
Backward slashes (\):
  for macro names, 206, 223
  for repeating in spreadsheets, 182
  for root directory, 24
Bar charts, 44, 130, 349
Base documents with desktop publishing, 351, 353
Batch files and programs, 24, 162
  for command programs, 159
  for operating systems, 49, 154–155
BAUD rate, 69
BCD format, 70, 150
Benefits in cost/benefit application, 251–265
Bike path system, CAD program for, 344–345
Binary data transmissions, 167
Blocks, programming, 50
Blueprint analogy, 89 (*see also* Development of applications)
Bond sales in construction case, 214–229
Boolean data types and expressions, 50, 52, 204
Bootstrap loaders, 59
Bottom-up approach, 230, 276

371

INDEX

BROWSE command (dBASE), 29
Budget preparations, 184–194
   for capital projects, 214–229
   spreadsheets for, 8, 12
Bulletin boards, for sharing of information, 127
Buses, 72
Business graphics, 44–46

Cables, 73
CAD programs, see Computer-aided design (CAD) programs
Calculations (see also Spreadsheets and spreadsheet programs):
   database fields for, 28
   order of, 52
Calendar forms for project management, 335
Capital projects:
   budgeting for, 214–229
   project management for, 334, 339
   tracking of, 195–206
CASE command (dBASE), 51, 157, 296, 298, 307
CATALOG feature (dBASE), 127
Catalogs of information, 147–148, 168
Cause and effect, statistical packages for, 38
Cells, spreadsheet, 32
   in formulas, 233
   naming of, 244
   protection of, 192
Central processing unit, 20, 56–57
   for communication/information retrieval systems, 78
   for desktop publishing, 76
   for information review workstations, 77
Centronics parallel standard, 54, 72
Chaining:
   of database fields, 117, 130
   with expert systems, 340–341
CHANGE command (dBASE), 29
Character data types, 28, 50, 280
ChartMaster graphics program, 347
Charts, 347–350 (see also Graphs and graphics)
   Bachman, 123–124
   bar and pie, 44, 130, 349–350
   Gantt, 40–41, 334, 335
   PERT, 334–335
   resource, 337–338
Chips, see Microprocessors
CLEAR command (dBASE), 295, 309, 311
Clip art, 47, 345
Clipboard, 154
Clout (Rbase), 149
COBOL programming language, 6
Coefficient with regression analysis, 237–238
Color laser printers, 67

Color video displays, 60–61, 75
Colossus telecommunications program, 167
Commands:
   batch files for, 159
   shells for, 153–154
   telecommunication, 167
Comments in databases, 287–288, 309
Common directories, 147
Communication, graphics for, 343
Communication/information retrieval systems, 77–78
Communications (see also Exchanging of data):
   micro-to-mainframe, 48, 68, 70, 168–169
   micro-to-micro, 68–71, 150, 163–168
   peripherals for, 68–71
   ports for, 72
   software for, 47–48
Compatibility and standards, 54–55
Complexity:
   of desktop publishing, 351
   and DSAs, 216
   of integrated programs, 162
   modules to reduce, 97
   of specialized software, 332–333
COM ports, 72
Compuserve database, 71
Computer-aided design (CAD)
   programs, 344–345
   monitors for, 60
   workstations for, 79–80
Computerphobia, 9
Concatenation of database fields, 283
Conceptual logic, 85
Conditional program control, 51
Confidence factors with expert systems, 341
Connectors:
   for information review workstations, 77
   standardization of, 54, 73
Consistency in design, 131–132, 146
Consoles, 59–60
Constants with regression analysis, 239
Construction, budgeting case for, 214–229
Consultants:
   for application development, 99
   for database design, 124–125
   expert systems as, 340
Control:
   program flow, 51–52
   remote links for, 168
Control Center (dBASE), 26, 31
Conversion of database files, 131
Coordination in database design, 131–132
Co-processors for engineering workstations, 80
COPY command (DOS), 23, 153

Copying:
   of database fields, 287
   of files, 23, 153, 164–166
   of spreadsheet formulas, 34–35, 180–181, 191, 239–240
COPY TO command (dBASE), 287
Cost/benefit case, 251–265
Cost breakdown reports, 336–337
@COUNT command (Lotus), 33
CPM, see Critical Path Method
C programming language, 6
CPU, see Central processing unit
CREATE command (dBASE), 279
CREATE FORMAT command (dBASE), 295
CREATE REPORT command (dBASE), 321
CREATE VIEW command (dBASE), 290
Criteria for database entries, 199–200, 292
Critical Path Method (CPM), 40, 334 (see also Project management, software for)
Critical success factors, 114, 134 (see also Solution models)
Cross-sectional graphs, 349 (see also Graphs and graphics, type)
Crosstalk telecommunications program, 69, 167
CSF (critical success factors), 114, 134
Cursor control vs. program flow, 262
Customized data-entry screens, 290–295

DADM (data administrators), 126–127
Daisy-wheel printers, 66–67
Data:
   access systems for, 147
   in database design, 27–28, 115, 134–135
   entering of, see Entering of data
   exchanging of, see Exchanging of data
   organization of, for MINAs, 275
   for programming, 50–51
   retrieval of, 147–149
   selection of, for graphics, 347–348
   sharing of, 127, 163
   for statistical package files, 37
   for training records case, 300–301
   transformations of, 12, 38, 149–151, 240
   types of, 28, 50, 94, 280
Data administrators, 126–127
Database administrators, 126
Database analysts, 168, 169
Databases and database management systems, 8, 26–31, 106–110
   access system to, 87–88
   for capital expenditures case, 197–198
   comments in, 287–288, 309
   data collection for, 115, 134–135

INDEX

373

Databases and database management systems *(continued)*
  data-entry for, 27, 28, 75, 128–129, 280–282
  for decision making case, 318–326
  description of data for, 27
  for DSAs, 212
  for economic development, 132–141
  fields for, *see* Fields, database
  generic categories in, 121
  for information management, 11–12
  for MINAs, 275
  multiple files for, 30, 108, 138–139, 284–290
  private, 109, 126, 131
  querying of, *see* Queries, database
  redundancies in, 122, 283–284, 286, 287
  reports for, 30, 130, 283–285
  spreadsheets as, 195, 197–198
  for telephone service cases, 278–280, 286–290
Data diagrams for database design, 135
Data dictionary/data directory, 111, 125–127, 136, 295
Data flow diagrams (DFD), 112
Data-intensive problems, 272
Data Interchange Format (DIF), 150
Data labels for graphs, 45
Data migration facility, 63
Data Queries command (Lotus), 199
DATA REGRESSION command (Lotus), 238
Data structures, 51
DATA TABLE command (Lotus), 226–227
Date arithmetic with databases, 318–319
Date data types, 28, 50, 280
DBA, *see* Database administrators, Database analysts
dBASE database program, 26–27
  add-in programs for, 49
  menu system for, 157–159
  with networks, 165
  programming of, 49, 51
  reserved words in, 279
  transferring of data with, 150
DBMS, *see* Databases and database management systems
DD, *see* Data dictionary/data directory
Decision making:
  expert systems for, 341–342
  for MINAs, 318–326
  programs for, 355
Decision support applications (DSA), 10–12, 90, 212–214
  capital projects budgeting case, 214–229
  cost/benefit case, 251–265
  highway financing case, 229–251
  problems for, 94

Default database entry format, 128, 280–282
Deletion anomalies in databases, 121–122, 303
Deletion of files, 23
Delimited file format, 150
Delimiters, 204
Demodulation, 69 (*see also* Micro-to-micro communications)
Dependencies:
  and database field normalization, 120, 122, 281
  network for, 40, 335
Designing:
  of databases, 27–28, 115–125, 136–141
  of decision support applications, 212–213
  of spreadsheets, 32
Desktop computers, 6
Desktop publishing (DTP), 43–44, 350–355
  printers for, 67
  systems for, 75–76
DesqView environment, 154 (*see also* Multitasking with OS/2)
Developmental problems, *see* Unstructured problems
Development of applications, 85
  defining of, 86–88
  framework for, 85
  illustration of, 100–103
  logic for, 88–100
  methods for, 95–96
Development of databases, 110–111
  consistency, coordination, and distribution in, 131–132
  data dictionaries and directories for, 125–127
  design for, 115–125, 136–141
  flexibility in, 116, 275
  implementation of, 127–131
  information requirements analysis for, 113–115, 133–136
  master plans for, 113–114
  models and diagrams for, 112–113
DFD, *see* Data flow diagrams
Diagrams:
  for database design, 111–113, 135
  of disk organization, 148
Dialog database, 71
Dictionaries, database data, 111, 125–127, 136, 295
DIF, *see* Data Interchange Format
Digitizers, 79, 80
DIR command (DOS), 23
Directories:
  common, 147
  database, 125–127, 136
  disk, 23–25, 148
  for Lotus, 160

Discounting of future dollars, 253–255 (*see also* Cost/benefit case)
Disjointed incrementalism, 93 (*see also* Solution models)
Disk operating systems (DOS):
  Batch language for, 49, 152
  functions of, 22–25
  graphics interface with, 20
Disks and disk drives, 63–65
  for communication/information retrieval systems, 78
  for data exchange, 55
  desktop publishing requirements for, 76
  floppy, 63–64, 72–73
  management and organization for, 22, 64, 148
  utilities for, 48
DISPLAY command (dBASE), 282–283
Displaying of spreadsheet data, 182–184
Distribution of databases, 111, 131–132
Divide and conquer method, 15, 90, 96–97, 103
  for capital expenditures case, 196–197
  for desktop publishing, 352
  for highway improvement financing case, 232–233
  for MINAs, 276
  for operational applications, 174
  for reduction in force application, 101
  for training records case, 305
DO CASE command (dBASE), 296, 298, 307
DO command (dBASE), 30–31, 287
Documentation, 125–127, 144, 145
Dollar sign ($):
  for absolute spreadsheet formulas, 35, 239–240
  as dBASE command, 324
Dominant database fields, 118, 121, 136–137
DOS, *see* Disk operating systems
DOS2OOLS menu system, 25
Dot-matrix printers, 66, 68, 75
DO WHILE command (dBASE), 52, 292, 294, 311
Download/upload process, 71, 167
Dr. Halo graphics program, 61, 343
DSA, *see* Decision support applications
DTP, *see* Desktop publishing
Dumb terminals, 70 (*see also* Micro-to-mainframe communications)
Duplication of databases, 131–132
DVORAK keyboard layout, 60
Dynamic linking of spreadsheet files, 36

EBCIDIC format, 70, 150
Economic development, database design for, 132–141
EDIT command (dBASE), 29
Editing:
  of databases, 29

INDEX

Editing *(continued)*
  of data entry, 129, 281, 292
  of spreadsheets, 192
  of text, 10–11
  with word processors, 41–42
Efficiency in database design, 116, 275
EGA Paint graphics program, 343
Electronic bulletin boards, 127
Electronic communications, *see* Communications
Electronic mail, 71, 166
ELSE command element (dBASE), 311
Emulation, terminal, 70, 167
Enable integrated program, 162
ENDDO command element (dBASE), 52, 292, 294
ENDIF command element (dBASE), 311
End user tools and computing, 5–7, 9
Energraphics program, 347
Engineering workstations, 79–80
Entering of data:
  for databases, 27, 28, 128–129, 280–282, 290–205
  devices for, 62
  macro for, 36
  for office automation, 75
  for spreadsheets, 32, 181, 192
  with statistical packages, 37
  for telephone service case, 290–295
  for training records case, 306
Environments, windowing, 154
Equal-level computer links, 163
Equal sign (=) in expressions, 52
Erasable laser disks, 65
Errors with database data entry, 129, 281, 292
Error traps for queries, 298
Excel spreadsheet program, 31, 36, 347
Exchanging of data, 149–150
  with Apple computers, 55
  with clipboard, 154
  communications for, 47–48
  in database files, 131, 150
  and disk formats, 63
  for highway financing case, 231–232
  micro-to-mainframe, 48, 68–71, 150, 168–169
  micro-to-micro, 68–71, 150, 163–168
  protocols for, 69, 70, 163, 167
  in spreadsheet files, 36
Expert systems, 6–7, 339–342
  complexity of, 332–333
  elements in, 333
  knowledge bases for, 339–341
  programming languages for, 6, 340
  rules in, 333, 339
  for training records case, 311–318
Expressions, 52 (*see also* Programming)
ExSys expert system program, 340
Extract area for database searches, 204–205

FIDO telecommunications program, 167
Fields, database, 27–28, 50, 108
  alternate names for, 128
  chaining of, 117, 130
  concatenation of, 283
  copying of, 287
  in database design, 115
  dictionaries and directories for, 111, 125–127, 136, 295
  for file linking, 289
  grouping of, 118–121, 136–141, 301–302
  linking of, 116–117, 302
  maximum and minimum values of, 129
  relationships between, 116–118, 124, 130
  for telephone service case, 278–279
  uniqueness of, 129
FILE COMBINE command (Lotus), 247
Files:
  backup, 23, 64–65, 129, 151
  copying of, 23, 153, 164–166
  database, *see* Databases and database management systems
  directories for, 23–25, 148
  locking of, 151, 164, 165
  management of, 20–24, 75
  organization of, 24–25, 147–148
  security for, 151
  servers for, 69, 78, 164
  spreadsheet, *see* Spreadsheets and spreadsheet programs
FILTER command (dBASE), 148
Filters, database, 148, 159
Financial calculations, 12 (*see also* Spreadsheets and spreadsheet programs)
FIND command (dBASE), 282, 298, 311
Fire and rescue training records case, 299–318
First Class expert system program, 340
Flexibility, in database design, 116, 275
Floating point numbers, 50 (*see also* Numeric data types)
Float time with CPM, 334
Floppy disks, 63–64, 72–73
Flow (of information) diagrams, 46
Forced database input, 129
FORMAT command (DOS), 22
Formats and formatting:
  ASCII, 70, 150
  conversion of, 150–151
  for database reports, 130
  for disks, 22, 63, 64
  for graphics data, 347–348
  with spreadsheets, 33, 181–182, 191–192
  of text, 10–11
  translation of, for data exchange, 70, 150, 168

Formats and formatting *(continued)*
  with word processors, 41–42
Formed-character printers, 66–67
Forms:
  for database entry, 128–129, 280–282, 290–205
  for data collection, 300–301
  software for, 88
Formulas, 33–35
  for budget requests case, 186–187
  cell references with, 233–234
  copying of, 34–35, 180–181, 191, 239–240
  for cost/benefit application, 263–265
  for database querying, 202–204
  for revenue inflow case, 178–180
FORTRAN programming language, 6
Forward chaining, with expert systems, 340
Fourth generation languages (4GL):
  for application development, 92, 95
  for databases, 109, 110
  for data flow diagrams, 112
  for prototyping, 115
  for querying, 161
Framework for development of applications, 85
  database design, 113–114
  illustration, 100–103
  logic for, 88–100
Framework integrated program, 162, 165
Free-form graphics software, 343–347
Freelance graphics program, 345, 347, 350
Freestyle outliner program, 43
Functions, spreadsheet, 33, 179
Future monetary values, 253–254

Gantt charts, 40–41, 334, 335
General applications, 10, 233–235
Generic categories, in databases, 121
{GETNUMBER} macro command (Lotus), 224
Gigabytes, 59
Goals:
  in database design, 133, 134
  with MINAs, 274
  PERT, 39–41, 334
  statement of, 96–97, 100–101
  for training records case, 299–300
GoldenGate integrated program, 71, 162, 168
Grammar checkers, 43
GrandView outliner program, 43
GRAPH command (Lotus), 236
Graphics data, format of, 347–348
Graphs and graphics:
  clip art, 47, 345
  for cost/benefit case, 257–258
  for database output, 130
  for data-entry systems, 75

INDEX

Graphs and graphics *(continued)*
    for desktop publishing, 76, 351, 355
    for engineering workstations, 80
    for information review workstations, 77
    interfaces for, 20, 21–22
    mouse for, 61
    presentation, 79, 342–350
    with Presentation Manager, 152
    printers for, 66
    for productivity systems, 78
    software for, 44–47
    type, selection of, 348–349
    workstations for, 79
Graphwriter program, 45
Greeked characters, 351 *(see also* Desktop publishing)
Green screens, 61
Grouping:
    of database fields, 118–121, 136–141, 301–302
    of files with DOS, 24–25
Group processes in micro-to-micro linking, 166

Hackers, 14
HAL add-in (Lotus), 149
Hard disks, 64
    for data-entry systems, 75
    for desktop publishing, 351
    management of, 153
    for productivity systems, 78
Hardware:
    central processing unit, 56–57
    for communications, 167
    configurations for, 73–80
    input-output devices, 59–62
    linkages for, 71–73
    memory, 58–59
    peripherals, 65–71
    standards for, 54–55
    storage media, 62–65
Harvard Graphics program, 45, 345, 347, 348–350
Harvard Total Project Manager program, 41, 334
Health and video screens, 61
HIDE command (Lotus), 182
Hierarchical database designs, 117
Hierarchical menus, 32
Hierarchy charts, 101, 305–306 *(see also* Divide and conquer method, Stepwise refinement)
High-density floppy disks, 63
High-resolution monitors:
    for desktop publishing, 76, 351
    for graphics, 79
    for productivity systems, 78
    for word processors, 75
Highway improvement financing case, 229–251

Highway improvement case *(continued)*
    critical assumptions for, 248, 250–251
    fees in, 241–246
    summary section for, 248–249
Hot Shot Graphics program, 345
Housekeeping tasks, 20–21, 309
Hyper-text programs, 355

IBM standard, 55
IC (information center), 99 *(see also* Development of applications)
Icons, 46 *(see also* Graphs and graphics, software for)
IDB database package, 71
Identification of database data, 27
IDIR menu system, 25
IDMS-R database package, 71
IF command (dBASE), 51, 311
IF command (Lotus), 202
IFRA, *see* Information requirements analyses
Image libraries, 345 *(see also* Graphs and graphics, Clip art)
Image scanners, 62
Impact printers, 65–67
Implementation:
    of databases, 111, 127–131
    vs. logic, 175
    of microcomputers, 12–13
Incinerator project, cost/benefit case for, 251–265
Independence of end user, and microcomputers, 7
INDEX command (dBASE), 29–30, 287, 289, 303, 311
Indexing:
    with databases, 29–30, 159, 282, 283, 287, 289, 303, 311
    with word processors, 43
Information, *see* Data, Databases and database management systems
Information management applications, 10–12
Information requirements analyses (IFRA), 111, 113–115, 118, 133–136
Information resources management, 126
Information review workstations, 77
Initialization of programs, 309–310
Ink-jet printers, 67, 76
Input, *see* Entering of data
Input area for database searches, 200
Input-output devices, 59–62
Input screens for database data entry, 128–129, 280–282, 290–295
Insertion anomalies in databases, 121–122, 303
Integers, 50 *(see also* Numeric data types)

Integration:
    of modules for highway financing case, 246–251
    of software packages, 89, 162
Integrity:
    of database fields, 125
    of spreadsheet data, 192
Intelligent terminals, 70
Intel microprocessors, 56–57
Interactive systems, 103
    for batch files, 159
    for database entries, 292
    DSAs, 212
Interest rates:
    in capital project budgeting case, 215, 226–229
    in cost/benefit application, 253, 256
Internal rate of return (IRR), 254, 263–264
Interrupts, 72
Interval/ratio graphic data, 347
Investments, expert systems for, 341
@IRR function (Lotus), 263

Job descriptions, modification of, 11
Joining of database files, 30

Keyboards, 60, 61 *(see also* Input-output devices)
Key database fields, 118, 136–137, 302
Keystrokes, *see* Macros
Knowledge engineers, 340 *(see also* Expert Systems)

Labels, spreadsheet, 32–33, 176, 182, 190
LAN, *see* Local Area Networks
Languages, programming, 6, 340
Laser disks:
    reusability of, 65
    storage, 64–65
Laser printers, 67, 68
    for desktop publishing, 76, 351
    for word processors, 75
LCD, *see* life cycle development
Learning curves for specialized software, 332
Legends for graphs, 45
Letter-quality printers, 66–67
Level of measurement for graphics data, 347
Libraries, mainframe, 168
Life cycle development (LCD), 99–100, 111–112
Light pens, 61, 75
Linear regression, 237–238
Line charts and graphs, 44, 130, 349
Linking *(see also* Exchanging of data):
    communications for, 48
    of database fields, 116–117, 302
    of database files, 288–290

376 INDEX

Linking *(continued)*
  of hardware, 71–73
  micro-to-main, 68–71, 150, 168–169
  micro-to-micro, 68–69
  of spreadsheet files, 36, 192–193, 247
LISP programming language, 6, 340
LIST command (dBASE), 289, 303, 311
Listing of files, 22–23
@LN function (Lotus), 240
Local Area Networks (LAN), 68–69, 163–166
Local highway financing case, 229–251
Locking of files, 151, 164, 165
Logarithmic functions:
  for data transformations, 38
  with regression analyses, 240
Logic, 85
  for application development, 88–100
  with expert systems, 339
  vs. implementation, 175
  relational, in database design, 116–118
Logical data type, 28, 50
Logical disk drives, 72–73
Longitudinal graphs, 349 (*see also* Graphs and graphics, type)
Looping, 52 (*see also* Programming)
Lotus 1-2-3 spreadsheet program, 31–32 (*see also* Spreadsheets and spreadsheet programs)
  add-ins for, 149
  directories for, 160
  formatting with, 182
  graphics with, 347
  as integrated program, 162
  menu system for, 157–159
  with networks, 165
  programming with, 35–36, 159–160
  reserved words in, 222
  transferring of data with, 150
LPT1 port, 72

Mace Utilities, 48
Machine-level security, 164
Macros:
  autoexecute, 159–160, 193
  for menu systems, 259–263
  names for, 206, 223
  for printing, 205–206
  for shells, 153
  spreadsheet, 36, 157–190, 193, 258–259
Mainframes, linking to, 68–71, 150, 168–169
Management:
  and advent of microcomputers, 9
  of files, 20–24, 75
  systems for, 76–78
Management information applications (MINA), 90, 273–276
  decision making case, 318–326
  problems for, 94–95

Management information applications *(continued)*
  telephone service case, 277–285, 285–299
  training records case, 299–318
Managerial tasks and microcomputer use, 5
Maneuverability with word processors, 42
Manipulation of information, 10, 12
Manuals, 144, 145 (*see also* Documentation)
Manuscript word processor, 42
Many-to-many database field relationships, 124
Master spreadsheet templates, 193
@MAX command (Lotus), 33
MD command (DOS), 24
Memory, 5–6, 58–59
  for communication/information retrieval systems, 78
  for desktop publishing, 76
  for engineering workstations, 80
  for productivity systems, 78
  with spreadsheets, 35
Memory variables, 50
MENUBRANCH command (Lotus), 259
Menus and menu systems, 87–88
  for access systems, 146, 157–159
  for communications, 167–168
  for cost/benefit application, 259–263
  for operating systems, 25, 154–156
  with programming, 51
  for spreadsheets, 32
  for telephone service case, 295–296
  for training records case, 306–307
Metadata, 125 (*see also* Data dictionary/data directory)
Micro-channel bus, 72
Microcomputers:
  early, 3
  in public organizations, growth and history of, 7–14, 9–10
  resistance to, 8–9, 14
  role of, 10–14
  technology of, 4–5
  as tools, 5–7
Micro-floppy disks, 63
Microprocessors, 5, 56–57
  for desktop publishing, 351
  for productivity systems, 78
Microsoft Project program, 334
Microsoft Windows program, 61
Microsoft Word word processor, 42, 44
Micro-to-mainframe communications, 48, 68, 70, 168–169
Micro-to-micro communications, 68–71, 150, 163–168
Milestones, PERT, 39–41, 334
MINA, *see* Management information applications

Models:
  for database design, 111, 112–114, 135
  for DSAs, 212
  for highway financing case, 231
  solution, 93–94, 114, 134
Modems, 69, 78
Modification anomalies for database fields, 121
MODIFY COMMAND command (dBASE), 287
MODIFY STRUCTURE command (dBASE), 28, 324
Modulation, 69 (*see also* Micro-to-micro communications)
Modules and modularity, 87–88
  for budget requests case, 188
  for desktop publishing, 352
  development of, 96, 97, 101–103
  integration of, 246–251
  with MINAs, 276
  programming, 49–50
  with project management, 338
  with word processors, 42
Monitors, 60–61 (*see also* Screen display)
  for communication/information retrieval systems, 78
  for data-entry systems, 75
  for desktop publishing, 76, 351
  for engineering workstations, 80
  for graphics, 79
  for information review workstations, 77
  for productivity systems, 78
  for word processors, 75
Monochrome monitors, 60
  for engineering workstations, 80
  for word processors, 75
Motorola microprocessors, 56
Mouse, 61
  for data-entry systems, 75
  for desktop publishing, 351
  for productivity systems, 78
MS-DOS, 21–25, 152
Multiple database files, 30, 108, 138–139, 284–290
Multitasking with OS/2, 152–154

Names:
  for cells, 244
  for criterion areas, 200
  for fields, 128
  for files, 27
  for formulas, 35, 186–187
  for macros, 206, 223
  for ranges, 205
  for statistical package files, 37
Natural log spreadsheet function, 240
Net present value, 33, 254, 256, 263

INDEX

Networks, 68–69
　for information review workstations, 77
　for micro-to-micro exchanges, 163–166
　for productivity systems, 78
　security for, 164–165
NeXT computer, 63, 65
Nodes:
　network, 69
　project management, 41
Nominal graphic data, 347
Nonimpact printers, 65, 67–68
Nonprogrammed problems, *see* Unstructured problems
Normalization for database design, 118–123, 137, 301–305
Norton Utilities, 48
"Not equal to" database operator, 29
NOT logical operator, 52
Novell's NetWare, 69, 164
NPV (net present value), 33, 254, 256, 263
@NPV function (Lotus), 33, 263
Nubus system, 72
Number signs (#):
　in database queries, 282
　for delimiters, 204
Numeric data types, 28, 50, 280

OA, *see* Office automation
Objectives (*see also* Goals):
　vs. goals, 274
　for training records case, 299–300
OCR, *see* Optical character readers
Office automation, 10–11, 74–76
One-to-many database field relationships, 124
One-to-one database field relationships, 124
OPA, *see* Operation-processing applications
Operating systems, 20–25
　access to, 49, 152–157
　compatibility with, 57
　for networks, 69, 164
Operational problems, *see* Structured problems
Operation-processing applications (OPA), 90, 94, 95, 174–175, 177–182
Operation stage of microcomputer implementation, 12
Operators, database, 29
Optical character readers (OCR), 62
Optical disks, 63, 64–65
Ordering with databases, 29
Ordinal graphic data, 347
Organization:
　of access systems, 146–147
　of data with MINAs, 275
　of disk files, 24–25, 64, 147–148

Organizations:
　charts of, 46
　commitment of, and systems configuration, 74
　effects of microcomputer implementation on, 13
OR operator, 52, 204
OS/2 operating system, 20, 152
　compatibility with, 57
　Presentation Manager in, 21–22
Outliners, 43
Outputs, database, 130–131, 204–205

PACK command (dBASE), 292
Page layout for desktop publishing, 76, 351, 353
PageMaker desktop publishing program, 351, 354
Paintbrush program, 46, 343
"Painting" of database screens, 129, 295
Paradox database program, 161
Parallel ports, 54, 72
Parameters, replaceable, 24, 31, 298
PARAMETERS command (dBASE), 31
Parentheses ( ) with calculations, 52
Parity, 69 (*see also* Communications)
PASCAL programming language, 6
PATH command (DOS), 147
PATHMINDER menu system, 25
Paths, PERT, 335
Pausing, macro prompts for, 36, 223, 262
PC-DOS, 21–25, 152
PC SAS (Statistical Analysis System), 6, 39
PC Paintbrush graphics program, 46, 343
PC Paint graphics program, 46, 61, 343
Peer-to-peer computer links, 163
Percentages, use of, in graph construction, 348
Percentage sign (%) for replaceable parameters, 24
Peripherals, 65–71
Personal computers, *see* Microcomputers
Personal productivity managers, 355
Personnel:
　for applications development, 98–99
　for database design, 113, 133–134
　databases for, 11
PERT, *see* Program Evaluation and Review Technique
Photobases, 347 (*see also* Scanners)
Physical disk drives, 72–73
Pie charts, 44, 130, 349–350
Pixels, 60, 62 (*see also* Image scanners, Monochrome monitors)
Pixie graphics program, 45
Planning:
　for microcomputers, 12–13
　project management for, 39–41, 331–339
Plotters, 67
　for desktop publishing, 76

Plotters *(continued)*
　for engineering workstations, 80
　for graphics, 79
Plus sign (+)
　for database field concatenation, 283
　for spreadsheet formulas, 34
PM software, *see* Project management software
Point and click feature, 154
Pointing method, in spreadsheets, 180
Polaris program, 39
PostScript page description language, 351 (*see also* Desktop publishing)
Power users, 162
Pre-implementation of microcomputers, 12–13
Presentation format for reports, 130
Presentation graphics, 79, 342–350
Presentation Manager, 21–22, 152–154
Preservation of files, 151
PRINT command (dBASE), 282
Printers, 65–68
　for communication/information retrieval systems, 78
　connections for, 72
　for desktop publishing, 76, 351
　for graphics, 79
　for information review workstations, 77
　for productivity systems, 78
　redirection of output to, 23
　for word processors, 75, 75
Printing:
　automatic, 205–206
　of database records, 282
　of screen, 145, 182–183
　of spreadsheet data, 182–184
　for telephone service case, 296–298
Private databases, 109, 126, 131
PRN device, 23, 72
Problems and problem-solving:
　components of, 87
　and database design, 112, 134
　identification of, 299–300
　logic for, 86
　microcomputers for, 4, 10
　programming for, 50
　understanding nature of, 91–93
Processes:
　with expert systems, 340
　graphics for, 46
Processors, 5 (*see also* Microprocessors)
ProComm communications software, 69, 167
Production databases, 169
Productivity:
　management systems for, 78
　microcomputers for, 4, 10
　and video screens, 61
Program Evaluation and Review Technique, 39–41, 333–335, 338

INDEX

Program flow, 51–52
  vs. cursor control, 262
Programmed problems, *see* Structured problems
Programming, 49–52
  of database managers, 30–31
  with DOS, 23–24
  languages for, 6, 340
  with spreadsheets, 35–36
  utilities for, 48–49, 147–151
Programming problems, *see* Semistructured problems
Projections, 236–237
Project management, 39–41
  concepts of, 39–40
  software for, 40–41, 333–339
Project Workbench management program, 41, 334
PROLOG programming language, 6, 340
Promis project management program, 41, 334
Prompts, macro, 36, 223, 262
Protection:
  of files, 151
  of spreadsheet cells, 192
Protocols, 69, 70, 163, 167
Prototyping, 99–100
  for database design, 111–112, 115, 135
  for DSAs, 213
Pseudocode, 50, 96, 97–98
  for capital expenditures case, 198–199, 203–204
  for capital projects budgeting case, 221–222
  as comments, 309
  for MINAs, 276
  for reduction in force application, 101–102
  for revenue inflow case, 178–179
  for training records case, 309, 314
Public databases, 109
Public organizations, microcomputers in:
  history of, 7–9
  status of, 9–14

QBE (query-by-example) database feature, 31, 149, 161
Quattro spreadsheet program, 31, 347
Queries, database, 29, 130, 282–283, 285
  for capital expenditures case, 198–204
  for telephone service case, 296–298
  for training records case, 307–311
Questioning for database design, 115
Question mark (?) in spreadsheet macro prompts, 36, 223, 262

RA, *see* Resource Allocation
Radio Shack computers, 7
RAM (Random Access Memory), 6, 58–59

RAM *(continued)*
  for communication/information retrieval systems, 78
  for engineering workstations, 80
  for productivity systems, 78
RAM-resident programs, 58
Rbase database, 149
RBBS, *see* Remote Bulletin Board Systems
RD command (DOS), 24
READ command (dBASE), 294–295
Read-Only Memory (ROM), 6, 59
Records, database, 27, 108, 165
Redirection of output, 23
Reduction in force, application for, 100–103
Reformatting of hard disks, 64
Regression analysis, 237–241
Relational logic in database design, 116–118
Relative copying of spreadsheet formulas, 34–35, 180–181, 240
Remote Bulletin Board Systems, 167–168
Remote links, 166–168
Repeating database fields, 120–121, 139, 301
Replaceable parameters, 24, 31, 298
REPLACE command (dBASE), 29, 319
Reports:
  for capital expenditures case, 203–205
  for databases, 30, 130, 283–285
  for decision making case, 321–324
  for project management, 336–338
Request system for telephone service:
  bare-bones, 277–285
  enhanced, 285–299
Reserved words:
  in dBASE, 279
  in Lotus, 222
Resolution:
  of displays, 60
  of image scanners, 62
Resource Allocation, 40 (*see also* Project management)
Resource charts for project management, 337–338
Resource Leveling, 40 (*see also* Project management)
Resources for computer support, 74
Retrieval of data, 147–149
Revenue inflow case, 176–184
RL, *see* Resource Leveling
ROM, *see* Read-Only Memory
Root directory, 24 (*see also* Disk operating system)
Rows, spreadsheet, 32
RS 232C standard, 54, 72

S100 bus, 54
SAA, *see* System Applications Architecture

@SAY command (dBASE), 292, 294, 296, 311
Scanners, 62, 346
Scope in database queries, 130
Screen display, 60–61 (*see also* Monitors)
  capture utilities for, 345–346
  database, 128–129
  for data-entry systems, 75, 128–129, 280–282, 290–295
  painting of, 295
  printing of, 145, 182–183
Scripts, telecommunication, 167
SDF, *see* System Data Format
Searching, in databases, *see* Queries, database
Sectors, disk, 22
Security, 14, 144, 151, 164–165
SELECT command (dBASE), 289
Semistructured problems, 91–94, 272
  capital projects budgeting case, 214–229
  and database design, 114
  decision making for MINAs, 318–326
  design for, 146
  DSAs for, 212
  expert systems for, 341
  project management for, 339
Sequencing with databases, 29
Sequential program control, 51
Serial ports, 72
Servers, network, 69, 78, 164
SET FILTER command (dBASE), 159, 303
SET INDEX command (dBASE), 159, 282, 283
SET RELATION command (dBASE), 289
SET TALK OFF command (dBASE), 309
SET UNIQUE ON command (dBASE), 287
Shading with image scanners, 62
Shared knowledge and access systems, 145
Shells, operating system, 153–154
Single-user systems, 165
Slack time with CPM, 334
Slash key (/) for spreadsheet menus, 32, 36
@SLN command (Lotus), 33
Slope with regression analysis, 237–238
Smart statistics, 38
Smart word processor features, 43
Software, 6
  in applications development, 86, 98
  categories of, 19–20
  communications, 47–48
  database management systems, 26–31
  graphics, 44–47
  for information review workstations, 77

INDEX

Software *(continued)*
    for micro-to-micro exchanges, 163
    for MINAs, 275
    for operating systems, 20–25
    for operational applications, 174–175
    and programming, 49–52
    project management, 39–41
    spreadsheets, 31–36
    statistical packages, 37–38
    upgrades for, 19
    utilities, 48–49
    word-processing, 41–44
Solution models, 93–94, 114, 134 (*see also* Critical success factors)
SORT command (dBASE), 29–30, 303
Sorting, 23, 29–30, 289, 303
Source database, 71
Sources of information for database design, 134
Specialized software, 331–332
    desktop publishing, 350–355
    expert systems, 339–342
    presentation graphics, 342–350
    for project management, 333–339
Specialized systems, 79–80
Spelling checkers, 43, 292
Spreadsheets and spreadsheet programs, 7, 8, 31–36
    with access systems, 165
    for budgeting, 8, 12, 186, 215–216
    for capital expenditures case, 195
    for capital projects budgeting case, 215–216
    columns, 32, 33, 182, 190–191
    combining and linking of files, 36, 192–193, 247–251
    for cost/benefit case, 258–259
    as databases, 195, 197–198
    data entry for, 32, 181, 192
    for desktop publishing, 352, 355
    displaying of, 182–184
    with DSAs, 213–214
    formatting of, 33, 181–182, 191–192
    formulas for, *see* Formulas
    graphics with, 347
    for highway financing case, 233–235
    macros with, 36, 157–190, 193, 258–259
    for operational applications, 174–175
    regression analysis with, 238–241
    for revenue inflow case, 176–177
SPSS/PC statistical package, 39
SPSSX (Statistical Package for Social Science), 6
SQL, *see* Structured Query Language
Standard data formats, 150
Standards, hardware, 54–55
STATGRAPH statistical package, 39
Statistical Analysis System, 6, 39
Statistical Package for Social Science, 6
Statistical packages, 6, 37–38
STATPAC statistical packages, 37–38

Stepwise refinement, 96, 97
    for budget requests case, 186
    for capital expenditures case, 198–199
    for database design, 114
    for desktop publishing, 352
    for operational applications, 174
    for programming, 50
    for revenue inflow case, 177–178
Storage media, 62–65
STORE command (dBASE), 310
Straight-line regression analysis, 237–238
Strategic planning for microcomputers, 12
Strategic problems, *see* Unstructured problems
Structured graphics, 347–350
Structured problems, 91–94, 173–175
    budget requests case, 184–194
    capital expenditures case, 195–206
    and database design, 114
    OPAs for, 90, 94, 95, 174–175, 177–182
    revenue inflow case, 176–184
Structured Query Language (SQL), 31, 161
Structures:
    data, 51
    database, 28, 111, 128, 279, 324
    graphics for, 46
Style checkers, 43
Style sheets for desktop publishing, 353
Subdirectories, 24–25
Subprojects with PERT, 338
Subtraction of spreadsheets, 192
@SUM function (Lotus), 180, 191
Superior-to-subordinate computer links, 163–164
Superkey macro program, 160
Symphony integrated program, 162
SYSTAT statistical package, 39
System Applications Architecture (SAA), 150–151
System buses, 72
System configurations, 73–80
System Data Format (SDF), 150
Systems analysis, 113
Systems components, 55
    central processing unit, 56–57
    input-output devices, 59–62
    memory, 58–59
    peripherals, 65–71
    storage media, 62–65

Tables as files, 115–116, 302
Tables of contents:
    for capital expenditures case, 197
    for highway financing case, 248
Tablets, graphic, 61
T. A. C. (The Applications Connection), 150, 168

Tactical problems, *see* Semistructured problems
Tags:
    database, 27
    for spreadsheet values, 244
Tape drive backups, 64
Tasks:
    appropriateness of, 73–74
    assessment of, 15, 73
    PERT, 39, 41, 334, 338
Team approach to database design, 124–125
Technology of microcomputers, 4–5
Telecommunications, 47–48, 69–70, 167
Telephone service cases:
    bare-bones, 277–285
    for decision making, 318–326
    enhanced, 285–299
Templates, spreadsheet, 188–190, 193
Terminal emulation, 70, 167
Testing:
    of alternative strategies, 220–221
    in decision making case, 319–321
Text:
    for desktop publishing, 353–355
    editing and formatting of, 10–11
    monitors for, 60
    scanners for, 62
Thermal printers, 68
Thesauruses, 43
Thinktank outliner program, 43
Tildes (~) in spreadsheet macros, 36, 193, 262
Time calculations, 318–319
TIMELINE project management program, 40–41
Time scheduling, 39–41, 331–339
Titles for graphs, 44–45
Top-down method, 276, 299
    for budget requests case, 188
    for desktop publishing, 352
Touch screens, 61
Toxic chemical problems, expert systems for, 341
TPA, *see* Transaction-processing applications
Tracking systems:
    for capital expenditures, 195–206
    for telephone service requests, 277–285
    for training records case, 299–318
Traffic congestion case, 229–251
Trailing spaces, trimming of, 283
Training records case, 299–318
    certification of performance in, 300, 304–306, 311–318
    data collection for, 300–301
Transaction files, 165–166
Transaction-processing applications (TPA), 90, 94, 95, 273
Transfer of data, *see* Exchanging of data

INDEX

Transformations of data, 149–151
  with databases, 12
  logarithmic, 38, 240
Translators for protocol matching, 70, 150, 168
Tree diagrams of disk organization, 148
TRIM command (dBASE), 283
TRS-80 computer (Radio Shack), 7
Tuples, 150
Types:
  of applications, 10, 94–95
  of data, 28, 50, 94, 280
  of frameworks, 89–93

Uncertainty with expert systems, 341
UNIX operating system, 21, 153
Unstructured problems, 91–94
  capital projects budgeting case, 214–229
  and database design, 114
  design for, 146
  DSAs for, 212
  expert systems for, 341
Updating:
  of databases, 129–130
  of network files, 164–166
Upgrades, software, 19
USE command (dBASE), 159, 282, 289, 309
User-designed spreadsheet formulas, 179
User interfaces:
  for access systems, 146

User interfaces *(continued)*
  for DSAs, 212
  for information review workstations, 77
  for integrated programs, 162
User-level security, 164–165
User manuals, 144, 145 (*see also* Documentation)
Utilities, 48–49, 147–151

Values, spreadsheet, transporting of, 223
Variability with statistical packages, 38
Variables:
  in batch files, 159
  database, 311
  programming, 50
VAX mainframes, terminals for, 70
VDT, *see* Video display terminals
Vectors, 150
Ventura Publisher desktop publishing program, 351
Video display terminals (VDT), 60 (*see also* Monitors, Screen display)
Viruses, 14
Vocabularies, user-specified, 149
Volatile memory, 58
VP-Expert expert system, 340
VT100 terminals, 70

WAIT command (dBASE), 311
What-if spreadsheet analyses, 31, 159
  for DSAs, 213, 215, 217, 233, 244, 246

What You See Is What You Get (WYSIWYG) systems, 75–76
Wild card character, *see* Asterisks
Windows, 148, 152–154
Word length, see Communications, micro-to-micro
WordPerfect word processor, 42
Word processors, 8, 10–11
  basic capabilities of, 42
  monitors for, 60
  for office automation, 74–75
  sophisticated facilities of, 42–43
WordStar word processor, 42, 44
Work breakdown hierarchy charts, 335–336
Work-group processing, 163
WORKSHEET command (Lotus), 32
Worksheets, *see* Spreadsheets and spreadsheet programs
Workstations, 7, 73, 79–80
Wraparound word processor feature, 42
Write-Once, Read Many (WORM) drives, 65

X coefficient with regression analysis, 239
XENIX operating system, 153
XTREE menu system, 25
X-Tree shell, 153
XYwrite word processor, 42, 44

Z-80 microprocessor, 56